»A Collector's Guide to MARILLION & FISH«

by

André Rostek

© I.P. Verlag Jeske/Mader GbR
Bruchwitzstr. 36
12247 Berlin
Germany

ISBN 3-931624-15-3
1. Auflage März 2002; First Edition March 2002

Table of Contents/Inhaltsverzeichnis: **Page**

Prologue:

Main Part:

Appendix:

Introduction

A big hello to all MARILLION fans out there!

First of all, I hope you will enjoy this book! In the process you might discover items in here which you've never heard about before or which are still missing in your collection.

I've tried to collect as much information as possible with regards to the different releases worldwide. Maybe I forgot the odd record, but as being a collector yourself, you know MARILLION and their different members put out so many recordings (released all over the world) that it was difficult enough for me to gather all the data for this book.

A very special "thank you" to the following MARILLION freaks. Without their help the book wouldn't have been possible:

Marcus Angermann
(for information on different releases)
Oliver Hülsmann
(for information on different releases)
Bert ter Steege
(for the complete MARILLION online discography)
Roberto Meloni (for song variations)
Bill Frech (for MARILLION tour dates)
The Company (for FISH tour dates)
and last but not least to my wife Christiane.

If you are aware of any mistakes, would like to add missing details or comment on the book, please contact me:

André Rostek
Josephstr. 18
44791 Bochum
Germany
rossi.chrissi@t-online.de

Bochum, March 2002

Einleitung

Hallo an alle MARILLION-Fans!

Ich hoffe, daß Euch dieses Buch gefällt und Ihr möglicherweise noch die eine oder andere Platte entdeckt, die Ihr noch nie gesehen, oder zumindest nicht in Eurer Sammlung zu stehen habt.

Ich habe versucht, so viele Informationen wie möglich über die verschiedenen Veröffentlichungen weltweit zu bekommen. Wahrscheinlich habe ich die eine oder andere Platte vergessen, aber als Plattensammler weißt Du, wie viele Aufnahmen es von MARILLION und den einzelnen Bandmitgliedern aus verschiedenen Ländern gibt. Es war bereits schwierig genug, alle vorhandenen Informationen zusammenzutragen.

Mein Dank geht deshalb an die folgenden MARILLION-Freaks, ohne deren großartige Unterstützung dieses Buch nicht möglich gewesen wäre:

Marcus Angermann
(für zahlreiche Infos zu verschiedenen Pressungen)
Oliver Hülsmann
(für zahlreiche Infos zu verschiedenen Pressungen)
Bert ter Steege
(für die größte MARILLION-Discographie im Internet)
Roberto Meloni
(für Infos zu den verschiedenen Song-Variationen)
Bill Frech (für MARILLION-Tourdaten)
The Company (für FISH-Tourdaten)
und natürlich an meine Frau Christiane.

So, falls Ihr noch irgendwelche Fragen oder Anregungen habt, könnt Ihr mich jederzeit postalisch erreichen:

André Rostek, Josephstr. 18,
44791 Bochum, Deutschland
rossi.chrissi@t-online.de

Bochum, März 2002

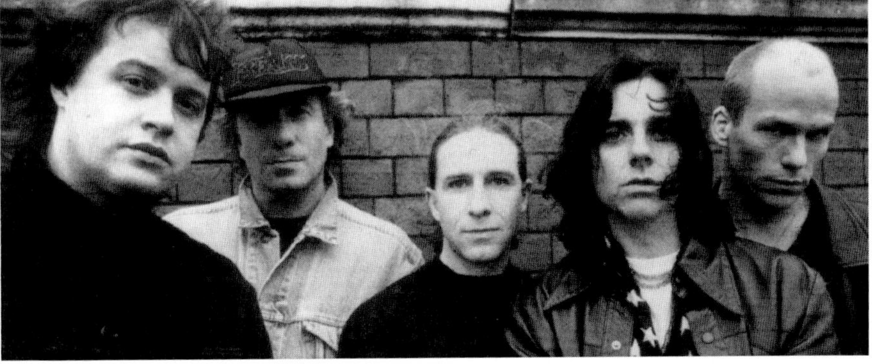

How to use the Book

I've tried to make the listings in the book easy to understand for everyone. You will see that some are in chronological (e.g. official releases) and some in alphabetical order (e.g. bootlegs).

Only vinyl and CD issues are specified, tapes or sound postcards and flexis from Eastern Europe are not listed because this section is much too obscure.

Firstly, all titles are listed with the original release date (mostly UK issue).

Secondly, the description of the different releases follows (singles are divided in 7" and 12" sections).

Firstly, all UK releases are mentioned. Secondly, all other European releases are listed. The third section is dedicated to releases from the rest of the world.

Please note that "EEC" is the abbreviation for all EMI records released in Holland and Germany. The reason being that EMI pressed the records for Germany in Holland. The only difference is the catalogue number for the early 7" singles. If the number starts with "1A...", the record is a German issue. But when the number is "1C...", then it's a Dutch release.

The abbreviations for the countries are the following:

A	Austria
ARG	Argentinia
AUS	Australia
BRA	Brazil
CAN	Canada
CH	Switzerland
COL	Columbia
CZ	Czech Republic
EEC	(means German or Dutch)
ESP	Spain
FRA	France
GER	Germany
GR	Greece
IRL	Ireland
ISR	Israel
ITA	Italy
JAP	Japan
KOR	Korea
LUX	Luxembourg
MEX	Mexico
NL	Netherlands
NZ	New Zealand
PER	Peru
POL	Poland
POR	Portugal
RSA	Rep. South Africa
RUS	Russia
SIN	Singapore
TAW	Taiwan
UK	United Kingdom
UKR	Ukraine
USA	United States of America
VEN	Venezuela
YUG	Yugoslavia
ZBM	Zimbabwe

Other abbreviations are:

foc = fold out cover
ltd. ed. = limited edition
no ps = no picture sleeve
ois = original inner sleeve
ps = picture sleeve

Über dieses Buch

Ich habe versucht, alle Auflistungen in diesem Buch so einfach und verständlich wie möglich zu erarbeiten. Ihr werdet sehen, daß manches in chronologischer Reihenfolge (z.B. offizielle Pressungen) gelistet ist. Andere Sachen dagegen lassen sich leichter in alphabetischer Reihenfolge (z.B. Bootlegs) darstellen.

Es wurden nur Vinyl und CD-Veröffentlichungen berücksichtigt, keine Cassetten oder Tonpostkarten und Flexis aus Osteuropa, da dieser Bereich unüberschaubar ist.

Alle Titel werden zunächst mit dem Erstveröffentlichungs-Datum (meistens UK-Pressungen) genannt. Danach folgt der Bereich mit den Beschreibungen der verschiedenen Veröffentlichungen (Singles sind noch in 7" und 12" unterteilt).

Bei der Reihenfolge der einzelnen Länder untereinander, werden zunächst immer alle UK-Pressungen genannt. Dann folgen in alphabetischer Reihenfolge andere europäische Länder. Zuletzt werden Pressungen aus anderen Kontinenten gelistet.

Beachtet bitte, daß die Länder-Abkürzung "EEC" für alle EMI-Pressungen aus Holland und Deutschland steht. Der Grund dafür ist, daß die EMI einen Großteil der Platten für den deutschen Markt in Holland pressen ließ. Der einzig ersicht-

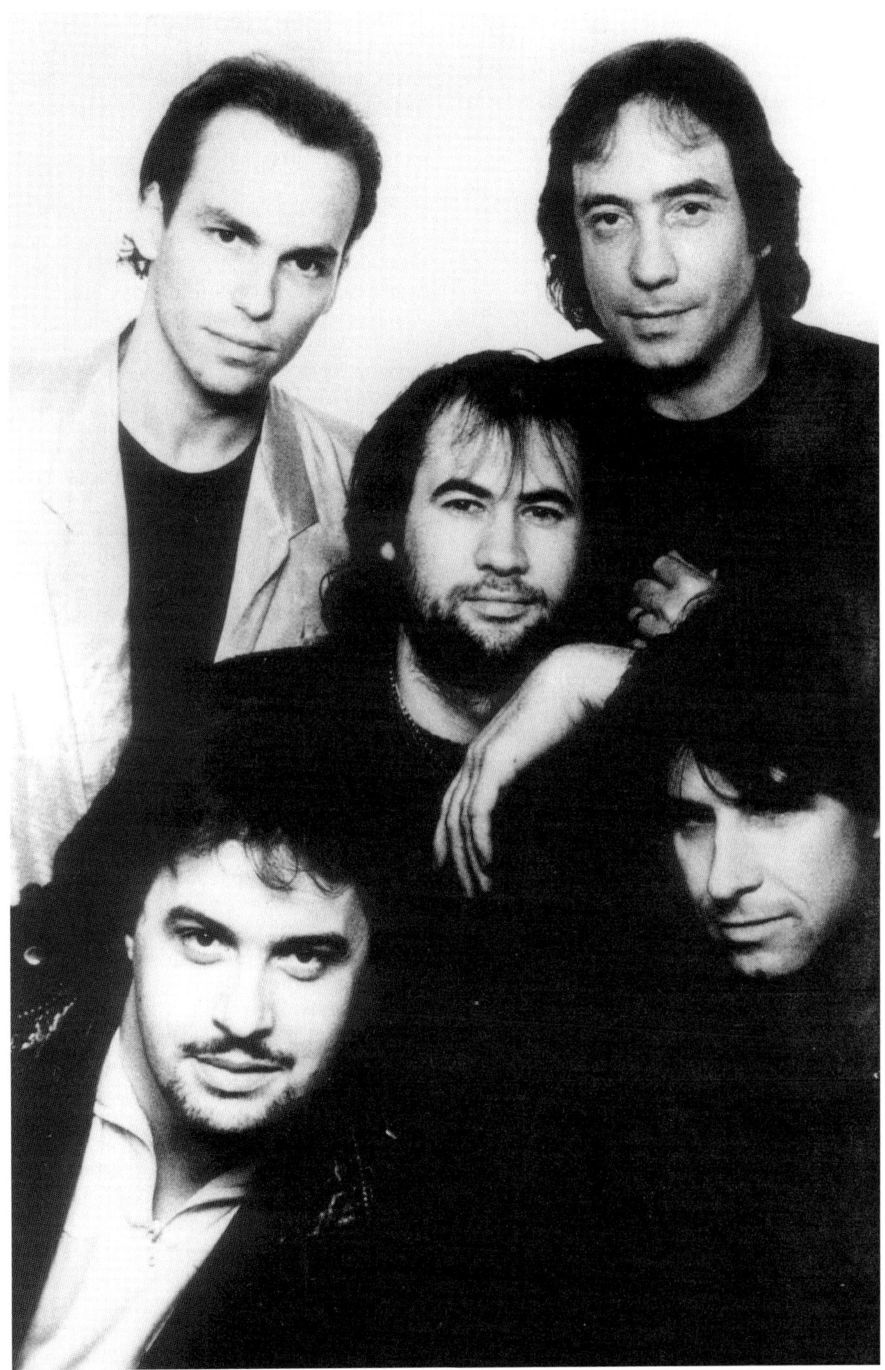

liche Unterschied ist bei den frühen 7"-Veröffentlichungen festzustellen. Eine deutsche Platte beginnt mit der Bestellnummer "1A..." und die holländische Veröffentlichung mit "1C...".

Die Abkürzungen für die Länder im einzelnen:

A	Österreich
ARG	Argentinien
AUS	Australien
BRA	Brasilien
CAN	Kanada
CH	Schweiz
COL	Kolumbien
CZ	Tschechische Republik
EEC	(deutsch oder holländisch)
ESP	Spanien
FRA	Frankreich
GER	Deutschland
GR	Griechenland
IRL	Irland
ISR	Israel
ITA	Italien
JAP	Japan
KOR	Korea
LUX	Luxemburg
MEX	Mexiko
GR	Griechenland
NL	Niederlande
PER	Peru
POL	Polen
POR	Portugal
RSA	Republik Südafrika
RUS	Russland
SIN	Singapur
TAW	Taiwan
UK	Großbritannien
UKR	Ukraine
USA	Amerika
VEN	Venezuela
YUG	Jugoslawien
ZBM	Simbabwe

Andere Abkürzungen sind:

foc	=	Klapp-Cover
ltd. ed.	=	limitierte Auflage
no ps	=	kein Bild-Cover
ois	=	Original-Innencover
ps	=	Bild-Cover

A (very short) Biography

In the late '70s there was a group called ELECTRIC GYPSY featuring Mick Pointer (drums), Doug Irvine (bass) and Andy Glass (guitar). The band, having no singer, made instrumental music. In 1979, Andy Glass left and founded SOLSTICE shortly after.

The rest of the band decided to change their name to SILMARILLION and recruited two new members. Steve Rothery (guitar) joined the outfit in the summer of 1979, followed by Brian Jelliman (keyboards) a few months later. In the winter of 1979/1980, they decided to change their monicker once more by dropping the "Sil". The name MARILLION was born.

Still looking for a singing frontman, Doug Irvine tried to do his best during 1980 but at the end of the year he left. Derek William Dick (vocals), better known as Fish, officially joined MARILLION on January 2nd, 1981, after having left his old band called BLEWITT. Also new was bass player Diz Minitt.

The band started touring all around the UK with this line-up. But at the end of 1981, keyboarder Brian Jelliman left MARILLION. He was replaced by Mark Kelly, who formerly played with the band CHEMICAL ALICE.

In March 1982, the former THE METROS member Pete Trewavas substituted bass player Diz Minnitt and MARILLION recorded their first single »Market square heroes«, released in the UK on the 25th of October 1982.

The group's line-up remained stable for the next two singles »Garden party« and »He knows you know« as well as for the first album »Script for a jester's tear«. Following, Mick Pointer split from the band. Many years later (in 1995) he founded ARENA.

Throughout the years, many musicians tried to fill the vacant drum position in MARILLION: e.g. Andy Ward (from CAMEL), John Martyr or Jonathan Mover but it was already November 1983, when Ian Mosley, who had played with DARRYL WAY'S WOLF, TRACE, GORDON GILTRAP BAND and STEVE HACKETT before, joined the band. As we all know, he is still there to this very day.

MARILLION managed to tour and record with great success over the following years but while working on the successor to the 1987 release »Clutching at straws«, vocalist Fish decided to leave the band in autumn 1988 in order to start a solo career a year later. This was a shock for most of the fans but the other band members worked hard to find a new singer with comparable qualities to Fish.

They found a replacement in Steve Hogarth, who had played with lots of different artists before and was a member of THE EUROPEANS and HOW WE LIVE. He joined the band officially on February 1st, 1989. Steve Hogarth wasn't "just a substitute" for Fish and his personality grew over the years.

The band did a few CDs with him, but with less success each album. This was the reason for the split with EMI after the release of »Afraid of sunlight« in 1995. MARILLION did a new contract with Castle Communications, but this contract ends with the release of »marillion.com« in 1999. They had offers from other "small labels" but they deceided to do something very special. The band asked their fans via internet to pay for their new CD in advance to be independent while producing the record. For the distribution of »Anoraknophobia« they signed again with EMI.

So let's see what's happening next...
(March2002).

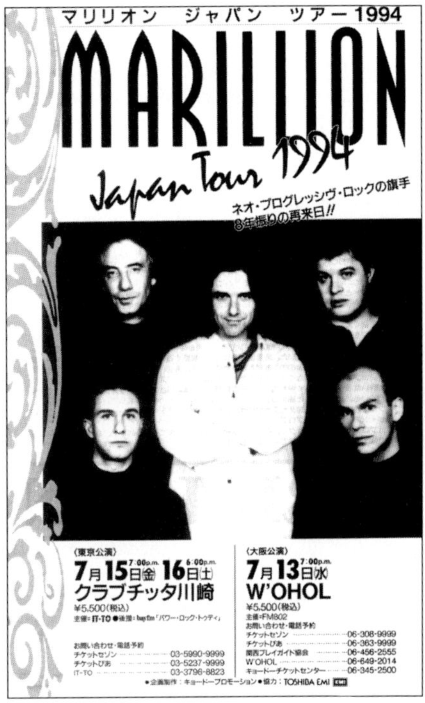

Eine (sehr kurze) Biographie

In den späten '70er Jahren gab es eine Band, die sich ELECTRIC GYPSY nannte, mit Mick Pointer (Schlagzeug), Doug Irvine (Bass) und Andy Glass (Gitarre). Die Band spielte Instrumental-Musik, da sie keinen Sänger hatten und im Jahr 1979 stieg Andy Glass aus, um später seine eigene Band (SOLSTICE) zu gründen.

Der Rest von ELECTRIC GYPSY entschloß sich, den Namen in SILMARILLION zu ändern, und zwei neue Musiker aufzunehmen. Steve Rothery (Gitarre) stieß im Sommer 1979 zur Band und nur zwei Monate später kam Brian Jelliman (Keyboards) hinzu.

Im Winter 1979/1980 wurde der Bandname erneut geändert. Sie entschlossen sich, das "Sil" im Namen wegzulassen, um sich ab sofort nur noch MARILLION zu nennen. Immer noch auf der Suche nach einem Sänger, versuchte sich Doug Irvine in dieser Position im Laufe des Jahres 1980, verließ aber gegen Ende des Jahres die Band.

Derek William Dick, besser bekannt als Fish, wurde am 02.01.1981 offizielles, neues Mitglied bei MARILLION, nachdem er zuvor bei BLEWITT gesungen hatte. Mit ihm kam auch ein neuer Bassist namens Diz Minnitt.

MARILLION waren mit dieser Besetzung überall in Großbritannien auf Tour, aber gegen Ende 1981 war es Brian Jelliman, der die Band verließ. Er wurde durch Mark Kelly ersetzt, der zuvor noch bei CHEMICAL ALICE gespielt hatte. Im März 1982 wurde Diz Minnitt durch den früheren THE METROS-Bassisten Pete Trewavas ersetzt. In dieser Besetzung bekamen MARILLION einen Plattenvertrag bei der EMI und veröffentlichten am 25.10.1982 ihre erste Single in England mit dem Titel »Market square heroes«.

Die Band blieb auch für die nächsten zwei Singles und das erste Album »Script for a jester's tear« zusammen, aber danach mußte Mick Pointer die Band verlassen. Viele Jahre später (1995) gründete er eine eigene Band mit dem Namen ARENA.

Viele Musiker haben versucht, den Platz von Mick Pointer bei MARILLION zu übernehmen, u.a. Andy Ward (CAMEL) oder auch John Martyr und Jonathan Mover. Es war mittlerweile September 1983, als Ian Mosley, der früher z.B. bei TRACE und STEVE HACKETT spielte, zu MARILLION stieß.

Mit diesem Line-up nahmen MARILLION in den kommenden Jahren erfolgreiche Alben auf, und tourten durch die ganze Welt. Als die Band jedoch mit den Aufnahmen für das Nachfolgealbum zu »Clutching at straws« (1987) beschäftigt war, entschied sich Fish, auszusteigen, um sich eine Solo-Karriere aufzubauen. Das war im Herbst 1988 sowohl für die anderen Bandmitglieder als auch für die Fans ein großer Schock. Es wurde schließlich lange und sorgfältig nach einem Ersatz für Fish gesucht.

Dieser Nachfolger wurde schließlich offiziell am 01.02.1989 der frühere EUROPEANS- und HOW WE LIVE-Sänger Steve Hogarth. Steve Hogarth war nie nur ein "Ersatz" für Fish, und hat sich schnell zu einer echten Führungspersönlichkeit in der Band entwickelt. Die Band veröffentlichte mit ihm diverse Alben, jedoch mit immer geringer werdendem Erfolg, was schließlich auch der Grund war, warum der Plattenvertrag mit der EMI nach dem 1995er Album »Afraid of sunlight« nicht verlängert wurde. MARILLION entschieden sich schließlich, einen Vertrag bei Castle Communications zu unterschreiben. Dieser Vertrag lief bis zur »marillion.com«-CD im Jahre 1999. Es lagen der Band danach Angebote von einigen anderen "kleinen" Plattenfirmen vor, doch die Bandmitglieder beschlossen, neue Wege zu gehen. In einer beispiellosen Aktion über das Internet ließen sie das neue Album von ihren Fans vorfinanzieren, um während der Produktion unabhängig zu sein. Für den Vertrieb von »Anoraknophobia« unterschreiben sie schließlich erneut einen Vertrag bei der EMI. Wir können also gespannt sein, was als nächstes passiert...

(März 2002)

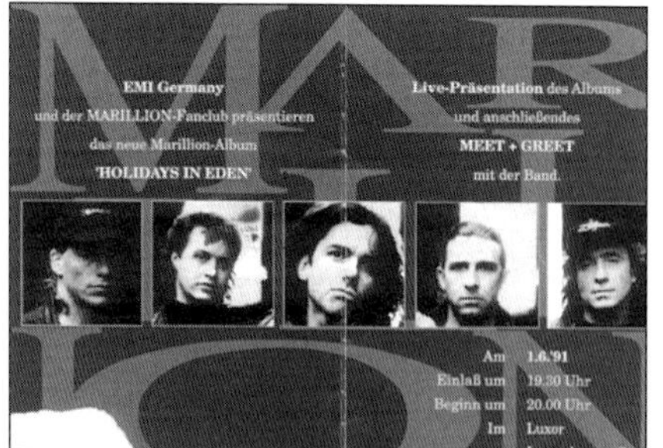

Official Releases and Promos

»Market square heroes«

(UK release 25.10.1982)

7" 7" 7" 7" 7" 7" 7" 7" 7" 7" 7" 7" 7" 7" 7" 7"

Side 1)	Market square heroes (Antichrist version)	4:15
Side 2)	Three boats down from the candy (7" version)	4:29

UK — EMI, EMI 5351
label yellow, push-out center

UK — EMI, EMI 5351
label yellow, small hole, no push-out

UK — EMI, EMI 5351
label black, re-release, no ps

Side 1)	Market square heroes (Antichrist version)	4:15
Side 2)	Market square heroes (Battlepriest version)	4:18

UK — EMI, EMI 5351 ADJ
label red, promo, no ps

12" 12" 12" 12" 12" 12" 12" 12" 12" 12" 12"

Side 1)	Market square heroes (Antichrist version)	4:15
	Three boats down from the candy (7" version)	4:29
Side 2)	Grendel (12" version)	17:14

UK — EMI, 12 EMI 5351
label white, promo

UK — EMI, 12 EMI 5351
label yellow, soft cover

UK — EMI, 12 EMI 5351
label black, soft cover

UK — EMI, 12 EMI 5351
label purple, soft cover

UK — EMI, 12 EMI P 5351
release 4/'83, picture disc, 3,000 copies, no ps

EEC — EMI, 052 0772 6
label yellow, hard cover

POR — EMI, 11C 052-07726
label yellow

»He knows you know«

(UK release 31.01.1983)

7" 7" 7" 7" 7" 7" 7" 7" 7" 7" 7" 7" 7" 7" 7" 7"

Side 1)	He knows you know (7" version)	3:30
Side 2)	Charting the single (7" version)	4:50

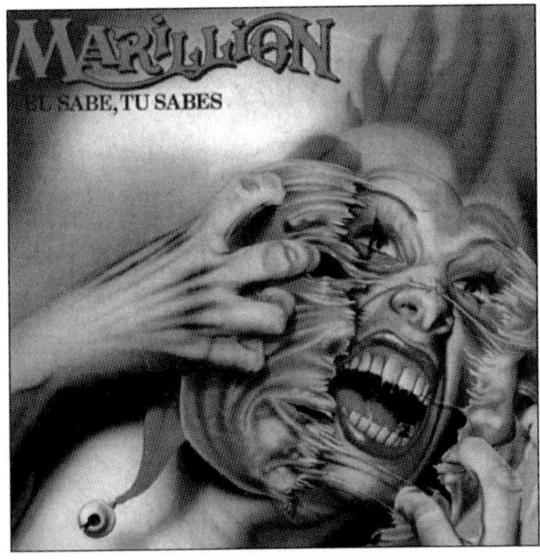

Spanish cover »He knows you know« promo 7"

UK — EMI, EMI 5362
label blue, hard cover
UK — EMI, EMI 5362
label yellow, push-out center, hard cover
UK — EMI, EMI 5362
label yellow, push-out center, soft cover
EEC — EMI, 1A 006-07713
label yellow, soft cover
EEC — EMI, 1C 006-07713
label yellow, soft cover
ESP — EMI, 10 C 006-007713
label yellow, promo, title "El sabe tu sabes"
ESP — EMI, 10 C 006-007713
label yellow, title "El sabe tu sabes"
AUS — EMI, EMI-1032
label yellow, no ps, promo
AUS — EMI, EMI-1032
label yellow, no ps
CAN — Capitol, 72926
label black, company sleeve

Side 1) He knows you know
Side 2) – not playable–

UK — Abbey Road
one-sided acetate

12" 12" 12" 12" 12" 12" 12" 12" 12" 12" 12"

Side 1) He knows you know (edited 12" version) 5:05
Side 2) Charting the single (7" version) 4:50

UK — EMI, 12 EMI 5263
label white, promo
UK — EMI, 12 EMI 5263
label yellow, soft cover
UK — EMI, 12 EMI 5263
label black, soft cover
UK — EMI, 12 EMI 5263
label purple, soft cover
UK — EMI, 12 EMI P 5263
number was given, but never released, picture disc
EEC — EMI, 052 Z 07713
label yellow, hard cover
EEC — EMI, 052 Z 07713
label yellow, soft cover

Side 1) He knows you know (edited version) 3:30
Side 2) Chelsea monday (edited version) 4:36

USA — Capitol, SPRO-9930/9931
label black, promo, stickered sleeve

Side 1) He knows you know (edited version) 3:30
Side 2) He knows you know (edited version) 3:30

USA — Capitol, SPRO-9964/9965
label black, promo, stickered sleeve

»Script for a jester's tear«

(UK release 14.03.1983)

LP LP LP LP LP LP LP LP LP LP LP LP LP LP

Side 1)	Script for a jester' s tear	7:40
	He knows you know	5:05
	The web	8:39
Side 2)	Garden party	7:00
	Chelsea monday	7:45
	Forgotten sons	8:00

UK — EMI, EMC 3429
label red, 250 promos in signed sleeve
UK — EMI, EMC 3429
label green, test pressing, no ps
UK — EMI, EMC 3429
label white, test pressing, no ps
UK — EMI, EMC 3429
label white, 2 one-sided test pressings
UK — EMI, EMC 3429
label black, foc
UK — EMI, EMC 3429
label yellow, foc
UK — EMI/Fame, FA 3235
release 5/'90, label black, foc
UK — EMI, EMC P 3429
release 6/'84, picture disc, no ps
UK — EMI, EMC P 3429
picture disc, mispressed, same picture on A+B, no ps
ESP — EMI, 6007715
label yellow, foc

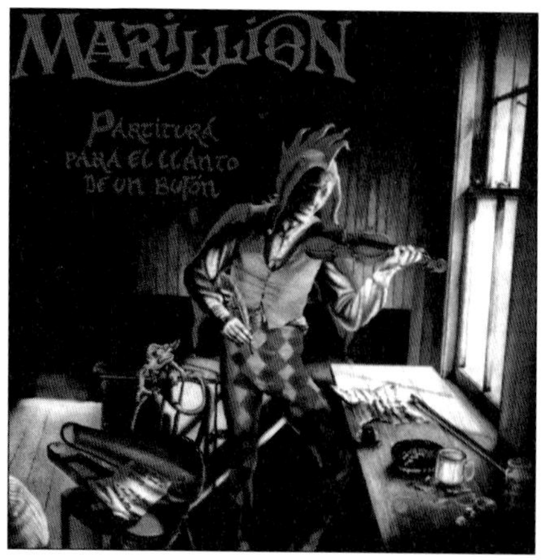

Argentinian cover »Scripf for a jester's tear« album

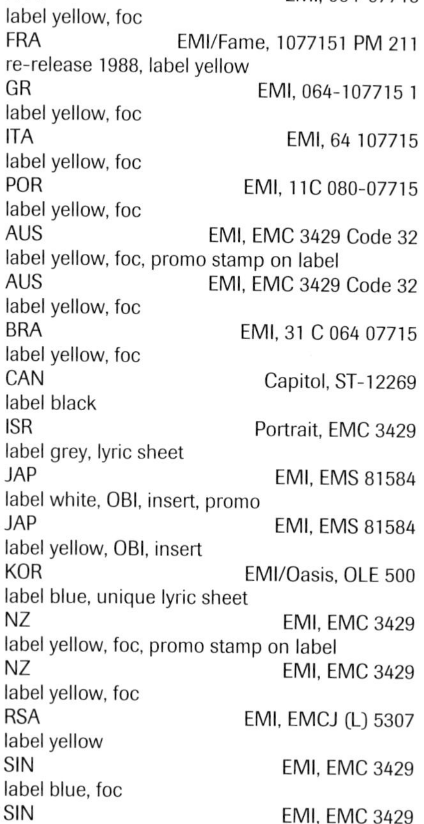

FRA EMI, 064-07715
label yellow, foc
FRA EMI/Fame, 1077151 PM 211
re-release 1988, label yellow
GR EMI, 064-107715 1
label yellow, foc
ITA EMI, 64 107715
label yellow, foc
POR EMI, 11C 080-07715
label yellow, foc
AUS EMI, EMC 3429 Code 32
label yellow, foc, promo stamp on label
AUS EMI, EMC 3429 Code 32
label yellow, foc
BRA EMI, 31 C 064 07715
label yellow, foc
CAN Capitol, ST-12269
label black
ISR Portrait, EMC 3429
label grey, lyric sheet
JAP EMI, EMS 81584
label white, OBI, insert, promo
JAP EMI, EMS 81584
label yellow, OBI, insert
KOR EMI/Oasis, OLE 500
label blue, unique lyric sheet
NZ EMI, EMC 3429
label yellow, foc, promo stamp on label
NZ EMI, EMC 3429
label yellow, foc
RSA EMI, EMCJ (L) 5307
label yellow
SIN EMI, EMC 3429
label blue, foc
SIN EMI, EMC 3429
label blue, foc, promo

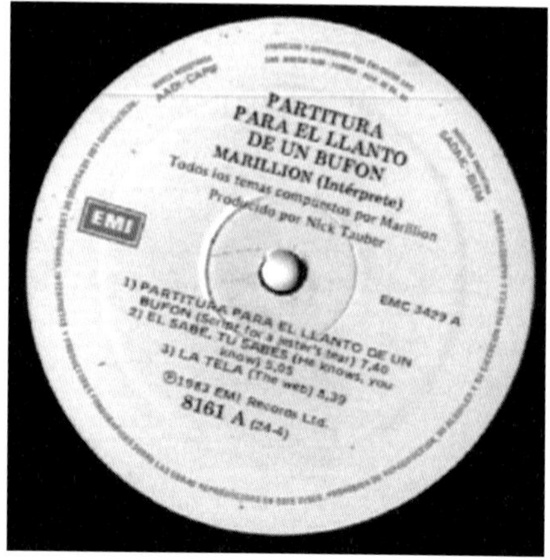

Argentinian label »Script for a jester's tear«

TAW Nova, 73004
label black with colour triangle
USA Capitol, ST-12269
label purple, golden promo stamp
USA Capitol, ST-12269
label purple

Side 1)	Script for a jester' s tear	8:37
	He knows you know	5:05
	The web	9:02
Side 2)	Garden party	7:12
	Chelsea monday	8:13
	Forgotten sons	8:18

EEC EMI, 1C 064-07 715
label yellow, foc

Side 1) Partitura para el llanto de un bufon
El sabe, tu sabes
La tela
Side 2) Fiesta en el jardin
Lunes en chelsea
Hijos olvidados

ARG EMI, EMI 8161
label yellow, promo
ARG EMI, EMI 8161
label yellow

Side 1) Script para la lagrina de un bufon
El sabe, tu sabes
La telarana
Side 2) Fiesta en el jardin
Lunes en chelsea
Hijos olvidados

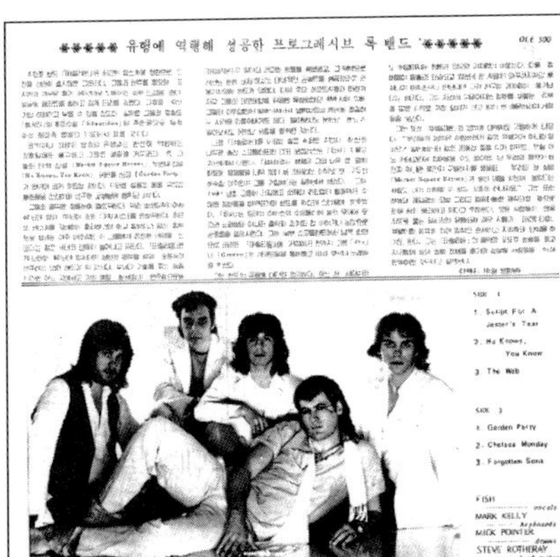

Korean lyric sheet »Scripf for a jester's tear« album

MEX — EMI, SLEM-1137
label yellow, promo stamp
MEX — EMI, SLEM-1137
label yellow

••

Side 1) Libreto para el ilanto de un bafon
El sabe, tu sabes
Tela de arana
Side 2) Fiesta en el jardin
Lunes en chelsea
Hijos olvidados

VEN — EMI, 103-04486
label yellow, foc

CD CD CD CD CD CD CD CD CD CD CD CD

Script for a jester' tear	8:39
He knows you know	5:22
The web	8:48
Garden party	7:15
Chelsea monday	8:16
Forgotten sons	8:21

UK — EMI, CDP 7 46237 2
release 27.12.1985
UK — EMI/Fame, CD FA 3235
release 5/'90
EEC — Disky, CD 867362
release 10/'96
ITA — EMI, CDPM 7 46237 2
RUS — EMI, CDP 746237
with russian print on back
UKR — BCVLX, 00030
counterfeit
JAP — EMI, CDP 7 46237 2
JAP — EMI, TOCP 8315
re-release
USA — Capitol, C 246237
USA — Capitol, DIDX 1298

2CD 2CD 2CD 2CD 2CD 2CD 2CD 2CD 2CD

Disc 1)	Script for a jester' tear	8:39
	He knows you know	5:22
	The web	8:48
	Garden party	7:15
	Chelsea monday	8:16
	Forgotten sons	8:21
Disc 2)	Market square heroes (battlepriest version)	4:18
	Three boats down from the candy (single version)	4:31
	Grendel (Fair-Deal studios demo)	19:10
	Chelsea monday (Manchester square demo)	6:55
	He knows you know (Manchester square demo)	4:29
	Charting the single (single version)	4:52
	Market square heroes (re-recorded version)	4:48

Disc 2 remastered bonus CD

UK — EMI, REMARIL 001
release 29.09.1997
EEC — EMI, 7243 8 57865 2 5
release 29.09.1997

»Garden party«

(UK release 06.06.1983)

7" 7" 7" 7" 7" 7" 7"7" 7" 7" 7" 7" 7" 7"7" 7"

Side 1) Garden party (edited version) 4:29
Side 2) Margaret (edited live version) 4:09
Edinburgh, Playhouse, 07.04.1983

UK — EMI, EMI 5593
label yellow, push-out centre
UK — EMI, EMI P 5593
shaped picture disc, uncut test pressing, no ps
UK — EMI, EMI P 5593
shaped picture disc, no ps
UK — EMI, EMI 5593
label yellow, with "Verkerke-kaard" NL
EEC — EMI, 1A 006-1077677
label yellow
EEC — EMI, 1C 006-1077677
label yellow
IRL — EMI, EMI 5593
label yellow, company sleeve

AUS EMI, EMI-1122
label yellow, promo stamp on label, no ps
AUS EMI, EMI-1122
label yellow

12" 12" 12" 12" 12" 12" 12" 12" 12" 12" 12"

Side 1) Garden party (alternative version) 7:15
Charting the single 6:30
London, Hammersmith Odeon 18.04.1983
Side 2) Margaret (full live version) 12:17
Edinburgh, Playhouse, 07.04.1983

UK EMI, 12 EMI 5393
label black, soft cover
UK EMI, 12 EMI S 5393
label yellow, ltd. ed. with poster
EEC EMI, 1A 062 Z 10 7766 6
label yellow, hard cover
EEC EMI, 1A 062 Z 10 7766 6
label yellow, soft cover

»Punch and Judy«

(UK release 30.01.1984)

7" 7" 7" 7" 7" 7" 7" 7" 7" 7" 7" 7"7" 7" 7" 7"

Side 1) Punch and Judy (7" version) 3:19
Side 2) Market square heroes
(edited re-recorded version) 3:56
Three boats down from the candy
(re-recorded version) 3:59

UK EMI, MARIL 1
label yellow, push-out centre
UK EMI, MARIL 1
label silver

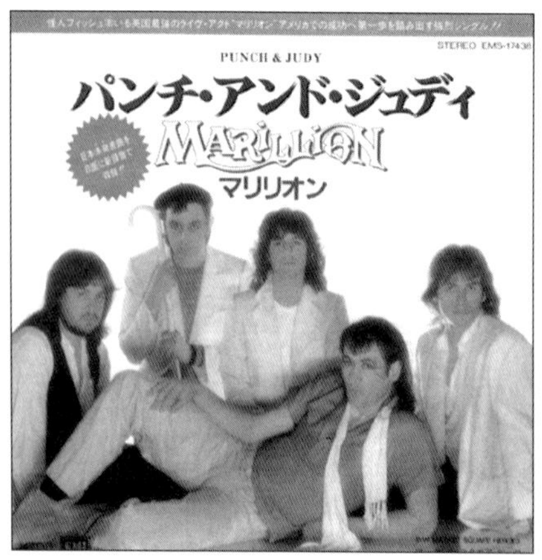

Japanese cover insert »Punch and Judy« 7"

EEC EMI, 1A 016-2000417
label yellow
EEC EMI, 1C 016-2000417
label yellow
ESP EMI, 006-200041 7
label yellow, promo, different back cover
ESP EMI, 006-200041 7
label yellow
RSA EMI, EMI J 4464
label yellow

Side 1) Punch and Judy (7" version) 3:19
Side 2) – not playable –

UK EMI
label green, one-sided test pressing

Side 1) Punch and Judy (7" version) 3:19
?
Side 2) ?
?

USA Capitol
4 track E.P.

Side 1) Punch and Judy (7" version) 3:19
Side 2) Market square heroes
(edited re-recorded version) 3:56

JAP EMI, EMS-1743
label white, unique photo insert as a cover, promo
JAP EMI, EMS-1743
label yellow, unique photo insert as a cover

12" 12" 12" 12" 12" 12" 12" 12" 12" 12" 12"

Side 1) Punch and Judy (7" version) 3:19
Side 2) Market square heroes
(re-recorded version) 4:45
Three boats down from the candy
(re-recorded version) 3:59

UK EMI, 12 MARIL 1
label white, promo
UK EMI, 12 MARIL 1
label yellow, soft cover
UK EMI, 12 MARIL 1
re-release, label black, no picture cover
UK EMI, 12 MARIL 1
same as before but with mispressed label
UK EMI, 12 MARIL P 1
picture disc, no ps
EEC EMI, 1 C K062-200158 6
label yellow, hard cover

»Fugazi«

(UK release 12.03.1984)

LP LP LP LP LP LP LP LP LP LP LP LP LP LP

Side 1)	Assassing	7:00
	Punch and Judy	3:17
	Jigsaw	6:46
	Emerald lies	5:06
Side 2)	She chameleon	6:52
	Incubus	8:28
	Fugazi	8:00

UK EMI, EMC 2400851
label red, 250 promos in signed sleeves
UK EMI, EMC 2400851
label white, promo
UK EMI, EMC 2400851
test pressing with different track order
UK EMI, EMC 2400851
label yellow, foc
UK EMI, EMC 2400851/MRL 1
label yellow, foc
UK EMI, EMCP 2400850/MRLP 1
picture disc, no ps
UK EMI/Fame, FA 3196
re-release 5/'88, foc
EEC EMI, 157739 1
label white, test pressing
EEC EMI, 157739 1
test pressing, plays side A on both sides, no ps
EEC EMI, 1C 064 2400851
label yellow, foc
EEC EMI, 1C 064 2400851
label yellow, foc, promo with 3 promo pages on blue paper
EEC EMI/Fame, 1C 038-1 57739 1
label yellow, foc, "Fame" sticker + ois
CZ EMI/Globus 210094-1 311
label black, vinyl black, promo
CZ EMI/Globus 210094-1 311
label black, vinyl black
CZ EMI/Globus 210094-1 311
label black, vinyl red
CZ EMI/Globus 210094-1 311
label black, vinyl pink
CZ EMI/Globus 210094-1 311
label black, vinyl blue-marbled, multicoloured
CZ EMI/Globus 210094-1 311
label black, vinyl clear, multicoloured
FRA EMI, 64 240085 1
label yellow, foc
GR EMI, 064 240085 1
label yellow, foc
ITA EMI, 64 240085 1
label yellow
POR EMI, 240085 1
label yellow
AUS EMI, EMC 240085
label yellow, foc, promo stamp on label
AUS EMI, EMC 240085
label yellow, foc
BRA EMI, 31C 064 240085
label yellow
CAN Capitol, ST-12331
label black, ois
ISR Portrait, EMC 240085
label grey, lyric sheet
JAP EMI, EMS 81647
label white, OBI, insert, promo
JAP EMI, EMS 81647
label yellow, OBI, insert
NZ EMI, EMC 219
label yellow, foc
RSA EMI, EMCJ (L) 240085 1
label yellow
TAW Nova, 73018
USA Capitol, ST-12331
label black, promo stamp, ois
USA Capitol, ST-12331
label black, ois
VEN EMI, 103 045 19
label yellow, foc

Side 1)	Asesinato (says the label) Asesinando (says the cover)
	Titeres
	Rompeca bezas
	Mentiras color esmeralda
Side 2)	Ella camaleon
	Incubo
	Fugazi

ARG EMI, EMI 8213
label yellow, foc, promo
ARG EMI, EMI 8213
label yellow, foc

Side 1)	Asesino
	Titeres
	Sierra de vaiven
	Yacimiento de esmeraldas
Side 2)	Ella camaleon
	Pesadilla
	Fugaz

MEX EMI, SLEM-1198
label yellow, foc

CD CD CD CD CD CD CD CD CD CD CD CD

	Assassing	7:01
	Punch and Judy	3:18
	Jigsaw	6:46
	Emerald lies	5:08
	She chameleon	6:53
	Incubus	8:30
	Fugazi	8:02

UK EMI, CDP 7 46027 2
UK EMI/Fame, CD FA 3196
EEC EMI, CDP 7 46027 2
EEC EMI/Fame, CDP 538-7 46027 2
RUS EMI, 746027
with russian print on back
UKR BCVLX, 00044
counterfeit
JAP EMI, CDP 7 46027 2
JAP EMI, TOCP 8316
re-release
USA Capitol, C 246027
USA Capitol, DIDX 910

2CD 2CD 2CD 2CD 2CD 2CD 2CD 2CD 2CD

Disc 1)	Assassing	7:01
	Punch and Judy	3:18
	Jigsaw	6:46
	Emerald lies	5:08
	She chameleon	6:53
	Incubus	8:30
	Fugazi	8:02
Disc 2)	Cinderella search (12" version)	5:32
	Assassing (alternate mix)	7:41
	Three boats down from the candy (re-recorded version)	4:01
	Punch and Judy *	3:50
	She chameleon *	6:34
	Emerald lies *	5:32
	Incubus	8:10

** Demo, previously unreleased, disc 2 remastered bonus CD*

UK EMI, 4933692
release 23.02.1998
EEC EMI, 7243 4 93369 2 3
release 23.02.1998

»Assassing«

(UK release 30.04.1984)

7" 7" 7" 7" 7" 7" 7" 7" 7" 7" 7" 7" 7" 7" 7" 7"

Side 1)	Assassing (7" version)	3:39
Side 2)	Cinderella search (7" version)	4:19

UK EMI, MARIL 2
label black, push-out centre
EEC EMI, 1A 006-2001577
label yellow
EEC EMI, 1C 006-2001577
label yellow
POR EMI, 2002977
label yellow
CAN Capitol, 729454
label black

12" 12" 12" 12" 12" 12" 12" 12" 12" 12" 12"

Side 1)	Assassing (full version)	7:00
Side 2)	Cinderella search (full version)	5:24

UK EMI, 12 MARIL 2
label white, promo
UK EMI, 12 MARIL 2
label black, soft cover
UK EMI, 12 MARIL P 2
picture disc, no ps
UK EMI, 12 MARIL P 2
same as before but mispressed with green colour only !

••

Side 1)	Assassing (full version)	7:02
Side 2)	Cinderella search (full version)	5:24
	Assassing (7" version)	3:35

EEC EMI, 1C K062 200158 6
label yellow, hard cover
EEC EMI, 1C K062 200158 6
same as before but cover print: “incl. hit single Assassing”

••

Side 1)	Assassing (edited remix)	3:36
Side 2)	Assassing (edited remix)	3:36

USA Capitol, SPRO-9132
label black, promo in “Fugazi cover” with promo stickers

••

Side 1)	Assassing (7" version)	3:35
Side 2)	Punch and Judy (7" version)	3:20
	Jigsaw (edited version)	3:59

CAN Capitol, SPRO 245
label black, promo, no ps

»Real to reel (live)«

(UK release 05.11.1984)

LP LP LP LP LP LP LP LP LP LP LP LP LP LP

Side 1)	Assassing	7:18
	Incubus	8:31

Cinderella search 5:24
Side 2) Forgotten sons 10:11
Garden party 6:30
Market square heroes 6:49

Side 1 recorded live in Montreal, Le Spectrum, 19./20.06.1984, side 2 recorded live in Leicester, De Montford Hall, 05.03.1984

UK EMI, JEST 1/EG 26 0303 1
label yellow, hard paper ois
UK EMI/Fame, FA 413142 1
re-release 11/'85, label yellow, "Fame" ois
UK EMI Gold
re-release
UK EMI, JEST P 1
picture disc, no ps
UK EMI, JEST P 1
picture disc with printing error, no ps
EEC EMI, 1C 038-26 0303 1
label yellow, soft paper ois
EEC EMI, 1C 038-26 0303 1
same as before but with tour dates sticker
EEC EMI/Fame, 1C 038-15 7623 1
label yellow, "Fame" sticker + ois
EEC EMI
mispressed, plays side B on both sides
EEC EMI, 26030 1
label white, test pressing
ESP EMI, 066-260303 1
label yellow
FRA EMI, 260303 1
label yellow, hard paper ois
GR EMI, 062-260303 1
label yellow
ITA EMI, 54 260303 1
label yellow
POR EMI, 2603031
label yellow, soft paper ois
BRA EMI, 31C 064-2603031
label yellow
CAN Capitol, SN 66174
label green
CAN Capitol, SQ 6516
label black
ISR Portrait, EG 260303
label grey
JAP EMI, EMS 81647
label white, OBI, insert, promo
JAP EMI, EMS 63038
label yellow, OBI, insert
RSA EMI, EMCJ (L) 2603031
label yellow
VEN EMI, EMI 25030
label yellow

••

Side 1) Asesinando
Incubo
En busqueda de la cenicienta
Side 2) Hijos olvidados
Fiesta en el jardin
Heroes de feria

ARG EMI, EMI 8375
label yellow, promo
ARG EMI, EMI 8375
label yellow

••

Side 1) – not playable –
Side 2) Forgotten sons 10:11
Garden party 6:30
Market square heroes 6:49

Live in Leicester, De Montford Hall, 05.03.1984

UK Townhouse, 2603031
label white, one-sided test pressing, side B, no ps

CD CD CD CD CD CD CD CD CD CD CD CD

Assassing 7:29
Incubus 8:43
Cinderella search 5:45
Emerald lies • 5:28
Forgotten sons * 10:36
Garden party * 6:32
Market square heroes * 7:32

*Recorded live in Montreal, Le Spectrum, 19./20.06.1984, except * recorded live in Leicester, De Montford Hall, 05.03.1984, • bonus track*

UK EMI/Fame, CD FA 3142
re-release 10/'87
EEC EMI, CDP 7 46027 2
EEC EMI, CDM 0777 7 52021 2 0
CAN EMI, 7243 8 56107 2 1
release 08.07.1997
JAP EMI, TOCP 8318

2CD 2CD 2CD 2CD 2CD 2CD 2CD 2CD 2CD

Disc 1) Assassing 7:29
Incubus 8:43
Cinderella search 5:45
Emerald lies • 5:28
Forgotten sons * 10:36
Garden party * 6:32
Market square heroes * 7:32
Disc 2) »Brief Encounter«
Lady Nina (extended version) 5:47
Freaks (7" version) 4:09
Kayleigh ° 4:11
Fugazi ° 8:32
Script for a jester's tear ° 8:52

*Disc 1 recorded live in Montreal, Le Spectrum, 19./20.06.1984, except * live in Leicester, De Montford Hall, 05.03.1984, disc 2 remastered bonus CD, ° recorded live in London, Hammersmith Odeon 01/1986, • bonus track*

UK — EMI, CDEM 1603
release 06.06.1997
EEC — EMI, 7243 8 56107 2 1
release 04.06.1997

»Kayleigh«

(UK release 07.04.1985)

7" 7" 7" 7" 7" 7" 7" 7" 7" 7" 7" 7" 7" 7" 7" 7"

Side 1) Kayleigh (single edit) 3:33
Side 2) Lady Nina (single edit) 3:41

UK — EMI, MARIL 3
label black
UK — EMI, MARIL 3
label silver
UK — EMI, MARIL P 3
picture disc, no ps
EEC — EMI, 2006387
label white, test pressing, no ps
EEC — EMI, 1A 006-20 0638 7
label yellow
EEC — EMI, 1C 006-20 0638 7
label yellow
ESP — EMI, 006 20 0638 7
label white, promo
ESP — EMI, 006 20 0638 7
label yellow

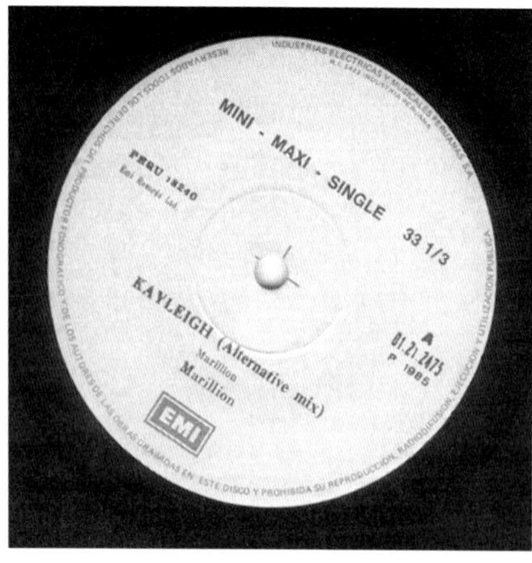

Peruvian label »Kayleigh« 7"

FRA — EMI, 20 0638 7
label silver
ITA — EMI, 06 20 0638 7
label yellow
POR — EMI, 20 0638 7
label yellow
AUS — EMI America, EMI-1534
label grey, promo, no ps
AUS — EMI America, EMI-1534
label grey, no ps
CAN — Capitol, B-72972
label black
JAP — EMI, PRP-1149
promo
NZ — EMI, EMI 932
label yellow, company sleeve
RSA — EMI, EMI J 4489
label yellow

Side 1) Kayleigh (single edit) 3:33
Side 2) Kayleigh (single edit) 3:33

USA — Capitol, P-B-5493
label white, promo, no ps

Side 1) Kayleigh (single edit) 3:33
Side 2) Heart of Lothian (single edit) 3:47

USA — Capitol, B-5493
label black

Side 1) Kayleigh (alternative mix)
Side 2) Lady Nina (12" mix)

PER — EMI, 01.21.2475/Peru 18240
label yellow, "mini maxi single", no ps

10" 10" 10" 10" 10" 10" 10" 10" 10" 10" 10"

Side 1) Kayleigh
Side 2) – not playable –

USA — Capitol
label white, one-sided test pressing

12" 12" 12" 12" 12" 12" 12" 12" 12" 12" 12"

Side 1) Kayleigh (alternative mix) 3:57
Kayleigh (extended version) 4:00
Side 2) Lady Nina (extended version) 5:46

UK — EMI, 12 MARIL 3
label black, soft cover
UK — EMI, 12 MARIL P 3
picture disc, no ps
EEC — EMI, 1C K 060 20 0639 6
label yellow, hard cover
ESP — EMI, 20 07026
label white, promo

ESP — EMI, 20 07026
label yellow
ESP — EMI, 20 07026
label yellow, cover with printing error
POR — EMI, 200 6396
label yellow
AUS — EMI
promo
NZ — EMI, GOOD 71

Side 1) Kayleigh (single version) 4:04
Side 2) Kayleigh (alternative mix) 4:00

USA — Capitol, SPRO 9417/9418
label black, promo, stickered sleeve

»Misplaced childhood«

(UK release 17.06.1985)

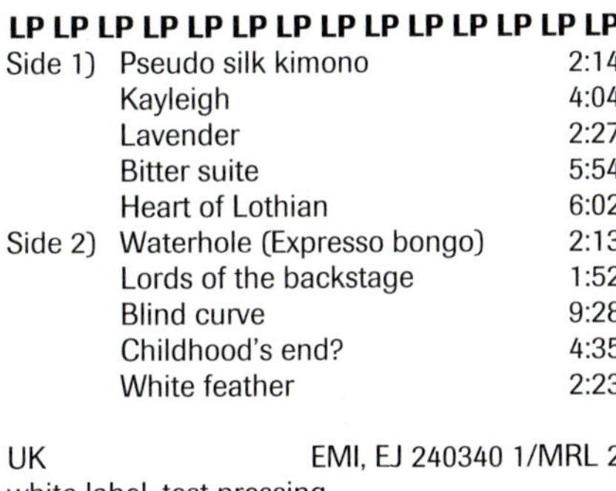

LP LP LP LP LP LP LP LP LP LP LP LP LP LP

Side 1)	Pseudo silk kimono	2:14
	Kayleigh	4:04
	Lavender	2:27
	Bitter suite	5:54
	Heart of Lothian	6:02
Side 2)	Waterhole (Expresso bongo)	2:13
	Lords of the backstage	1:52
	Blind curve	9:28
	Childhood's end?	4:35
	White feather	2:23

UK — EMI, EJ 240340 1/MRL 2
white label, test pressing
UK — EMI, EJ 240340 1/MRL 2
red and green label, test pressing
UK — Townhouse
one-sided acetate
UK — Townhouse
2 one-sided acetates
UK — EMI, EJ 240340 1/MRL 2
label black, foc
UK — EMI, EJ 240340 1/MRL 2
label purple, foc
UK — EMI, 100 CENT 26
release 11/'97, label black, foc, 180 gram vinyl
UK — EMI, EJ 240340 0/MRL P 2
picture disc, no ps
EEC — EMI, 1C 064-240340 1
label yellow, foc
EEC — EMI, 1C 064-240340 1
label yellow, foc, "Kayleigh" print on cover
EEC — EMI, 1C 064-240340 1
same as before but with tour dates sticker
EEC — EMI, 42 703 9
label yellow, foc, club edition

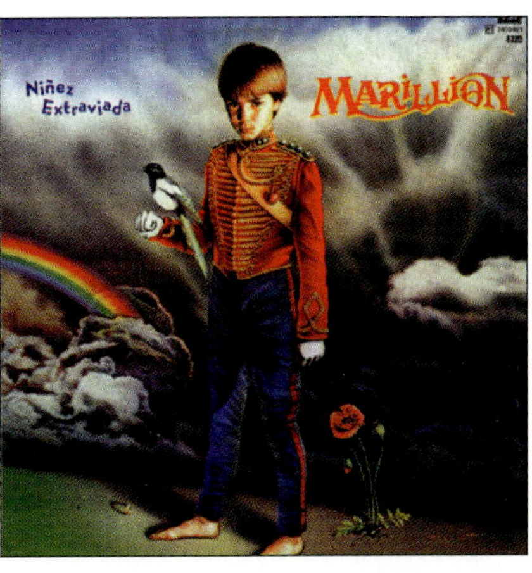

Argentinian cover »Misplaced childhood« album

EEC — EMI, 32 306-3
label yellow, foc, different club edition
ESP — EMI, 066-240340 1
label white, foc, promo
ESP — EMI, 066-240340 1
label yellow, foc
FRA — EMI, 50 999 240340 1
label yellow, foc
GR — EMI, 064-240340 1
label yellow, foc
ITA — EMI, 64 240340 1
label yellow, foc
POR — EMI, 240340 1
label yellow, foc
YUG — EMI, LSEMI 11145
label yellow, foc
AUS — EMI, EMC 240340
label yellow, foc, promo stamp on label
AUS — EMI, EMC 240340
label yellow, foc
BRA — EMI, 31C 064-240340
label yellow, foc
CAN — Capitol, ST-12431
label black, ois, the track "Blind curve" part v.) is called "Tschub" on the label
COL — EMI, 111027
label red/grey, logo in black
ISR — Portrait, EJ 240340
label black, lyric sheet
JAP — EMI, EMS-81728
label white, insert, OBI, promo
JAP — EMI, EMS-81728
label yellow, insert, OBI
KOR — EMI, EKPL-0225
label red, korean lyric sheet, promo stamp on cover

KOR EMI, EKPL-0225
label red, korean lyric sheet
MEX EMI, SLEM-1315
label yellow
NZ EMI, EMI 259
label yellow, foc
RSA EMI, EMCJ (D) 240340 1
label yellow, foc
USA Capitol, ST-12431
label black, ois, the track "Blind curve" part v.) is called "Tschub" on the label
USA Capitol, ST-12431
label black, ois, golden promo stamp, the track "Blind curve" part v.) is called "Tschub" on the label
USA Capitol, ST-12431
label black, ois, promo, virgin vinyl, the track "Blind curve" part v.) is called "Tschub" on the label
USA Capitol, DJ-12431
label black, ois, promo, banned for airplay, the track "Blind curve" part v.) is called "Tschub" on the label
USA Capitol
test pressing with different cover, the track "Blind curve" part v.) is called "Tschub" on the label
VEN EMI, 25044
label yellow, foc, logo with different colour
ZBW EMI, EMCJ (D) 240340 1
label yellow, foc

••

Side 1) Falso kimono de seda
Kayleigh
Lavanda
Bittersuite
Corazon seductor
Side 2) Charco-Expresso bongo
Amos de la trastienda
Curva sin salida
Fin de la ninez
Pluma blanca

ARG EMI, EMI 56320
label yellow, promo, title »Ninez estraviada«
ARG EMI, EMI 56320
label yellow, title »Ninez estraviada«

CD CD CD CD CD CD CD CD CD CD CD CD

	Pseudo silk kimono	2:13
	Kayleigh	4:03
	Lavender	2:27
	Bitter suite	5:53
	Heart of Lothian	6:02
	Waterhole (Expresso bongo)	2:12
	Lords of the backstage	1:52
	Blind curve	9:29
	Childhood's end?	4:32
	White feather	2:23

UK EMI, CDEMS 1518
UK EMI, CDP 746160 2
EEC EMI, CDP 7 46160 2
FRA EMI, 7461602
CAN Capitol, C2 46160
JAP EMI, CDP 7 46160 2
JAP EMI, TOCP 8317
re-release
UKR BCVLX, 00043
counterfeit
USA Capitol, C 246160
USA Capitol, DIDX 1251

2CD 2CD 2CD 2CD 2CD 2CD 2CD 2CD 2CD

Disc 1)	Pseudo silk kimono	2:13
	Kayleigh	4:03
	Lavender	2:27
	Bitter suite	5:53
	Heart of Lothian	6:02
	Waterhole (Expresso bongo)	2:12
	Lords of the backstage	1:52
	Blind curve	9:29
	Childhood's end?	4:32
	White feather	2:23
Disc 2)	Lady Nina (extended 12" version)	5:50
	Freaks (single version)	4:03
	Kayleigh (alternative mix)	4:03
	Lavender blue (remix)	4:22
	Pseudo silk kimono *	2:11
	Kayleigh *	4:06
	Lavender *	2:27
	Bitter suite *	2:54
	Lords of the backstage *	1:46
	Blue angel *	1:46
	Misplaced rendezvous *	1:56
	Heart of Lothian *	3:49
	Waterhole (Expresso bongo) *	2:00
	Passing strangers *	9:17
	Childhood's end? *	2:23
	White feather *	2:18

** Demo 2/'85, disc 2 remastered bonus CD*

UK EMI, 497 0342
release 17.10.1998
EEC EMI, 7243 4 97034 2 1
release 17.10.1998

»Lavender«

(UK release 27.08.1985)

7" 7" 7" 7" 7" 7" 7" 7" 7" 7" 7" 7" 7" 7" 7" 7"

Side 1)	Lavender (7" version)	3:40
Side 2)	Freaks (7" version)	4:04

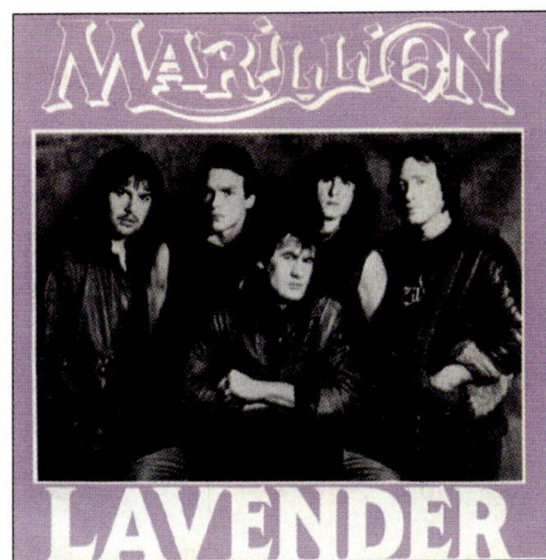

Canadian cover »Lavender« 7"

UK — EMI, MARIL 4
label white, promo

UK — EMI, MARIL 4
label silver

UK — EMI, MARIL 4
label black, small center hole

UK — EMI, MARIL 4
label black, big center hole

EEC — EMI, 1A 006-20 0777 7
label yellow

EEC — EMI, 1C 006-20 0777 7
label yellow

ESP — EMI, 6 200777 7
label white, promo

ESP — EMI, 6 200777 7
label yellow

FRA — EMI, 2007777
label silver, with promo stamp

FRA — EMI, 2007777
label silver

IRL — EMI, MARIL 4
label black, company sleeve

POR — EMI, 200 7777
label yellow, back cover black/white

CAN — Capitol, B-72290
label black, different cover

AUS — EMI, EMI-1578
label yellow, promo, no ps

AUS — EMI, EMI-1578
label yellow, no ps

NZ — EMI, EMI 922
label yellow, company sleeve

RSA — EMI, EMI J 200777 7
label yellow

USA — Capitol, B-5539
label black

ZBW — EMI, EMI J 200777 7
label yellow, company sleeve

Side 1)	Lavender (7" version)	3:40
Side 2)	Lavender (7" version)	3:40

USA — Capitol, P-B-5539
label white, promo, no ps

12" 12" 12" 12" 12" 12" 12" 12" 12" 12" 12"

Side 1)	Lavender blue	4:18
Side 2)	Freaks (7" version)	4:04
	Lavender (7" version)	3:40

UK — EMI, 12 MARIL 4
label black, soft cover

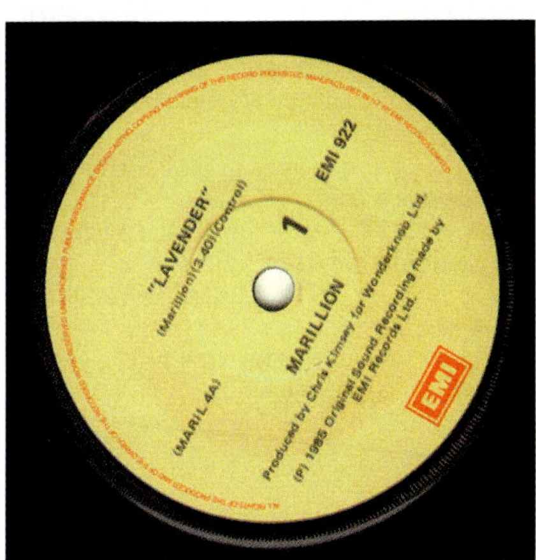

New Zealand label »Lavender« 7"

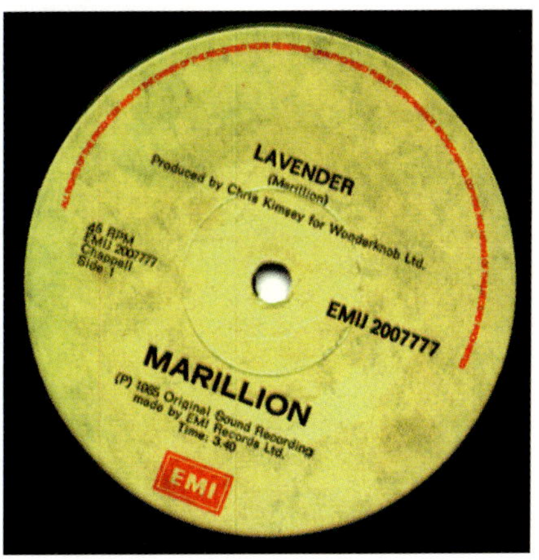

Zimbabwean label »Lavender« 7"

UK EMI, 12 MARIL 4
label purple, soft cover
UK EMI, 12 MARIL P 4
picture disc, no ps
UK EMI, 12 MARIL P 4
same as before but mispressed with the same picture on A+B
EEC EMI, 20 0778 6
test pressing, label white, no ps
EEC EMI, 1C K 060 20 0778 6
label yellow, hard cover
ESP EMI, 052-200778 6
label yellow
POR EMI, 200 7786
label yellow
AUS EMI, ED-134
label yellow, promo
AUS EMI, ED-134
label yellow
NZ EMI, GOOD 82
label yellow, promo

Side 1) Lavender (single version) 3:40
Side 2) Lavender blue (extended version) 4:20

USA Capitol, SPRO 9510/9511
label black, promo, stickered sleeve

»Heart of Lothian«

(UK release 18.11.1985)

7" 7" 7" 7" 7" 7" 7" 7" 7" 7" 7" 7" 7" 7" 7" 7"

Side 1) Heart of Lothian (7" version) 3:40
Side 2) Chelsea monday 7:23
Utrecht, Vredenburg, 15.10.1985

UK EMI, MARIL 5
label silver
UK EMI, MARIL 5
label black
UK EMI, MARIL 5
label black but no label on A-side
EEC EMI, 2009587
label white, test pressing, no ps
EEC EMI, 1A 006-20 0958 7
label yellow
EEC EMI, 1C 006-20 0958 7
label yellow
EEC EMI, 1C 006-20 0958 7
label yellow but with Kate Bush "Cloudbusting" label (20 0899 7) on A-side
AUS EMI, EMI-1649
label yellow, promo, no ps
AUS EMI, EMI-1649
label yellow

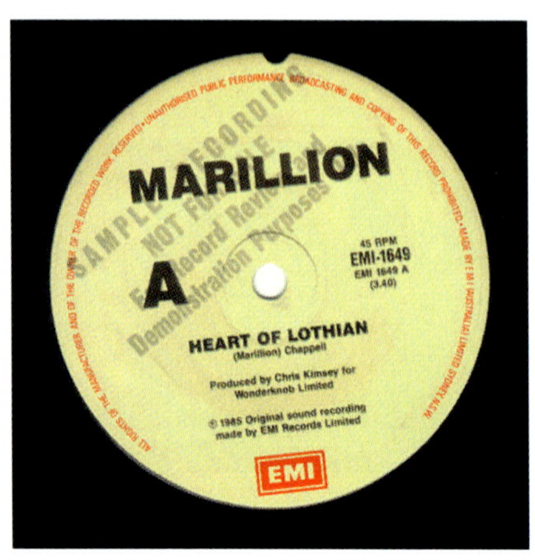

Australian label »Heart of Lothian« 7"

CAN Capitol, B-72993
label black
RSA EMI, EMI J 200958 7
label yellow, with promo stamp
RSA EMI, EMI J 200958 7
label yellow

Side 1) – not playable –
Side 2) Chelsea Monday 7:23
Utrecht, Vredenburg, 15.10.1985

UK EMI, MARIL 5 B
one-sided test pressing, side B

12" 12" 12" 12" 12" 12" 12" 12" 12" 12" 12"

Side 1) Heart of Lothian (full version) 5:43
Side 2) Chelsea Monday 7:23
Utrecht, Vredenburg, 15.10.1985
Heart of Lothian (7" version) 3:40

UK EMI, 12 MARIL 5
label black, soft cover
UK EMI, 12 MARIL 5
label white, test pressing
UK EMI, 12 MARIL P 5
picture disc, no ps
EEC EMI, 1C K 060 20 0959 6
label yellow, hard cover
POR EMI
label yellow
AUS EMI, ED-159
label yellow, promo
AUS EMI, ED-159
label yellow

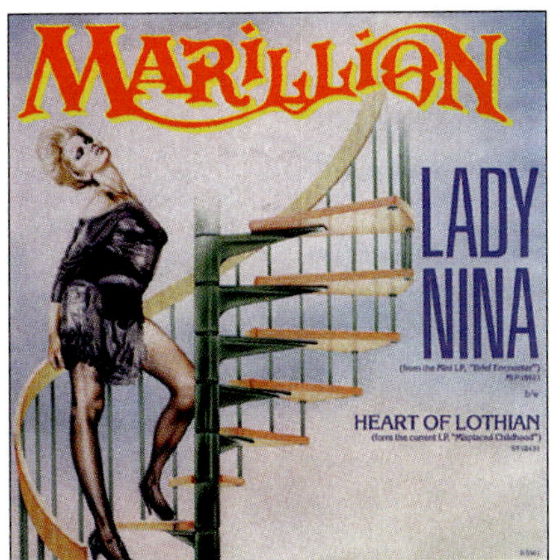

American cover »Lady Nina« 7"

»The story so far«

(CAN promo release only 1985)

LP LP LP LP LP LP LP LP LP LP LP LP LP LP

Side 1)	Market square heroes (»Real to reel« live version)	7:08
	He knows you know (12" version)	5:06
	Garden party (album version)	7:14
Side 2)	Punch and Judy (album version)	3:19
	Kayleigh (alternative mix)	4:04
	Lavender (7" version)	3:40

CAN Capitol, SPRO-281
made for promotional use only

»Lady Nina«

(USA-only release 4/'86)

7" 7" 7" 7" 7" 7" 7" 7" 7" 7" 7" 7" 7" 7" 7" 7"

Side 1)	Lady Nina (7" version)	3:39
Side 2)	Heart of Lothian (edit)	3:47

USA Capitol, B 5561
label black

Side 1)	Lady Nina (7" version)	3:39
Side 2)	Lady Nina (7" version)	3:39

USA Capitol, P-B-5561
label white, promo

12" 12" 12" 12" 12" 12" 12" 12" 12" 12" 12"

Side 1)	Lady Nina (extended version)	5:45
Side 2)	Lady Nina (7" version)	3:39

USA Capitol, SPRO-9593/9594
label black, promo, stickered sleeve
UK Abbey Road
acetate

»Brief encounter«

(USA-only release 4/'86)

LP LP LP LP LP LP LP LP LP LP LP LP LP LP

Side 1)	Lady Nina (extended version)	5:46
	Freaks (7" version)	4:08
	Kayleigh *	4:10
Side 2)	Script for a jester's tear *	8:31
	Fugazi *	8:52

** Live London, Hammersmith Odeon 1/'86*

USA Capitol, MLP-15023
label black, test pressing, different cover
USA Capitol, MLP-15023
label white, test pressing, promo stamp
USA Capitol, MLP-15023
label black, with golden promo stamp
USA Capitol, MLP-15023
label black

CD CD CD CD CD CD CD CD CD CD CD CD

Only released as the bonus CD of the »Real to reel« remaster (04.06.1997)

»Interview with Fish«

(EEC-only release 1986)

LP LP LP LP LP LP LP LP LP LP LP LP LP LP

There are two different picture discs with interviews featuring Fish

EEC Baktabak, BAK 2021
picture disc, die-cut sleeve
EEC Red Door, RD PD 23
picture disc, no ps

CD CD CD CD CD CD CD CD CD CD CD CD

There is one interview CD with Fish, release date unknown

FRA Talking Records, TRCD 001
ltd. ed. of 1,000 copies

»Welcome to the garden party«

(GER-only release 6/'86)

7" 7" 7" 7" 7" 7" 7" 7" 7" 7" 7" 7" 7" 7" 7" 7"

Side 1)	Garden party (edited version)	4:29

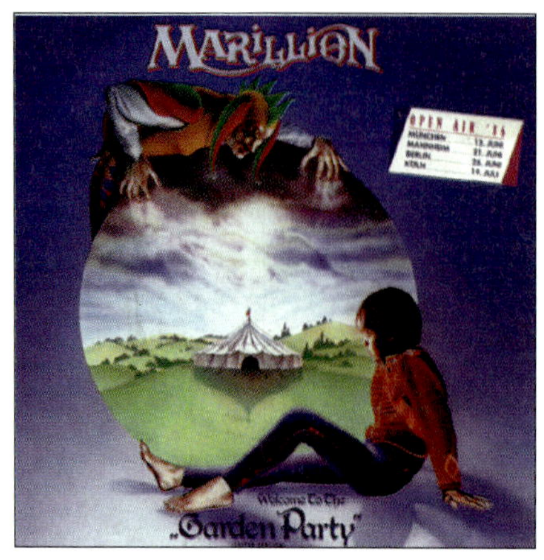

German cover »Welcome to the garden party« 7"

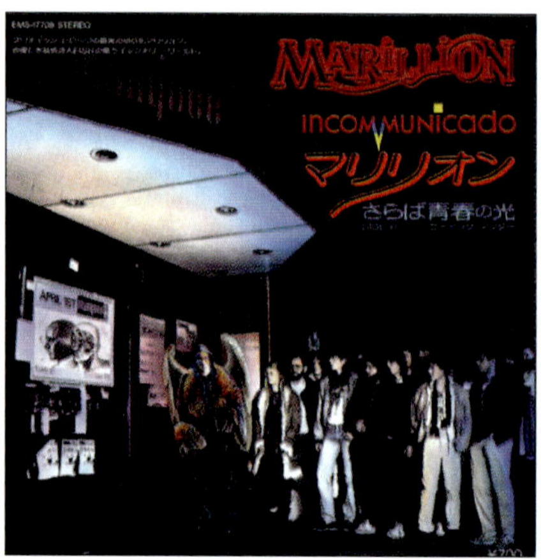

Japanese cover »Incommunicado« 7"

Side 2) Market square heroes (edit, re-recorded) 3:58

EEC EMI, 1 C 006-20 1189 7
label yellow

12" 12" 12" 12" 12" 12" 12" 12" 12" 12" 12"

Side 1) Garden party 6:56
Side 2) Kayleigh 4:10
Script for a jester's tear 8:50

Side 1 recorded live in Leicester, 05.03.1984, side 2 recorded live in London, Hammersmith Odeon, 1/'86

EEC EMI, 1 C K 060-20 1190 6
label yellow, tour sticker on cover

»Incommunicado«

(UK release 11.05.1987)

7" 7" 7" 7" 7" 7" 7" 7" 7" 7" 7" 7" 7" 7" 7" 7"

Side 1) Incommunicado 3:56
Side 2) Going under 2:47

UK EMI, MARIL 6
label silver, hard cover, small centre hole
UK EMI, MARIL 6
label silver, soft cover, small centre hole
UK EMI, MARIL 6
label silver, hard cover, big centre hole
UK EMI, MARIL 6
label silver, soft cover, big centre hole
EEC EMI, 1 C 006-20 1817 7
label black
ESP EMI, 006-2018177
label white, promo
ESP EMI, 006-2018177
label yellow
FRA EMI, 1 C 006-20 1817 7
label black, french tour dates sticker
IRL EMI, MARIL 6
label black, company sleeve
ITA EMI, 06 2018177
label yellow
POR EMI, 2018177
label yellow, back cover black/white
AUS EMI, EMI 1953
label yellow, promo
AUS EMI, EMI 1953
label yellow
JAP EMI, EMS-17709
label white, lyric sheet, promo
JAP EMI, EMS-17709
label yellow, lyric sheet
NZ EMI, EMI 880
label yellow
RSA EMI, EMI J 2018177
label yellow

12" 12" 12" 12" 12" 12" 12" 12" 12" 12" 12"

Side 1) Incommunicado (album version) 5:16
Side 2) Incommunicado (alternative mix) 5:56
Going under 2:46

UK EMI, 12 MARIL 6
label white, test pressing, no ps
UK EMI, 12 MARIL 6
label black, soft cover
UK EMI, 12 MARIL P 6
picture disc, no ps
UK EMI, 12 MARIL P 6
same as before but mispressed, plays side A on both sides

EEC EMI, 1 C K 060-20 1816 6
label black, hard cover
ESP EMI, 052 20 1816 6
label white, hard cover, promo
ESP EMI, 052 20 1816 6
label yellow, hard cover
FRA EMI, 1 C K 060-20 1816 6
label black, french tour dates sticker
ITA EMI, 14 2018166
label yellow
POR EMI, 201 9366
label yellow
AUS EMI, ED 268
label yellow, hard cover
NZ EMI, GOOD 182
label yellow, hard cover
VEN EMI, EMI 25144
label yellow

CD CD CD CD CD CD CD CD CD CD CD CD

Incommunicado (album version)	5:16
Incommunicado (alternative mix)	5:56
Going under	2:46

UK EMI, CD MARIL 6
cardboard sleeve, foc
EEC EMI, CDP 560 201 816 2
cardboard sleeve, foc, CD made in UK, cover in EEC

»Clutching at straws«

(UK release 22.06.1987)

LP LP LP LP LP LP LP LP LP LP LP LP LP LP

Side 1)	Hotel hobbies	3:37
	Warm wet circles	4:23
	That time of the night (The short straw)	5:56
	Just for the record	3:08
	White russian	6:26
Side 2)	Incommunicado	5:14
	Torch song	4:05
	Slainte mhath	4:40
	Sugar mice	5:44
	The last straw (incl. Happy ending)	5:48

UK EMI, EMD 1002
label white, test pressing, hard ois
UK EMI, EMD 1002
cocktail label, structure cover, hard ois
UK EMI, ATAK 135
re-release
UK EMI, EMD P 1002
picture disc, die cut sleeve
UK EMI, EMD P 1002
same as before but mispressed with different side B
UK Sony, 450290 0 / EMD P 1002
Michael Jackson »Bad« picture disc mispressed, plays "Clutching at straws", black rim around the record
EEC EMI, 1 C 064-24 0785 1
cocktail label, structured cover, soft ois
EEC EMI, 1 C 064-24 0785 1
same as before but with "Loreley" sticker
EEC EMI, 038-74 6866 1
re-release, cocktail label, soft ois
EEC EMI, 14 672 0
club edition, cocktail label, soft ois
ESP EMI, 2407851
white label, promo
ESP EMI, 2407851
yellow label
GR EMI, 062-240785 1
yellow label with english print, ois
GR EMI, 062-240785 1
yellow label with greek print, ois
ITA EMI, 64-240785 1
cocktail label, hard ois
POR EMI, 2407851
cocktail label, soft ois
RUS P 94, RAT 30780
label black, slightly different cover
YUG EMI, LSEMI 78049
cocktail label, structure cover, hard ois
AUS EMI, EMC 240785
label yellow
CAN Capitol, ST-12539
label black, soft ois
ISR EMI, EMD 1002-1
cocktail label, lyric sheet
JAP EMI, EMS-91230
cocktail label, insert, OBI, promo stamp
JAP EMI, EMS-91230
cocktail label, insert, OBI
NZ EMI, EMI 3533
ois
RSA EMI, EMC J (D) 2407851
cocktail label, soft ois, gold promo stamp
RSA EMI, EMC J (D) 2407851
cocktail label, soft ois
USA Capitol, ST-12539
cocktail label, golden promo stamp
USA Capitol, ST-12539
cocktail label
VEN EMI, EMI 25148
cocktail label

Side 1) Hobbies de hotel
Circulos humedos y calidos
Aquel tiempo de la noche - Insignificante
Solo para el record
Ruso blanco

Side 2) Incomunicado
Cancion ardiente
Slainte mhath
Ratones de azucar
El colmo

ARG EMI, EMI 10026
label yellow, ois, promo print, title »Pendiendo de un hilo«
ARG EMI, EMI 10026
label yellow, ois, title »Pendiendo de un hilo«

Side 1) Diversion en el hotel
Circulos, humedos y calientes
Tiempo de la noche (el pequeno popote)
Sora pala la estadistica
Ruso blanco
Side 2) Incomunicado
La cancion de la Antorch
Ratones de dulce
El ultimo popote
Final feliz

MEX EMI, EMI SLEM 1464

CD CD CD CD CD CD CD CD CD CD CD CD

Hotel hobbies	3:37
Warm wet circles	4:23
That time of the night (The short straw)	5:56
Going under •	2:47
Just for the record	3:08
White russian	6:26
Incommunicado	5:14
Torch song	4:05
Slainte mhath	4:40
Sugar mice	5:44
The last straw (incl. Happy ending)	5:48

• *Bonus track*

UK EMI, CD EMD 1002
UK EMI, CDP 7 46866 2
UK EMI, CZ 214
re-release
EEC EMI, CDP 7 46866 2
? EMI, CDP 7 46866 2
mispressed CD plays The Beatles
? EMI, CDP 7 46866 2
mispressed CD plays Queensryche
UKR BCVLX, 00042
counterfeit
JAP EMI, CP 32-5449
insert, OBI
USA Capitol, C 246866
USA Capitol, DIDX 1638

2CD 2CD 2CD 2CD 2CD 2CD 2CD 2CD 2CD

Disc 1)	Hotel hobbies	3:37
	Warm wet circles	4:23
	That time of the night (The short straw)	5:56
	Going under •	2:47
	Just for the record	3:08
	White russian	6:26
	Incommunicado	5:14
	Torch song	4:05
	Slainte mhath	4:40
	Sugar mice	5:44
	The last straw (incl. Happy ending)	5:48
Disc 2)	Incommunicado (alternative version)	5:57
	Tux on	5:13
	Going under (extended version)	2:48
	Beaujolais day *	4:51
	Story from a thin wall *	6:47
	Shadows on the Barley *	2:07
	Sunset hill *	4:21
	Tic-tac-toe *	2:59
	Voice in the crowd *	3:29
	Exile on Princess Street *	5:29
	White Russian (demo version) *	6:15
	Sugar mice in the rain *	5:56
	Warm wet circles (Rock'n'roll) (instrumental) **	2:20

• *Bonus track, * previously unreleased, ** multimedia hidden track, disc 2 remastered bonus CD*

UK EMI, 498611 2
release 22.03.1999
EEC EMI, 7243 4 98611 2 1
release 19.03.1999

Video-CD Video-CD Video-CD Video-CD

Hotel hobbies	3:35
Warm wet circles	4:25
That time of the night	5:57
Incommunicado **	3:57

*** Video, PAL format*

UK EMI, EMCDV 1
video CD, test pressing

»Sugar mice«

(UK release 13.07.1987)

7" 7" 7" 7" 7" 7" 7" 7" 7" 7" 7" 7" 7" 7" 7" 7"

Side 1)	Sugar mice (album version)	5:47
Side 2)	Tux on	5:09

UK EMI, MARIL 7
label silver, small center hole, hard cover

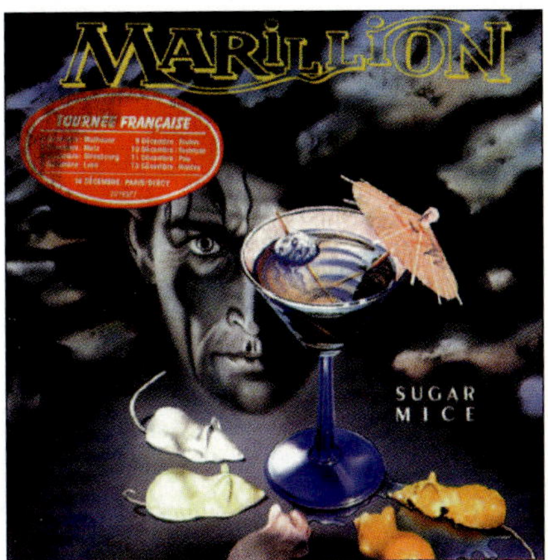

French cover »Sugar Mice« 7"

UK — EMI, MARIL 7
label silver, big center hole, hard cover
UK — EMI, MARIL 7
label black, hard cover, "QFH" promo sample sticker on cover
EEC — EMI, 1 C 016-20 1937 7
label yellow, soft cover, but mispressed label with time for "Sugar mice" 4:59
ESP — EMI, 006-2019377
label yellow, soft cover
FRA — EMI, 2019377
label silver, promo stamp
FRA — EMI, 2019377
label silver, french tour dates sticker
IRL — EMI, MARIL 7
label black, company sleeve
POR — EMI, 201 9377
label yellow, back cover black/white

••

Side 1) Sugar mice (edited version) 4:57
Side 2) Tux on 4:59

UK — EMI, MARIL DJ 7
label white, test pressing, no ps
UK — EMI, MARIL DJ 7
label silver, test pressing, no ps
UK — EMI, MARIL DJ 7
label black, promo, no ps
UK — EMI, MARIL P 7
picture disc + poster, no ps
USA — Capitol, B-44060
label black
CAN — Capitol, B-44060
label black

••

Side 1) Sugar mice (edit) 4:57
Side 2) Sugar mice (edit) 4:57

USA — Capitol, P-B- 44060
label white, promo

10" 10" 10" 10" 10" 10" 10" 10" 10" 10" 10"

Side 1) Sugar mice
Side 2) ?

UK — Abbey Road
acetate

12" 12" 12" 12" 12" 12" 12" 12" 12" 12" 12"

Side 1) Sugar mice (extended version) 6:08
Side 2) Sugar mice (album version) 5:45
Tux on 5:12

UK — EMI, 12 MARIL 7
label black, soft cover
UK — EMI, 12 MARIL P 7
picture disc, no ps
EEC — EMI, 1C K 060-20 1936 6
label yellow, hard cover
POR — EMI, 201 9366
label yellow

CD CD CD CD CD CD CD CD CD CD CD CD

Sugar mice (radio edit) 5:00
Tux on 5:09
Sugar mice (extended version) 6:09

UK — EMI, CD MARIL 7
cardboard sleeve, with promo sticker
UK — EMI, CD MARIL 7
cardboard sleeve
UK — EMI, CD MARIL 7

»Warm wet circles«

(UK release 26.10.1987)

7" 7" 7" 7" 7" 7" 7" 7" 7" 7" 7" 7" 7" 7" 7" 7"

Side 1) Warm wet circles (7" remix) 4:23
Side 2) White russian 6:09
Loreley, 18.07.1987

UK — EMI, MARIL 8
label silver, hard cover
UK — EMI, MARIL 8
label silver, soft cover
EEC — EMI, 006-20 2158 7
label yellow, censored back cover
EEC — EMI, 006-20 2158 7
same as before, with "Clutching" advert
EEC — EMI, 1 C 016-20 2158 7
label yellow, censored back cover

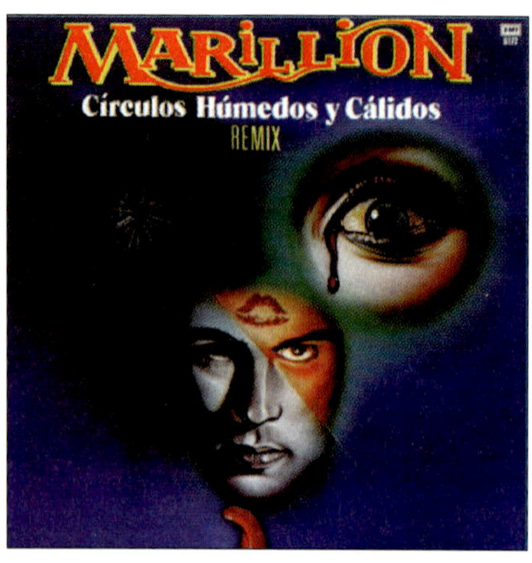

Argentinian cover »Warm wet circles« 12"

IRL EMI, MARIL 8
label black, company sleeve

Side 1) Warm wet circles
Side 2) – not playable –

UK Abbey Road
one-sided metal acetate in factory sleeve, no number

12" 12" 12" 12" 12" 12" 12" 12" 12" 12" 12"

Side 1) Warm wet circles (7" remix) 4:23
Side 2) White russian * 6:09
Incommunicado * 5:27
** Recorded live in Loreley, 18.07.1987*

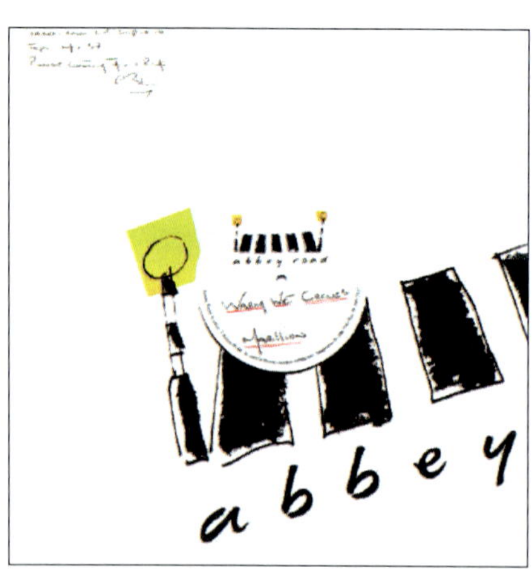

UK metal acetate »Warm wet circles« 12"

UK EMI, 12 MARIL 8
label black, "Warning" sticker
UK EMI, 12 MARIL P 8
picture disc, "Warning" sticker
EEC EMI, 1C K 060-20 2168 6
label yellow, censored cover

Side 1) Circulos humedos y calidos
Side 2) Ruso blanco
Incomunicado

ARG EMI, EMI 6177
label yellow

Side 1) Warm wet circles (tape mix 37)
Side 2) – not playable –

UK Abbey Road
one-sided metal acetate in factory sleeve, no number

CD CD CD CD CD CD CD CD CD CD CD CD

Warm wet circles (7" remix) 4:23
White russian * 6:09
Incommunicado * 5:27
** Recorded live in Loreley, 18.07.1987*

UK EMI, CD MARIL 8
cardboard sleeve

»B'sides themselves«

(UK release 04.01.1988)

LP LP LP LP LP LP LP LP LP LP LP LP LP LP

Side 1) Grendel 17:14
Charting the single 4:46
Market square heroes
(re-recorded edit) 3:56
Three boats down from the candy
(re-recorded) 3:57
Side 2) Cinderella search (full version) 5:24
Lady Nina (7" edit) 3:41
Freaks 4:02
Tux on 5:10
Margaret 12:17
Edinburgh, 07.04.1983

UK EMI, EMS 1295
label black
UK EMI, ATAK 113
re-release
EEC EMI, 1C 064-74 8807 1
label yellow
EEC EMI/Fame, 1C 038-1 57734 1
label yellow, "Fame" sticker + "Fame" ois

FRA EMI, 74 8807 1 PM 254
label yellow
GR EMI, 7488 071
label yellow
ITA EMI, 74 8807 1
label yellow
POR EMI, 74 8807 1
label yellow
CAN Capitol, C1 48807
label purple
BRA EMI, 064 74 8807 1
label yellow
ISR EMI, EMS 12951
label black
VEN EMI, EMI 25159
label yellow

CD CD CD CD CD CD CD CD CD CD CD CD

Grendel	17:14
Charting the single	4:46
Market square heroes (re-recorded edit)	3:56
Three boats down from the candy (re-recorded version)	3:57
Cinderella search (edit)	4:22
Lady Nina (7" edit)	3:41
Freaks	4:02
Tux on	5:10
Margaret	12:17
Edinburgh, 07.04.1983	

UK EMI, CZ 39
EEC EMI, CDP 7 48807 2
UKR BCVLX, 00041
counterfeit

»Freaks (live)«

(UK release 21.11.1988)

7" 7" 7" 7" 7" 7" 7" 7" 7" 7" 7" 7" 7" 7" 7"

Side 1)	Freaks	4:10
	Mannheim, Maimarkt, 21.06.1986	
Side 2)	Kayleigh	3:53
	London, Hammersmith Odeon 09./10.01.1986	

UK EMI, MARIL 9
label black
UK EMI, MARIL P 9
shaped picture disc, uncut test pressing, no ps
UK EMI, MARIL P 9
shaped picture disc, insert, no ps
EEC EMI, 006-20 3087 7
label yellow
EEC EMI, 006-20 3087 7
label yellow, but no label on B-side
EEC EMI, 006-20 3087 7
label yellow, but with confound label A-side and B-side
ESP EMI, 006 2030877
label yellow
POR EMI, 2030877
label yellow

10" 10" 10" 10" 10" 10" 10" 10" 10" 10" 10"

Side 1)	Freaks
	Mannheim, Maimarkt, 21.06.1986
Side 2)	– not playable –

USA Capitol
label white, one-sided test pressing

12" 12" 12" 12" 12" 12" 12" 12" 12" 12" 12"

Side 1)	Freaks	4:11
	Mannheim, Maimarkt, 21.06.1986	
	Kayleigh *	4:05
Side 2)	Childhood's end? *	2:52
	White feather *	4:16

** Recorded live in London, Hammersmith Odeon 09./10.01.1986*

UK EMI, 12 MARIL 9
label black, soft cover
EEC EMI, 060-20 3088 6
label yellow, hard cover
ITA EMI, 14 2031886
label yellow

CD CD CD CD CD CD CD CD CD CD CD CD

Freaks	4:11
Mannheim, Maimarkt, 21.06.1986	
Kayleigh *	4:05
Childhood's end? *	2:52
White feather *	4:16

** Recorded live in London, Hammersmith Odeon 09./10.01.1986*

UK EMI, CD MARIL 9
EEC EMI, 560 20 3088 2

»The thieving magpie – La gazza ladra (live)«

(UK release 29.11.1988)

2LP 2LP 2LP 2LP 2LP 2LP 2LP 2LP 2LP 2LP

Side 1)	Intro: La gazza ladra *	2:44
	Slainte mhath *	4:47
	He knows you know	5:06
	Chelsea monday **	8:00
Side 2)	Pseudo silk kimono °	2:16
	Kayleigh °	3:50
	Lavender °	2:38

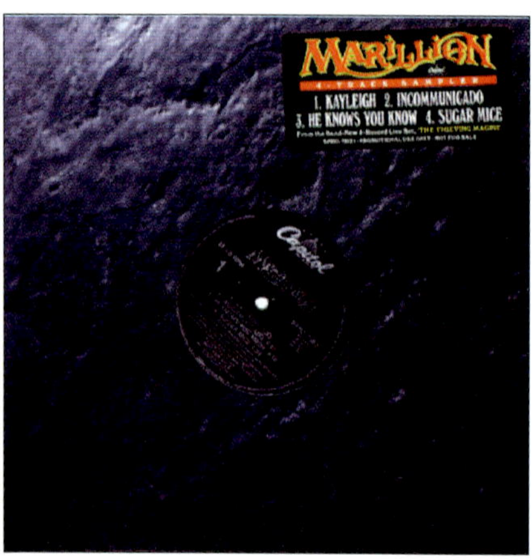

US cover »The thieving magpie« promo sampler 12"

	Bitter suite °	6:13
	Heart of Lothian °	6:13
Side 3)	Jigsaw	6:20
	Punch and Judy	3:21
	Sugar mice *	6:00
	Fugazi	8:34
Side 4)	Script for a jester's tear	8:41
	Incommunicado *	5:24
	White russian *	6:12

*Recorded live in Sheffield, City Hall, 06.03.1984, except * live in Edinburgh, Playhouse, 17.-19.12.1987, live in ** Leicester, De Montfort Hall, 05.03.1984,° live in live London, Hammersmith Odeon 09./10.01.1986*

UK EMI, MARL 1
label white, test pressing, foc, ois
UK EMI, MARL 1
label black, foc, ois, merchandise sheet
EEC EMI, 164-79 1465 1
label yellow, foc, ois
EEC EMI, 606913
label yellow, foc, ois, club edition
EEC EMI, 32 845 0
label yellow, foc, club edition, cover made in UK
FRA EMI/Pathe Marconi, 164-7914631
label yellow, foc, ois, promo
FRA EMI/Pathe Marconi, 164-7914631
label yellow, foc, ois
ITA EMI, 2 62 791463 1
label yellow, foc, ois
ITA EMI, 2 62 791463 1
label yellow, foc, ois, promo print on cover
POR EMI, 7914631
label yellow, foc, ois
BRA EMI, 164 7914631
label yellow, foc
ISR EMI, MARL 1-1
label black, foc, promo sticker
ISR EMI, MARL 1-1
label black, foc
USA Capitol, C1-01463 2
label purple, ois, golden promo stamp
USA Capitol, C1-01463 2
label purple, ois
VEN EMI, EMI 25169
label yellow, foc
VEN EMI, EMI 25169
label yellow

12" 12" 12" 12" 12" 12" 12" 12" 12" 12"

Side 1)	Kayleigh	3:52
	London, Hammersmith Odeon 09./10.01.1986	
	Incommunicado *	4:57
	He knows you know	4:58
	Sheffield, City Hall, 06.03.1984	
	Sugar mice *	5:55

** Recorded live in Edinburgh, Playhouse, 17.-19.12.1987*

USA Capitol, SPRO-79521
label purple, promo, stickered sleeve, double side 1

2CD 2CD 2CD 2CD 2CD 2CD 2CD 2CD 2CD

Disc 1)	Intro: La gazza ladra	2:44
	Slainte mhath	4:47
	He knows you know *	5:06
	Chelsea Monday **	8:00
	Freaks °	4:11
	Jigsaw *	6:20
	Punch and Judy *	3:21
	Sugar mice	6:00
	Fugazi *	8:34
	Script for a jester's tear *	8:41
	Incommunicado	5:24
	White russian	6:12
Disc 2)	Pseudo silk kimono	2:16
	Kayleigh	3:50
	Lavender	2:38
	Bitter suite	6:13
	Heart of Lothian	6:13
	Waterhole	2:16
	Lords of the backstage	6:07
	Blind curve	5:34
	Childhoods end?	3:47
	White feather	4:22

*Disc 1 recorded live in Edinburgh, Playhouse, 17.-19.12.1987, except * live in Sheffield, City Hall, 06.03.1984, ** live in Leicester, De Montfort Hall, 05.03.1984, ° live in Mannheim, Maimarkt, 21.06.1986, disc 2 recorded live in London, Hammersmith Odeon 09./10.01.1986*

UK EMI, CD MARL 1
booklet, poster

CH EMI, CDS 7914632
booklet, poster
JAP EMI, CP 25 5767/68
release 1989, OBI, booklet, poster
USA Capitol, CDP 7 91463 2
2 separate CDs in long pack cover, booklet, poster

»Hooks in you«

(UK release 24.08.1989)

7" 7" 7" 7" 7" 7" 7" 7" 7" 7" 7" 7" 7" 7" 7" 7"

Side 1) Hooks in you (7" version) 2:57
Side 2) After me 3:24

UK EMI, MARIL 10
label white, hard cover
UK EMI, MARIL 10
label black, hard cover
UK EMI, MARIL 10
label silver, hard cover
EEC EMI, 006-20 3495 7
label yellow, soft cover
FRA EMI, 006-20 3495 7
label yellow, promo stamp
ITA EMI, 06-20 3495 7
label yellow
POR EMI, 2034957
label yellow
AUS EMI, EMI 2322
label yellow, company sleeve

Side 1) Hooks in you (7" version) 2:54
Side 2) Hooks in you (Meaty Mix) 3:51
USA Capitol, 7PRO-79911
label white, promo, company sleeve

Side 1) Engachado en ti (7" version) 2:53
Side 2) Engachado en ti (7" version) 2:53

MEX EMI, SEC-803
label yellow, promo, no ps

12" 12" 12" 12" 12" 12" 12" 12" 12" 12" 12"

Side 1) Hooks in you (Meaty Mix) 3:57
Side 2) Hooks in you (7" version) 2:57
After me 3:24

UK EMI, 12 MARIL 10
label white, promo, no ps
UK EMI, 12 MARIL 10
label black, soft cover
UK EMI, 12 MARIL P 10
label black, ltd. ed. posterbag
EEC EMI, K 060 20-3495 6
label yellow, hard cover
FRA EMI, PM 212 20 3495 6
label yellow, hard cover

CD CD CD CD CD CD CD CD CD CD CD CD

Hooks in you (Meaty Mix) 3:57
Hooks in you (7" version) 2:57
After me 3:24

UK EMI, CD MARIL 10
EEC EMI, 552 20 3495 2
A EMI, 552 20 3495 3
3" CD, cardboard sleeve

Hooks in you (7" version) 2:55

USA Capitol, DPRO-79751
orange promo CD, no ps

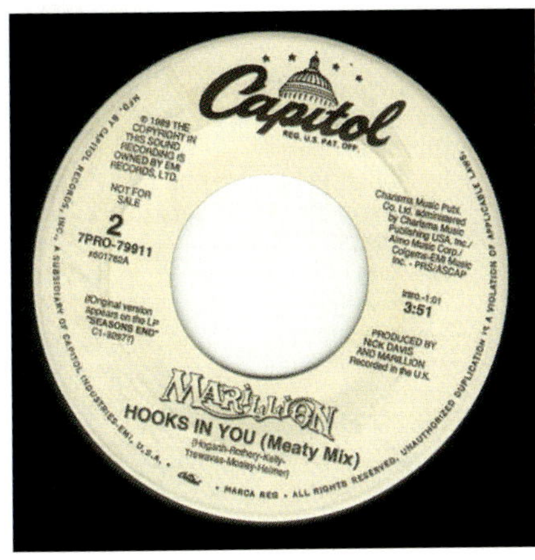

US label »Hooks in you« promo 7"

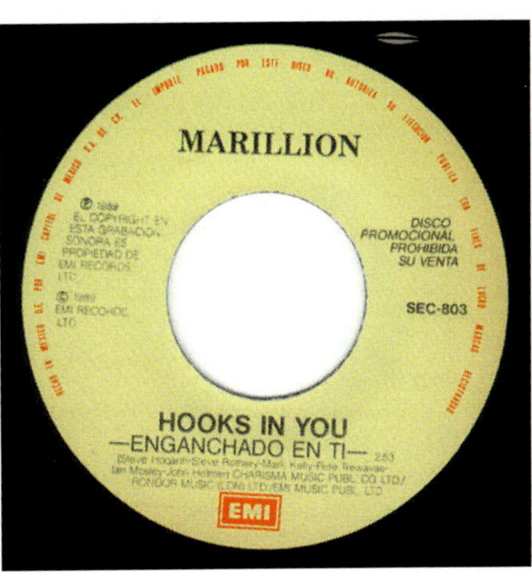

Mexican label »Hooks in you« promo 7"

»Seasons end«

(UK release 25.09.1989)

LP LP LP LP LP LP LP LP LP LP LP LP LP LP

Side 1) The king of sunset town 7:55
Easter 5:56
The uninvited guest 3:49
Seasons end 8:11
Side 2) Holloway girl 4:27
Berlin 7:43
Hooks in you 2:54
The space 6:13

UK EMI, EMD 1011
label white, test pressing
UK EMI, EMD 1011
label white, foc, promo sticker
UK EMI, EMD 1011
label white, foc
UK EMI, EMD PD 1011
white vinyl test pressing for picture disc, no ps
UK EMI, EMD PD 1011
picture disc, insert, no ps
UK EMI, EMD PD 1011
same as before, same picture on A+B, no ps
EEC EMI, 064-79 2877 1
label yellow, foc
EEC EMI, 25039 1
label yellow, foc, club edition
EEC EMI, 064-79 2877 0
picture disc, insert, no ps
ESP EMI, 006-792877 1
ITA EMI, 7928771
ois
POR EMI, 79 28771
label white, foc
AUS EMI, EMC 792877
BRA EMI, 066-7928771
label yellow, foc
KOR EMI/Jeil Records, EKPL 0030
label white, lyric sheet
RSA EMI, EMCJ (L) 7928771
label yellow
USA Capitol, C1-92877
label purple, ois
VEN EMI, EMI 25170
label yellow
ZBW EMI/Gramma, EMCJ (L) 7928771
label yellow

••

Side 1) El rey del pueblo de sunset
Pascua
El huesped no invitado
El fin de las estaciones
Side 2) Chica de holloway
Berlin
Enganchado en ti
El espacio

MEX EMI, LEMSE 1669
label yellow, foc, promo stamp
MEX EMI, LEMSE 1669
label yellow, foc

CD CD CD CD CD CD CD CD CD CD CD CD

The king of sunset town 7:55
Easter 5:56
The uninvited guest 3:49
Seasons end 8:11
Holloway girl 4:27
Berlin 7:43
After me • 3:19
Hooks in you 2:54
The space 6:13

• Bonus track

UK EMI, CD EMD 1011
with special promo cardbox
UK EMI, CD EMD 1011
UK EMI, 792877 2
EEC EMI, CDP 00777 7 92877 2 7
JAP EMI, TOCP-5929
OBI, promo
JAP EMI, TOCP-5929
OBI
USA Capitol, CDP 7 92877 2

2CD 2CD 2CD 2CD 2CD 2CD 2CD 2CD 2CD

Disc 1) The king of sunset town 7:55
Easter 5:56
The uninvited guest 3:49
Seasons end 8:11
Holloway girl 4:27
Berlin 7:43
After me • 3:19
Hooks in you 2:54
The space 6:13
Disc 2) Uninvited guest
(extended 12" version) 5:03
The bell in the sea (7" version) 4:19
The release (7" version) 3:44
The king of sunset town * 5:32
Holloway girl * 4:47
Seasons end * 8:01
The uninvited guest * 3:53
Berlin * 8:02
The bell in the sea * 4:52

*• Bonus track, * Mushroom farm demo, 3/89, disc 2 remastered bonus CD*

UK EMI, REMARIL 005
release 29.09.1997

EEC EMI, 7243 8 57713 2 3
release 29.09.1997
CAN EMI, 7243 8 57713 2 3
release 21.04.1998
USA Sanctuary, 4510
release 07.03.2000

»The uninvited guest«

(UK release 27.11.1989)

7" 7" 7" 7" 7" 7" 7" 7" 7" 7" 7" 7" 7" 7" 7" 7"

Side 1) The uninvited guest (7" version) 3:44
Side 2) The bell in the sea 4:21

UK EMI, MARIL 11
label black, hard cover
UK EMI, MARIL 11
label black, promo sticker on cover
UK EMI, MARIL PD 11
clear vinyl test pressing for the shape, no ps
UK EMI, MARIL PD 11
shaped picture disc, uncut test pressing, no ps
UK EMI, MARIL PD 11
same as before, but “Seasons end” picture on side B, no ps
UK EMI, MARIL PD 11
shaped picture disc, insert, logo white background, no ps
UK EMI, MARIL PD 11
shaped picture disc, insert, logo black background, no ps
EEC EMI, 006-20 3582 7
label yellow, soft cover

••

Side 1) The uninvited guest (7" version) 3:50
Side 2) The uninvited guest (7" version) 3:50

USA Capitol
label white, promo

12" 12" 12" 12" 12" 12" 12" 12" 12" 12" 12"

Side 1) The uninvited guest (12" version) 5:04
Side 2) The bell in the sea 4:21
The uninvited guest (7" version) 3:44

UK EMI, 12 MARIL 11
label black, soft cover
UK EMI, 12 MARIL S 11
label black, “Open door” cover
EEC EMI, K 060-20 3582 6
label yellow, hard cover

CD CD CD CD CD CD CD CD CD CD CD CD

The uninvited guest (7" version) 3:44
The uninvited guest (12" version) 5:04
The bell in the sea 4:21

UK EMI, CD MARIL 11
EEC EMI, 552 20 3582 2
A EMI, 552 20 3582 3
3" CD, cardboard sleeve

••

The uninvited guest (7" version) 3:50

USA Capitol, DPRO-79922
pink , promo, backing card

»Easter«

(UK release 26.03.1990)

7" 7" 7" 7" 7" 7" 7" 7" 7" 7" 7" 7" 7" 7" 7" 7"

Side 1) Easter (7" edit) 4:29
Side 2) The release 3:39

UK EMI, MARIL 12
label black, promo
UK EMI, MARIL 12
label silver, hard cover
UK EMI, MARIL 12
label white, hard cover
UK EMI, MARIL PD 12
picture disc, insert, no ps
EEC EMI, 006-20 3760 7
label yellow, soft cover
FRA EMI, 2037607
label silver, hard cover, promo stamp
FRA EMI, 2037607
label silver, hard cover
ITA EMI, 06 2037607
label yellow, soft cover

12" 12" 12" 12" 12" 12" 12" 12" 12" 12" 12"

Side 1) Easter (12" edit) 5:58
Side 2) The release 3:39
Uninvited guest 4:44
Glasgow, Barrowlands, 04.12.1989

UK EMI, 12 MARIL 12
label black, soft cover
EEC EMI, 060-20 3760 6
label yellow, hard cover

••

Side 1) Easter (7" edit) 4:29
Uninvited guest * 4:44
Side 2) Warm wet circles * 5:40
That time of the night * 4:36

* *Recorded live in Glasgow, Barrowlands, 04.12.1989*

UK EMI, 12 MARIL G 12
label black, foc, numbered ltd. ed.

Side 1) Easter (12" edit) 5:58
The release 3:39
Side 2) Warm wet circles * 5:40
That time of the night * 4:36
Recorded live in Glasgow, Barrowlands, 04.12.1989

UK EMI, 12 MARIL S 12
ltd. ed. of 5,000 copies

CD CD CD CD CD CD CD CD CD CD CD CD
Easter (12" edit) 5:58
The release 3:39
Uninvited guest 4:44
Glasgow, Barrowlands, 04.12.1989

UK EMI, CD MARIL 12
EEC EMI, 560 20 3760 2

»Cover my eyes«

(UK release 28.05.1991)

7" 7" 7" 7" 7" 7" 7" 7" 7" 7" 7" 7" 7" 7" 7" 7"
Side 1) Cover my eyes (Pain and heaven) 3:54
Side 2) How can it hurt 4:08

UK EMI, MARIL 13
label silver, hard cover
EEC EMI, 006-20 4348 7
label yellow, soft cover

Side 1) Cubro mis ojos 3:54
Side 2) Cubro mis ojos 3:54

MEX EMI, 7001072
promo, no ps

12" 12" 12" 12" 12" 12" 12" 12" 12" 12" 12"
Side 1) Cover my eyes (Pain and heaven) 3:52
Side 2) How can it hurt 4:10
The party 5:36

UK EMI, 12 MARIL P 13
label black, poster
EEC EMI, 204348 6
label white, test pressing, no ps
EEC EMI, 060-20 4348 6
label yellow

CD CD CD CD CD CD CD CD CD CD CD CD
Cover my eyes (Pain and heaven) 3:52
How can it hurt 4:10
The party 5:36

UK EMI, CD MARIL 13
blue CD
UK EMI, CD MARIL 13
pink CD
UK EMI, CD MARIL S 13
in blue box with poster
EEC EMI, CDP 560 20 4348 2
blue CD

Cover my eyes (Pain and heaven) 3:48

USA I.R.S., DPRO-67084
silver/blue CD, promo, no ps

»Holidays in Eden«

(UK release 24.06.1991)

LP LP LP LP LP LP LP LP LP LP LP LP LP LP
Side 1) Splintering heart 6:51
Cover my eyes (Pain and heaven) 3:55
The party 5:35
No one can 4:39
Side 2) Holidays in Eden 5:27
Dry land 4:41
Waiting to happen 4:55
This town 3:19
The rake's progress 1:54
100 nights 6:41

UK EMI, EMD 1022
picture label, hard ois
UK EMI, EMD 1022
same as before, with "Hit-singles" sticker
EEC EMI, 796822 1
label white, test pressing, no ps
EEC EMI, 064-7 96822 1
picture label, soft ois
EEC EMI, 064-7 96822 1
same as before, with "Tourdates" sticker
CZ Popron, 50 135-1
picture label, soft ois
ITA EMI, 7968221
picture label, soft ois
POR EMI, 7968221
picture label, hard ois
BRA EMI, 7968221
promo
BRA EMI, 7968221
COL EMI,
KOR EMI, EKPL-0153
with lyric sheet
VEN EMI, EMI 25191
picture label, ois

CD CD CD CD CD CD CD CD CD CD CD CD
Splintering heart 6:51
Cover my eyes (Pain and heaven) 3:55
The party 5:35

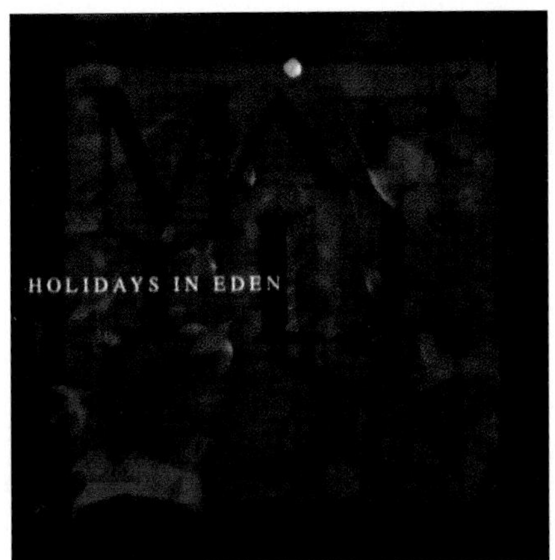

US cover »Holidays in Eden« CD

No one can	4:39
Holidays in Eden	5:27
Dry land	4:41
Waiting to happen	4:55
This town	3:19
The rake's progress	1:54
100 nights	6:41

UK — EMI, CDEMD 1022
UK — EMI, CDP 796822 2
EEC — EMI, CDP 7 96822 2
pink CD, first edition
EEC — EMI, CDP 7 96822 2
blue CD, second edition
CAN — Capitol, C2 96822
JAP — EMI, TOCD-6784
OBI, promo
JAP — EMI, TOCD-6784
OBI

••

Cover my eyes (Pain and heaven)	3:55
No one can take you away from me	4:39
Splintering heart	6:51
The party	5:35
A collection	2:58
Holidays in Eden	5:27
How can it hurt	4:10
Dry land	4:41
Waiting to happen	4:55
This town	3:19
The rake's progress	1:54
100 nights	6:41

USA — I.R.S., X2-13138
different cover, different tracks
USA — I.R.S., X2-13138
same as before but with long cover

2CD 2CD 2CD 2CD 2CD 2CD 2CD 2CD 2CD

Disc 1)	Splintering heart	6:51
	Cover my eyes (Pain and heaven)	3:55
	The party	5:35
	No one can	4:39
	Holidays in Eden	5:27
	Dry land	4:41
	Waiting to happen	4:55
	This town	3:19
	The rake's progress	1:54
	100 nights	6:41
Disc 2)	Sympathy (single version)	3:30
	How can it hurt (single version)	4:11
	A collection (single version)	3:00
	Cover my eyes (acoustic single version) **	2:34
	Sympathy (acoustic single version) **	2:30
	I will walk on water (alternative '98 remix)	5:14
	Splintering heart *	6:42
	You don't need anyone *	4:04
	No one can *	4:51
	The party *	5:45
	This town *	4:16
	Waiting to happen *	5:31
	Eric (Stanbridge Video Soundtrack)	2:32
	The epic (Fairground) (Mushroom farm demo 3/'89)	8:31

** Moles Club demo 12/'90, ** Racket Club, 5/'92, disc 2 remastered bonus CD*

UK — EMI, 493 3722
release 1998
EEC — EMI, 7243 4 93372 2 0
release 1998

»No one can«

(UK release 22.07.1991)

7" 7" 7" 7" 7" 7" 7" 7" 7" 7" 7" 7" 7" 7" 7" 7"

Side 1)	No one can	4:39
Side 2)	A collection	2:58

UK — EMI, MARIL S 14
label black, red box, badge, 4 prints
UK — EMI, MARIL 14
label silver, hard cover, golden rim around cover
EEC — EMI, 006-20 4409 7
label yellow, soft cover, brown rim around cover
FRA — EMI, 006-20 4409 7
label yellow, soft cover

12" 12" 12" 12" 12" 12" 12" 12" 12" 12" 12"

Side 1)	No one can	4:39
Side 2)	A collection	2:58

Splintering heart 7:22
Bath, Moles Club, 11.12.1990

UK EMI, 12 MARIL 14
label black, soft cover
EEC EMI, 204409 6
label white, test pressing, no ps
EEC EMI, 060-20 4409 6
label yellow, hard cover

CD CD CD CD CD CD CD CD CD CD CD CD
No one can 4:39
A collection 2:58
Splintering heart 7:22
Bath, Moles Club, 11.12.1990

UK EMI, CD MARIL 14
golden rim around cover
EEC EMI, 560 20 4409 2
light brown rim around cover

»Dry land«

(UK release 23.09.1991)

7" 7" 7" 7" 7" 7" 7" 7" 7" 7" 7" 7" 7" 7" 7" 7"
Side 1) Dry land (7" edit) 4:02
Side 2) Holloway girl * 3:41
After me * 3:25
** Recorded live in London, Borderline Club, 22.05.1991*

UK EMI, MARIL 15
label silver, hard cover

••

Side 1) Dry land (7" edit) 4:02
Side 2) Holloway girl * 3:41
** Recorded live in London, Borderline Club, 22.05.1991*

EEC EMI, 006-20 4542 7
label yellow, soft cover

10" 10" 10" 10" 10" 10" 10" 10" 10" 10" 10"
Side 1) Dry land (LP version) 4:43
Side 2) Waiting to happen * 4:25
Easter * 3:12
Sugar mice * 3:05
** Recorded live in London, Borderline Club, 22.05.1991*

UK EMI, 10 MARIL 15
clear vinyl, numbered foc

12" 12" 12" 12" 12" 12" 12" 12" 12" 12" 12"
Side 1) Dry land (LP version) 4:43
Holloway girl * 3:48
Side 2) King of sunset town * 3:30
Substitute * 2:25
** Recorded live in London, Borderline Club, 22.05.1991*

UK EMI, 12 MARIL 15
label black, soft cover
UK EMI, 12 MARIL P 15
picture disc, die-cut sleeve
EEC EMI, 060-204542 6
label yellow, hard cover

CD CD CD CD CD CD CD CD CD CD CD CD
Dry land (7" edit) 4:03
Holloway girl * 3:48
Easter * 3:12
Dry land (LP version) 4:43
** Recorded live in London, Borderline Club, 22.05.1991*

UK EMI, CD MARIL 15

••

Dry land (7" edit) 4:03
Holloway girl * 3:48
Easter * 3:12
Sugar mice * 3:05
** Recorded live in London, Borderline Club, 22.05.1991*

EEC EMI, 5 0999 204 542 2 7

»Sympathy«

(UK release 11.05.1992)

7" 7" 7" 7" 7" 7" 7" 7" 7" 7" 7" 7" 7" 7" 7" 7"
Side 1) Sympathy 3:28
Side 2) Kayleigh 4:03
Birmingham, Leisure Centre, 27.09.1990

UK EMI, MARIL 16
label silver, soft cover
EEC EMI, 006-88 0008 7
label yellow, soft cover

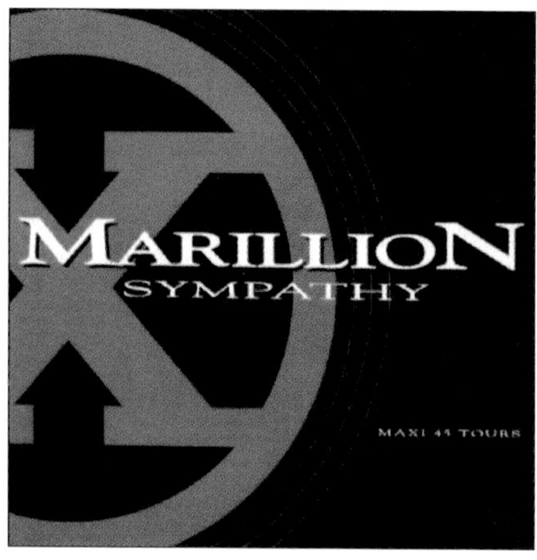

French cover »Sympathy« promo 12"

Side 1) Sympathy (Compasion) 3:28
Side 2) Sympathy (Compasion) 3:28

MEX EMI, 700 1194
label yellow, promo, »Singles collection« cover

12" 12" 12" 12" 12" 12" 12" 12" 12" 12" 12"

Side 1) Sympathy 3:28
Side 2) Kayleigh 4:03
Birmingham, Leisure Centre, 27.09.1990
Dry land 4:56
London, Hammersmith Odeon, 29.09.1990

UK EMI, 12 MARIL PD 16
picture disc, insert, no ps

Side 1) Sympathy 3:27
Side 2) – not playable –
FRA EMI, SP 1596
one-sided promo

CD CD CD CD CD CD CD CD CD CD CD CD

Sympathy 3:27
Kayleigh 4:05
(Argentinian TV-version, 30.02.1992)
I will walk on water (mix) 4:08

UK EMI, CD MARIL S 16
digi pack part 1

Sympathy 3:28
Kayleigh 4:03
Birmingham, Leisure Centre, 27.09.1990
Dry land 4:56
London, Hammersmith Odeon, 29.09.1990

UK EMI, CD MARIL 16
digi pack part 2
UK EMI, CD MARIL 16
promobox + tape + sheet
EEC EMI, CDP 564 880008 2

Sympathy 3:28
Kayleigh 4:03
Birmingham, Leisure Centre, 27.09.1990

FRA EMI, PM 110 880 6162
promo

Sympathy 3:28

UK EMI
test pressing, no number, factory sleeve

»A singles collection 1982-1992«

(UK release 08.06.1992)

LP LP LP LP LP LP LP LP LP LP LP LP LP LP

Side 1) Cover my eyes (Pain and heaven) 3:55
(album version)
Kayleigh (7" version) 3:32
Easter (album version) 5:56
Warm wet circles (7" version) 4:22
Uninvited guest (7" version) 3:43
Assassing ('92 remix) 7:39
Hooks in you (album version) 2:54
Side 2) Garden party ('92 remix) 7:09
No one can (album version) 4:40
Incommunicado (album version) 5:14
Dry land (album version) 4:41
Lavender (7" version) 3:40
I will walk on water (album version) 4:11
Sympathy (single version) 3:27

UK EMI, EMD 1033
label yellow
EEC EMI, 799370 1
label white, test pressing, no ps
EEC EMI, 064-799370 1
label yellow
POL MJM Music, MJM 141
label white
POR EMI, 7993701
label yellow
KOR EMI, EKPL-0249
label yellow
KOR EMI, EKPL-0249
picture label, korean lyric sheet, promo stamp on cover

CD CD CD CD CD CD CD CD CD CD CD CD

Cover my eyes (Pain and heaven) 3:55
(album version)
Kayleigh (7" version) 3:32
Easter (album version) 5:56
Warm wet circles (7" version) 4:22
Uninvited guest (7" version) 3:43
Assassing ('92 remix) 7:39
Hooks in you (album version) 2:54
Garden party ('92 remix) 7:09
No one can (album version) 4:40
Incommunicado (album version) 5:14
Dry land (album version) 4:41
Lavender (7" version) 3:40
I will walk on water 4:11
Sympathy (single version) 3:27

UK EMI, CD EMD 1033
EEC EMI, CDP 7 99370 2
ITA EMI, 072 7993702
RUS KJF, 31-867
counterfeit

BRA EMI, 368 799370 2
promo
JAP EMI, TOCP-7262
OBI
JAP Toshiba EMI, TOCP-7262
OBI, promo, japanese lyrics, purple promo print around the hole of the CD
USA I.R.S., X-2 13157
title »6 of 1, half a dozen of the other«

»No one can« (new release)

(UK release 13.07.1992)

7" 7" 7" 7" 7" 7" 7" 7" 7" 7" 7" 7" 7" 7" 7" 7"

Side 1) No one can 4:39
Side 2) Cover my eyes (Pain and heaven) 4:06
(Mike Stone-remix)

UK EMI, MARIL 17
label silver, hard cover
UK EMI, MARIL 17
label silver, hard cover, promo sticker on cover

12" 12" 12" 12" 12" 12" 12" 12" 12" 12" 12"

Side 1) No one can 4:39
Side 2) Cover my eyes (Pain and heaven) 4:06
(Mike Stone-remix)
Sympathy * 2:28
** Racket Club acoustic session 5/'92*

UK EMI, 12 MARIL PD 17
picture disc, insert, no ps

CD CD CD CD CD CD CD CD CD CD CD CD

No one can 4:39
Cover my eyes (Pain and heaven) * 2:33
Sugar mice * 3:01
** Racket Club acoustic session 5/'92*

UK EMI, CD MARIL S 17
digi pack, part 1

••

No one can 4:39
Cover my eyes (Pain and heaven) 4:06
(Mike Stone-remix)
Sympathy * 2:28
** Racket Club acoustic session 5/'92*

UK EMI, CD MARIL 17
release 20.07.1992, digi pack, part 2
EEC EMI, CDP 560 8 80149 2 2

••

No one can (radio edit) 4:41

USA I.R.S., DPRO-67096
blue/purple CD, promo, backing card

»Live at the Borderline«

(UK-only release 20.08.1992)

CD CD CD CD CD CD CD CD CD CD CD CD

Splintering heart 7:22
Easter 6:10
King of sunset town 5:27
Waiting to happen 5:09
Sympathy 4:34
Kayleigh 3:52
Lavender 2:41
Heart of Lothian 2:49
Uninvited guest 3:50
Slainte mhath 5:17
The release 4:08
Hooks in you 3:58
Garden party 7:04
Recorded live in London, Borderline Club, 09.05.1992

UK Racket Records, RACKET 1
ltd. ed. of 2,000 copies
UK Racket Records, RACKET 1
re-release 1/'98

»Marillion 3-CD-Box«

(UK-only release 27.11.1992)

3CD 3CD 3CD 3CD 3CD 3CD 3CD 3CD 3CD

Disc 1) »Script for a jester's tear«
Disc 2) »Fugazi«
Disc 3) »Misplaced childhood«

UK EMI, 777 78 0634 2 1
3-CD-Box with original albums

»Music collection«

(ITA-only release 1993)

CD CD CD CD CD CD CD CD CD CD CD CD

Grendel (single version) 17:15
Lady Nina (single version) 3:43
Freaks (album version) 4:05
Sugar mice (album version) 5:47
She chameleon (album version) 6:53
Hotel hobbies (album version) 3:40
Forgotten sons (album version) 8:24
La gazza ladra/Slainte mhath 7:33
Edinburgh, Playhouse, 17/19.12.1987
Chelsea Monday (album version) 8:18
The pseudo silk kimono
(album version) 2:20

ITA EMI, 0 777 78 9346 2 2
compilation with unique cover

»Live in Caracas«

(UK-only release 08.02.1993)

CD CD CD CD CD CD CD CD CD CD CD CD

Splintering heart	6:11
Holidays in Eden	4:56
Script for a jester's tear	11:26
Easter	6:03
Hotel hobbies	1:42
Warm wet circles	5:34
That time of the night	5:08
Kayleigh	3:51
Lavender	2:28
Heart of Lothian	2:50
Cover my eyes	4:09
Slainte mhath	5:23
The space	7:54
Waiting to happen	4:52
Hooks in you	2:49

Recorded live in Caracas, The Poliedro Arena, 30.09.1992

UK — Racket Records, RACKET 2
ltd. ed. of 1,000 copies
UK — Racket Records, RACKET 2
re-release 1/'98

»Live in Glasgow«

(UK-only release 23.11.1993)

CD CD CD CD CD CD CD CD CD CD CD CD

King of sunset town	7:10
Slainte mhath	4:58
Uninvited guest	4:38
Easter	6:03
Warm wet circles	5:40
That time of the night	4:36
Holloway girl	6:20
Seasons end	7:58
Berlin *	8:32
The space *	6:44

*Recorded live in Glasgow, Barrowland Ballroom, 04.12.1989, except * live in Bradford, St. Georges Hall, 10.12.1989*

UK — Racket Records, RACKET 3
ltd. ed. of 1,000 copies
UK — Racket Records, RACKET 3
re-release 1/'98

»The great escape«

(UK release 10.01.1994)

CD CD CD CD CD CD CD CD CD CD CD CD

The great escape (alternative ending)	4:39
Alone again in the lap of luxury (edit)	5:45
Hard as love	6:41
The hollow man	4:08

UK — EMI, CD BRAVE 1
promo

••

The great escape (alternative ending)	4:39
Made again	5:01
Marouatte jam	9:55

EEC — EMI, 7243 8 81164 28

»Brave«

(UK release 07.02.1994)

2LP 2LP 2LP 2LP 2LP 2LP 2LP 2LP 2LP 2LP

Side 1)	Bridge	2:52
	Living with the big lie	6:46
	Runaway	4:40
	Goodbye to all that	12:26
	a) Wave	
	b) Mad	
	c) The opium den	
Side 2)	d) The slide	
	e) Standing in the swing	
	Hard as love	6:41
	The hollow man	4:08
Side 3)	Alone again in the lap of luxury	8:13
	a) Now wash your hands	
	Paper lies	5:49
	Brave	7:54
Side 4*)	The great escape	6:29
	a) The last of you	
	b) Falling from the moon	

Marillion
Brave: 3 Track Album Sampler
RadioCD
Title: Marillion
Cat No: CDEMDDJ 1054
Track 1. Brave: An Introduction
Track 2. Hollow Man 4.08
Composer: Steve Hogarth/John Helmer/Marillion
Producer: Dave Meegan & Marillion
Publisher: Charisma Music Publ./Rondor Music
Track 3. Lap Of Luxury 8.13
Composer: Steve Hogarth/Marillion
Producer: Dave Meegan & Marillion
Publisher: Charisma Music Publ./Rondor Music
Track 4. The Great Escape 6.29
Composer: Steve Hogarth/John Helmer/Marillion
Producer: Dave Meegan & Marillion
Publisher: Charisma Music Publ./Rondor Music

UK cover »Brave« promo sampler CD

	Made again	5:01
Side 4*)	The great escape	
	(alternative ending)	4:39
	"Water sounds" (untitled)	7:00

** Double groove on side 4, two possibilities to play this side*

UK — EMI, EMD 1054
ltd. ed., foc

CD CD CD CD CD CD CD CD CD CD CD CD

Bridge	2:52
Living with the big lie	6:46
Runaway	4:40
Goodbye to all that	12:26
a) Wave	
b) Mad	
c) The opium den	
d) The slide	
e) Standing in the swing	
Hard as love	6:41
The hollow man	4:08
Alone again in the lap of luxury	8:13
a) Now wash your hands	
Paper lies	5:49
Brave	7:54
The great escape	6:29
a) The last of you	
b) Falling from the moon	
Made again	5:01

UK — EMI, CD EMD 1054
EEC — EMI, 7243 8 28032 2 5
ITA — EMI, LC 0542
RUS — EMI, 7243
counterfeit
CAN — EMI, 7243 8 28032 2 5
JAP — EMI, TOCP-8186
OBI
USA — I.R.S., DPRO-6729
promo, no ps
USA — I.R.S., X2-28032

Brave (an introduction)	5:29
spoken biography during	
"The great escape"	
The hollow man	4:08
Alone again in the lap of luxury	8:13
The great escape	6:29

UK — EMI, CD EMD DJ 1054
CD album sampler, promo

2CD 2CD 2CD 2CD 2CD 2CD 2CD 2CD 2CD

Disc 1)	Bridge	2:52
	Living with the big lie	6:46
	Runaway	4:40
	Goodbye to all that	12:26
	a) Wave	
	b) Mad	
	c) The opium den	
	d) The slide	
	e) Standing in the swing	
	Hard as love	6:41
	The hollow man	4:08
	Alone again in the lap of luxury	8:13
	a) Now wash your hands	
	Paper lies	5:49
	Brave	7:54
	The great escape	6:29
	a) The last of you	
	b) Falling from the moon	
	Made again	5:01
Disc 2)	The great escape (orchestral version)	5:18
	Marouatte jam (single version)	9:44
	The hollow man	
	(french acoustic version)	4:10
	Winter trees (single version)	1:47
	Alone again in the lap of luxury	
	(french acoustic version)	2:43
	Runaway (french acoustic version)	4:27
	Hard as love (instrumental)	6:48
	Living with the big lie *	5:12
	Alone again in the lap of luxury *	3:17
	Dream sequence *	2:36
	The great escape (Spiral remake)	4:39

** Racket Club demo, 23.01.1993, disc 2 remastered bonus CD*

UK — EMI, 4 97038 2
release 17.10.1998
EEC — EMI, 7243 4 97038 2 7
release 17.10.1998
USA — Sanctuary, 4512
release 10.02.2000, remastered

»Marillion acoustic«

(FRA-only release 07.02.1994)

CD CD CD CD CD CD CD CD CD CD CD CD

Alone again in the lap of luxury	
(acoustic version)	2:46
Runaway (acoustic version)	4:30
The hollow man (acoustic version)	4:25

FRA — EMI, SPCD 1714
promo, ltd. ed.

»The hollow man«

(UK release 14.03.1994)

7" 7" 7" 7" 7" 7" 7" 7" 7" 7" 7" 7" 7" 7" 7" 7"

Side 1)	The hollow man (album version)	4:09
Side 2)	Brave (album version)	7:54

UK EMI, EM 307
label silver

10" 10" 10" 10" 10" 10" 10" 10" 10" 10" 10"

Side 1) The hollow man (album version) 4:09
Side 2) Brave (album version) 7:54

UK Abbey Road
acetate

CD CD CD CD CD CD CD CD CD CD CD CD

The hollow man (album version) 4:09
Brave (album version) 7:54
Marouatte jam 9:51

UK EMI, CD EMS 307
part 1 of a two-CD-set

The hollow man (album version) 4:09
The great escape (orchestral version) 5:17
Winter trees (instrumental) 1:45

UK EMI, CD EM 307
part 2 of a two-CD-set
EEC EMI, 7243 8 81244 2
release 21.03.1994

»Alone again in the lap of luxury«

(UK release 25.04.1994)

12" 12" 12" 12" 12" 12" 12" 12" 12" 12" 12"

Side 1) Alone again in the lap of luxury (12" version) 7:12
Side 2) Living with the big lie (album version) 6:46
The space 6:42
Cambridge, 02.03.1994

UK EMI, 12 EMPD 318
picture disc, insert, no ps

CD CD CD CD CD CD CD CD CD CD CD CD

Alone again in the lap of luxury (radio edit) 4:27
River (instrumental) * 1:32
Bridge * 2:51
Living with the big lie * 6:36

* *Recorded live in London, Forum, 05.03.1994*

UK EMI, CD EMS 318
part 1 of a two-CD-set

Alone again in the lap of luxury (12" version) 7:12
Cover my eyes * 4:03
Slainte mhath * 4:33
Uninvited guest * 3:55

* *Recorded live in London, Forum, 05.03.1994*

UK EMI, CD EM 318
release 02.05.1994, part 2 of a two-CD-set

Alone again in the lap of luxury (radio edit) 4:27
Cover my eyes * 4:03
Slainte mhath * 4:33
Uninvited guest * 3:55

* *Recorded live in London, Forum, 05.03.1994*

EEC EMI, 7243 8 81354 2 0
release 09.05.1994

Alone again in the lap of luxury (radio edit) 4:26

UK EMI, CD EMDJ 318
promo

Alone again in the lap of luxury (edit) 5:43

USA I.R.S., DPRO-10746
green CD, promo, no ps

»Live from Loreley«

(UK-only release 06.03.1995)

CD/VHS CD/VHS CD/VHS CD/VHS CD/VHS

Slainte mhath 5:25
Assassing 6:39
Script for a jester's tear 9:40
Sugar mice 5:56
Hotel hobbies 3:55
Warm wet circles 5:58
That time of the night 4:32
Kayleigh 4:31
Lavender 8:15
Heart of Lothian 6:29
The last straw 6:32
Incommunicado 7:00

Recorded live in St. Goarshausen, Loreley-Freilichtbühne, 18.07.1987

UK EMI, 7243 8 3169 6 2 7
CD only available with video/box

»The making of Brave«

(UK-only release 22.05.1995)

2CD 2CD 2CD 2CD 2CD 2CD 2CD 2CD 2CD

Disc 1) Jones, the fog 1:20

	Early sketch for "Bridge"	1:10
	You get used to it	0:26
	Big lie	0:28
	Musical theme guitar	0:33
	Musical string theme 1	1:53
	Guitar solo	0:43
	Tube train	0:25
	Musical string theme 2	0:50
	Argument	0:25
	Runaway	2:21
	Good-bye to all that	1:15
	Magma	1:12
	Wave	1:42
	Mad 1	0:59
	Mad 2	0:26
	Mad 3	0:27
	Mad 4	1:25
	Opium den	3:08
	The slide	1:53
	Standing in the swing	2:04
	Hard as love	6:35
	Hollow man	3:38
	Lap of luxury	5:25
	Echo jam	1:06
	Now wash your hands 1	0:53
	Now wash your hands 2	2:47
	Paper lies	5:38
	The great escape	4:39
	Falling from the moon	6:27
	Made again	2:37
	Cabin fever	0:50
Disc 2)	Bridge	2:26
	Living with the big lie	6:15
	Runaway	4:20
	Goodbye to all that	0:44
	Wave	1:18
	Mad	1:36
	The opium den	1:34
	The slide	2:31
	Standing in the swing	1:46
	Hard as love	6:14
	The hollow man	4:04
	Alone again in the lap of luxury	5:46
	a) Now wash your hands	0:58
	Paper lies	4:43
	Brave	6:06
	The great escape	5:56
	a) The last of you	
	b) Falling from the moon	
	Made again	5:24

UK Racket Records, RACKET 6
UK Racket Records, RACKET 6
re-release 1/'98

»Marillion 3-CD-Box«

(EEC-only release 29.05.1995)

3CD 3CD 3CD 3CD 3CD 3CD 3CD 3CD 3CD

Disc 1) »Misplaced childhood«
Disc 2) »Clutching at straws«
Disc 3) »Holidays in Eden«

EEC EMI, MA CD BX 3
3-CD-box with the original albums

»Beautiful«

(UK release 29.05.1995)

CD CD CD CD CD CD CD CD CD CD CD CD

Beautiful	5:17
Live forever	4:36
The great escape (demo version)	5:50
Hard as love (demo version)	6:12

UK EMI, CD MARIL S 18
part 1 of a two-CD-set
EEC EMI, 7243 8 82183 2 0

Beautiful	5:17
Afraid of sunrise	5:04
Icon	6:10

UK EMI, CD MARIL 18
part 2 of a two-CD-set

Beautiful	5:17
Icon	6:10

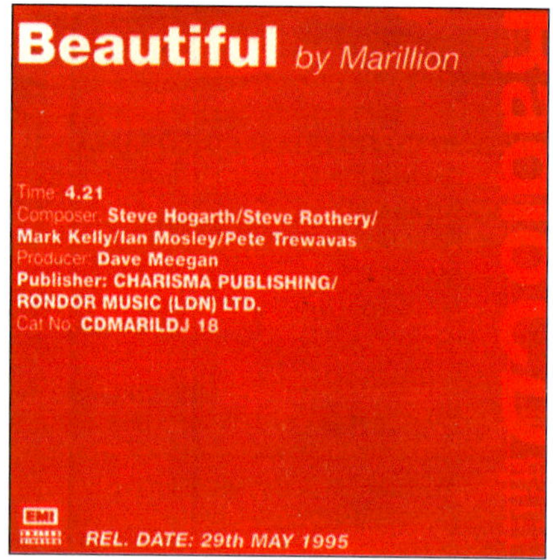

UK cover »Beautiful« promo CD

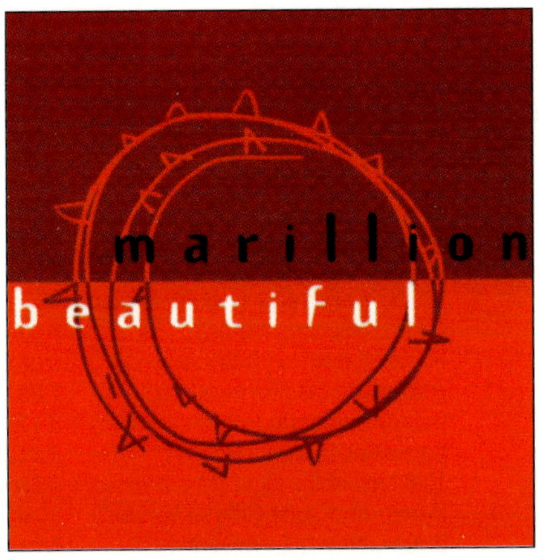

EEC cover »Beautiful« promo CD

FRA — EMI, 882182 2
release 06.06.1995

Beautiful (edit) — 4:21

UK — EMI, CD MARIL DJ 18
promo

Beautiful (radio edit) — 3:58

EEC — EMI, CDP 519 482
promo

»Cannibal surf babe«

(Promo-only release 6/'95)

CD CD CD CD CD CD CD CD CD CD CD CD

Cannibal surf babe (special mix)
Beautiful
Sugar mice
A collection
Easter

UK — EMI
test pressing-only
EEC — EMI, 882408 2
test pressing-only

Cannibal surf babe (radio edit) — 3:47
Cannibal surf babe (album version) — 5:44

USA — I.R.S./El Dorado, DPRO-10769
promo, backing card

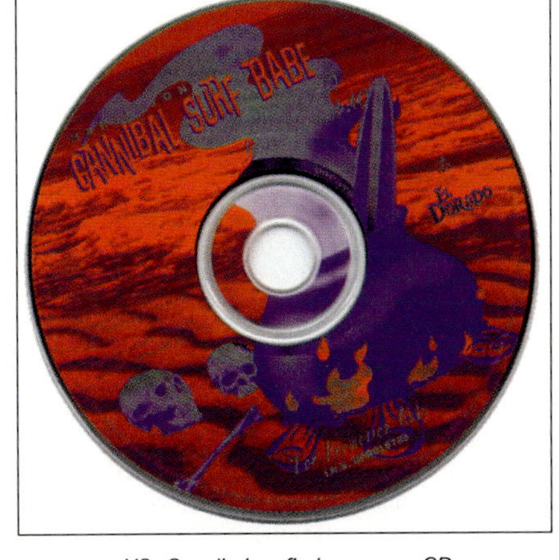

US »Cannibal surfbabe« promo CD

»Afraid of sunlight«

(UK release 24.06.1995)

LP LP LP LP LP LP LP LP LP LP LP LP LP LP

Side 1)	Gazpacho	7:28
	Cannibal surf babe	5:46
	Beautiful	5:13
	Afraid of sunrise	5:02
Side 2)	Out of this world	7:55
	Afraid of sunlight	6:50
	Beyond you	6:11
	King	7:04

UK — EMI, EMD 1079
label purple, ois

CD CD CD CD CD CD CD CD CD CD CD CD

Gazpacho	7:28
Cannibal surf babe	5:46
Beautiful	5:13
Afraid of sunrise	5:02
Out of this world	7:55
Afraid of sunlight	6:50
Beyond you	6:11
King	7:04

UK — EMI, CD EMD 1079
EEC — EMI, 7243 8 33874 2 7
CAN — EMI, 7243 8 33874 2 7
USA — I.R.S./El Dorado, DPRO-10764
promo, no ps
USA — I.R.S./El Dorado, 8338742
promo with original sleeve
USA — I.R.S./El Dorado, IRS-33874

	Gazpacho	7:28
	Cannibal surf babe	5:46
	Beautiful	5:13
	Afraid of sunrise	5:02
	Out of this world	7:55
	Afraid of sunlight	6:50
	Beyond you (mono version)	6:11
	King	7:04

JAP EMI, TOCP-8568
OBI, japanese lyrics
JAP EMI, TOCP-8568
OBI, japanese lyrics, purple promo print around the hole of the CD

2CD 2CD 2CD 2CD 2CD 2CD 2CD 2CD 2CD

Disc 1)	Gazpacho	7:28
	Cannibal surf babe	5:46
	Beautiful	5:13
	Afraid of sunrise	5:02
	Out of this world	7:55
	Afraid of sunlight	6:50
	Beyond you	6:11
	King	7:04
Disc 2)	Icon	6:04
	Live forever	4:34
	Second chance aka Beautiful *	5:14
	Beyond you (demo) *	5:17
	Cannibal surf babe (studio outtake) *	5:59
	Out of this world (studio outtake) *	7:27
	Bass frenzy *	1:17
	Mirages (demo) *	6:02
	Afraid of sunlight (acoustic demo) *	6:51
	Sympathy (for the roadcrew) **	3:41

** Previously unreleased, ** multimedia hidden track, disc 2 remastered bonus CD*

UK EMI, 498 614 2
release 21.03.1999
EEC EMI, 7243 4 98614 2 8
release 18.03.1999
USA Sanctuary, 4510
release 21.03.2000, remastered

»The originals«

(UK-only release 25.09.1995)

3CD 3CD 3CD 3CD 3CD 3CD 3CD 3CD 3CD

Disc 1) »Script for a jester's tear«
Disc 2) »Fugazi«
Disc 3) »Misplaced childhood«

UK EMI, CD OMB 015
3 CD box, each with CD-size foc

»The best of Marillion«

(release 1996)

CD CD CD CD CD CD CD CD CD CD CD CD

Kayleigh (single version)	3:34
Market square heroes (B-side version)	3:59
Freaks (album version)	4:04
Garden party (1992 remix)	7:10
Warm wet circles (album version)	4:25
Fugazi (album version)	8:02
Heart of Lothian (album version)	6:06
Assassing (album version)	7:03
Incommunicado (album version)	5:17
Lavender (album version)	3:41
That time of the night (album version)	5:58
Punch and Judy (album version)	3:18
Sugar mice (album version)	5:46
Chelsea Monday (album version)	8:17

POL CDK-3356-41
pirate compilation with unique cover
RUS 012451-07
pirate compilation with unique cover

»Made again«

(UK release 25.03.1996)

2CD 2CD 2CD 2CD 2CD 2CD 2CD 2CD 2CD

Disc 1)	Splintering heart	6:33
	Easter	6:28
	No one can	4:44
	Waiting to happen	5:09
	Cover my eyes	4:06
	The space	6:35
	Hooks in you *	3:02
	Beautiful *	5:35
	Kayleigh *	4:04
	Lavender *	4:20
	Afraid of sunlight *	6:55
	King *	7:27
Disc 2)	Bridge	3:26
	Living with the big lie	6:49
	Runaway	4:46
	Goodbye to all that	0:41
	a) Wave	1:22
	b) Mad	1:24
	c) The opium den	2:38
	d) The slide	4:10
	e) Standing in the swing	2:12
	Hard as love	6:58
	The hollow man	4:33
	Alone again in the lap of luxury	6:44
	a) Now wash your hands	1:15
	Paper lies	5:34

Brave 8:39
The great escape 1:18
a) The last of you 2:42
b) Falling from the moon 3:27
Made again 5:25

*Disc 1 recorded live in London, Hammersmith Odeon, 29.09.1991, except * live in Rotterdam, Ahoy, 29.09.1995, disc 2 recorded live in Paris, La Cigalle, 29.04.1994*

UK EMI, CD EMD 1094
ltd. ed.
EEC EMI, 7243 8 37678 2 3
with cardboard box + poster
EEC Castle, RAW DD 111
with cardboard box + poster
USA Castle, 117-2
release 09.04.1996

CD CD CD CD CD CD CD CD CD CD CD CD

No one can 4:44
London, Hammersmith Odeon, 29.09.1991
Beautiful 5:35
Rotterdam, Ahoy, 29.09.1995
Made again 5:25
Paris, La Cigalle, 29.04.1994

EEC Castle, RAW P 1019
promo album sampler

»Kayleigh«

(EEC release 28.05.1996)

CD CD CD CD CD CD CD CD CD CD CD CD

Grendel (single version) 17:16
He knows you know (album version) 5:23
Jigsaw (album version) 6:50
Punch and Judy (album version) 3:22
Cinderella search (edited 7" version) 4:22
Kayleigh (edited 7" version) 3:32
Lavender (edited 7" version) 3:40
Lady Nina (edited 7" version) 3:43
Torch song (album version) 4:05

EEC Disky, DC 867182
CAN Disky, E2 86718

»Essential collection«

(UK-only release 07.10.1996)

CD CD CD CD CD CD CD CD CD CD CD CD

Grendel (single version) 17:16
He knows you know (album version) 5:23
Jigsaw (album version) 6:50
Punch and Judy (album version) 3:22
Cinderella search (edited 7" version) 4:22
Kayleigh (edited 7" version) 3:32
Lavender (edited 7" version) 3:40
Lady Nina (edited 7" version) 3:43
Torch song (album version) 4:05

UK EMI Gold, 7243 85359 2 2 3
compilation with unique cover

»Marillion Box«

(FRA-only release 1996)

2CD 2CD 2CD 2CD 2CD 2CD 2CD 2CD 2CD

Disc 1) »Clutching at straws«
Disc 2) »Seasons end«

FRA EMI, 8-53158-2
2 CD-set in a box

»Best of both worlds«

(UK release 24.02.1997)

2CD 2CD 2CD 2CD 2CD 2CD 2CD 2CD 2CD

Disc 1) Script for a jester's tear (album version) 8:45
Market square heroes (re-recorded edit) 3:57
He knows you know (album version) 5:23
Forgotten sons (album version) 8:19
Garden party (album version) 7:16
Assassing (7" version) 3:38
Punch and Judy (album version) 3:19
Kayleigh (7" version) 3:34
Lavender (7" version) 3:41
Heart of Lothian (7" version) 3:37
Incommunicado (album version) 5:16
Warm wet circles (7" version) 4:24
That time of the night (album version) 5:58
Sugar mice (album version) 5:46

Disc 2) The uninvited guest (album version) 3:46
Easter (7" version) 4:31
Hooks in you (Meaty mix) 3:54
The space (album version) 6:15
Cover my eyes (album version) 3:55
No one can (album version) 4:40
Dry land (album version) 4:43
Waiting to happen (album version) 4:56
The great escape (album version) 6:28
Alone again in the lap of luxury (radio edit) 4:29
Made again (album version) 5:04
King (album version) 7:06
Afraid of sunlight (album version) 6:51

	Beautiful (radio edit)	4:23
	Cannibal surf babe (album version)	5:18

UK — EMI, CD EMC 3761
UK — EMI, CD ADV 103
promo-set, backing card, no ps
EEC — EMI, 7243 8 55184 2 3
CAN — EMI, 7243 8 55184 2 3
release 18.03.1997

»Best of both worlds – The Fish years«

(UK-only release 24.03.1997)

2LP 2LP 2LP 2LP 2LP 2LP 2LP 2LP 2LP 2LP

Side 1)	Script for a jester's tear (album version)	8:45
	Market square heroes (re-recorded edit)	3:57
	He knows you know (album version)	5:23
Side 2)	Forgotten sons (album version)	8:19
	Garden party (album version)	7:16
	Assassing (7" version)	3:38
Side 3)	Punch and Judy (album version)	3:19
	Kayleigh (7" version)	3:34
	Lavender (7" version)	3:41
	Heart of Lothian (7" version)	3:37
Side 4)	Incommunicado (album version)	5:16
	Warm wet circles (7" version)	4:24
	That time of the night (album version)	5:58
	Sugar mice (album version)	5:46

UK — EMI, EMCF 3761
2 picture discs in die-cut foc

»Best of both worlds – The Hogarth years«

(UK-only release 24.03.1997)

2LP 2LP 2LP 2LP 2LP 2LP 2LP 2LP 2LP 2LP

Side 1)	The uninvited guest (album version)	3:46
	Easter (7" version)	4:31
	Hooks in you (Meaty mix)	3:54
	The space (album version)	6:15
	Cover my eyes (album version)	3:55
Side 2)	No one can (album version)	4:40
	Dry land (album version)	4:43
	Waiting to happen (album version)	4:56
	The great escape (album version)	6:28
Side 3)	Alone again in the lap of luxury (radio edit)	4:29
	Made again (album version)	5:04
	King (album version)	7:06
Side 4)	Afraid of sunlight (album version)	6:51
	Beautiful (radio edit)	4:23
	Cannibal surf babe (album version)	5:18

UK — EMI, EMCH 3761
2 picture discs in die-cut foc

»This strange engine«

(UK release 21.04.1997)

CD CD CD CD CD CD CD CD CD CD CD CD

Man of a thousand faces	7:33
One fine day	5:31
80 days	5:00
Estonia	7:57
Memory of water	3:01
An accidental man	6:12
Hope for the future	5:11
This strange engine	15:41

UK — Castle, RAW PR 121
promo, no ps
UK — Castle, RAW DP 121
digi pack
UK — Castle, RAW 121
UK — Eagle, CMEDD 071
re-release 19.02.2001
CAN — EMI,
release 07.10.1997
RUS — MN, 3004 SF
counterfeit
USA — Velvel, VEL-79791-2
release 3/'97
USA — Velvel, VEL-79791-2
release 12/'97, "bonus tracks" sticker, but bonus not on CD

••

Man of a thousand faces	7:33
One fine day	5:31
80 days	5:00
Estonia	7:57
Memory of water	3:01
An accidental man	6:12
Hope for the future	5:11
This strange engine	15:41
Beautiful (unplugged) •	4:50
Made again (unplugged) •	5:16

• *Bonus tracks*

JAP — Pony Canyon, PCCY-01098
OBI, japanese lyrics

••

Man of a thousand faces	7:33
One fine day	5:31
80 days	5:00
Estonia	7:57

Memory of water 3:01
An accidental man 6:12
Hope for the future 5:11
This strange engine 15:41
Estonia (THE POSITIVE LIGHT mix) • 11:49
80 days (acoustic) • 4:35

• *Bonus tracks*

USA Velvel, VEL-79791-2
correct release with bonus tracks

••

Man of a thousand faces (exerpt) 1:26
This strange engine (exerpt) 2:38
One fine day (exerpt) 1:09
An accidental man (exerpt) 2:11

UK Castle, RAW P 1047
promo, no ps

»Man of a thousand faces«

(UK release 15.05.1997)

CD CD CD CD CD CD CD CD CD CD CD CD

Man of a thousand faces (radio edit) 3:38
Beautiful (unplugged) 4:50
Made again (unplugged) 5:16
Man of a thousand faces (extended version) 8:20

UK Castle, RAW X 1044
with release sticker, no ps
UK Castle, RAW X 1044
digi pack
EEC Castle, RAW X 1044
digi pack

»80 days«

(UK release 29.09.1997)

CD CD CD CD CD CD CD CD CD CD CD CD

80 days (album version) 5:00
This strange engine * 16:17
The bell in the sea * 4:23

* *Recorded live in Paris, Bataclan, 20.05.1997*

UK Castle, RAW X 1049
UK Castle, RAW X 1049
no ps but with promo sticker
EEC Castle, RAW X 1049
release 13.10.1997

»Memory of water«

(UK-only release 12/'97)

12" 12" 12" 12" 12" 12" 12" 12" 12" 12" 12"

Side 1) Memory of water (remixed by THE POSITIVE LIGHT) 9:40
Side 2) – not playable –

UK Eagle Records
one-sided white label acetate, no ps, no number

»Tales from the engine room«

(UK release 21.01.1998)

CD CD CD CD CD CD CD CD CD CD CD CD

Estonia 11:43
The memory of water 9:36
This strange engine 20:37

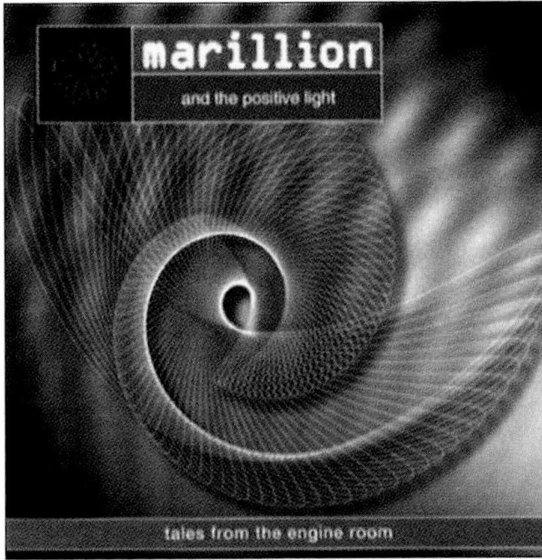

UK cover »Tales from the engine room« CD Eagle

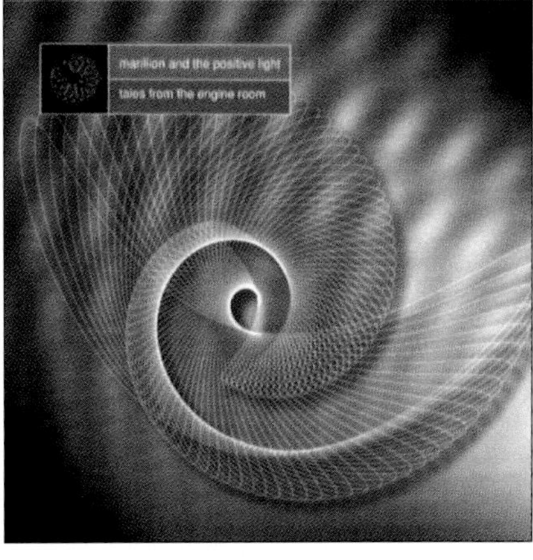

UK cover »Tales from the engine room« CD Racket

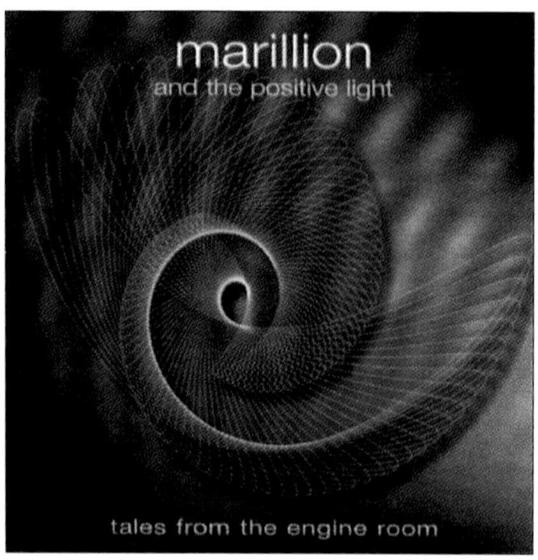

UK cover »Tales from the engine room« CD test pressing

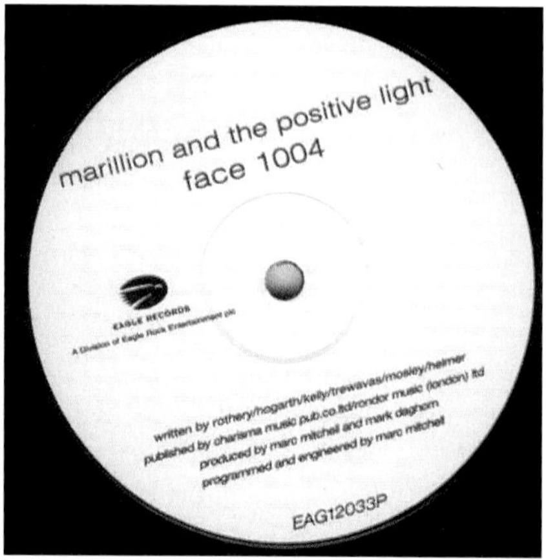

UK label »Face 1004« promo 12"

One fine day	8:20
Face 1004	8:40

All tracks by MARILLION and THE POSITIVE LIGHT

UK — Racket Records, RACKET 7
first edition, ltd.
USA — Cleopatra, PURP 375
release 29.09.1998, first edition

Estonia	11:43
The memory of water	9:36
This strange engine	20:37
One fine day	8:20
Face 1004	8:40
80 days •	8:46

• *Bonus track*

UK — Eagle Records
silver test pressing, no number, factory sleeve
UK — Eagle Records
golden test pressing, no number, different cover
UK — Eagle Records, EAG CD 033
release 01.06.1998
EEC — Eagle Records, EAG CD 033
release 30.06.1998
USA — Cleopatra, PURP 375
release 12/'98

»Face 1004«

(UK-only release 21.01.1998)

12" 12" 12" 12" 12" 12" 12" 12" 12" 12" 12"

Side 1)	Face 1004 (THE POSITIVE LIGHT REMIX)	8:40
Side 2)	– not playable –	

UK — Eagle Records, 12033 P
one-sided 12" promo, no ps, given away with the first 1,500 copies of »Tales from the engine room«

»Marillion Rochester«

(USA-only release 04.05.1998)

2CD 2CD 2CD 2CD 2CD 2CD 2CD 2CD 2CD

Disc 1)	Emmanuel/Seasons end	9:01
	Alone again in the lap of luxury	5:45
	Hard as love	7:48
	80 days	5:12
	Kayleigh	4:11
	Lavender	4:18
	Afraid of sunlight	6:59
	Man of a thousand faces/Estonia	18:15
	Easter	6:56
Disc 2)	This town	5:30
	100 nights	4:41
	Slainte mhath	5:08
	King	7:38
	This strange engine	22:18
	The great escape	3:58
	Falling from the moon	2:08
	Garden party	8:00

Recorded live in Rochester (NY), The Spectrum, 31.08.1997

USA — Racket Records, RACKET 8
first ltd. ed. of 1,000 copies, numbered and signed; this was given away free by the band to all people who took part in spending money for the tour fund.
USA — Racket Records, RACKET 8
next ltd ed. of 1,000 copies; those unnumbered and unsigned copies of the CD-set were sold by Racket Records during a ltd. period of time.

»Kayleigh - The essential Marillion collection«

(UK-only release 5/'98)

CD CD CD CD CD CD CD CD CD CD CD CD

Kayleigh (single version)	3:34
Lavender (single version)	3:42
He knows you know (album version)	5:24
Garden party (1992 remix)	7:11
Punch and Judy (single version)	3:19
Market square heroes (re-recorded edit)	3:57
Cinderella search (full version)	5:30
Cover my eyes (album version)	3:56
No one can (album version)	4:39
Freaks (single version)	4:06
Sympathy (single version)	3:28
Hooks in you (album version)	2:56
Dry land (album version)	4:42
100 nights/The rake's progress (reprise)	7:03
Cannibal surf babe (album version)	5:19
Afraid of sunlight (album version)	6:49

UK — EMI, 7243 4 94564 2 6
sold at "Woolworth's" UK only

»Piston Broke«

(UK-only release 05.06.1998)

2CD 2CD 2CD 2CD 2CD 2CD 2CD 2CD 2CD

Disc 1)	Man of a thousand faces	8:14
	Hard as love	5:27
	Gazpacho	4:53
	Afraid of sunlight	7:06
	80 days °	6:29
	Estonia	8:49
	Alone again in the lap of luxury *	6:37
	The space	2:38
	Easter *	6:22
	Brave °	8:42
	The great escape *	6:08
Disc 2)	This strange engine °	19:40
	Sugar mice **	6:22
	This town/The rakes progress/ 100 nights ∞	11:25
	The bell in the sea *	5:46
	Hope for the future *	6:49
	King *	9:29

*Recorded live in Gent, Vooruit, 19.05.1997, except * live in Geleen, Hanenhof, 23.05.1997, ** live in Hannover, Capitol, 14.10.1997, ° live in Paris, Bataclan, 20.05.1997, ∞ live in Hamburg, Docks, 13.10.1997*

UK — Racket Records, RACKET 9
2CD-set, mailorder or sold at concerts

»These chains«

(UK release 14.09.1998)

CD CD CD CD CD CD CD CD CD CD CD CD

These chains	4:28
Fake plastic trees	4:56
Oswestry, The Wall's, 25./26.06.1998	
Memory of water (big beat mix)	8:05

UK — Castle, RAW X 1051
EEC — Castle, RAW X 1051
release 05.10.1998

»Radiation«

(UK release 21.09.1998)

CD CD CD CD CD CD CD CD CD CD CD CD

Costa del slough	1:24
Under the sun	4:13
Answering machine	3:48
Three minute boy	5:59
Now she'll never know	4:59
These chains	4:49
Born to run	5:12
Cathedral wall	7:19
A few words for the dead	10:31

UK — Castle, RAW PR CD 126
promo, no ps
UK — Castle, RAW CD 126
UK — Raw Power, RAW CD 126
CD-R test pressing, company sleeve
UK — Eagle, CMEDD 113
re-release 19.02.2001
EEC — Castle, RAW CD 126

••

Costa del slough	1:24
Under the sun	4:13
Answering machine	3:48
Three minute boy	5:59
Now she'll never know	4:59
These chains	4:49
Born to run	5:12
Cathedral wall	7:19
A few words for the dead	10:31
The space •	4:12
Fake plastic trees •	4:56

• Bonus tracks, recorded live in Oswestry, The Walls Restaurant, 25./26.06.1998

JAP — Pony Canyon, PCCY-01281
OBI, japanese lyrics, promo
JAP — Pony Canyon, PCCY-01281
OBI, japanese lyrics

••

Costa del slough	1:24
Under the sun	4:13
Answering machine	3:48
Three minute boy	5:59
Now she'll never know	4:59
These chains	4:49
Born to run	5:12
Cathedral wall	7:19
A few words for the dead	10:31
Estonia (acoustic) •	6:43
Memory of water (big beat mix)	8:05

• *Bonus track*

USA Velvel, 63467-79769-2
release 27.10.1998

»Marillion & The web Christmas 1998«

(UK-only release 15.12.1998)

CD CD CD CD CD CD CD CD CD CD CD CD

Introduction	3:52
Tumble down the years (demo)	0:49
Interior Lulu (demo, part 1)	2:50
Interior Lulu (demo, part 2)	1:03
Karaoke introduction	2:05
Cover my eyes (karaoke version)	4:20
No one can (karaoke version)	5:02
Beautiful (karaoke version)	5:18
Dave Meegan-mix	
These chains (karaoke version)	4:28
Outro	0:18

UK Racket Records, WEBFREE 01
free fan club CD, no ps

»Unplugged at The Walls«

(UK-only release 23.03.1999)

2CD 2CD 2CD 2CD 2CD 2CD 2CD 2CD 2CD

Disc 1)	Beautiful	4:51
	Beyond you	5:58
	Afraid of sunlight	4:13
	Runaway	6:36
	Now she'll never know	5:18
	Alone again in the lap of luxury	3:52
	The space	4:09
	Fake plastic trees	5:09
	Holloway girl	4:13
	King	6:32
Disc 2)	The answering machine	4:29
	Gazpacho	5:38
	Cannibal surf babe	7:11
	Black bird	2:54
	Abraham, Martin and John	8:09
	Hooks in you	3:48
	80 days	4:17

Recorded live in Oswestry, The Walls Restaurant, 25./26.06.1998

UK Racket Records, RACKET 10
2CD-set, mailorder-only

»Marillion«

(UK promo release only 9/'99)

CD-R CD-R CD-R CD-R CD- CD-R CD-R

Rich
Deserve
Memory of water
Beautiful
Answering machine
Now she'll never know

UK
CD-R, only 1 copy exists

»marillion.com«

(UK release 18.10.1999)

CD CD CD CD CD CD CD CD CD CD CD CD

A legacy	6:16
Deserve	4:23
Go!	6:11
Rich	5:42
Enlightened	4:59
Built-in bastard radar	4:52
Tumble down the years	4:33
Interior Lulu	15:14
House	10:15

UK Castle Intact
CD-R with release date print, no ps
UK Castle Intact, RAWCDP 144
promo CD in cardboard sleeve
UK Castle Intact, RAWCD 144
digi pack in special cardboard sleeve
UK Castle Intact, RAWCD 144
same as before, but fully signed (1,000 copies for mailorder)
EEC Castle Intact, RAWSD 144
USA Sanctuary Records, NR 4505
full promo CD with insert
USA Sanctuary Records, 4505
release 16.11.1999

••

Deserve	4:23
Rich	5:42
A legacy	6:16

UK Castle Intact, RAW P 2144
3 track promo CD in cardboard sleeve

A legacy 6:16
Deserve 4:23
Go! 6:11
Rich 5:42
Enlightened 4:59
Built-in bastard radar 4:52
Tumble down the years 4:33
Interior Lulu 15:14
House 10:15
Kayleigh •
Market square heroes •
Freaks •
Garden party •

• Bonus tracks

RUS Castle Intact, RAWCD 144
counterfeit

»Zodiac«

(UK-only release 11/'99)

CD CD CD CD CD CD CD CD CD CD CD CD

Rich 5:42
The uninvited guest 4:38
Goodbye to all that 9:19
Afraid of sunlight 8:00
Deserve * 5:03
Sugar mice 5:49
The answering machine * 4:11
Berlin * 8:33
Cathedral wall 7:20
Waiting to happen 5:53
Garden party 7:37

*Recorded live in Oxford, The Zodiac, between the 24. and 27.07.1999, * featuring Ben Castle on Saxophone*

UK Racket Records, RACKET 11
mailorder or sold at concerts

»marillion.christmas«

(UK-only release 12/'99)

CD CD CD CD CD CD CD CD CD CD CD CD

Gabriel's message 4:09
The answering machine (single edit 1999) 3:19
Interior Lulu ** 8:41
Tumble down the years ** 4:36
Memory of water (Technopox remix by Silent Buddhas 1998) 10:02
Abraham, Martin and John * 4:34
Runaway * 4:43
Estonia * 6:41
Beautiful (by Anne Bond and Cradley CE Primary school, October 1999) 5:03
Marillion christmas greetings and introduction of the songs 3:00

** Racket Club acoustic session 1999, ** »Radiation« version 1998*

UK Racket Records, WebFree 2
free fan club CD, with ps but no backing card

»Heroes, villains, millenium predictions«

(release 22.12.1999)

CD CD CD CD CD CD CD CD CD CD CD CD

This CD contains a (promo) interview with Steve Hogarth

? Masterpiece Title
including a promo letter

»marillion.co.uk«

(UK-only release 3/'00)

CD CD CD CD CD CD CD CD CD CD CD CD

The answering machine (from »Unplugged at the Walls«) 3:44
Afraid of sunrise (from »Unplugged at the Walls«) 4:15
The great escape (from »The making of Brave«) 7:01
The space (from »Live in Caracas«) 5:54
Afraid of sunlight (from »Piston Broke«) 7:17
Berlin (from »Zodiac«) 8:54
The bell in the sea (live, previously unreleased) 3:47
Interviewcuts with music 8:55
Deserve *
The bell in the sea *

*This is an enhanced CD with video clips *, a promo video trailer with interviewcuts and music. There are also files with biography, diary and explanations of songs from »marillion.com«*

UK Racket Records, RACKET 12
free mailorder CD, no backing card

»Rarities Vol. 1«

(RUS-only release 2000)

CD CD CD CD CD CD CD CD CD CD CD CD

Market square heroes (battlepriest version) 4:18

Three boats down from the candy (single version) 4:31
Grendel (Fair-Deal studios demo) 19:10
Chelsea monday (Manchester square demo) 6:55
He knows you know (Manchester square demo) 4:29
Charting the single (single version) 4:52
Market square heroes (re-recorded version) 4:48

RUS MRCD 030002
counterfeit, ltd. ed., same as »Script for a jester's tear« remaster bonus CD

»More rarities Vol. 2«

(RUS-only release 2000)

CD CD CD CD CD CD CD CD CD CD CD CD

Cinderella search (12" version) 5:32
Assassing (alternate mix) 7:41
Three boats down from the candy (re-recorded version) 4:01
Punch and Judy * 3:50
She chameleon * 6:34
Emerald lies * 5:32
Incubus * 8:10

** Demo*

RUS MRCD 030200008
counterfeit, ltd. ed., same as »Fugazi« remaster bonus CD

»Rarities again Vol. 3«

(RUS-only release 2000)

CD CD CD CD CD CD CD CD CD CD CD CD

Lady Nina (extended 12" version) 5:50
Freaks (single version) 4:03
Kayleigh (alternative mix) 4:03
Lavender blue (remix) 4:22
Pseudo silk kimono * 2:11
Kayleigh * 4:06
Lavender * 2:27
Bitter suite * 2:54
Lords of the backstage * 1:46
Blue angel * 1:46
Misplaced rendezvous * 1:56
Heart of Lothian * 3:49
Waterhole (Expresso bongo) * 2:00
Passing strangers * 9:17
Childhood's end? * 2:23
White feather * 2:18

** Demo 2/'85*

RUS MRCD 04000212
counterfeit, ltd. ed., same as »Misplaced childhood« remaster bonus CD

»The CD singles '82-'88«

(UK release 21.07.2000)

12CD 12CD 12CD 12CD 12CD 12CD 12CD

Disc 1) »Market square heroes« (8886682)
Market square heroes 4:15
Three boats down from the candy 4:29
Grendel 17:14

Disc 2) »He knows you know« (8886692)
He knows you know (7" edit) 3:30
Charting the single 5:40
He knows you know (12" edit) 5:05

Disc 3) »Garden party« (8886702)
Garden party (7"edit) 4:29
Margaret (live edit) 4:09
Edinburgh, 07.04.83
Garden party 7:15
Charting the single 6:30
London, 18.04.83
Margaret 12:17
Edinburgh, 07.04.83

Disc 4) »Punch and Judy« (8886712)
Punch and Judy (7" version) 3:19
Market square heroes (re-recording edit) 3:56
Three boats down from the candy (re-recording) 3:59
Market square heroes (re-recording) 4:45

Disc 5) »Assassing« (8886722)
Assassing (7" version) 3:39
Cinderella search (7" version) 4:19
Assassing 7:01
Cinderella search 5:24

Disc 6) »Kayleigh« (8886732)
Kayleigh (single edit) 3:33
Lady Nina (single edit) 3:41
Kayleigh (alternative mix) 3:57
Kayleigh (extended version) 4:00
Lady Nina (extended version) 5:46

Disc 7) »Lavender« (8886742)
Lavender 3:40
Freaks 4:04
Lavender blue 4:18

Disc 8) »Heart of Lothian« (8886752)
Heart of Lothian (7" edit) 3:49
Chelsea monday 7:23
Utrecht, 15.10.85
Heart of Lothian 5:43

Disc 9) »Incommunicado« (8886762)
Incommunicado (single version) 3:56
Going under 2:47
Incommunicado (album version) 5:16
Incommunicado (alternate version) 5:57

Disc 10) »Sugar mice« (8886772)

	Sugar mice	5:47
	Tux on	5:12
	Sugar mice (radio edit)	5:00
	Sugar mice (extended version)	6:08

Disc 11) »Warm wet circles« (8886782)

	Warm wet circles (7" remix)	4:23
	White russian	6:09
	Loreley, 18.07.87	
	Incommunicado	5:27
	Loreley, 18.07.87	

Disc 12) »Freaks (live)« (8886792)

	Freaks	4:12
	Mannheim, 21.06.86	
	Kayleigh *	4:08
	Childhoods end? *	3:10
	White feather *	4:00

** Recorded live in London, 09./10.01.86*

UK Abbey Road, Disc 1-12
12 test pressing CDs, each packed seperately
UK EMI, 888 6672
12 picture CDs with seperate ps and number in cardboard box
EEC EMI, 7243 8 88667 2 9
12 picture CDs with seperate ps and number in cardboard box
FRA EMI, PM 568
12 picture CDs with seperate ps and number in cardboard box

4CD 4CD 4CD 4CD 4CD 4CD 4CD 4CD 4CD

Disc 1)	Market square heroes	4:15
	Three boats down from the candy	4:29
	Grendel	17:14
	He knows you know (7" edit)	3:30
	Charting the single	5:40
	He knows you know (12" edit)	5:05
	Garden party (7"edit)	4:29
	Margaret (live edit)	4:09
	Edinburgh, 07.04.83	
	Garden party	7:15
	Charting the single	6:30
	London, 18.04.83	
	Margaret	12:17
	Edinburgh, 07.04.83	
Disc 2)	Punch and Judy (7" version)	3:19
	Market square heroes (re-recording edit)	3:56
	Three boats down from the candy (re-recording)	3:59
	Market square heroes (re-recording)	4:45
	Assassing (7" version)	3:39
	Cinderella search (7" version)	4:19
	Assassing	7:01
	Cinderella search	5:24
	Kayleigh (single edit)	3:33
	Lady Nina (single edit)	3:41
	Kayleigh (alternative mix)	3:57
	Kayleigh (extended version)	4:00
	Lady Nina (extended version)	5:46
Disc 3)	Lavender	3:40
	Freaks	4:04
	Lavender blue	4:18
	Heart of Lothian (7" edit)	3:49
	Chelsea monday	7:23
	Utrecht, 15.10.85	
	Heart of Lothian	5:43
	Incommunicado (single version)	3:56
	Going under	2:47
	Incommunicado (album version)	5:16
	Incommunicado (alternate version)	5:57
Disc 4)	Sugar mice	5:47
	Tux on	5:12
	Sugar mice (radio edit)	5:00
	Sugar mice (extended version)	6:08
	Warm wet circles (7" remix)	4:23
	White russian	6:09
	Loreley, 18.07.87	
	Incommunicado	5:27
	Loreley, 18.07.87	
	Freaks	4:12
	Mannheim, 21.06.86	
	Kayleigh *	4:08
	Childhoods end?*	3:10
	White feather *	4:00

** Recorded live in London, 09./10.01.86*

UK EMI
4 CD-R, company sleeve

»Marillion christmas 2000: A piss-up in a brewery«

(UK-only release 29.01.2001)

CD CD CD CD CD CD CD CD CD CD CD CD

Go!	6:12
After me	3:53
Alone again in the lap of luxury	5:17
Cinderella search	3:46
The space	4:50
A collection	3:53
Sympathy *	4:44
Number one *	3:29
Dry land *	6:16
Gazpacho	5:55
How will you go *	5:09
Cannibal surf babe	5:52

*Recorded live and acoustic in Burton-upon-Trent, Bass Museum, 16./17.11.2000, * feat. Stephany Sobey-Jones on cello*

UK Racket Records, WebFree 03
free fan club CD, no backing card

»Crash course – An introduction to Marillion«

(UK-only release 2/'01)

CD CD CD CD CD CD CD CD CD CD CD CD

This is the 21st century (»Anoraknophobia« version)	10:52
Rich (»marillion.com« version)	5:42
Afraid of sunlight (»Afraid of sunlight« version)	6:50
A legacy (»marillion.com« version)	6:16
Under the sun (»Radiation« version)	4:13

UK Racket Records, RACKET 15
sold at UK-University tour 2001 for 1 pound, one copy each person, 1,000 copies
UK Racket Records, RACKET 15
re-release without tourdates on sleeve, mail-order-only for the people who ordered the »Between you and me/Map of the world« CD-single, no backing card, 1 pound each

»marillion.com – millenium collection«

(release 2001)

CD CD CD CD CD CD CD CD CD CD CD CD

Kayleigh
Cover my eyes (Pain and heaven)
Warm wet circles
Beautiful
Deserve
Sugar mice
King
Enlightened
Assassing
Alone again in the lap of luxury
Lavender
Hooks in you
Built-in bastard radar
Uninvited guest
Heart of Lothian
House
Incommunicado

Eastern Europe pirate compilation

»Anoraknophobia«

(UK release 07.05.2001)

CD CD CD CD CD CD CD CD CD CD CD CD

Between you and me	6:27
Quartz	9:06
Map of the world	5:02
When I meet god	9:17
The fruit of the wild rose	6:57
Separated out	6:13
This is the 21st century	11:07
If my heart were a ball it would roll uphill	9:28

UK Liberty
test pressing, no number, printed CD with info sheet
UK EMI, CDLRL 048
promo, cardboard sleeve, some with promo folder and/or promo sheet(s) and/or promo photo(s)
UK EMI
EEC EMI
FRA EMI
test pressing, no number, printed CD with info sheet
USA Sanctuary, 84506
release 14.05.2001

··

Between you and me (radio edit)	4:25
Map of the world (radio edit)	4:16

UK EMI, CDLRL 049
2-track sampler, promo, cardboard sleeve, some with promo folder and/or promo sheet and/or promo photo(s) and/or sticker

2CD 2CD 2CD 2CD 2CD 2CD 2CD 2CD 2CD

Disc 1)	Between you and me	6:27
	Quartz	9:06
	Map of the world	5:02
	When I meet god	9:17
	The fruit of the wild rose	6:57
	Separated out	6:13
	This is the 21st century	11:07
	If my heart were a ball it would roll uphill	9:28
Disc 2)	Number one	2:48
	The fruit of the wild rose (demo)	6:19
	Separated out (demo)	6:03
	Between you and me (Mark Kelly remix)	5:08
	Number one (recording video)	
	Map of the world (recording video)	

UK Intact Records, 12674-001/002
ltd. ed. book cover, mailorder-only for the 12,674 people who pre-ordered and paid the album in autumn 2000, large booklet with all the names of the first nearly 8,000 people who ordered, comes in special "Anorak" cardboard box with Racket-catalogue

»Refracted – The making of "Afraid of sunlight" – From dusk 'til dot, Vol. 1«

(UK-only release 5/'01)

2CD 2CD 2CD 2CD 2CD 2CD 2CD 2CD 2CD

Disc 1)	Gazpacho	7:32
	Cannibal surf babe	5:33
	Beautiful	6:34
	Afraid of sunrise	5:14
	Out of this world	7:06
	Beyond you	6:04
	Afraid of sunlight	6:42
	King	7:04
Disc 2)	Gazpacho mid-8	1:03
	Gazpacho shuffle	0:22
	Heavy groove Gazpacho	1:29
	Gazpacho guitar	0:34
	Gazpacho chorus	1:31
	Big soul surf babe	0:41
	X-ray surf babe	0:37
	Jangly surf babe	2:54
	Beautiful piano	1:08
	AOS cabaret	0:29
	Out of this world original end	4:36
	Out of this world actual end	2:27
	Pulse beyond you	1:30
	Beyond you piano version	0:40
	Beyond Blade Runner	0:59
	Beyond the 80's	0:20
	Beyond the Stones	1:35
	Beautifully disturbing	1:16
	Latin AOS	1:17
	Work on AOS	0:38
	More AOS	1:33
	The electronix king	1:03
	Heavy king	0:25
	Hendrix king	1:01
	Funkadelic king	0:47
	Talking kings	2:25
	Hero king	0:38

UK Racket Records, RACKET 17
mailorder-only or sold at concerts

»Between you and me/ Map of the world«

(UK-only release 08.10.2001)

CD CD CD CD CD CD CD CD CD CD CD CD

Between you and me (Mark Kelly radio mix)	4:27
Map of the world (radio edit)	4:15
Quartz	9:22
Manchester, 19.05.2001	
If my heart were a ball it would roll uphill (Pete Trewavas edit)	4:44

UK Intact Records, Intact 011001
cardboard sleeve, people who bought the record via mailorder before the official release got one extra copy for free with each CD they ordered

»Another DAT at the office – The making of "This strange engine" – From dusk 'til dot, Vol. 2«

(UK-only release 10/'01)

2CD 2CD 2CD 2CD 2CD 2CD 2CD 2CD 2CD

Disc 1)	Man of 1000 faces	6:33
	One fine day	4:47
	Memory of water	3:10
	Accidental man (AOS demo)	6:15
	This strange engine	34:02
Disc 2)	The monkee song	2:25
	McCartney faces	0:29
	Tribal faces	1:00
	1000 faces piano intro	0:56
	Man of 1000 crows	1:05
	Voice of command	2:11
	Beyond 80 days	0:39
	Acoustic beyond 80 days	1:35
	79 days	0:57
	Estonia groove	0:24
	Estonia rock	1:46
	Estonia engine	0:40
	Accidental groove	1:57
	Accidental acoustic man	1:15
	Accidental Duke of York	0:29
	Accidental guitar riff	0:31
	Accidental chorus	1:30
	Chord workshop man	1:31
	New accident	2:19
	Chill for the future	1:54
	Hope for The Pretenders	0:49
	Hope for Ry Cooder	1:38
	Hope for Jeff Buckley	2:12
	Hope for a chorus	1:24
	Strange Stones engine	0:31
	Acoustic lamb engine	1:06
	This strange jam	0:39
	This strange intro	1:53
	Wax on wood	1:03
	Ever since an idea	1:43
	The louge navy	0:37
	Cloud of bees jam	1:38
	Acoustic mummy daddy	0:43
	Electric mummy daddy	0:54
	Blue pain guitar solo	1:16
	Red coat ending	0:53
	Run like hell ending	1:16
	Groove ending	1:23
	The strange ending	1:29

UK Racket Records, RACKET 18
mailorder-only or sold at concerts

Compilation Tracks

MARILLION Tracks on Compilation Albums

"Alone again in the lap of luxury"
»Capitol Promo Sampler # 4«, CD, 1994
CAN Capitol, CDPRO VOL 4

"Assassing"
»EMI 4 tracks Mini-LP«, LP, 1984
ITA EMI, 50 240146 1
»Kerrang! Compilation«, 2LP, 1985
UK EMI/Virgin KER 1
»Rock Collection - Rock Solid«, 2LP, 1985
EEC Time Life, TL 527/20
»Rock Hits and Ballads«, 3CD, 1996
EEC Disky, HR 869 112
»Rock me tonight«, promo, LP, 1985
ARG EMI, 8269/81 2604051
»Rock 'n' ride – Hits only«, CD
EEC 27400143 H

"Assassing" (live)
»Live Rock«, LP, 1985
GR EMI, MT 12002

"Beautiful"
»Kippevel«, CD, 1996
EEC Eva
»Promo Dial 11 Septembro 95«, 2CD, 1995
BRA PP 0065

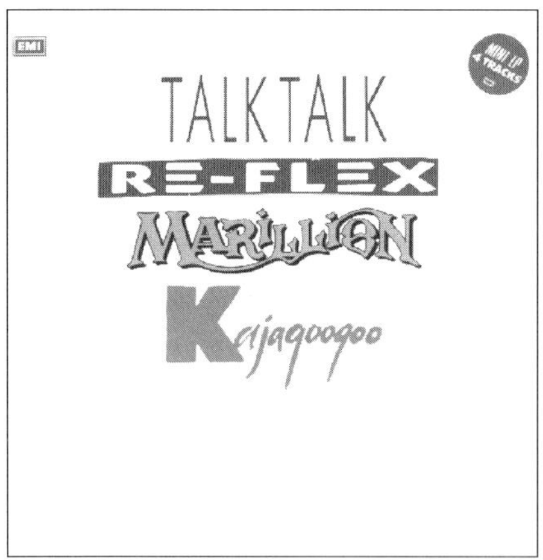

Italian cover »Mini-LP« 12"

"Between you and me" (edit)
»Tips, Trends, News 18/19«, CD, 2001
GER EMI, KW 18/19-2001
»Very important products 16.KW«
GER EMI, 16.KW 17.04.2001

"Built-in bastard radar"
»Hard Rock«, promo, CD, 1999
FRA

"Cannibal surfbabe"
»Capitol Promo Sampler # 22«, CD, 1995
CAN Capitol, CDPRO VOL 22
»Capitol Promo Sampler # 23«, CD, 1995
CAN Capitol, CDPRO VOL 23
»The best things in life are free«, CD, 1995
USA
»Tune-up Vol. 135«, promo, CD, 1995
USA Album Network, VOL 135

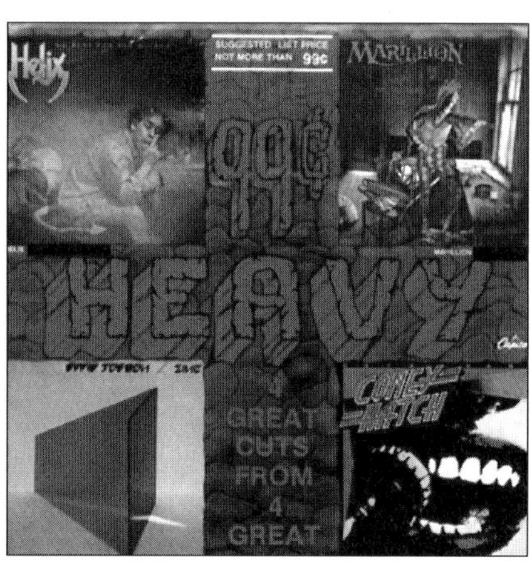

Canadian cover »The 99C Heavy E.P.« 7"

"Chelsea monday"
»99 C Heavy – 4 great cuts from 4 great albums«, 7", 1983
CAN Capitol 72928

"Cover my eyes"
»Disco promocional mix invendavel«, promo, no ps, 12", 1991
BRA EMI, 9951 260

"Deserve"
»The corner (February 2k)«, promo, CD, 2000
USA

"Dry land"
»Capitol Promo Sampler # 7«, CD, 1992
CAN Capitol, CDPRO VOL 7

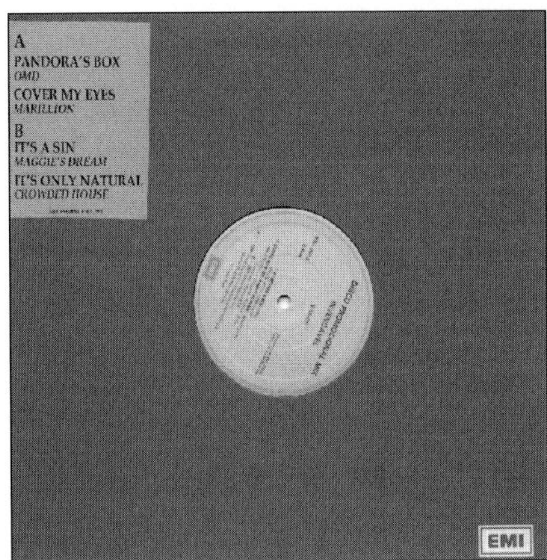

Brazilian cover »Cover my eyes« promo 12"

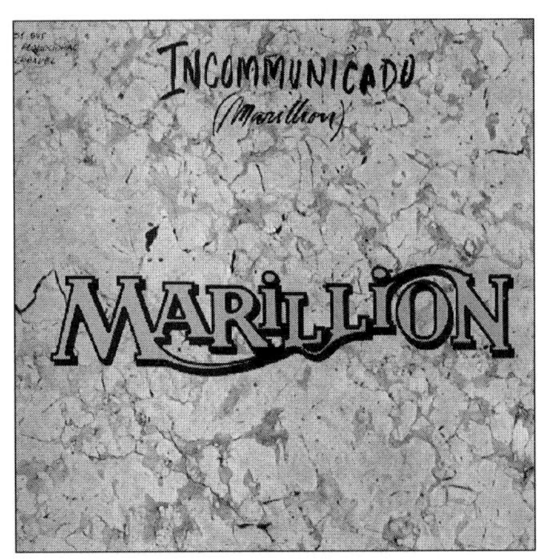

Brazilian cover »Incommunicado« promo 12"

»Flights of fantasy«, 2CD, 1995
EEC Columbia/Sony, 480406-2

"Easter"
»EMI Hot shots Nr. 2« promo, CD, 1990
EEC EMI, CDP 519006

"Face 1004" (fade out edit)
(with THE POSITIVE LIGHT)
»Fly like an eagle« promo, CD, 1998
UK Eagle Records, EAGPKS 1

"Garden party"
»25 years of Rock 'n' Roll - 1983«, 2LP, 1988
UK Connoisseur Collection, YRNRLP 83
»A time to remember – 1983«, CD
EEC EMI
»Born to be wild 3«, CD, 1994
EEC Bellaphon, MUSCD 023
»Essential Rock«, CD, 1996
EEC EMI, 8520272
»Kneipen Hits – Rock Classics«, 2CD
EEC Disky
»Rock Collection - Hard 'n' Heavy«, 2CD
EEC Time Life, TL 527/14

"Heart of Lothian"
»A time to remember - 1985«, CD
EEC EMI
»Pop on Top 01/1986«, LP, 1986
GER S*R International, 42 640 3

"He knows you know"
»A time to remember – 1983«, CD
EEC EMI
»Plenty good music« promo, LP, 1983
USA Capitol, SPRO-9937

"He knows you know" (live)
»Marquee-Collection Vol. 3«, LP, 1983
UK England Rec., MAR 3
»Marquee-Collection Vol. 3«, LP, 1984
ITA Disco Magic, MAR 3
»Marquee-Collection Vol. 4«, LP
ESP D 30.302
»Reading Rock '82«, 2LP, 1983
UK Mean, MNLP 82
»Remember 25 years in Rock«, 3LP, 1983
ESP 9021/3

"Hooks in you"
»EMI Hot shots Nr. 9« promo, CD, 1989
CH EMI, CDP 518937
»The final countdown«, 2LP, 1991
UK Telstar, STAR 2431
»The final countdown«, CD, 1991
UK Telstar, TCD 2431
»The very best of Soft Metal«, 2LP, 1991
UK Telstar, STAR 2431
»The very best of Soft Metal«, CD, 1991
UK Telstar, TCD 2431

"Incommunicado"
»Air freshner Vol. 2« promo, LP, 1987
RSA EMI, LP 104
»A time to remember – 1987«, CD
EEC EMI
»Best of 1980-1990 Vol.12«, 2CD, 1997
EEC EMI, 8535702
»Chart show - Rock the nation«, 2LP, 1988
UK ADD 2
»Club Top 13 International«, LP, 1987
EEC 13 398 3
»Essential Rock«, 3CD, 1997
EEC Disky, EH 885 082

»Kneipen Hits – Die Zweite«, 2CD, 1998
EEC Disky, GDO 852 122
»New«, LP, 1987
EEC EMI, 1C 058 Y 7 48138 1
»On the road again«, CD
EEC
»Pur Hits«, CD, 1996
EEC EMI, 8 53395 2-538
»Rock Anthems«, 2CD, 1994
UK Dino Entert., DINCD101
»Rock City Nights«, LP, 1989
UK Vertigo, RCNTV 1
»Rock City Nights«, CD, 1989
UK Vertigo, 840 622-2
»Rock Classics«, CD, 1996
UK MCI, MUSCD 028
»Rock met ballen«, CD
EEC
»Split with DAVID BOWIE«, 7", promo, no ps,1987
ARG EMI, DIF 469-A/B
»Split with WHITESNAKE«, 12", promo, 1987
BRA EMI, 995515045-A/B
»The Hits - Album 6«, 1988
UK HITS 6
»Wild at heart 1«, CD, 1996
EEC Bellaphon, MUSCD 028

"Incommunicado" ("Thieving Magpie"-Version live)

»Live 'n' kickin'«, CD, 1994
EEC EMI, 7243 829604323
»Rock met ballen«, 2CD
EEC

"Kayleigh"

»20th century - Hits for a mill…«, 2CD
EEC Disky
»80's Superhits«, 2CD, 1997
EEC Disky, DOU 878252
»A time to remember«, CD
EEC EMI
»Ballads from the heart«, 2CD, 1997
EEC Disky, DOU 882432
»Chart Hit History«, 3CD, 1996
EEC Disky, HR 873902
»Classic Rock«, 2CD
EEC Disky
»Das Hit-Paket der '80er Jahre«, 2CD, 1997
EEC Disky, DU 876022
»Die Mega Schmuse-Box«, 6CD, 1998
EEC TV shop order-only
»Dreams of glory«, CD, 1994
EEC Intercord, INT 870.020
»Een portret van Jaap Stam«, CD, 1998
EEC Disky, DC 887702
»Everyday hurts«, CD, 1997
EEC Koch Int., CRMIDCD19
»FAME greatest Popsongs 2«, CD, 1992
EEC EMI, BOSPCD121
»Fetenhits (The ballads)«, 2CD, 1997
EEC Polystar, 555 067-2
»Greatest hits of the 80's«, 8CD, 1999
EEC Disky
»Greatest Love«, 3CD, 1995
EEC Disky, HR 861542
»Greatest Love 3«, CD, 1996
EEC Disky, DC 869642
»Greatest Popballads 1«, CD, 1996
EEC Disky, DC 877422
»Greatest Popballads«, 3CD, 1996
EEC Disky, HR 877412
»Heart Beat«, CD
EEC RCA Ariola, 887 569-901
»Heart Beats«, 2CD, 1997
EEC Disky, DOU 878262
»Heart Rock«, CD, 1996
EEC Disky, DC 865742
»Herzschmerz«, 2CD
EEC Polystar
»Hitbreaker 16 Formel Top Hits«, LP, 1985
GER S*R International, 42 327 7
»Hits der '80er Jahre«, 3CD
EEC Disky
»Hits der '80er Vol.2«, 2CD, 1994
EEC BMG Ent., 74321203882
»Ich steh' auf Rock Vol. 2«, CD, 1997
EEC BMG/Ariola, 21 46548 2-283
»Ich liebe dich«, 2CD, 1997
EEC Disky, DU 876032
»International Pop Gold«, CD, 1988
EEC EMI, CDP 654-746455 2
»Just the best (20-35)«, CD, 1996
EEC Disky, DC 869722
»Kneipen Hits – Ballads«, 2CD, 1998
EEC Disky, GDO 852162
»Kuschelrock 4«, 3LP, 1990
EEC Sony/CBS, 467475 1
»Kuschelrock 4«, 2CD, 1990
EEC Sony/CBS, 467475 2
»Life in the fast lane«, LP, 1988
UK Telstar, TCD 2315
»Mal Sondock's Hitparade«, 3CD
EEC Disky
»Marquee 30 legendary years«, 2LP, 1988
UK Polydor, MQTV 1
»Marquee 30 legendary years«, CD, 1988
UK Polydor, 840 101-2
»Megastars«, 2CD, 1997
EEC Disky, DU 883112
»Megastars und ihre No.1 Hits«, 2CD, 1997
EEC Disky, GDU 883702
»Metal Ballads Vol. 4«, CD, 1991
EEC RCA/Ariola, PD 75194
»Missing you« promo, LP, 1991
ARG EMI, 58560

»More than a feeling«, 3LP, 1990
UK TV mailorder-only
»More than a feeling«, 3CD, 1990
UK TV mailorder-only
»Music machine '86«, LP, 1986
EEC SMMC 149
»My generation (Rockin' ...)«, 2CD, 1994
EEC EMI/Intercord, 890.005
»Now 1985 - Millenium series«, 2CD
UK Virgin
»Now that's what I call music 5«, 2LP, 1985
UK EMI/Virgin, NOW 5
»Now this is music Vol. 3«, 2LP, 1985
UK EMI/Virgin, 158-2607793
»O. Bierhoff: Ich steh' auf Rock«, CD
EEC Ariola
»ON LINE Flexi Disc«, 7", promo, one-sided flexi-disc, no number, no ps, 1985
UK ON LINE
»Perfect CD-Collection Nr. 10«, CD, 1988
EEC Ariola/Hitmaster, 259.074
»Peter's Pop Hits 1985«, 2CD, 1999
EEC Disky
»Pop Classics 2- The 70's + 80's«, 2CD
EEC EVA, 795484
»Pop Ballads«, CD, 1997
EEC Disky, HR 877412
»Pop Giganten: Hits der '80er«, 2CD
EEC Media Markt
»Premiere CD: International '88«, CD, 1988
EEC Dureco, 1988376
»Pur Ballads«, CD, 1996
EEC EMI, 724385342622
»Rock & Love«, CD
EEC Zyx
»Rock Anthems Vol.2«, CD, 1995
EEC Dino, DICD 110
»Rock Ballads Forever Gold«, 2CD, 2000
EEC Diamond Records
»Rock Collection – Rock Stars«, 2CD
EEC Time Life, TL 527/01
»Rock Dreams«, LP, 1988
A CBS, 4601012
»Rock Hits and Ballads«, CD, 1996
EEC Disky, DC 86152
»Rock Hits and Ballads«, 3CD, 1996
EEC Disky, HR 869112
»Rock 'n' Ride – Symphonic Rock«, CD
EEC 27400204 H
»Rock 'n' Romance«, 4CD
EEC Polystar
»Rock 'n' Romance 2«, 2CD, 1997
EEC Polystar, PMS
»Rock Pop Music Hall - Herbst«, 2LP, 1985
EEC K-tel, TG 1575
»Rock Romance«, CD
UK Arc
»Rock Super Stars Vol.2«, 8CD, 1995
ITA EMI, 7243 840949 2
»Rock Super Stars Vol.2«, CD
UK Virgin
»Schmuse Rock«, 2CD, 1997
EEC Disky, DU 883022
»Soft Metal«, LP, 1989
UK Stylus Music, SMD 862
»Soft Rock Collected«, CD, 1997
EEC Disky, DC 881482
»Split with TALKING HEADS«, 7", promo, no ps,1985
ARG EMI, DIF 355-A/B
»Split with DURAN DURAN«, 7", promo, no ps,1985
ITA EMI Nescafe, 1792447
»Stereoplay: Highlights - Artrock«, CD
EEC Phono
»Styles« orange vinyl, LP, 1986
EEC Sparkasse, 07-980014-20
»Super Hit Sensation«, LP, 1988
UK Ariola, 207 101 502
»The 80's Love Collection«, 2CD
UK Virgin
»The best Love Songs ever«, 2CD, 1998
EEC Disky, DOU 882452
»The best of 1980-1990 Vol. 1«, 3LP, 1990
EEC EMI, 1C 152- 7 94147 1
»The best of 1980-1990 Vol. 1«, 2CD, 1990
EEC EMI, 652-7 94147 2
»The greatest love Vol. 2«, LP, 1989
UK Telstar, TCD 2352
»The Love Collection«, CD, 1989
? MOD CD 1031
»The Originals Vol. 10«, LP, 1990
EEC EVA
»The Power of Love«, 2LP, 1986
UK West Five Records, WEF4
»The Rock Masterpieces 2«, promo, CD, 1997
GR EMI, 7243 8 23104 2 6
»Top 100 aller tijden«, 2CD, 1989
EEC Magnum, 471 613 2
»Top Rock«, CD, 1997
EEC EMI, 8 55822 2-888
»Totally 80's«, CD, 1997
EEC EMI, 7243 83303328
»Trailer Disc«, promo, 7", 1985
BRA BIZZ 549 201 003
»Vibraciones '86«, LP, 1985
ARG EMI 8339/81 2607631

"Kayleigh" (live)
»Rock Progression«, 2CD
UK Snapper
»Rock Progression«, 2CD, 1998
EEC Edel, 0000114SMD
»World's greatest live album«, CD, 1997
EEC Disky, DOU 882512
»World's greatest live tour«, CD, 1998
EEC Disky, DC , 887022

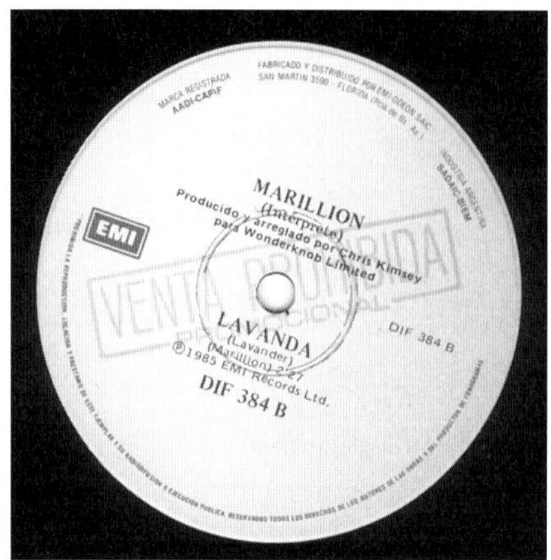

Argentinian label »Lavanda« promo 7"

"Kayleigh" (Steve Hogarth vocal demo)
»Retro-spective«, promo, 2CD, 1997
UK EMI, CAT PRO 100

"Lavender"
»17 Hot Winners '86«, LP, 1986
ARG EMI, 58400/81 2609941
»Classic Rock«, 2CD
EEC Disky
»Classic Rock Ballads«, CD, 1998
EEC Koch Int., CRMCD0120
»Club Top 13 – 1985 Extra«, LP, 1985
EEC Buch-Club, 41 667 7
»Formel 1 – Herbst '85«, LP, 1985
EEC EMI, 1C 088 26 0800 1
»Greatest hits of the '80's«, 8CD
EEC Disky
»Hitbreaker«, LP, 1985
GER S*R International, 42819
»Hot City Nights«, 1989
EEC Vertigo, 836-057-2
»Now that's what I call music 6«, 2LP, 1985
UK EMI/Virgin, NOW6
»Rock Classics from the 80's«, 2CD
EEC Disky
»Rock Collection - Rock Groups«, 2CD
EEC Time Life, TL 527/09
»Rock Diamonds Vol. 2«, CD
EEC Kiosk
»Ronny's Pop Show 1985«, LP, 1985
EEC CBS, 24 053
»Sound Pieces«, LP, 1987
EEC Sparkasse, 07-9803151-20
»Split with QUEEN«, 7", promo, no ps, 1985
ARG EMI, DIF 384-A/B
»The Love Collection 2«, CD, 1989
MODCD 1032

"Map of the world" (edit)
»Tips, Trends, News 18/19«, CD, 2001
GER EMI, KW 18/19-2001
»Very important products 16.KW«, CD, 2001
GER EMI, 16.KW 17.04.2001

"Market square heroes"
»A time to remember – 1982«, CD
EEC EMI

"No one can"
»Banana Jack Vol. 2«, 2CD
EEC EMI, 7 97965 2-686
»Capitol Promo Sampler # 2«, CD, 1992
CAN Capitol, CDPRO VOL 2
»Cool – Die Musik zum Brunch«, 2CD, 1996
EEC EMI, 8 52776 2-634
»Solo para difusion«, promo, LP, company sleeve, 1991
ARG EMI, DIFLP 051

"Punch and Judy"
»A time to remember – 1984«, CD
EEC EMI
»Symphonic Rock«, 2CD, 1998
EEC Disky, DOU 882422

"Sugar mice"
»Now that's what I call music10«, 2LP, 1987
UK EMI/Virgin, NOW10
»Pop on Top – Ausgabe 4/87«, LP, 1987
EEC S*R International, 14 437
»Soft Metal«, CD
UK Temple
»Soft Rock«, LP, 1989
UK Telstar, STAR 2397

"Sugar mice" (live)
»Live Wired«, CD, 1997
UK EMI, CDEMS 1609

"Sympathy"
»Capitol Promo Sampler # 18«, CD, 1992
CAN Capitol, CDPRO VOL 18
»Is this love?«, CD, 1993
EEC EMI, 7 81400 2-564

"Sympathy" (unplugged)
»Unplugged«, CD
EEC EMI, 7 89660 2-564

"The great escape"
»Promo Dial 5«, CD, 1995
BRA 5-9951 359

"This is the 21st century" (edit)
»The art of Sysyphus Vol. 7«, CD, 2001
EEC Sysyphus Records, CD 2001-7

"This is the 21st century" (edit)
»Tips, Trends, News 18/19«, promo, CD, 2001
GER EMI, KW 18/19-2001
»Very important products 16.KW«, promo, CD, 2001
GER EMI, 16.KW 17.04.2001

"Three boats down from the Candy" (live)
»Reading Rock '82«, 2LP, 1983
UK Mean, MNLP 82

"Under the sun"
»Rock Sound Vol. 1«, Magazine + CD, 1998
EEC Freeway, RSCDH 001

"Uninvited guest"
»Capitol Promo Sampler # 3«, CD, 1990
CAN Capitol, CDPRO VOL 3

"Waiting to happen"
»Heartbeat 2«, CD
EVA, PD 75203

Fish Tracks on Compilation Albums

"3D"
»The art of Sysyphus Vol. 7«, CD, 2001
GER Sysyphus Records, CD 2001-7

"A gentleman's excuse me"
»EMI Hot shots Nr. 2« promo, CD, 1990
GER EMI, CDP 519 006
»Fast 90's«, 3CD, 199?
EEC
»Hot Hits of the '90s Vol. 2«, CD, 1996
EEC
»Missing you Vol. 2«, CD, 199?
EEC
»Schmuse Rock«, 2LP
EEC
»Schmuse Rock«, 2CD
EEC
»Scotland the brave«, CD, 199?
UK

"Big wedge"
»Symphonic Rock«, 2CD, 1998
EEC
»Tie up«, LP, 1990
GER
»Tie up«, LP, 1990
ITA BMG, ZL 74537
»Fish/ Tina Turner«, 7", promo, no ps, 1989
ITA EMI, 1793797

"Boston tea party"
»Park Pop«, promo, CD, 1993
EEC

"Internal exile"
»Jamo Collection Vol. 1«, CD, 1992
EEC
»On the road again Vol. 2«, CD, 199?
EEC

"Somebody special"
»Voiceprint Promo Sampler 18«, CD, 1998
UK Voiceprint, VP 9808 CD

"State of mind"
»BBC Top of the Pops # 1304«, LP, 1989
USA
»EMI Hot shots Nr. 10«, promo, CD, 1989
GER EMI, CDP 518 947

Europeans Tracks on Compilation Albums

"Animal Song" (Cross Country version)
»Hit that perfect beat Vol. 1«, CD, 1984
UK Oglio, OPCD-1689

"Drinc Pink Zinc" (demo)
»The Snoopies album«, LP, 1981
UK private pressing, RSB 1

How We Live Tracks on Compilation Albums

"All the time in the world"
»Rock Pop in Concert«, 2LP, 1987
EEC BMG Ariola, 303103
»Rock over London #426«, LP, 28.06.1987
USA Radioshow

“Games in Germany”
»Rock Pop in Concert«, 2LP, 1987
EEC BMG Ariola, 303103

“Dry land”
»Rock over London #429«, LP, 19.07.1987
USA Radioshow

Toni Childs Tracks on Compilation Albums

“Stop your fussin’ ”
»Zartbitter (Büchergilde Gutenberg)«, LP, 1989
GER Polydor, 21624/0

“Stop your fussin’ ” (edit)
»Alf’s Super Hitparade«, 2LP, 1988
GER Polystar, 840 098-1
»Alf’s Super Hitparade«, CD, 1988
GER Polystar, 840 098-2
»High Life«, 2LP, 1988
GER Polystar, 816 907-1
»High Life«, CD, 1988
GER Polystar, 816 907-2

Transatlantic Tracks on Compilation Albums

“All of the above” (edit)
»Progressive springtime 2000«, promo, CD, 2000
EEC SPV/Inside Out, A-23238

“Duel with the devil” (edit)
»Bridge across forever tour«, promo, CD, 2001
EEC SPV/Inside Out,TODPRCD-01
»The art of Sysyphus Vol. 9 «, CD , 2001
EEC Sysyphus Records, CD 2001-5

“My new world” (edit)
»Progressive springtime 2000«, promo, CD, 2000
EEC SPV/Inside Out, A-23238

“We all need some light”
»The art of Sysyphus Vol. 2 «, CD, 2000
EEC Sysyphus Records, CD 2000-2

“We all need some light” (edit)
»Progressive springtime 2000«, CD, promo, 2000
EEC SPV/Inside Out, A-23238

Marillion Radio Shows

»BBC Transcription Services In Concert-331«

LP LP LP LP LP LP LP LP LP LP LP LP LP LP
Side 1) Assassing 6:55
Script for a jester’s tear 8:55
Incubus 8:43
Side 2) He knows you know 5:00
Fugazi 8:18
Garden party/Market square heroes 9:40
(Medley called “Petrushka”)
Recorded live in Chippenham, Gold Diggers Club, 12.03.1984, air date week 25 of 1984

UK BBC, CN 04387 S
vinyl black, yellow die-cut sleeve, 4 pages cue sheets

»BBC Transcription Services In Concert-353«

LP LP LP LP LP LP LP LP LP LP LP LP LP LP
Side 1) Garden party 6:35
Cinderella serach 5:43
Jigsaw 6:44
Chelsea Monday 8:05
Side 2) Pseudo silk kimono/Kayleigh/
Bitter suite (i, ii, iv, v)/
Heart of Lothian 15:55
Incubus 8:30
The record includes an introduction by Richard Skinner, recorded live in London, Hammersmith Odeon, 14.12.1984, air date week 17 of 1985.

UK BBC, 155103/4-S (CN 4557/S)
vinyl black, label green/white, yellow die-cut sleeve, 4 pages cue sheets, Matrix “155103/4-S”

»BBC Transcription Services In Concert-431«

LP LP LP LP LP LP LP LP LP LP LP LP LP LP
Side 1) Slainte mhath 4:42
White russian 5:50
Incubus 8:50
Sugar mice 5:45
Side 2) Fugazi 7:40
Hotel hobbies/Warm wet circles/
That time of the night 14:12
The last straw 6:00
The record includes an introduction by Richard

Skinner, recorded live in London, Wembley Arena, 04./05.11.1987, air date week 16 of 1988

UK BBC, 159206/7-S (CN 5129/S)
vinyl black, label green/white, yellow die-cut sleeve, 4 pages cue sheets, Matrix "12 FPS 159206/7"

»BBC Transcription Services In Concert-548«

CD CD CD CD CD CD CD CD CD CD CD CD

Holidays in Eden
Waiting to happen
The party
Easter
Incommunicado
No one can
Kayleigh
Lavender
Heart of Lothian
Cover my eyes
Slainte mhath

Recorded live in London, Wembley Stadium, 1992

UK BBC, TCD-0382
2 large cue sheets, less than 100 copies

»King Biscuit Flower Hour Show 631«

2LP 2LP 2LP 2LP 2LP 2LP 2LP 2LP 2LP 2LP

Side 1) THE DEL FUEGOS
Longest day
Hold us down
Don't run wild
Back seat nothing
Shame
Side 2) Night on the town
Sound of our town
I still want you
It's all right
Side 3) MARILLION
Waterhole (Expresso bongo)
Lords of the backstage
Blind curve
Side 4) – not playable –

The records include commercial breaks by "Budweiser", "U.S. Army", "Pioneer", "Hawaiian Punch" and introductions, the MARILLION side was recorded live in Cardiff, St.David's Hall, 12.01.1986, air date 08.06.1986

USA DIR Braoadcasting Corporation
vinyl black, label light blue, no ps, 2 pages cue sheets, Matrix "KB-631 A/B/C"

»London Wavelength BBC Rock Hour Show 521«

LP LP LP LP LP LP LP LP LP LP LP LP LP LP

Side 1)	Assassing	6:55
	Script for a jester's tear	8:50
	Fugazi	8:20
Side 2)	Incubus	8:41
	Garden party/Market square heroes	9:53
	(Medley called "Petrushka")	

The record includes commercial breaks by "Certs", "Coors", "Hubba-Bubba", "U.S. Navy", "Jensen", an introduction by Richard Skinner and a fade-in and fade-out by Phil Harvey, recorded live in Chippenham, Gold Diggers Club, 12.03.1984, air date 20.05.1984.

USA BBC, BC 521
vinyl black, label yellow, no ps, 1 page cue sheet, Matrix "BBC Rock Hour….."

an "A" version and a version "B" of this record are known, but there are no differences in the music.

»Westwood One In Concert Show 85-24«

2LP 2LP 2LP 2LP 2LP 2LP 2LP 2LP 2LP 2LP

Side 1) MARILLION
Assassing
Garden party
Side 2) Cinderella search
Punch and Judy
Jigsaw
Emerald lies
Side 3) Misplaced childhood (part 1)
Side 4) GO WEST
And it's raining
SOS
Don't look now
Here's one you'll know
Call me
We close our eyes

The records include commercial breaks by "Budweiser", "Panasonic", "U.S. Army", "Levis", "Starbrust", "Bubblicious" and spoken fade-in and fade-out., the MARILLION sides were recorded live in London, Hammersmith Odeon, 14.12.1984, air date 25.10.1985

USA Westwood One, IC 85-24
vinyl black, label black/white, no ps, 2 pages cue sheets, Matrix "IC-85-24 1/2/3/4"

»Westwood One In Concert Show 86-08«

2LP 2LP 2LP 2LP 2LP 2LP 2LP 2LP 2LP 2LP

Side 1) THE ALARM
Marching on
Howling wind
Where were you hiding...
68 guns
Side 2) Spirit of '76
Strength
The stand
Side 3) MARILLION
Assassing
Garden party
Side 4) Pseudo silk kimono
Kayleigh
Bitter suite
Heart of Lothian

The records include commercial breaks by "Budweiser", "Certs", "U.S. Army", "Levis" and spoken fade-in and fade-out., the MARILLION sides were recorded live in London, Hammersmith Odeon, 14.12.1984, air date 28.04.1986

USA Westwood One, IC 86-08
vinyl black, label black/white, no ps, 1 page cue sheet, Matrix "IC-86-08-1/2/3/4".

»BBC Top of the Pops«

USA # 1006
LP, (15.02.1984) including MARILLION with "Punch & Judy"
USA # 1019
LP, (16.05.1984) including MARILLION with "Assassing"
USA # 1072
LP, (22.05.1985) including MARILLION with "Kayleigh"
USA # 1086
LP, (28.08.1985) including MARILLION with "Lavender"
USA # 1098
LP, (21.11.1985) including MARILLION with "Heart of Lothian"
USA # 1176
LP, (21.05.1987) including MARILLION with "Incommunicado"
USA # 1185
LP, (23.07.1987) including MARILLION with "Sugar mice"
USA # 1200
LP, (05.11.1987) including MARILLION with "Warm wet circles"
USA # 1256
LP, (01.12.1988) including MARILLION with "Freaks"
USA # 1297
LP, (15.09.1989) including MARILLION with "Hooks in you"
USA # 1328
LP, (20.04.1990) including MARILLION with "Easter"

»Rock over London«

USA # 004
LP, (10.07.1983) including MARILLION with "Garden party"
USA # 114
LP, (01.04.1984), including MARILLION (Fish-Interview)
USA # 122
LP, (27.05.1984) including MARILLION with "Assassing" and introduction by Fish
USA # 223
LP, (09.06.1985) including MARILLION with "Kayleigh"
USA # 224
LP, (16.06.1985) including MARILLION with "Kayleigh"
USA # 225
LP, (23,06.1985) including MARILLION with "Kayleigh"
USA # 226
LP, (30.06.1985) including MARILLION with "Kayleigh"
USA # 231
LP, (04.08.1985) including MARILLION (Fish-Interview about "Kayleigh")
USA # 236
LP, (08.09.1985) including MARILLION with "Lavender"
USA # 238
LP, (22.09.1985) including MARILLION with "Lavender"
USA # 240
LP, (06.10.1985) including MARILLION with "Lavender"
USA # 250
LP, (15.12.1985) including MARILLION with "Heart of Lothian" and introduction by Fish

USA # 421
LP, (24.05.1987) including MARILLION with "Incommunicado"
USA # 427
LP, (05.07.1987) including MARILLION with "Just for the record"
USA # 429
LP, (19.07.1987) including MARILLION with "Sugar mice" and introduction by Fish
USA # 431
LP, (02.08.1987) including MARILLION with "Sugar mice"
USA # 432
LP, (09.08.1987) including MARILLION with "Sugar mice"
USA # 433
LP, (16.08.1987) including MARILLION with "Sugar mice"
USA # 446
LP, (15.11.1987) including MARILLION with "Incommunicado"
USA # 447
LP, (22.11.1987) including MARILLION with "Warm wet circles"
USA, ROL 92-09
CD, (24.02.1992) including MARILLION with exclusive acoustic versions of "Holloway girl" and "Easter" + Interview with Steve Hogarth

»Olon Repertoire Service«

NL Olon
LP, promo-sampler, no ps (13.06.1991) including MARILLION with "Cover my eyes"

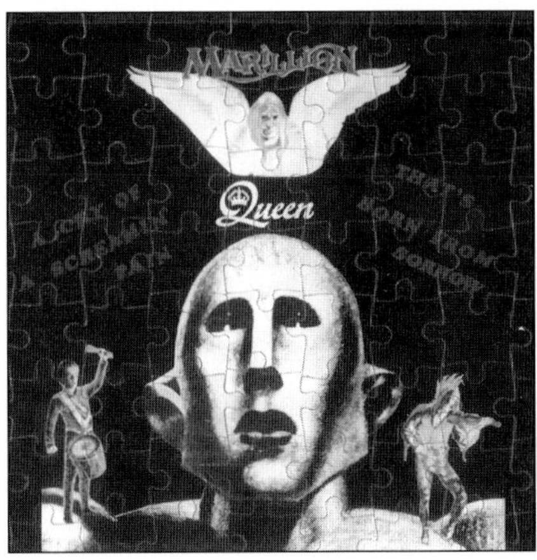

Cover »A cry of a screamin' pain...« album

MARILLION Vinyl Bootlegs

»Acoustic concert Luxor Cologne«

LP LP LP LP LP LP LP LP LP LP LP LP LP LP

Side 1) Holloway girl
Sugar mice
After me
The party
Easter
Waiting to happen
Side 2) The king of sunset town
Substitute
Cover my eyes (not live, but from the video clip)
Assassing *
Script for a jester's tear *

*Recorded live in Cologne, Luxor, 01.06.1991, except * live St.Gallen, Open Air, 27.05.1985*

EEC Sirius Records, SR 002
vinyl black, 1,000 copies, Matrix "MAR-1/2"
EEC Sirius Records, 002
picture disc, 1,000 copies, Matrix "MAR-1/2"
EEC Sirius Records
same as before, but plays music by SEPULTURA, Matrix "SAA 2530 CD-A/B"

»A cry of a screamin' pain that's born from sorrow«

LP LP LP LP LP LP LP LP LP LP LP LP LP LP

Side 1) QUEEN - live in Newcastle, 22.11.1973
Procession
Father to son
Son and daughter
Orge battle
Hangman
Side 2) MARILLION - Demo Spring, 3/'80
The hounting of gill house
Herne the hunter
Scott's porridge

EEC
vinyl clear/pink, first 39 numbered copies have jigsaw (88 pieces) instead of a cover and 1 insert as back cover , Matrix "TFKRL 9102"
EEC
vinyl clear/pink, next 313 numbered copies have 2 inserts instead of a cover, Matrix "TFKRL 9102"

»Alive«

2LP 2LP 2LP 2LP 2LP 2LP 2LP 2LP 2LP 2LP

Side 1)	Assassing	7:00
	Cinderella search	5:50
	Script for a jester's tear	9:50
	Punch and Judy	3:42
Side 2)	Jigsaw	7:25
	Emerald lies	5:20
	Pseudo silk kimono	2:48
	Kayleigh	3:52
	Lavender	2:30
	Bitter suite (i, ii, iii)	6:00
Side 3)	Bitter suite (iv, v)	2:13
	Heart of Lothian	3:40
	Incubus	9:15
	Fugazi	10:00
Side 4)	Garden party	9:40
	Market square heroes	10:20

Recorded live in Milano, Rolling Stone, 17.06.1985

EEC "Jump" mid-price, SPELP 4/SPEMC
vinyl black, the declarations on the cover are mostly wrong. Matrix "SG-4-A/B/C/D

»Another Chelsea evening«

LP LP LP LP LP LP LP LP LP LP LP LP LP LP

Side 1)	Script for a jester's tear	8:25
	Chelsea Monday	7:25
	The web	9:44
Side 2)	He knows you kwow	5:49
	Forgotten sons	12:59
	Market square heroes	8:00

Recorded live in London, Hammersmith Odeon, 18.04.1983 (video recording)

EEC Laughing Clown
first edition, vinyl black, cover red/blue, Matrix "LC 48065"
EEC Laughing Clown
re-release with Fish photo on cover, vinyl black, Matrix "LC 48065"
EEC Laughing Clown
re-release with Fish photo on cover, vinyl clear/multicoloured, Matrix "LC 48065"

••

Side 1)	Script for a jester's tear	8:25
	Chelsea Monday	7:25
	The web	9:44
Side 2)	Forgotten sons	12:59
	Skyline drifter *	9:30
	Bicester, Red Lion Pub, 14.03.1981	

*Recorded live in London, Hamersmith Odeon, 18.04.1983 (video recording), * a sticker on the cover says, that the track is called "Time for sale"*

EEC Laughing Clown
second edition, vinyl black, cover yellow/blue, Matrix "CHELSEA"
EEC Laughing Clown
second edition, vinyl red, cover yellow/blue, Matrix "CHELSEA"
EEC Laughing Clown
third edition, vinyl black, cover orange/red, Matrix "CHELSEA"
EEC Laughing Clown
third edition, vinyl blue/multicoloured, cover orange/red, Matrix "CHELSEA"
EEC Laughing Clown
fourth edition, vinyl black, cover orange xerox, Matrix "CHELSEA"

»At Rome - Incommunicado«

LP LP LP LP LP LP LP LP LP LP LP LP LP LP

Side 1) Fugazi
Hotel hobbies
Warm wet circles
That time of the night (The short straw)
Side 2) Kayleigh
Lavender
Bitter suite
Heart of Lothian
Incommunicado

Recorded live in Rome, Theatre Pallazzo Scallinata, 03.07.1987, re-release of »Go Fish« 2LP-Bootleg sides 3+4

EEC YRC 019
vinyl black, Matrix "CR 0019 C/D"

»BBC Transcription Services«

LP LP LP LP LP LP LP LP LP LP LP LP LP LP

Side 1) Slainte mhath
White russian
Incubus
Sugar mice
Side 2) Fugazi
Hotel hobbies
Warm wet circles
That time of the night
The last straw

Recorded live in London, Wembley Arena, 03./04.11.1987

UK BBC CN 5129/S
vinyl black, yellow die-cut sleeve, Matrix "159206", this is a bootleg copy of the official »BBC Transcription Services In Concert 431« radio show with black/white labels (the original has green/white labels)

»Childhood mysteries«

2LP 2LP 2LP 2LP 2LP 2LP 2LP 2LP 2LP 2LP

Side 1) Waterhole (Expresso bongo)
Lords of the backstage
Blind curve (i Vocal under bloodlight)
Intro
Emerald lies/Script for a jester's tear
Assassing
Side 2) Pseudo silk kimono
Kayleigh
Lavender
Bitter suite
Heart of Lothian
Side 3) Incubus
Garden party
Market square heroes
Side 4) Fugazi
White feather

Recorded live at The Monsters of Rock, Castle Donington, 17.08.1985

EEC Homestead Records
vinyl black, Matrix "LAVENDER A/B/C/D"
EEC TAKRL 2147/2148
re-release of 100 copies with insert instead of a cover, Matrix "LAVENDER A/B/C/D"
EEC Homestead Records
re-release as a picture disc (record 1 only), Matrix "LAVENDER A/B"

»Childhood's end«

3LP 3LP 3LP 3LP 3LP 3LP 3LP 3LP 3LP 3LP

Side 1) La gazza ladra
Intro
Emerald lies/Script for a jester's tear
Incubus
Side 2) Chelsea Monday
The web
Side 3) Pseudo silk kimono
Kayleigh
Lavender
Bitter suite
Heart of Lothian
Side 4) Waterhole (Expresso bongo)
Lords of the backstage
Blind curve
Childhood's end?
White feather
Side 5) Fugazi
Garden party
Market square heroes
Side 6) Punch and Judy
Assassing
Incubus

Sides 1-5 recorded live in Stockholm, Eriksdalhallen, 11.10.1985, side 6 recorded live at The Pink Pop Festival, Geleen, 11.06.1984

EEC Dharma Records
vinyl black, Matrix "DH-11 A/B/C/D/E/F"
EEC Dharma Records
re-release with foc, vinyl black, Matrix "DH-11 A/B/C/D/E/F"

»Definitely Loganastan«

LP LP LP LP LP LP LP LP LP LP LP LP LP LP

Side 1) Incubus
Chelsea Monday
The web
Side 2) Bitter suite
Heart of Lothian
Waterhole (Expresso bongo)
Lords of the backstage
Blind curve
Childhood's end?

Recorded live in Hannover, Stadthalle, 23.11.1985

EEC
vinyl black, black cover with red sticker, grey insert with tracklist

»Demories«

LP LP LP LP LP LP LP LP LP LP LP LP LP LP

Side 1) The web (Leyland Farm Studios, 198?)
Charting the single
(Watlington, Roxon Studios, 18./19.07.1981)
Market square heroes
(London, EMI Studios, 06.09.1982)
The institution waltz *
Side 2) I know what I like *
Herne the hunter
Bicester, Red Lion Pub, 14.03.1981

** Milton Keynes, Starting Gate, 24.12.1981*

ESP A&J Records
PF 2705 J, vinyl black, Matrix "257071"
ESP A&J Records
PF 2705 J, vinyl grey-marbled, Matrix "257071"

»Double o charity«

LP LP LP LP LP LP LP LP LP LP LP LP LP LP

Side 1) Garden party
Market square heroes/Let's twist again

Script for a jester's tear (cut)
Side 2) Script for a jester's tear (continues)
Fuagzi
Shadow on the wall

Recorded live in London, Hammersmith Odeon, 02.02.1986, special guests: Mike Oldfield, Roger Chapman, Steve Hackett and Peter Hammill

ESP A&J Records
NJ 1903/55, vinyl black, Matrix "MARILLION"

»Elvis Costello and Marillion«

LP LP LP LP LP LP LP LP LP LP LP LP LP LP

Side 1) ELVIS COSTELLO, Flip City Studio demos, 1975
Imagination is a powerful deceiver 4:14
Third rate romance (with no piano) 3:26
Knocking on heaven's door 4:20
I'm packing up (version 1) 3:13
I'm packing up (version 2) 2:48
(Please Mr.) don't stop the band 5:07
ELVIS COSTELLO, third John Peel Session 23.10.1978/30.10.1978
I just don't know what to do with myself 2:40
Side 2) MARILLION; live in Bangor, University, 12.02.1982
Chelsea Monday 8:11
Three boats down from the candy 6:12
Forgotten sons 11:27

Side 1 is the second side of the ELVIS COSTELLO bootleg "Our aim is true", side 2 is the second side of the MARILLION bootleg »Grendel's Garden Party«

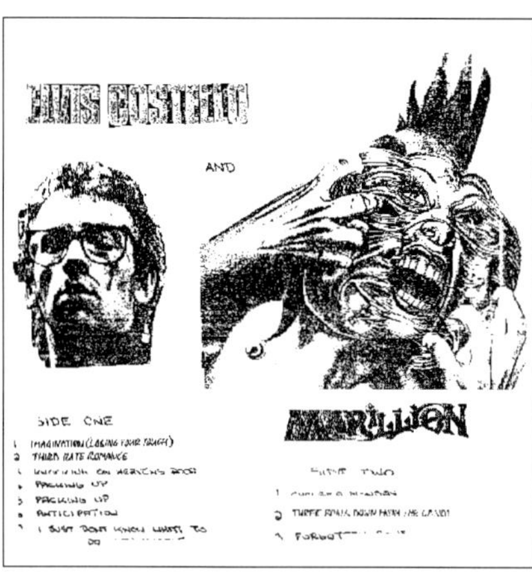

Cover insert »Elvis Costello & Marillion« album

EEC
vinyl black, 2 white inserts instead of a cover, Matrix "S-3230-B/MAR 101 B"
EEC
vinyl black, 2 yellow inserts instead of a cover, Matrix "S-3230-B/MAR 101 B"

»Eyes of Cinderella«

LP LP LP LP LP LP LP LP LP LP LP LP LP LP

Side 1) Assassing 7:10
Punch and Judy 3:35
Jigsaw 6:18
Cinderella search 6:30
Side 2) Incubus 8:55
Garden party/Market square heroes 14:45

Recorded live in Zürich, Schlüfwegzentrum, 21.11.1984 (TV-recording)

EEC Vinyl Virus
VV LP 028, vinyl black, Matrix "VV 028 LP"

»First service«

LP LP LP LP LP LP LP LP LP LP LP LP LP LP

Side 1) Script for a jester's tear 8:25
Chelsea Monday 7:25
The web 9:44
Side 2) Forgotten sons 12:59
Skyline drifter * 9:30

*Recorded live in London, Hammersmith Odeon, 18.04.1983 (video recording), except * Bicester, Red Lion Pub, 14.03.1981, re-release of »Another chelsea evening« bootleg LP*

EEC TAKRL 2073
re-release of 100 copies with yellow insert instead of a cover, Matrix "CHELSEA"

»Fish ahoy«

3LP 3LP 3LP 3LP 3LP 3LP 3LP 3LP 3LP 3LP

Side 1) Garden party
Freaks
Assassing
Chelsea Monday
Side 2) Script for a jester's tear
Pseudo silk kimono
Kayleigh
Lavender
Bitter suite (i, ii, iii)
Side 3) Bitter suite (iv, v)
Heart of Lothian

Waterhole (Expresso bongo)
Lords of the backstage
Blind curve
Childhood's end?
White feather

Side 4) Forgotten sons
Incubus

Side 5) Fugazi
Market square heros
incl. "She loves you/Let's twist again"

Side 6) Soundcheck
incl. "Pieces of Incubus", "Freaks", "Garden party", "Script for a jester's tear"...

Recorded live in Rotterdam, Ahoy, 19.06.1986

EEC All Day Music
each record has different multicoloured vinyl, 50 copies in box with insert, Matrix "KANT A/B/C/D/E/F"

EEC All Day Music
each record has black vinyl, 450 copies in regular sleeve, Matrix "KANT A/B/C/D/E/F"

EEC All Day Music
each record has a different colour (white, yellow and green/black), this seems to be a test pressing, only 1 copy is known, Matrix "KANT A/B/C/D/E/F"

»Fish and chips«

LP LP LP LP LP LP LP LP LP LP LP LP LP LP

Side 1) Incubus
Garden party
Market square heroes

Side 2) Fugazi
White feather

Re-release of the »Childhood mysteries« 2LP bootleg (side 3+4), recorded live at The Monsters of Rock, Castle Donington, 17.08.1985

EEC TAKRL
re-release of 100 copies with yellow insert instead of a cover, no number, Matrix "LAVENDER"

»Fish for president«

LP LP LP LP LP LP LP LP LP LP LP LP LP LP

Side 1) Assassing
Garden party
Cinderella search

Side 2) Jigsaw
Chelsea Monday
Emerald lies

Recorded live in Geneva, Salle de Fetes de Thonex, 29.11.1984

EEC
vinyl black, 150 copies, Matrix "GENF"

»Fishing behind the wall«

2LP 2LP 2LP 2LP 2LP 2LP 2LP 2LP 2LP 2LP

Side 1) Slainte mhath
Assassing
White russian
Sugar mice

Side 2) Fugazi
Hotel hobbies
That time of the night (The short straw)
Warm wet circles

Side 3) Waterhole (Expresso bongo)
Lords of the backstage
Blind curve
Childhoods end?
White feather
Kayleigh

Side 4) Lavender
Heart of Lothian
The last straw
Incommunicado
Garden party
Market square heroes
incl. "Let's twist again"

Recorded live in East-Berlin, Radrennbahn Weissensee, 18.06.1988

EEC Quaak Records, QR 010
vinyl black, Matrix "MEB"

»Fish out of water – rarities«

LP LP LP LP LP LP LP LP LP LP LP LP LP LP

Side 1) Grendel 20:05
(London, EMI Studios 06.09.1982)
The institution waltz 4:10
Aston Clinton,Village Hall, 11/'81

Side 2) Lady Fantasy * 6:55
Alice * 5:00
Garden party ** 9:32
Time for sale ** 3:12

** "Demo Summer", 06.06.1980, ** Bicester, Red Lion Pub, 14.03.1981*

EEC Homestead/Northlake Records
(label "See for miles Records")
vinyl green, Matrix "GRENDEL"

EEC Homestead/Northlake Records (label "See for miles Records")
vinyl black, Matrix "GRENDEL"
EEC Homestead/Northlake Records (label "Laughing Records")
vinyl black, Matrix "GRENDEL"
EEC TAKRL 2279
re-release of 100 copies with pink insert instead of a cover, Matrix "GRENDEL"

»Fish out of water – rarities – part two«

LP LP LP LP LP LP LP LP LP LP LP LP LP LP

Side 1)	Market square heroes *	4:05
	Three boats down from the candy *	4:55
	Interview	2:50
	Snow angel **	5:58
	The web **	6:55
Side 2)	Assassing	6:15
	Reading Rock Festival, 27.08.1983	
	Interview	2:00
	Charting the single	4:50
	(Watlington, Roxon Studios,18/19.07.1981)	
	Forgotten sons	8:30
	(Friday Rock Show, 29.01.1982)	

** London, EMI Studios 06.09.1982, ** Bicester, Red Lion Pub, 14.03.1981*

EEC Homestead Records, HMS 148322-86
vinyl black, Matrix "030"

»Fish out of water – rarities – part three«

LP LP LP LP LP LP LP LP LP LP LP LP LP LP

Side 1)	Shadow on the wall *	7:30
	I know what I like *	6:42
	Auld lang syne	3:52
Side 2)	Geesabun	4:22
	Script for a jester's tear	9:51
	Cinderella search	6:24

*Recorded live in Aylesbury, Friars, 22.12.1984, except * live in London, Hammersmith Odeon, 06.02.1986*

EEC Northlake Records, 235246-1286
vinyl black, Matrix "GEESABUM"

»Flying exhibition«

2LP 2LP 2LP 2LP 2LP 2LP 2LP 2LP 2LP 2LP

Side 1)	Slainte mhath
	Assassing
	White russian
	Sugar mice
Side 2)	Fugazi
	Hotel hobbies
	Warm wet circles
	That time of the night (The short straw)
Side 3)	Pseudo silk kimono
	Kayleigh
	Lavender
	Bitter suite
	Heart of Lothian
Side 4)	The last straw
	Incommunicado
	Garden party

Recorded live in Essen, Grugahalle, 23.11.1987

EEC Movement/Observation Records, R 29788
vinyl black, Matrix "911 002"

»Forgotten songs«

LP LP LP LP LP LP LP LP LP LP LP LP LP LP

Side 1)	Close *	9:40
	Lady Fantasy *	6:37
	Alice *	5:50
Side 2)	Institution waltz **	3:59
	I know what I like **	6:48
	He knows you know °	3:24
	Garden party °	6:35

** "Demo Summer", 06.06.1980, ** Aston Clinton,Village Hall, 11/'81, ° Watlington, Roxon Studios, 18/19.07.1981*

There are lots of different versions known concerning the cover or the colour of the records. Some people mixed up some records and covers and changed them amongst each another, so that it is quite difficult to say which cover belongs to which record colour. All records have Matrix "MAR 002". Here they are:

- vinyl blue (original version)
- vinyl black
- vinyl red
- vinyl yellow
- vinyl clear/multicoloured
- vinyl white/multicoloured
- vinyl yellow/multicoloured
- cover red with black print
- cover red with yellow and white print
- cover orange with black print

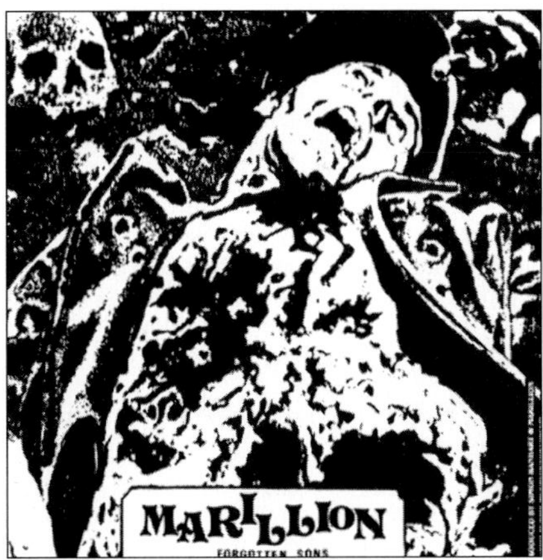

Cover »Forgotten sons« 7"

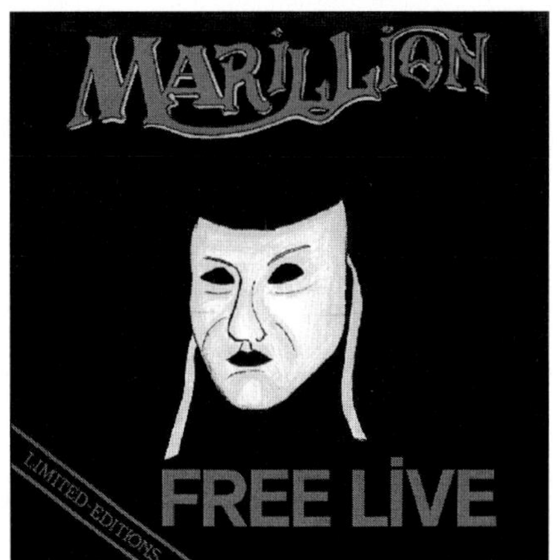

Cover »Free live« album

- no cover, but green insert with black print
- picture cover with shoes look like feet

(please note that some covers have round red stickers "Surprise vinyl")

»Forgotten sons«

7" 7" 7" 7" 7" 7" 7" 7" 7" 7" 7" 7" 7" 7" 7" 7"

Side 1) Forgotten sons (part 1)
Side 2) Forgotten sons (part 2)

Recorded live in Mannheim, Maimarkt, 21.06.1986

EEC Azimuth, AM 30375
vinyl black, Matrix "AM 30375"

»Free live«

LP LP LP LP LP LP LP LP LP LP LP LP LP LP

Side 1) Pseudo silk kimono
Kayleigh
Lavender
Bitter suite
Chelsea Monday
Side 2) Blind curve (iv, v)
Childhoods end?
White feather
Fugazi

Recorded live in Milano, Teatro Tenda, 24.10.1985

UK Original Sound Records, LTD 058 X
vinyl black, no Matrix

»From Hammersmith Odeon 08.01.86«

LP LP LP LP LP LP LP LP LP LP LP LP LP LP

Side 1) The web
Pseudo silk kimono
Kayleigh
Lavender
Side 2) Bitter suite
Heart of Lothian
Waterhole (Expresso bongo)
Lords of the backstage
Blind curve (i, ii)

Recorded live in London, Hammersmith Odeon, 08.01.1986

AUS M 11685
vinyl black, first edition, green cover, Matrix "A/B"
AUS M 11685
vinyl black, second edition, orange cover, Matrix "A/B"

»From Pink Pop Festival, Geleen, Holland«

LP LP LP LP LP LP LP LP LP LP LP LP LP LP

Side 1) Punch and Judy
Assassing
Jigsaw
Script for a jester's tear
Side 2) Incubus
Cinderella search

Recorded live at The Pink Pop Festival, Geleen, 11.06.1984

AUS M 11684
vinyl black, Matrix "MA 111"

»Garden party – The great cucumber massacre«

2LP 2LP 2LP 2LP 2LP 2LP 2LP 2LP 2LP 2LP

Side 1) Script for a jester's tear
Garden party
Side 2) Three boats down from the candy
The web
Side 3) Charting the single
Chelsea Monday
He knows you know
Side 4) Forgotten sons
Market square heroes

Recorded live in Norwich, University of East Anglia, 15.03.1983

JAP (but could also be EEC release)
vinyl black, Matrix "XL 1541/XL 1542"

»Go Fish«

2LP 2LP 2LP 2LP 2LP 2LP 2LP 2LP 2LP 2LP

Side 1) Assassing
Freaks
Script for a jester's tear
Side 2) White russian
Incubus
Sugar mice
Side 3) Fugazi
Hotel hobbies
Warm wet circles
That time of the night (The short straw)
Side 4) Kayleigh
Lavender
Bitter suite
Heart of Lothian
Incommunicado

Recorded live in Rome, Theatre Pallazzo Scallinata, 03.07.1987

EEC Easy Flight Records, Flight 110
vinyl black, Matrix "FLI 110"

»Good run«

LP LP LP LP LP LP LP LP LP LP LP LP LP LP

Side 1)	Garden party	7:09
	Freaks	5:40
	Assassing	6:23
Side 2)	Pseudo silk kimono	2:12
	Kayleigh	4:01
	Lavender	2:22
	Bitter suite	8:07
	Heart of Lothian	2:54

Re-release of »Tell me a story« 2LP-Bootleg (side 1+2), recorded live in Mannheim, Maimarkt, 21.06.1986

EEC Northlake Records
vinyl black, 200 copies with small blue insert (DIN A4) instead of a cover, Matrix "PICTURE"
EEC Northlake Records
vinyl green, 200 copies with small blue insert (DIN A4) instead of a cover, Matrix "PICTURE"

»Grendel's garden party«

LP LP LP LP LP LP LP LP LP LP LP LP LP LP

Side 1)	Grendel	
Side 2)	Chelsea Monday	8:11
	Three boats down from the candy	6:12
	Forgotten sons	11:27

Recorded live in Bangor, University, 12.05.1982

EEC
vinyl black, large (30x50 cm) green/black insert with Marillion picture instead of a cover, Matrix "MAR 101"
EEC
vinyl black, large (30x50 cm) green/black insert with Fish picture instead of a cover, Matrix "MAR 101"
EEC
vinyl black, small (20x30 cm) black/white insert with Fish picture instead of a cover, Matrix "MAR 101"

»Incubus«

LP LP LP LP LP LP LP LP LP LP LP LP LP LP

Side 1) Pseudo silk kimono
Kayleigh
Lavender
Bitter suite
Heart of Lothian
Side 2) Jigsaw
Incubus
Fugazi

Recorded live in Bologna, Arena Puccini, 18.06.1985

EEC Clean Sound, CS 1015
vinyl black, no Matrix

»In the realm of Asgard«

LP LP LP LP LP LP LP LP LP LP LP LP LP LP

Side 1) Pseudo silk kimono °
Kayleigh °
Lavender °

Bitter suite (i) °
Pseudo silk kimono ∞
Kayleigh ∞
Lavender ∞
Bitter suite (i, ii, iii, iv, v (cut) ∞
Side 2) Lords of the backstage ∞
Blind curve (iv, v) ∞
Childhoods end? *
White feather *
Charting the single **

** Recorded live in Hannover, Stadthalle, 23.11.1985, ** live in Baunatal, Rundsporthalle, 01.10.1983, ° 11/'85, ∞ 12/85; no further information*

EEC
vinyl black, 150 copies, Matrix "MN 1/2"

»Jester«

LP LP LP LP LP LP LP LP LP LP LP LP LP LP

Side 1) Garden party
Script for a jester's tear
Charting the single
Assassing
Side 2) Forgotten sons
Market square heroes
Margaret * 12:17

*Recorded live in Den Haag, Zuiderpark, 3.07.1983, except *; is taken from the official »Garden party« 12", live in Edinburgh, Playhouse, 07.04.1983*

EEC Keri Records (on label), MJ 783
vinyl black, Matrix "MJ-783"
EEC Night-side and Day-side (on label), MJ 783
vinyl black, Matrix "MJ-783"
EEC White label, MJ 783
vinyl black, Matrix "MJ-783"

»Jigsaw«

LP LP LP LP LP LP LP LP LP LP LP LP LP LP

Side 1) Punch and Judy
Assassing
Jigsaw
Incubus
Cinderella search
Side 2) Fugazi
Garden party
Market square heroes

Recorded live at The Pink Pop Festival, Geleen, 11.06.1984

EEC Keri Records, MJ 784
vinyl black, blue and white label, Matrix "MJ-784 A/B"

EEC Keri Records, MJ 784
vinyl black, grey and white label, Matrix "MJ-784 A/B"

»Juggernauts on BBC«

LP LP LP LP LP LP LP LP LP LP LP LP LP LP

Side 1) Forgotten sons * 8:30
Three boats down from the candy * 4:55
The web *
Side 2) Assassing **
Market square heroes **
Margaret ° 12:17

** London, Friday Rock Show, 29.01.1982, ** recorded live in Den Haag, Zuiderpark, 03.07.1983, ° is taken from the official »Garden party« 12", live in Edinburgh, Playhouse, 07.04.1983*

EEC Ventriloquists, BMI,
30 copies on multicoloured vinyl, orange cover with sticker, Matrix "M1/M2"
EEC Ventriloquists, BMI
120 copies on black vinyl, orange cover with sticker, Matrix "M1/M2"

»Keyboard landscape«

2LP 2LP 2LP 2LP 2LP 2LP 2LP 2LP 2LP 2LP

Side 1) Assassing 6:23
Garden party 7:09
Freaks 5:40
Side 2) Pseudo silk kimono 2:12
Kayleigh 4:01
Lavender 2:22
Bitter suite 8:07
Heart of Lothian 2:54
Side 3) Waterhole (Expresso bongo) 3:30
Lords of the backstage 1:50
Blind curve 9:30
Childhoods end? 2:45
White feather 6:08
Side 4) Forgotten sons 10:17
Market square heroes 8:34
incl. "She loves you"/"Let's twist again"
Fugazi * 8:15

*Recorded live in Mannheim, Maimarkt, 21.06.1986, except * is taken from the official version of »Brief encounter«, live in London, Hammersmith Odeon 1/'86*

EEC Trap Records, 1C 064 24 0340 1
vinyl black, foc, Matrix "240340 A/B/C/D"

»Lavender«

2LP 2LP 2LP 2LP 2LP 2LP 2LP 2LP 2LP 2LP

Side 1) La gazza ladra
Intro
Emerald lies/Script for a jester's tear
Incubus
Chelsea Monday
Side 2) The web
Pseudo silk kimono
Kayleigh
Lavender
Bitter suite
Heart of Lothian (cut)
Side 3) Heart of Lothian (continues)
Waterhole (Expresso bongo)
Lords of the backstage
Blind curve
Childhood's end?
White feather
Side 4) Fugazi
Garden party
Market square heroes

Recorded live in Utrecht, Vredenburg, 15.10.1985

EEC Fancy Records, MJ 1510185
vinyl black, Matrix "MJ 151085"

»Lavender blue«

2LP 2LP 2LP 2LP 2LP 2LP 2LP 2LP 2LP 2LP

Side 1) Blind curve *
Childhood's end? *
White feather *
Side 2) Assassing
Garden party
Freaks **
Side 3) Pseudo silk kimono
Kayleigh
Bitter suite
Heart of Lothian
Cinderella search
Side 4) Punch and Judy
Jigsaw
Emerald lies
Lavender blue **

*Recorded live in London, Hammersmith Odeon, 14.12.1984, except * live in Cardiff, St.David's Hall, 12.01.1986, ** is taken from the official »Lavender« 12" single*

EEC Magician Wood, ML 86
vinyl black, Matrix "ML 86 A/B/C/D"

»Lay the blame on Genesis«

LP LP LP LP LP LP LP LP LP LP LP LP LP LP

Side 1) Assassing
Garden party
Cinderella search
Side 2) Punch and Judy
Jigsaw
Emerald lies

Recorded live in London, Hammersmith Odeon, 14.12.1984

EEC Genesis music ltd., MAR 1
picture disc, no sleeve, Matrix "MARI"

»Live (dedicated to all cucumber lovers)«

LP LP LP LP LP LP LP LP LP LP LP LP LP LP

Side 1) He knows you know
Garden party
Script for a jester's tear
Side 2) Three boats down from the candy
Assassing
Chelsea Monday

Recorded live in Baunatal, Rundsporthalle, 01.10.1983

There are lots of different versions known concerning the cover or the colour of the records. Some people mixed up some records + covers and changed them amongst each other, so that it is quite difficult to say which cover belongs to which record colour. All records have Matrix "MAR 001". Here they are:

- vinyl black
- vinyl blue
- vinyl dark-green
- vinyl light green
- vinyl yellow green
- vinyl red
- vinyl yellow
- vinyl clear
- vinyl clear/multicoloured
- vinyl white/multicoloured
- yellow cover with dark-red print
- yellow cover with light-red and black print
- no cover, but two inserts, yellow and black print

»Live (for radio station airplay only)«

LP LP LP LP LP LP LP LP LP LP LP LP LP LP

Side 1) Assassing 6:55
Script for a jester's tear 8:55
Incubus 8:43
Side 2) He knows you know 5:00

Fugazi 8:18
Garden party/Market square heroes 9:40

Recorded live in Chippenham, Gold Diggers Club, 12.03.1984

FRA FC 001
vinyl black, Matrix "FC 001", demonstration record - not for sale

»Live at Hammersmith Odeon«

LP LP LP LP LP LP LP LP LP LP LP LP LP LP

Side 1) Assassing 7:13
Garden party 7:04
Cinderella search 6:52
Punch and Judy 3:37
Jigsaw 4:54
Side 2) Pseudo silk kimono/Kayleigh/
Bitter suite/Heart of Lothian 19:35
Fugazi 10:11

Recorded live in London, Hammersmith Odeon, 14.12.1984

EEC Fat Man
vinyl black, Matrix "HOT CHILDHOOD A/B"
EEC Fat Man
vinyl clear, Matrix "HOT CHILDHOOD A/B"
EEC Fat Man
vinyl yellow, Matrix "HOT CHILDHOOD A/B"
EEC Fat Man
vinyl blue, Matrix "HOT CHILDHOOD A/B", 50 copies
EEC Fat Man
vinyl red/multicoloured, Matrix "HOT CHILDHOOD A/B", 100 copies
EEC Fat Man
vinyl white/multicoloured, Matrix "HOT CHILDHOOD A/B", 100 copies
EEC Fat Man
vinyl white with blue stripes, Matrix "HOT CHILDHOOD A/B", 50 copies

»Live in Europe 1985«

LP LP LP LP LP LP LP LP LP LP LP LP LP LP

Side 1) La gazza ladra
Intro
Emerald lies/Script for a jester's tear
Incubus
Chelsea Monday
Side 2) The web
Pseudo silk kimono
Kayleigh
Lavender
Bitter suite
Heart of Lothian (cut)

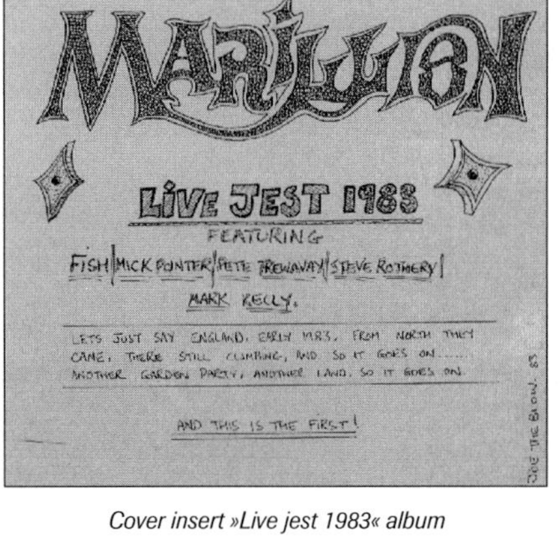

Cover insert »Live jest 1983« album

Re-release of »Lavender« bootleg sides 1+2, recorded live in Utrecht, Vredenburg, 15.10.1985,

EEC TAKRL 2171
vinyl black, red insert instead of a cover, 100 copies, Matrix "MJ 151085"

»Live jest 1983«

LP LP LP LP LP LP LP LP LP LP LP LP LP LP

Side 1) Script for a jester's tear
Garden party
Three boats down from the candy
Side 2) Chelsea Monday
He knows you know
Grendel

Recorded live in London, Hammersmith Odeon, 18.04.1983

EEC
orange insert instead of a cover, 20 copies, Matrix "KD 001"

»Live at Sheffield City Hall«

3LP 3LP 3LP 3LP 3LP 3LP 3LP 3LP 3LP 3LP

Side 1) La gazza ladra
Slainte mhath
Assassing
White russian
Side 2) Sugar mice
Fugazi
Hotel hobbies (cut)
Side 3) Hotel hobbies (continues)

Warm wet circles
That time of the night
Geesabun
Waterhole (Expresso bongo)
Side 4) Lords of the backstage
Blind curve (i, ii, iii)
Side 5) Blind curve (iv, v)
Childhoods end?
White feather
Kayleigh
Lavender (cut)
Side 6) Incommunicado
Garden party
Market square heroes

Recorded live in Sheffield, City Hall, 15.02.1988

EEC Tina B. discjockey service
vinyl black, Matrix " MARL 1/2/3/4/5/6"

»Live at the Rolling Stone«

2LP 2LP 2LP 2LP 2LP 2LP 2LP 2LP 2LP 2LP

Side 1)	Assassing	7:00
	Cinderella search	5:50
	Script for a jester's tear	9:50
	Punch and Judy	3:42
Side 2)	Jigsaw	7:25
	Emerald lies	5:20
	Pseudo silk kimono	2:48
	Kayleigh	3:52
	Lavender	2:30
	Bitter suite (i, ii, iii)	6:00
Side 3)	Bitter suite (iv, v)	2:13
	Heart of Lothian	3:40
	Incubus	9:15
	Fugazi	10:00
Side 4)	Garden party	9:40
	Market square heroes	10:20

Re-release of the »Alive« bootleg with unfinished cover, recorded live in Milano, Rolling Stone, 17.06.1985

EEC Jump Records
vinyl black, Matrix "SG-4-A/B/C/D"

»Live Walsall 1990«

LP LP LP LP LP LP LP LP LP LP LP LP LP LP

Side 1) Intro: Mission Impossible
Splintering heart
The uninvited guest
Slainte mhath
The party (cut)
Side 2) The party (continues)
Easter
Warm wet circles
That time of the night
No on can

Recorded live in Walsall, Junction 10, 22.12.1990

EEC Sirius Records, SR 001
vinyl black, 1,000 copies, Matrix "MEFW 01"

»Long songs«

LP LP LP LP LP LP LP LP LP LP LP LP LP LP

Side 1)	Forgotten sons	13:47
	Market square heroes	8:21
Side 2)	Charting the single	10:48
	She chameleon *	6:13
	Herne the hunter **	11:03

*Recorded live in Baunatal, Rundsporthalle, 01.10.1983, except * live in Glasgow, The Mayfair, 13.09.1982, ** live in Bicester, Red Lion Pub, 14.03.1981*

EEC HC 00286-3
vinyl black, Matrix "LONG A/B"
EEC HC 00286-3
vinyl white/multicoloured, Matrix "LONG A/B"
EEC TAKRL 2150
vinyl black, white insert instead of a cover, 100 copies, Matrix "LONG A/B"

»Lothian's heart «

2LP 2LP 2LP 2LP 2LP 2LP 2LP 2LP 2LP 2LP

Side 1) Script for a jester's tear
Incubus
Chelsea Monday (cut)
Side 2) Chelsea Monday (continues)
The web
Pseudo silk kimono
Kayleigh
Lavender
Bitter suite (cut)
(Part of U2 – "Pride in the name of love" live)
Side 3) Bitter suite (continues)
Heart of Lothian
Waterhole (Expresso bongo)
Lords of the backstage
Blind curve
Side 4) Childhoods end?
White feather
Fugazi

Recorded live in Frankfurt, Festhalle, 05.11.1985

EEC Duck production
vinyl black, Matrix "DUCK-MA"

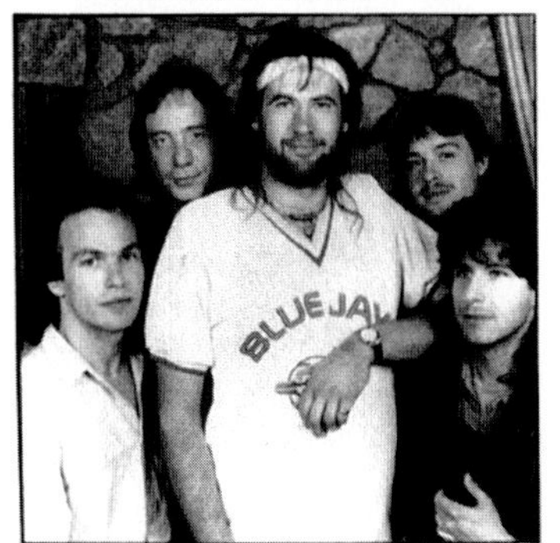

Cover »Marillion & Iron Maiden live« 7"

EEC Duck production
vinyl white/multicoloured, Matrix "DUCK-MA"
EEC TAKRL 2102/2103
vinyl black, yellow insert instead of a cover, 100 copies, Matrix "DUCK-MA", bootleg called »Lothean's Heart«

»Marillion & Iron Maiden live«

7" 7" 7" 7" 7" 7" 7" 7" 7" 7" 7" 7" 7" 7" 7" 7" 7"
Side 1) The boys are back in town
Side 2) With a little help from my friends
Recorded live in London, Wembley Arena, 05.11.1987

EEC MAR 01
vinyl black, Matrix "MAR 01"

»Marquee '83 «

2LP 2LP 2LP 2LP 2LP 2LP 2LP 2LP 2LP 2LP
Side 1) Garden party
Punch and Judy
Script for a jester's tear
Side 2) Emerald lies
He knows you know
Assassing
Side 3) She chameleon
Jigsaw
Side 4) Incubus
Market square heroes
incl. Margaret/Jean Jeanie
Recorded live in London, Marquee, 30.10.1983, MARILLION performed under the name of LUFTHANSA AIR TERMINAL.

ITA Jolly Joker Records, JJ 0056
vinyl black, Matrix "M 741 A/B S 870 A/B"

»Other Fish to fry«

LP LP LP LP LP LP LP LP LP LP LP LP LP LP
Side 1) Assassing
Garden party
Cinderella search
Side 2) Punch and Judy
Jigsaw
Chelsea Monday
Emerald lies
Recorded live in Lyon, Palais d' Hiver, 28.11.1984

EEC
vinyl black, 150 copies, Matrix "M1/M2"

»Passport «

2LP 2LP 2LP 2LP 2LP 2LP 2LP 2LP 2LP 2LP
Side 1) Assassing
Garden party
Cinderella search
Punch and Judy
Jigsaw
Side 2) Chelsea Monday
Emerald lies
Pseudo silk kimono
Kayleigh
Bitter suite
Heart of Lothian
Side 3) Script for a jester's tear
Incubus
Forgotten sons
Side 4) Fugazi
Market square heroes
Recorded live in Stockholm, Göta Lejon, 19.11.1984

EEC Picture Records, 191-184
vinyl black, Matrix " 191 184"

»Pink Pop live 1984«

LP LP LP LP LP LP LP LP LP LP LP LP LP LP
Side 1) Punch and Judy
Assassing
Jigsaw
Incubus
Cinderella search
Side 2) Fugazi
Garden party
Market square heroes
Re-release of the »Jigsaw« bootleg, recorded live at The Pink Pop Festival, Geleen, 11.06.1984

EEC TAKRL 2156
vinyl black, yellow insert instead of a cover, 100 copies, Matrix “MJ-784 A/B”

»Radio broadcast«

2LP 2LP 2LP 2LP 2LP 2LP 2LP 2LP 2LP 2LP

Side 1) Garden party
Freaks
Assassing
Side 2) Pseudo silk kimono
Kayleigh
Lavender
Bitter suite
Heart of Lothian
Side 3) Waterhole (Expresso bongo)
Lords of the backstage
Blind curve
Childhoods end?
White feather
Side 4) Forgotten sons
Market square heroes
incl. “She loves you”/“Let’s twist again”

Re-release of the »Tell me a story« bootleg, recorded live in Mannheim, Maimarkt, 21.06.1986

EEC TAKRL 2180/2181
vinyl red, yellow insert instead of a cover, 100 copies, Matrix “PICTURE A/B/C/D”

»Reflections on a child«

2LP 2LP 2LP 2LP 2LP 2LP 2LP 2LP 2LP 2LP

Side 1) Chelsea Monday
The web
Pseudo silk kimono
Kayleigh
Lavender
Bitter suite (cut)
Side 2) Bitter suite (continues)
Heart of Lothian
Waterhole (Expresso bongo)
Lords of the backstage (cut)
Side 3) Heart of Lothian (continues)
Waterhole (Expresso bongo)
Lords of the backstage
Blind curve
Childhood’s end?
White feather
Side 4) Garden party *
Charting the single **

*Side 1 and 2 and * recorded live in Berlin, Eissporthalle, 18.11.1985, ** live in Berlin, Metropol, 05.07.1984; side 3 live in Utrecht, Vredenburg, 15.10.1985. This bootleg is nearly the same as »Reflections on a child on a Chelsea Monday« (on side 1, 2 and 4), but side 3) is »Lavender« bootleg side 3*

EEC TAKRL 2196/2197
vinyl black, yellow insert instead of a cover, 100 copies, Matrix “REFLECTIONS A/B/C/D”, the number on Side 3 (151085 C) was crossed out and replaced by “REFLECTIONS C”

»Reflections on a child on a Chelsea Monday«

2LP 2LP 2LP 2LP 2LP 2LP 2LP 2LP 2LP 2LP

Side 1) Chelsea Monday
The web
Pseudo silk kimono
Kayleigh
Lavender
Bitter suite (cut)
Side 2) Bitter suite (continues)
Heart of Lothian
Waterhole (Expresso bongo)
Lords of the backstage (cut)
Side 3) Lords of the backstage (continues)
Blind curve
Childhoods end?
White feather
Fugazi
Side 4) Garden party
Charting the single *

*Recorded live in Berlin, Eissporthalle, 18.11.1985, except * live in Berlin, Metropol, 05.07.1984*

EEC Collectorecord
vinyl black, Matrix “REFLECTIONS A/B/C/D”

»Rock ‘n’ roll (with Queen)«

7" 7" 7" 7" 7" 7" 7" 7" 7" 7" 7" 7" 7" 7" 7"

Side 1) Crazy little thing called love
Side 2) Tutti frutti (with Fish on backing vocals)

Recorded live in Mannheim, Maimarkt, 21.06.1986

EEC
vinyl black, 1,000 copies, for the Queen fan club (?), Matrix “A/B”

»Second service«

LP LP LP LP LP LP LP LP LP LP LP LP LP LP

Side 1) Close ° 9:40
Lady Fantasy ° 6:37
Alice ° 5:50
Side 2) Institution waltz * 3:59

I know what I like * 6:48
He knows you know ** 3:24
Garden party ** 6:35

° *"Demo Summer", 06.06.1980, re-release of the »Forgotten songs« bootleg, * recorded live Aston Clinton, Village Hall, 11/'81; ** Watlington, Roxon Studios, 18/19.07.1981*

EEC TAKRL 2166
vinyl black, yellow insert instead of a cover, 100 copies, Matrix "MAR 002"

»Selling Fish live Vol. 1«

LP LP LP LP LP LP LP LP LP LP LP LP LP LP

Side 1) Script for a jester's tear
Garden party
Three boats down from the candy
Side 2) Chelsea Monday
He knows you know
Grendel

Re-release of the »Live jest« bootleg, recorded live in London, Hammersmith Odeon, 18.04.1983

EEC Doktor Dyper Records
vinyl black, deluxe colour cover, first edition, Matrix "KD001"
EEC Doktor Dyper Records
vinly black, with purple insert, 500 copies, second edition, Matrix "KD 001"
EEC Doktor Dyper Records
vinyl black, 2 pink xeroxed inserts instead of a cover, third edition, Matrix "KD 001

»Selling Fish live Vol. 2«

LP LP LP LP LP LP LP LP LP LP LP LP LP LP

Side 1) Emerald lies
She chameleon
Assassing
Side 2) Punch and Judy
Incubus
Forgotten sons

Recorded live in London, Marquee, 30.10.1983, MARILLION performed under the name of LUFTHANSA AIR TERMINAL

EEC Doktor Dyper Records (label "Jester Records")
vinyl black, 500 copies, red sticker with tracklist on back cover, Matrix "DLP 02"
EEC Doktor Dyper Records
white label, vinyl black, 500 copies, tracklist is printed on back cover, Matrix "DLP 02" (but this edition was pressed from a different master)

»Selling Fish live Vol. 3«

LP LP LP LP LP LP LP LP LP LP LP LP LP LP

Side 1) Pseudo silk kimono
Kayleigh
Lavender
Bitter suite
Heart of Lothian (i)
Side 2) Heart of Lothian (ii)
Waterhole (Expresso bongo)
Lords of the backstage
Blind curve
Childhoods end?
White feather

Recorded live in London, Hammersmith Odeon, 08.01.1986

EEC
vinyl black, Matrix "MBE-1"

»Selling Fish live Vol. 4«

LP LP LP LP LP LP LP LP LP LP LP LP LP LP

Side 1) Intro
Emerald lies/Script for a jester's tear
Incubus
Side 2) Jigsaw
The web
Fugazi

Recorded live in London, Hammersmith Odeon, 08.01.1986

EEC
vinyl black, Matrix "COD-99"

»Shadowplays in Switzerland«

LP LP LP LP LP LP LP LP LP LP LP LP LP LP

Side 1) Splintering heart
Garden party
Dry land
The party
The space
Side 2) A collection
Waiting to happen
Cover my eyes
Lords of the backstage
Blind curve (i, ii, iii)
This town
The rakes progress

Recorded live in Lausanne, Salle de Fetes Beaulieu, 19.10.1991

EEC Metal Mess, MMR 9210
picture disc, Matrix "MM PLP 9210"

»Tell me a story«

2LP 2LP 2LP 2LP 2LP 2LP 2LP 2LP 2LP 2LP

Side 1) Garden party
Freaks
Assassing
Side 2) Pseudo silk kimono
Kayleigh
Lavender
Bitter suite
Heart of Lothian
Side 3) Waterhole (Expresso bongo)
Lords of the backstage
Blind curve
Childhoods end?
White feather
Side 4) Forgotten sons
Market square heroes
incl. "She loves you"/"Let's twist again"
Recorded live in Mannheim, Maimarkt, 21.06.1986

EEC See for miles Records
vinyl black, Matrix "PICTURE A/B/C/D"
EEC Northlake Records
vinyl green, Matrix "PICTURE A/B/C/D"

»The game is over«

LP LP LP LP LP LP LP LP LP LP LP LP LP LP

Side 1) Grendel
Garden party
Side 2) Script for a jester's tear
Assassing
Charting the single
Recorded live at the Reading Festival, Thames-side Arena, 27.08.1983

EEC ARC 0077
vinyl black, Matrix "ARC 0077"

»The juggler and the ventriloquist«

LP LP LP LP LP LP LP LP LP LP LP LP LP LP

Side 1) Assassing
Punch and Judy
Jigsaw
Side 2) Script for a jester's tear
Emerald lies
Cinderella search
Recorded live in Offenbach, Stadthalle, 07.05.1984

EEC
clear sleeve with yellow sticker, clear vinyl, 50 copies, Matrix "III"

EEC
clear sleeve with red sticker, clear/multicoloured vinyl, 30 copies, Matrix "III"

»The night Marillion went down to Stockholm«

3LP 3LP 3LP 3LP 3LP 3LP 3LP 3LP 3LP 3LP

Side 1) La gazza ladra
Intro
Emerald lies/Script for a jester's tear
Incubus
Side 2) Chelsea Monday
The web
Side 3) Pseudo silk kimono
Kayleigh
Lavender
Bitter suite
Heart of Lothian
Side 4) Waterhole (Expresso bongo)
Lords of the backstage
Blind curve
Childhood's end?
White feather
Side 5) Fugazi
Garden party
Market square heroes
Side 6) Punch and Judy
Assassing
Incubus
Sides 1-5 recorded live in Stockholm, Eriksdalhallen, 11.10.1985, side 6 live at The Pink Pop Festival, Geleen, 11.06.1984

EEC
vinyl black, Matrix "DH 11 A/B/C/D/E/F"

»The one and only«

LP LP LP LP LP LP LP LP LP LP LP LP LP LP

Side 1) Garden party
Market square heroes/ Let's twist again
Script for a jester's tear (cut)
Side 2) Script for a jester's tear (continues)
Fugazi
Shadow on the wall
Recorded live in London, Hammersmith Odeon, 02.02.1986, with special guests: Mike Oldfield, Roger Chapman, Steve Hackett and Peter Hammill

EEC
white insert instead of a cover, re-release of "Double o charity", Matrix "MARILLION"

»The web«

LP LP LP LP LP LP LP LP LP LP LP LP LP LP

Side 1) Heart of Lothian (continues)
Waterhole (Expresso bongo)
Lords of the backstage
Blind curve
Childhood's end?
White feather
Side 2) Fugazi
Garden party
Market square heroes

Re-release of »Lavender« bootleg sides 3+4, recorded live in Utrecht, Vredenburg, 15.10.1985

EEC Explosive
red insert instead of a cover, 100 numbered copies, Matrix "151085"

»Volume one of the greatest puppet show on earth«

LP LP LP LP LP LP LP LP LP LP LP LP LP LP

Side 1) Assassing
Punch and Judy
Jigsaw
Script for a jester's tear
Side 2) Emerald lies
Chelsea Monday
Incubus

Recorded live in Edinburgh, Playhouse, 19.02.1984

EEC
black/white xerox copy of "Assassing" picture disc instead of a cover, vinyl black, Matrix "BMX PD"
EEC
picture disc, yellow card with tracklist, Matrix "BMX PD"

»ZZ TOP - Live at Hammersmith Odeon«

2LP 2LP 2LP 2LP 2LP 2LP 2LP 2LP 2LP 2LP

This is a mispressed bootleg, starting side 1 with the Marillion live version of "She chameleon" recorded in Glasgow, The Mayfair, 13.09.1982 for about 10 seconds (maybe taken from the »Long songs«-bootleg). After that you will hear ZZ Top the rest of the bootleg.

EEC, large black/white insert instead of a cover, Matrix "BEARD A/B/C/D"

Marillion CD Bootlegs

»Acoustic Concert«

CD CD CD CD CD CD CD CD CD CD CD CD

Vocal introduction	0:58
Holloway girl	3:29
Sugar mice	3:32
After me	4:34
The party	5:45
Easter	3:31
Waiting to happen	4:53
King of sunset town	4:25
Substitute	3:11
Cover my eyes (video clip)	3:57
Assassing *	7:32
Script for a jester's tear *	8:57

*Recorded live in Cologne, Luxor, fan club convention "The Release", 01.06.1991, except * live in St. Gallen, Open Air Festival, 27.05.1985*

Sirius Records, CD 002
1992

»Another secret gig«

CD CD CD CD CD CD CD CD CD CD CD CD

Splintering heart	9:11
Easter	7:40
King of sunset town	6:09
Waiting to happen	5:48
Sympathy	4:03
Kayleigh	4:46
Lavender	2:22
Heart of Lothian	2:59
Uninvited guest	3:59
Slainte mhath	7:59
The release	4:09
Hooks in you	6:45
Garden party	7:48

Recorded live in London, Borderline Club, 09.05.1992

Rockland, ROLA 12
1992

»Assassination at Garden Party«

CD CD CD CD CD CD CD CD CD CD CD CD

Garden party	7:00
Script for a jester's tear	8:32
Three boats down from the Candy	5:07

Chelsea Monday	6:53
He knows you know	5:39
Grendel	18:41

Recorded live in London, Hammersmith Odeon, 18.04.1983

ITA Buy Or Die Records, BOD CD 216
1991

»Brave Tour«

2CD 2CD 2CD 2CD 2CD 2CD 2CD 2CD 2CD

Disc 1)	Bridge	2:30
	Living with the big lie	6:49
	Runaway	4:43
	Goodbye to all that	11:58
	a) Wave	
	b) Mad	
	c) The opium den	
	d) The slide	
	e) Standing in the swing	
	Hard as love	6:45
	The hollow man	4:30
	Alone again in the lap of luxury	7:56
	a) Now wash your hands	
	Paper lies	5:16
	Brave	9:27
	The great escape	7:55
	a) The last of you	
	b) Falling from the moon	
	Made again	5:31
Disc 2)	Cover my eyes	4:10
	Slainte mhath	4:54
	Easter	7:54
	Garden party	8:04
	Waiting to happen	5:06
	Hooks in you	3:05
	Sugar mice *	6:28
	Freaks **	7:41
	Gimme some lovin' **	4:39
	Substitute °	2:48
	Eric ∞	6:01

*Recorded live in Genova, Teatro Verdi, Sestri Ponente, 15.04.1994, except * live in Milwaukee, Riverside Theatre, 23.02.1990, ** live in Utrecht, Tivoli, 22.09.1990, ° live in Cologne, Luxor, 01.06.1991, ∞ live in London, Town & Country Club, 22.12.1990*

Banzai, BZCD 015/16
1994

»Childhood mysteries«

CD CD CD CD CD CD CD CD CD CD CD CD

Waterhole (Expresso Bongo)/ Lords of the backstage/Blind curve: Vocal under a bloodlight	5:19
Intro: Emerald lies/ Intro to Script for a jester's tear	1:30
Script for a jester's tear	8:31
Assassing	6:46
Incubus	11:28
Garden party	7:05
Market square heroes	6:50
Fugazi	9:08
White feather	4:14

Recorded live at Castle Donington, Monsters of Rock Festival, 17.09.1985

Classic Ltd., CL001
1992

»Childhood rehearsals«

CD CD CD CD CD CD CD CD CD CD CD CD

Garden party	7:18
Cinderella search	6:09
Jigsaw	7:48
Misplaced childhood (part 1)	16:34
- Pseudo silk kimono	
- Kayleigh	
- Bitter suite	
i Brief encounter	
ii Lost weekend	
iii Misplaced rendezvous	
iv Windswept thumb	
- Heart of Lothian	
i Wide boy	
ii Curtain call	
Incubus	8:40
Chelsea Monday	8:12

Recorded live in London, Hammersmith Odeon, 14.12.1984

Papercorn, PC 010
1993

»Cinderella search«

CD CD CD CD CD CD CD CD CD CD CD CD

Assassing	7:12
Punch & Judy	3:35
Jigsaw	6:18
Cinderella search	6:30

Incubus	8:58
Garden party/	
Market square heroes	14:44

Recorded live in Zürich, Schlüfwegzentrum, 21.11.1984

Oh Boy, 1-9140

1992, version a) CD with yellow print, version b) CD with blue print

»Daffodils«

CD CD CD CD CD CD CD CD CD CD CD CD

Charting the single *	8:20
She chameleon **	5:18
Garden party	7:54
The web	10:30
Chelsea Monday	8:21
Three boats down from the candy	4:41
He knows you know	3:28
Margaret	6:20
Charting the single	5:44
Forgotten sons	11:27

*Recorded live in Glasgow, Mayfair, 02.05.1982, except * live in Baunatal, Rundsporthalle, 01.10.1983, ** live in Glasgow, Mayfair, 13.09.1982*

Axe Records, AXE 001

1991

»Fairy-land«

CD CD CD CD CD CD CD CD CD CD CD CD

Garden party	6:18
Script for a jester's tear	8:27
Three boats down from the Candy	4:50
Chelsea Monday	6:48
He knows you know	5:23
Grendel	18:36

Recorded live in London, Hammersmith Odeon, 18.04.1983

Poetry in Motion, POET 9213

1992

»Fishing behind the Wall«

CD CD CD CD CD CD CD CD CD CD CD CD

Slainte mhath	4:30
Assassing	6:09
White russian	5:52
Sugar mice	5:51
Fugazi	4:03

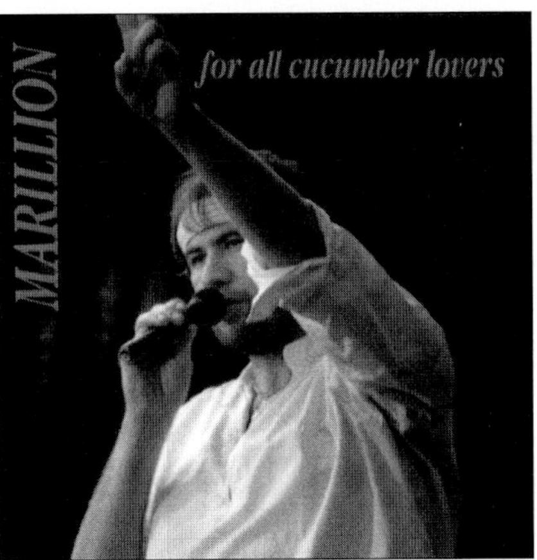

Cover »For all cucumber lovers« CD

Forgotten sons *	12:40
Market square heroes *	6:36
Lavender	2:34
Heart of Lothian	4:06
Incommunicado	5:04
Garden party	6:51

*Recorded live in East-Berlin, Radrennbahn Weissensee, 18.06.1988, except * live in Baunatal, Rundsporthalle, 01.10.1983*

CD without any information, 1990

»For all cucumber lovers«

CD CD CD CD CD CD CD CD CD CD CD CD

He knows you know	7:36
Garden party	7:49
Script for a jester's tear	10:32
Three boats down from the Candy	5:37
Assassing	7:37
Chelsea Monday	10:09
Forgotten sons	12:55
Market square heroes	6:59

Recorded live in Baunatal, Rundsporthalle, 01.10.1983

Stoned Records, 013 CD

1989, original release with a photo cover, re-release with a black CD box

»Forgotten Sons«

CD CD CD CD CD CD CD CD CD CD CD CD

Garden party	7:32
Script for a jester's tear	9:59

Charting the single	5:27
Assassing	8:29
Forgotten sons	10:39
Market square heroes	5:21

Recorded live in Den Haag, Parkpop, Zuiderpark, 03.07.1983

Rocks, ROCKS 92041
1993

»Garden party - In UK 1984«

2CD 2CD 2CD 2CD 2CD 2CD 2CD 2CD 2CD

Disc 1)	Assassing	7:54
	Script for a jester's tear	12:15
	Incubus	8:59
	He knows you know	5:44
	Fugazi	9:26
	Garden party	6:42
	Market square heroes	3:18
Disc 2)	Garden party	7:22
	Cinderella search	6:25
	Jigsaw	6:57
	Chelsea Monday	8:21
	Pseudo silk kimono/Kayleigh	8:39
	Bitter suite	4:38
	i Brief encounter	
	ii Lost weekend	
	iii Misplaced rendezvous	
	iv Windswept thumb	
	Heart of Lothian	4:40
	i Wide boy	
	ii Curtain call	
	Incubus	8:54

Disc 1 recorded live in Chippenham, Golddiggers Club, 12.03.1984, disc 2 live in London, Hammersmith Odeon, 14.12.1984

Sirius Records, SR 006/007
1992

»Genesis: The story so far«

2CD 2CD 2CD 2CD 2CD 2CD 2CD 2CD 2CD

Disc 1)	Slainte mhath	6:10
	Assassing	7:45
	Script for a jester's tear	11:22
	White russian	6:02
	Incubus	9:05
	Sugar mice	6:28
	Torch song	3:55
	Fugazi	8:19
Disc 2)	Hotel hobbies	4:14
	Warm wet circles/That time of the night (The short straw)	10:28
	Kayleigh	4:22
	Lavender	2:55
	Bitter suite	7:59
	Heart of Lothian	4:18
	The last straw	5:50
	Incommunicado	5:12
	Garden party	6:32
	Market square heroes (part 1)	4:29
	Let's twist again	2:56
	Market square heroes (part 2)	2:41

Recorded live in Milwaukee, Billy's Old Mill, 25.09.1987

Limes, LIMES 3013
2CD-Box with playing cards, lighter..., 1993

»Golden tears«

CD CD CD CD CD CD CD CD CD CD CD CD

Garden party	4:49
Freaks	4:21
Assassing	6:23
Misplaced childhood (part 1)	18:53
a) Pseudo silk kimono	
b) Kayleigh	
c) Lavender	
d) Bitter suite	
e) Heart of Lothian	
Misplaced childhood (part 2)	17:34
a) Waterhole	
b) Lords of the backstage	
c) Blind curve	
d) Childhood's end?	
White feather	6:51
Forgotten sons	8:28
Market square heroes	8:28

Recorded live in Mannheim, Maimarktgelände, 21.06.1986

Kiss The Stone, KTS 070
1992

»Goodbye Fish/USA 1987«

CD CD CD CD CD CD CD CD CD CD CD CD

Slainte mhath	6:05
Assassing	7:45
Script for a jester's tear	9:23
Kayleigh	4:28
Lavender	2:24
Bitter suite	6:24
Heart of Lothian	5:55
Garden party	6:22

Incubus 9:04
Sugar mice 5:59
Fugazi 8:29

Recorded live in Milwaukee, Billy's Old Mill, 25.09.1987

The Concert Series, TCS-CD-12
1995, re-release from 1992

»Happy ending«

CD CD CD CD CD CD CD CD CD CD CD CD

Slainte mhath 4:46
White russian 6:06
Incubus 9:46
Sugar mice 5:55
Fugazi 8:14
Hotel hobbies/Warm wet circles/
That time of the night 14:47
The last straw/Happy ending 6:31

Recorded live in London, Wembley Arena, 04.11.1987

Rising Sun Records, RSR 001
1992

»Haunters' having lots of fun«

CD CD CD CD CD CD CD CD CD CD CD CD

The haunting of Gill House * 7:39
Herne the hunter * 12:04
Scott's porridge * 2:23
Lady Fantasy * 6:48
Alice * 5:55

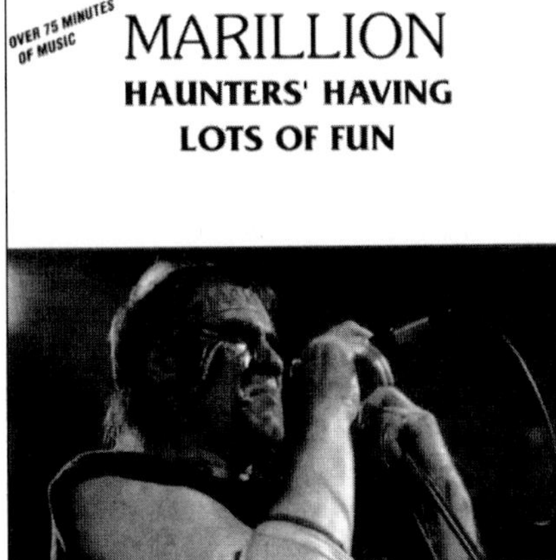

Cover »Haunters having lots of fun« CD

Skyline drifter ** 4:24
Time for sale ** 10:13
He knows you know ° 3:44
Charting the single ° 4:51
Institution waltz ∞ 3:55
I know what I like
(In your Wardrobe) ∞ 6:17
Market square heroes • 3:46
Three boats down from
the Candy • 4:28

** Hertford, Enid's Studio-demo, 06.06.1980, ** Bicester, Red Lion Pub, 14.03.1981, ° Oxfordshire, Roxon Studios-demo, 18./19.07.1981), ∞ Aston Clinton, Village Hall-demo, 11/'81, • EMI-demo, 06.09.1982)*

Rockland, ROLA 5
1992, version a) cover white, version b) cover red

»Heaven & hell«

CD CD CD CD CD CD CD CD CD CD CD CD

Garden party 4:48
(cut in the middle of the song)
Freaks 4:20
Assassing 6:22
Misplaced childhood (part 1) 18:52
a) Pseudo silk kimono
b) Kayleigh
c) Lavender
d) Bitter suite
e) Heart of Lothian
Misplaced childhood (part 2) 17:33
a) Waterhole
b) Lords of the backstage
c) Blind curve
d) Childhood's end?
White feather 6:50
Forgotten sons 8:27
Market square heroes 8:25

Recorded live in Mannheim, Maimarktgelände, 21.06.1986

Baby Capone, BC 029
1994

»Hogi's time«

CD CD CD CD CD CD CD CD CD CD CD CD

Splintering heart 6:27
Cover my eyes 3:52
Slainte mhath 4:26
Uninvited guest 4:46

The party 6:37
Easter 6:28
No one can 5:27
This town 3:17
Kayleigh/King of Sunset Town 8:11
Holidays in Eden/Hooks in you 7:22

Recorded live in Cologne, Live Music Hall, 24.07.1991

CD without any information, 1992

»In search of forever«

CD CD CD CD CD CD CD CD CD CD CD CD

Garden party 7:00
He knows you know 4:25
Three boats down from the Candy 4:12
Market square heroes 5:14
Forgotten sons 9:09
Margaret 5:52
She chameleon (incomplete) 3:06
Forgotten sons * 10:48
Margaret * 10:10
Forgotten sons ** 9:23

*Recorded live at Reading Rock Festival, 29.08.1982, except * live at Roskilde Festival, 01.07.1983, ** Old grey whistle test (TV), 20.05.1983*

Music with Love, MWL 002
1993

»In session tonight«

CD CD CD CD CD CD CD CD CD CD CD CD

Forgotten sons * 7:42
Three boats down from the Candy * 4:19
The web * 8:30
He knows you know ** 3:37
Garden party ** 6:56
Charting the single ** 4:37
Grendel ° 18:31
Market square heroes ° 3:44
Three boats down from the Candy ° 4:29

** Friday Rock Show, 29.01.1982, ** Oxfordshire, Roxon Studios demo, 18./19.07.1981, ° EMI-demo, 06.09.1982*

Take It Or Leave It Music, T 9411
1994

»Japanese whispers«

CD CD CD CD CD CD CD CD CD CD CD CD

Bridge 2:30
Living with the big lie 6:49
Runaway 4:43
Goodbye to all that 11:58
a) Wave
b) Mad
c) The opium den
d) The slide
e) Standing in the swing
Hard as love 6:45
The hollow man 4:30
Alone again in the lap of luxury 7:56
a) Now wash your hands
Paper lies 5:16
Brave 9:27
The great escape 7:55
a) The last of you
b) Falling from the moon
Made again 5:31

Recorded live in Bonn, Biskuithalle, 17.03.1994

On the Air, OTA-004
1995, release in plastic bag with paper inlay

»Just slip across«

CD CD CD CD CD CD CD CD CD CD CD CD

Freaks 9:04
Easter 8:18
This town 6:16
Kayleigh/Lavender/Heart of Lothian 9:51
Hooks in you 3:14
Splintering heart 7:37
Incommunicado 7:41
Gimme some lovin' 4:54
Freaks (reprise) 10:21

Recorded live in Utrecht, Tivoli, fan club convention "Freaks", 22.09.1990

Rockland, ROLA 4
1992

»Live in Liverpool«

CD CD CD CD CD CD CD CD CD CD CD CD

Forgotten sons 10:22
Garden party 7:52
She chameleon 5:44
He knows you know/The web 10:12
Institution waltz 5:53
Three boats down from the Candy 4:55
Market square heroes 7:00
Margaret 7:12

Recorded live in Liverpool, Warehouse, 26.08.1982

Triangle Records, PYCD 075
1992

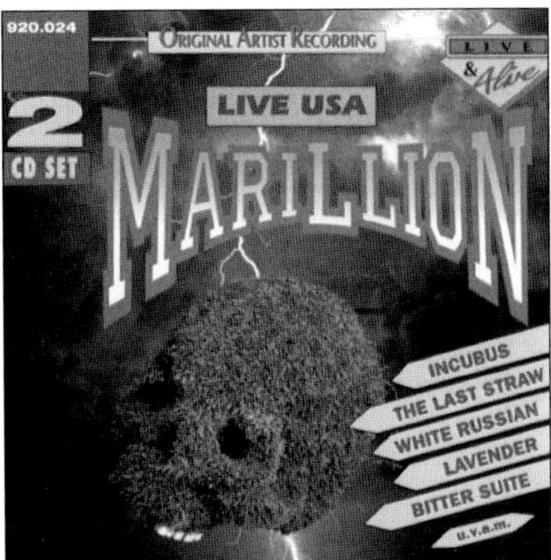

Cover »Live USA« double CD

»Live USA«

2CD 2CD 2CD 2CD 2CD 2CD 2CD 2CD 2CD

Disc 1)	Slainte mhath	4:55
	Assassing	6:29
	Script for a jester's tear	9:02
	White russian	5:45
	Incubus	8:55
	Sugar mice	5:54
	Torch song	3:47
	Fugazi	8:05
Disc 2)	Hotel hobbies	3:58
	Warm wet circles/That time of the night (The short straw)	10:15
	Kayleigh	3:56
	Lavender	2:37
	Bitter suite	8:09
	Heart of Lothian	4:00
	The last straw	5:30
	Incommunicado	4:42
	Garden party	6:23
	Market square heroes/My generation/Let's twist again	10:01

Recorded live in Milwaukee, Billy's Old Mill, 25.09.1987

Imtrat Live & Alive, 920.024

1992

»Live Walsall 1990«

CD CD CD CD CD CD CD CD CD CD CD CD

Intro: Mission Impossible	0:54
Splintering heart	7:15
The uninvited guest	5:42
Slainte mhath	6:38
The party	6:12
Easter	6:23
Warm wet circles	4:06
That time of the night (The short straw)	5:46
No one can	5:52
Holloway girl	6:09
Berlin	8:58
Kayleigh	4:20
Holidays in Eden	5:35

Recorded live in Walsall, Junction 10, 20.12.1990, six more tracks are listed on the cover, which are not on the CD

Sirius Records, CD 001

1992

»Misplaced rendez vous«

2CD 2CD 2CD 2CD 2CD 2CD 2CD 2CD 2CD

Disc 1)	Intro	
	Assassing	7:12
	Cinderella search	5:50
	Script for a jester's tear	9:58
	Punch & Judy	3:53
	Jigsaw	6:52
	Emerald lies	5:24
	Misplaced childhood (part 1)	
	a) Pseudo silk kimono	2:40
	b) Kayleigh	3:34
	c) Bitter suite	6:50
	d) Heart Of Lothian	5:13
	Incubus	8:27
Disc 2)	Fugazi	9:34
	Forgotten sons	11:59
	Garden party	6:18
	Market square heroes	12:09
	The web *	8:22
	Grendel **	18:21
	Market square heroes °	3:38

*Recorded live in Nice, 15.06.1985, except * Friday Rock Show, 29.01.1982, ** Fair Deal Studio-demo, 06.09.1982, ° EMI-demo, 06.09.1982*

Kobra Records, KR 19

1997

»My first temptation«

CD CD CD CD CD CD CD CD CD CD CD CD

Slainte mhath	6:10

Assassing	7:45
Script for a jester's tear	11:22
White russian	6:02
Incubus	9:05
Sugar mice	6:28
Torch song	3:55
Fugazi	8:19

Recorded live in Milwaukee, Billy's Old Mill, 25.09.1987

American Concert Series, ACS 015
1994, re-release from 1992, part 1 of the concert, see also »The last Fish« CD for part 2

»One off show«

2CD 2CD 2CD 2CD 2CD 2CD 2CD 2CD 2CD

Disc 1)	Bridge	2:30
	Living with the big lie	6:49
	Runaway	4:43
	Goodbye to all that	11:58
	a) Wave	
	b) Mad	
	c) The opium den	
	d) The slide	
	e) Standing in the swing	
	Hard as love	6:45
	The hollow man	4:30
	Alone again in the lap of luxury	7:56
	a) Now wash your hands	
	Paper lies	5:16
	Brave	9:27
	The great escape	7:55
	a) The last of you	
	b) Falling from the moon	
	Made again	5:31
Disc 2)	Splintering heart	7:22
	Easter	6:10
	King of sunset town	5:27
	Waiting to happen	5:09
	Sympathy	4:34
	Kayleigh	3:52
	Lavender	2:41
	Heart of Lothian	2:49
	Uninvited guest	3:50
	Slainte mhath	5:17
	The release	4:08
	Hooks in you	3:58
	Garden party	7:04

Recorded live in Oxford, Apollo Theatre, 11.05.1995

Insect, IST 77/78
1995, cover with OBI, looks japanese

»Paris 1987«

CD CD CD CD CD CD CD CD CD CD CD CD

Slainte mhath	5:23
Script for a jester's tear	10:18
White russian	6:02
Incubus	9:49
Sugar mice	6:15
Fugazi	8:26
Hotel hobbies	3:59
Warm wet circles	5:58
That time of the night (The short straw)	4:09
Kayleigh	4:34
Lavender	2:32
The last straw	6:13
Incommunicado	5:25

Recorded live in Paris, Le Zenith, 09.07.1987

Red Line - Post Script, PSCD 1135
1991

»Pinkpop, Geleen June 11th 1984«

CD CD CD CD CD CD CD CD CD CD CD CD

Punch & Judy	3:56
Assassing	7:23
Jigsaw	6:59
Incubus	9:12
Cinderella search	5:47
Fugazi	9:25
Garden party	8:53
Market square heroes	5:12

Recorded live in Geleen, Pinkpop (Burgermeester Daamen Sportpark), 11.06.1984

Take it or Leave it Music, T 9406
1994

»Reflections«

CD CD CD CD CD CD CD CD CD CD CD CD

Splintering heart	6:16
Cover my eyes	3:48
Slainte mhath	4:43
Uninvited guest	4:56
Warm wet circles	9:47
No one can	5:10
Script for a jester's tear	8:18
This town	3:40
Kayleigh	3:45
King of sunset town	3:38

Holidays in Eden	5:01
Hooks in you	1:43

Recorded live in Workington, Derwent Park Rugby Stadium, Cumbria Rock Festival, 13.07.1991

Robespierre Records, RBCD 011

1992

»Shadowplays in Switzerland«

CD CD CD CD CD CD CD CD CD CD CD CD

Splintering heart	6:46
Garden party	7:23
Dry land	4:34
The party	6:11
The space	6:28
A collection	4:10
Waiting to happen	4:52
Cover my eyes	3:54
Lords of the backstage	1:48
Blind curve	4:13
This town	4:20
The rake's progress	2:46
100 nights	4:34
No one can	5:03
Holidays in Eden	4:44

Recorded live in Lausanne, Salle de Fetes Beaulieu, 19.10.1991

Rarities Special, RS 9204

1992

»Something fishy going on«

CD CD CD CD CD CD CD CD CD CD CD CD

Slainte mhath	5:03
Script for a jester's tear	9:21
Easter	6:24
Warm wet circles	4:10
That time of the night (The short straw)	6:20
Holloway girl	4:59
Kayleigh	3:16
Lavender	1:48
Heart of Lothian	2:53
Hooks in you	3:30
The space	6:50
Incommunicado	5:04
After me	4:04
Market square heroes/School's out	8:42

Recorded live in Paris, Le Zenith, 25.10.1989

Metal Memory Records, MM 90024

1991

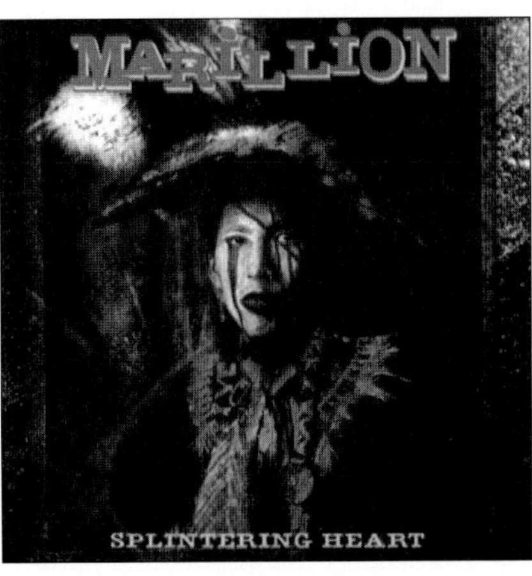

Cover »Splintering heart« CD version 1

»Splintering heart«

CD CD CD CD CD CD CD CD CD CD CD CD

Splintering heart	6:46
Garden party	7:23
Dry land	4:34
The party	6:11
The space	6:28
A collection	4:10
Waiting to happen	4:52
Cover my eyes	3:54
Lords of the backstage	1:48
Blind curve	4:13
This town	4:20
The rake's progress	2:46

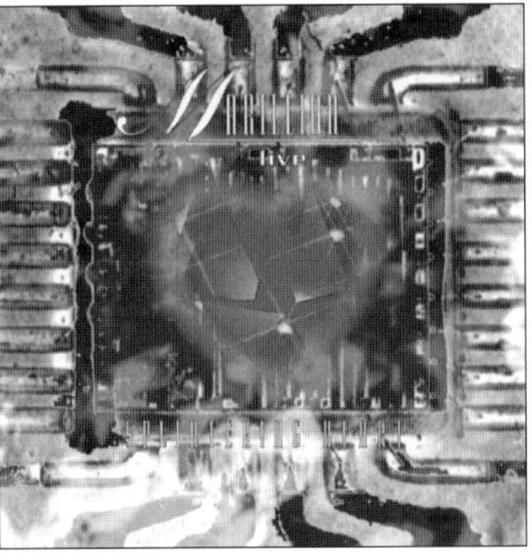

Cover »Splintering heart« CD version 2

100 nights	4:34
No one can	5:03
Holidays in Eden	4:44

Recorded live in Lausanne, Salle de Fetes Beaulieu, 19.10.1991

Metal Mess, MMR 9210
1993

Live Line Records, LL 15474
1994, re-release with different cover

»Tell me a story (1991)«

2CD 2CD 2CD 2CD 2CD 2CD 2CD 2CD 2CD

Disc 1)	Garden party	7:09
	Freaks	5:40
	Assassing	6:23
	Misplaced childhood part 1	19:36
Disc 2)	Misplaced childhood part 2	23:44
	Forgotten sons	10:17
	Market square heroes/ "She loves you"/"Let's twist again"	8:34

Recorded live in Mannheim, Maimarktgelände, 21.06.1986

Three Cool Cats, TCC 041/042

»The brave on stage«

2CD 2CD 2CD 2CD 2CD 2CD 2CD 2CD 2CD

Disc 1) Bridge
Living with the big lie
Runaway
Goodbye to all that
a) Wave
b) Mad
c) The opium den
d) The slide
e) Standing in the swing
Hard as love
The hollow man
Alone again in the lap of luxury
a) Now wash your hands
Paper lies
Brave
The great escape
a) The last of you
b) Falling from the moon
Made again
Disc 2) Cover my eyes
Slainte mhath
The uninvited guest
Easter
Garden party

Recorded live in Oslo, Sentrum Scene, 24.05.1995

EGG, EGG 2002-1
1995

»The last fish«

CD CD CD CD CD CD CD CD CD CD CD CD

Hotel hobbies	4:14
Warm wet circles/That time of the night (The short straw)	10:28
Kayleigh	4:22
Lavender	2:55
Bitter suite	7:59
Heart of Lothian	4:18
The last straw	5:50
Incommunicado	5:12
Garden party	6:32
Market square heroes (part 1)	4:29
Let's twist again	2:56
Market square heroes (part 2)	2:41

Recorded live in Milwaukee, Billy's Old Mill, 25.09.1987

American Concert Series, ACS 016
1992, part 2 of the concert, see also »My first temptation« CD for part 1

»The low fat yoghurts«

CD CD CD CD CD CD CD CD CD CD CD CD

This town (long version) *	5:57
Splintering heart *	7:27
Eric (The party)	5:48
No one can	4:42
This town (short version)	3:56
You don't need anyone	3:54
Holidays in Eden	5:57
This town (extended version)	15:07

*Recorded live in Bath, Moles Club, 12.12.1990, except * live in Utrecht, Tivoli, fan club convention "Freaks", 22.09.1990*

Rockland, ROLA 10
1992

»Unforgotten truth«

CD CD CD CD CD CD CD CD CD CD CD CD

Assassing	6:55
Garden party	6:52

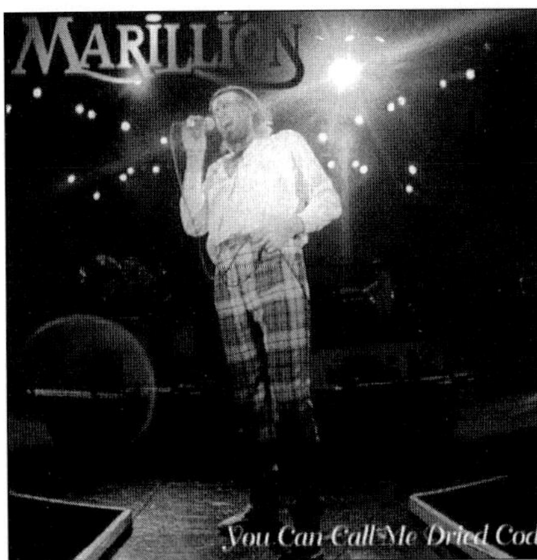

Cover »You can call me dried cod« double CD

	Cinderella search	6:13
	Punch & Judy	3:33
	Jigsaw	7:12
	Emerald lies	5:37
	Blind curve *	9:54
	Childhood's end? *	3:28
	White feather *	4:07
	Misplaced childhood (part 1)	16:26
	- Pseudo silk kimono	
	- Kayleigh	
	- Bitter suite	
	i Brief encounter	
	ii Lost weekend	
	iii Misplaced rendezvous	
	iv Windswept thumb	
	- Heart of Lothian	
	i Wide boy	
	ii Curtain call	

*Recorded live in London, Hammersmith Odeon, 14.12.1984, except * live in Cardiff, St David's Hall, 12.01.1986*

Classical Shots On CD, CSCD 006
1993

»You can call me dried cod«

2CD 2CD 2CD 2CD 2CD 2CD 2CD 2CD 2CD

Disc 1)	Garden party	6:18
	Script for a jester's tear	8:27
	Three boats down from the Candy	4:50
	Chelsea Monday	6:48
	He knows you know	5:23
	Grendel	18:36
Disc 2)	Slainte mhath	6:10
	Assassing	7:45
	Script for a jester's tear	11:22
	White russian	6:02
	Incubus	9:05
	Sugar mice	6:28
	Torch song	3:55
	Fugazi	8:19

Disc 1 recorded live in London, Hammersmith Odeon, 18.04.1983, disc 2 live in Milwaukee, Billy's Old Mill, 25.09.1987

Sound Carrier System, SCD 84705/06
1994

Dream Theater »Uncovered«

2CD 2CD 2CD 2CD 2CD 2CD 2CD 2CD 2CD

Disc 1)	Elton John medley
	- Funeral for a friend
	- Love lies bleeding
	Red hill mining town
	Led Zeppelin medley
	- The Rover
	- Achilles' last stand
	- The song remains the same
	Tears
	Damage Inc.
	Happines is a warm gun (with Steve Hogarth on vocals)
	Easter (with Steve Hogarth on vocals and Steve Rothery on guitar)
	Winter
	In the dead of night
Disc 2)	Yes medley
	- Machine messiah
	- Heart of the sunrise
	- Close to the edge
	- Siberian khatru
	- Starship trooper
	The Big medley
	- In the flesh
	- Carry on wayward son
	- Bohemian rhapsody
	- Lovin' touchin' squeezin'
	- Cruise control
	- Turn it on again
	- Pull me under
	Space dye vest *
	Carry that weight **
	Golden slumbers ("The night") **
	Don't look past me **

Mission: Impossible ***
To live forever (acoustic) °
Indulge in reverie ∞
A late summer's rain (Schizophrenia) ∞

*Recorded live in London, Ronnie Scott's, 31.01.1995, except * Kevin Moore demo 1995, ** demos 1988 – 1990, *** John Petrucci demo 1994, ° demo 1993, ∞ John Petrucci flexi disc for "Guitar Player" magazine*

Kobra Records, KRCD 08//9
release 1995

IRON MAIDEN »Blaze or glory«

2CD 2CD 2CD 2CD 2CD 2CD 2CD 2CD 2CD

Disc 1) Man on the edge
Wrathchild
Heaven can wait
Lord of the flies
Fortunes of war
Blood on the world's hands
Afraid to shoot strangers
The evil that men do
The aftermath
Sign of the cross
2 minutes to midnight
Sanctuary

Disc 2) Fear of the dark
The clairvoyant
Iron Maiden
Number of the beast
Hallowed be thy name
The trooper
Running free
The boys are back in town *
With a little help from my friends *
Rhythm of the beast °
Beehive boogie °
2 minutes to midnight **
Caught somewhere in time **

*Recorded live in Weert, Bospop-Festival, 13.07.1996, except * live in London, Wembley Arena, 05.11.1987 (MARILLION with IRON MAIDEN), ** live in Bristol, 08.10.1986, ° Nicko's »Rhythm of the beast« single*

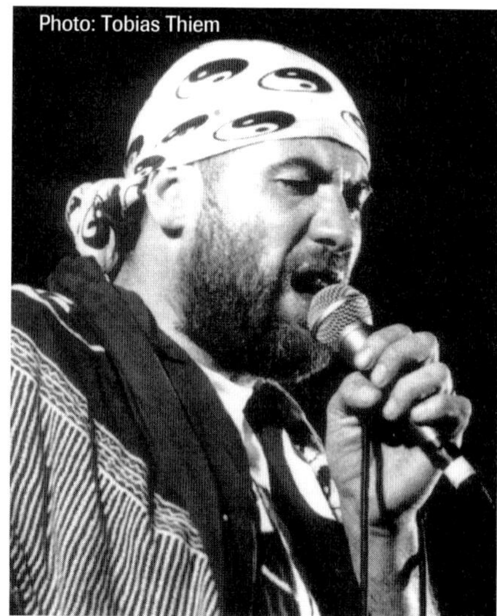
Photo: Tobias Thiem

FISH CD-Bootlegs

»A voice in the crowd part 1«

CD CD CD CD CD CD CD CD CD CD CD CD

Fearless	6:07
Big wedge	5:32
Boston tea party	4:03
Credo	7:25
Medley: View from the hill/	7:44
He knows you know/	4:56
She chameleon/	3:48
Kayleigh	3:58
White russian	6:36
The company	5:01
Just good friends	6:03
Hold your head up	3:10
Lucky	5:05
Internal exile	4:31

Recorded live in Ludwigshafen, 31.03.1993

Rob Roy Records, RR 001
1993

»Bagpipe disaster«

CD CD CD CD CD CD CD CD CD CD CD CD

Vigil in a wilderness of mirrors	9:18
Credo	9:12
Incubus	11:16
Shadowplay	7:53

Lucky	5:20
Heart of Lothian	5:20
Fugazi	11:21
Internal exile	4:26
Market square heroes (incl. the laugh)	5:59

Recorded live in Utrecht, Vredenburg, 17.12.1991

Rarities Special, RS 9205

1992

»External inside«

2CD 2CD 2CD 2CD 2CD 2CD 2CD 2CD 2CD

Disc 1)	Fearless	6:22
	Big wedge	5:41
	Boston tea party	4:00
	Credo	7:36
	Family business	6:30
	Medley: View from the hill/ He knows you know/	4:07
	She chameleon	3:56
	Kayleigh	4:17
	White russian	7:15
	The company	6:42
	Just good friends	6:11
Disc 2)	Jeepster	4:00
	Hold your head up	8:13
	Internal exile	5:21
	Cliche	7:17
	The last straw	5:43
	Five years	6:42
	MARILLION- Garden party / Market square heroes *	14:46

*Recorded live in Paris, 15.03.1993, except * live in Zürich (1984?) (MARILLION)*

Star Records, OHM 021

1993

»Fishing all over the world«

CD CD CD CD CD CD CD CD CD CD CD CD

Intro: Muppets	0:56
Credo	7:55
The voyeur (I like to watch)	4:30
Punch & Judy	7:09
Just good friends	8:23
Pipeline	8:33
Out of my life	3:54
Incubus	10:05
Raw meat	6:04
Something in the air	6:48
Lady Nina	5:52
The company	3:55

Recorded live in Ulm, Gorki Park Festival, 25.06.1992

Internal Exile Records, DRA 2506

1992

»Forgotten songs«

CD CD CD CD CD CD CD CD CD CD CD CD

Intro	0:38
Tongues	7:28
Just good friends (Close)	7:49
Dear friend	6:53
Big wedge	6:03
Forgotten sons	8:42
"Introducing the band"	0:47
Internal exile	4:51
Market square heroes	5:44
Outro	0:44
Kayleigh *	3:59
Lavender *	2:49
Heart of Lothian *	3:06
Script for a jester's tear **	8:57
Incommunicado °	4:48

*Recorded live in Utrecht, Tivoli, 26.10.1991, except * live in Rotterdam, Ahoy, 10.08.1990, ** live in Utrecht, Vredenburg, 05.12.1991 (MARILLION), ° live in Brussels, Ancienne Belgique, 21.10.1991 (MARILLION)*

Jolly Joker Music, JJM 002

part 2 of the release, 1993, see also »No place for children« bootleg CD for part 1

»In the company of freaks«

CD CD CD CD CD CD CD CD CD CD CD CD

Punch & Judy	4:57
State of mind	4:41
Assassing	7:17
The company	3:46
Script for a jester's tear	10:18
Incubus	10:34
A gentleman's excuse me	4:01
Sugar mice	7:16
Vigil in a wilderness of mirrors	8:54
Big wedge	6:17
Internal exile	5:22

Recorded live in Rotterdam, Ahoy, 10.03.1990

Rockland, ROLA 11

1992

»Good company«

CD CD CD CD CD CD CD CD CD CD CD CD

Kayleigh *	3:59
Lavender *	3:37
Heart of Lothian *	3:08
Faith healer	3:46
Dunfermline, East End Park, 13.05.1990 (with NAZARETH)	
The company	5:42
Soundcheck, Rotterdam, Ahoy, 10.03.1990	
The voyeur (I like to watch) **	5:04
Vigil in a wilderness of mirrors **	8:32
Fugazi **	7:12
Heart of Lothian **	5:09
Tongues °	6:22
Kayleigh ∞	11:41
Lavender ∞	3:22
The voyeur (I like to watch) ∞	6:55
O sole mio ∞	1:27
Punch & Judy ∞	6:10

** Recorded live in Rotterdam, Ahoy, 10.03.1990, ** soundcheck, Siegburg, Schulzentrum, Neuenburg, 25.05.1991, ° live in London, Hammersmith Odeon, 23.11.1991, ∞ live at Aviemore, Crofter's Pub, 26.11.1989*

Rockland, ROLA 19

with sticker, 1992

»Live Germany '90«

CD CD CD CD CD CD CD CD CD CD CD CD

The voyeur (I like to watch)	5:39
The company	4:03
Script for a jester's tear	12:18
A gentleman's excuse me	4:46
Sugar mice	6:40
Vigil in a wilderness of mirrors	8:57
Kayleigh	3:59
Lavender	2:26
Heart of Lothian	3:26

Recorded live in Hamburg, CCH 3, 20.03.1990

Capitol, CAP 1008

1992

»Live USA - Live in Holland«

CD CD CD CD CD CD CD CD CD CD CD CD

Vigil in a wilderness of mirrors	9:18
Credo	9:12
Incubus	11:16
Shadowplay	7:53
Lucky	5:20
Heart of Lothian	5:20
Fugazi	11:21
Internal exile	4:26
Market square heroes	5:59

Recorded live in Utrecht, Vredenburg, 17.12.1991

Imtrat, 900.139

1993

»Lucky bastards«

2CD 2CD 2CD 2CD 2CD 2CD 2CD 2CD 2CD

Disc 1)	Intro: The Teddy Bear's picnic	2:20
	Vigil in a wilderness of mirrors	9:23
	Credo	8:23
	Family business	7:32
	Incubus	12:35
	Dear friend	7:20
	The company	4:05
Disc 2)	Lucky	6:52
	Big wedge	6:25
	Heart of Lothian	6:10
	Shadowplay	9:47
	Internal exile	4:36
	Market square heroes	6:24
	Kayleigh *	3:57
	Dear friend*	4:12
	Out of my life *	3:58

*Recorded live in Geleen, Hanehof, 18.12.1991, except * recorded acoustic in studio (?)*

Take it or leave it, T 9404/9405

1994

»No place for children«

CD CD CD CD CD CD CD CD CD CD CD CD

Intro	0:31
Vigil in a wilderness of mirrors	9:01
Credo	8:19
State of mind	5:18
Family business	5:55
Incubus	10:31
Shadowplay	6:12
Kayleigh	5:05
Lucky	5:43
Fugazi	8:11
Heart of Lothian	3:28
The company	4:51

Recorded live in Utrecht, Tivoli, 26.10.1991

Jolly Joker Music, JJM 001

part 1 of the release, 1992 , see also »Forgotten songs« bootleg CD for part 2

»Plenty of fish in the sea«

CD CD CD CD CD CD CD CD CD CD CD CD

	Faith healer	6:27
	The voyeur (I like to watch)	4:57
	Punch & Judy	4:23
	The company	4:25
	Script for a jester's tear	9:15
	Vigil in a wilderness of mirrors	9:15
	Big wedge	5:29
	Fugazi	8:05
	Kayleigh	4:10
	Lavender	2:30
	Heart of Lothian	3:27

Recorded live in London, Town & County Club, 11.11.1989

Metal Memories, MM90036
1992

»Raw meat«

2CD 2CD 2CD 2CD 2CD 2CD 2CD 2CD 2CD

Disc 1)	Intro: Muppets/	
	Credo	8:18
	The voyeur (I like to watch)	4:40
	Punch & Judy	6:17
	Just good friends	6:54
	Pipeline	8:18
	Out of my life	4:09
	Incubus	9:36
Disc 2)	Raw meat	6:31
	Something in the air	7:16
	Lady Nina	6:25
	The company	5:48
	Lucky	5:25
	Big wedge	5:43

Recorded live in Hamburg, Grosse Freiheit, 23.06.1992

ITA FISH 009/010
1993

»Take a view from the hill!«

CD CD CD CD CD CD CD CD CD CD CD CD

	Fearless	6:25
	Boston tea party	4:03
	Credo	7:26
	Family business	6:40
	View from the hill	4:37
	She chameleon	3:47
	Kayleigh	4:05
	The company	4:34
	Just good friends	6:08
	Internal exile	5:28
	Cliche	7:19
	The last straw	5:47
	Five Years	6:30

Recorded live in Paris, 15.03.1993

Klondyke Records
1993

»The mask Vol. 1 – Hammersmith live«

2CD 2CD 2CD 2CD 2CD 2CD 2CD 2CD 2CD

Disc 1)	The voyeur (I like to watch)	6:31
	Punch and Judy	5:17
	State of mind	6:17
	Family business	5:50
	Assassing	6:41
	The company	7:06
	Intro to Script for a jester's tear	5:34
	Script for a jester's tear	7:13
	A gentleman's excuse me	4:23
Disc 2)	Sugar mice	8:53
	Vigil in a wilderness of mirrors	9:43
	Kayleigh	4:04
	Lavender	2:22
	Heart of Lothian	4:58
	Cliche	7:20
	Big wedge	6:24

Recorded live in London, Hammersmith Odeon, 02.04.1990

ITA FISH 001/002
1993

»The mask Vol. 2 – Haddington convention«

2CD 2CD 2CD 2CD 2CD 2CD 2CD 2CD 2CD

Disc 1)	Vigil in a wilderness of mirrors	9:48
	Credo	7:58
	State of mind	6:57
	Tongues	8:02
	Family business	7:13
	Incubus	11:10
	Shadowplay	6:38
Disc 2)	Dear friend	7:02
	Lucky	5:22
	Big wedge	7:35
	Fugazi	8:49

	Heart of Lothian	5:36
	The company	5:20
	Forgotten sons	12:33

Recorded live in Haddington, Corn Exchange, 03.11.1991 at the first convention of the Company Scotland

ITA FISH 003/004
1993

»The mask Vol. 3 – Zürich Volkshaus«

2CD 2CD 2CD 2CD 2CD 2CD 2CD 2CD 2CD

Disc 1)	Vigil in a wilderness of mirrors	9:18
	Credo	8:08
	Tongues	7:47
	Family business	6:45
	Incubus	11:37
	The company	3:54
Disc 2)	Shadowplay	10:49
	Dear friend	5:46
	Lucky	5:04
	Big wedge	6:36
	Heart of Lothian	5:41
	Fugazi	10:46
	Internal exile	4:31
	Market square heroes	5:12

Recorded live in Zürich, Volkshaus, 05.12.1991

ITA FISH 005/006
1993

»The mask Vol. 4 – Edinburgh Playhouse«

2CD 2CD 2CD 2CD 2CD 2CD 2CD 2CD 2CD

Disc 1)	Vigil in a wilderness of mirrors	9:10
	Credo	8:38
	Tongues	7:38
	Family business	7:36
	Incubus	10:16
	Geesabun	4:26
	The company	7:56
	Shadowplay	6:37
Disc 2)	Dear friend	8:33
	The bells/Happy new year	4:35
	Lucky	4:55
	Big wedge	6:33
	Heart of Lothian	5:25
	Forgotten sons	9:46
	Flower of Scotland	3:55
	Internal exile *	4:36
	Market square heroes *	6:48

*Recorded live in Edinburgh, Playhouse, 31.12.1991, except * live in Paris, Olympia, 09.12.1991*

ITA FISH 007/008
1994

»The mask Vol. 1 – 4«

CD CD CD CD CD CD CD CD CD CD CD CD

There was also a ltd. ed. of boxes made in 1993, including all 4 parts of »The mask«

»There's a guy works down the chip shop swears he's Fish«

CD CD CD CD CD CD CD CD CD CD CD CD

Vigil in a wilderness of mirrors	10:07
Credo	7:57
Tongues	7:03
Incubus	9:48
The company	4:16
Big wedge	6:49
Internal exile/ Market square heroes	10:32
Heart of Lothian	4:01

Recorded live in Nottingham, Royal Centre, 15.11.1991

Kiss The Stone, KTS 062
1992

»Virgil«

CD CD CD CD CD CD CD CD CD CD CD CD

Shadowplay	7:02
Kayleigh	4:40
Lucky	5:11
Fugazi	8:42
Heart of Lothian	4:15
The company	3:57
Vigil in a wilderness of mirrors	9:34
Credo	7:33
State of mind	5:45
Family business	5:52
Incubus	9:25

Recorded live in Utrecht, Tivoli, 26.10.1991

Crocodile Beat, 53040
1993

FISH Discography

FISH FISH FISH FISH FISH FISH FISH FISH

Born 25.04.1958 as Derek William Dick in Dalkeith (near Edinburgh) Scotland.

He first played with a band called NOT QUITE RED FOX in March 1980. In late spring/summer 1980 he sung in BLEWITT (with Frank Usher). Next came the STONE DOME BAND with Diz Minnit in September 1980.

Fish joined MARILLION on 02.01.1981. Some work with Tony Banks in 1986. Over the next years he took part in some charity projects. He left MARILLION in September 1988 to start a solo career.

Fish wurde am 25.04.1958 als Derek William Dick in Dalkeith (nahe Edinburgh) in Schottland geboren.

Zunächst spielte er mit seiner ersten eigenen Band NOT QUITE RED ab März 1980. Etwa im Frühjahr/Sommer 1980 sang er bereits bei BLEWITT (u.a. mit Frank Usher). Danach spielte er in der STONE DOME BAND u.a. mit Diz Minnit (September 1980).

Fish stieg offiziell am 02.01.1981 als Sänger bei MARILLION ein.

Im Jahr 1986 begann er mit Tony Banks zusammenzuarbeiten. In den Jahren darauf folgten einige Wohltätigkeits-Projekte.

Er verließ MARILLION im September 1988, um eine Solo-Karriere zu beginnen.

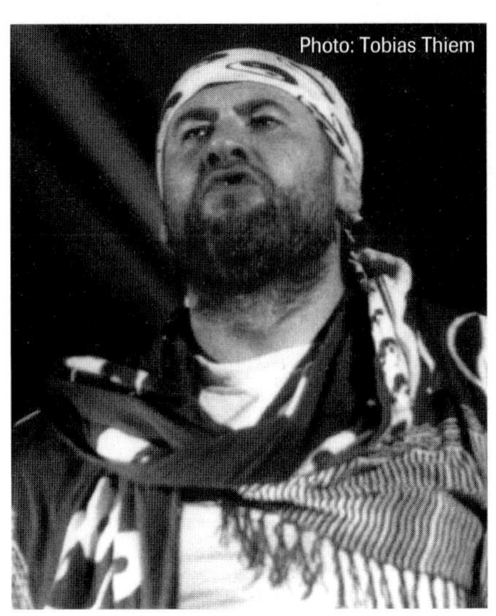
Photo: Tobias Thiem

»State of mind«

(UK release 16.10.1989)

7" 7" 7" 7" 7" 7" 7" 7" 7" 7" 7" 7" 7" 7" 7" 7"

Side 1) State of mind (edited version) 4:11
Side 2) The voyeur (I like to watch) 4:41

UK EMI, EM 109
EEC EMI, 006-20 3562 7

••

Side 1) State of mind "Estado de mente" (edited version) 4:11
Side 2) Big wedge "Gran cuna" (7" version) 4:23

MEX EMI, SEC 830
label yellow, promo, no ps

12" 12" 12" 12" 12" 12" 12" 12" 12" 12" 12"

Side 1) State of mind (Presidental Mix) 5:48
Side 2) State of mind (edited version) 4:11
The voyeur (I like to watch) 4:41
UK EMI, 12 EM 109
UK EMI, 12 EM PD 109
picture disc
UK EMI, 12 EM PD 109
same as before but misspressed, plays MADONNA »Cherish« 12"
EEC EMI, 060-20 3562 6
ITA EMI, 14 203562 6

CD CD CD CD CD CD CD CD CD CD CD CD

State of mind (album version) 4:45
The voyeur (I like to watch) 4:41
State of mind (Presidental Mix) 5:48

UK EMI, CD EM 109
EEC EMI, 056 20 3562 2
EEC EMI, CDP 552-20 3562 3
foc, (3"CD)

»Big wedge«

(UK release 27.12.1989)

7" 7" 7" 7" 7" 7" 7" 7" 7" 7" 7" 7" 7" 7" 7" 7"

Side 1) Big wedge (7" version) 4:23
Side 2) Jack and Jill 4:22
UK EMI, EM 125
UK EMI, EMS 125
ltd. ed., numbered "wallet", foc
EEC 006-20 3655 7

••

Side 1) Big wedge (edit) 3:06
Side 2) Big wedge (edit) 3:06

FRA EMI, SP 1455
promo with different ps

12" 12" 12" 12" 12" 12" 12" 12" 12" 12" 12"

Side 1)	Big wedge (12" remix)	8:12
Side 2)	Jack and Jill	4:22
	Faith healer	5:42

UK — EMI, 12 EM 125
UK — EMI, 12 EM PD 125
picture disc
EEC — EMI, 060-20 3655 6

CD CD CD CD CD CD CD CD CD CD CD CD

Big wedge (album version)	5:15
Jack and Jill	4:22
Faith healer	5:42

UK — EMI, CD EM 125
green Fish-logo
EEC — EMI, 560-20 3655 2
blue Fish-logo

»Vigil in a wilderness of mirrors«

(UK release 19.01.1990)

LP LP LP LP LP LP LP LP LP LP LP LP LP LP

Side 1)	Vigil	8:43
	Big wedge	5:19
	State of mind	4:42
	The company	4:04
Side 2)	A gentleman's excuse me	4:15
	Family business	5:14
	View from the hill	6:38
	Cliche	7:01
	Jack and Jill	4:28

UK — EMI, EMD 1015
foc, with promo stickers
UK — EMI, EMD 1015
foc
UK — EMI, EMPD 1015
picture disc, poster
EEC — EMI, 064-793634-1
foc
EEC — EMI, 66682 6
foc, label yellow, club edition
ESP — EMI, 072-7936341
foc
ITA — EMI, 64 7936341
foc
BRA — EMI, 068-793634 1
MEX — EMI, EMI LEMP 1679
VEN — EMI, EMI 25176

CD CD CD CD CD CD CD CD CD CD CD CD

Vigil	8:43
Big wedge	5:19
State of mind	4:42
The company	4:04
A gentleman's excuse me	4:15
The voyeur (I like to watch)•	4:42
Family business	5:14
View from the hill	6:38
Cliche	7:01

• Bonus track

UK — EMI, CD EMD 1015
EEC — EMI, CDP 7936342
some with tour sticker
JAP — EMI, TOCP 6103
promo
JAP — EMI, TOCP 6103

••

Vigil	8:43
Big wedge	5:19
State of mind	4:42
The company	4:04
A gentleman's excuse me	4:15
The voyeur (I like to watch) •	4:42
Family business	5:14
View from the hill	6:38
Cliche	7:01
Jack and Jill •	4:28
Internal exile •	4:52
The company (demo) •	4:29
A gentleman's excuse me (demo) •	3:55
Whiplash •	4:21

Remastered, • bonus tracks
UK — Dick Bros, DDick 28CD
release 18.12.1997
EEC — Roadrunner, RR 8687 2
release 28.10.1998

»A gentleman's excuse me«

(UK release 05.03.1990)

7" 7" 7" 7" 7" 7" 7" 7" 7" 7" 7" 7" 7" 7" 7" 7"

Side 1)	A gentleman's excuse me	4:14
Side 2)	Whiplash	4:12

UK — EMI, EM 135
UK — EMI, EMS 135
ltd. ed., red vinyl, insert
UK — EMI, EMS PD 135
ltd. ed., shaped picture disc, insert
UK — EMI, EMS PD 135
same as before but uncut test pressing
EEC — EMI, 006-20 3755 7
ITA — EMI, 06 203 7557

12" 12" 12" 12" 12" 12" 12" 12" 12" 12" 12"

Side 1)	A gentleman's excuse me (album version)	4:16

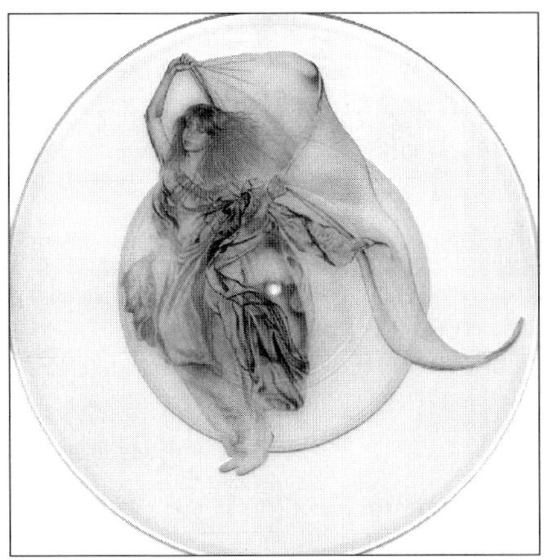

UK »A gentleman's excuse me« uncut shape

Side 2) Whiplash 4:12
A gentleman's excuse me (demo) 3:53

UK EMI, 12 EM 135
UK EMI, 12 EMPD 135
picture disc, insert
EEC EMI, 060-20 3755 6

CD CD CD CD CD CD CD CD CD CD CD CD
A gentleman's excuse me
(album version) 4:16
Whiplash 4:12
A gentleman's excuse me (demo) 3:53

UK EMI, CDEM 135
EEC EMI, 560-20 3755 2

»The company«

(UK release 18.07.1990)

7" 7" 7" 7" 7" 7" 7" 7" 7" 7" 7" 7" 7" 7" 7" 7"
Side 1) The company (album version) 4:06
Side 2) Punch and Judy 4:16
Rotterdam, Ahoy, 10.03.1990

EEC EMI, 016-20 3946 7

12" 12" 12" 12" 12" 12" 12" 12" 12" 12" 12"
Side 1) The company (album version) 4:06
Family business * 5:19
Side 2) Punch and Judy * 4:16
The company (demo) 4:30
** Rotterdam, Ahoy, 10.03.1990*

EEC EMI, 060-20 3946 6

German cover »The company« CD

CD CD CD CD CD CD CD CD CD CD CD CD
The company (album version) 4:06
Family business * 5:19
Punch and Judy * 4:16
The company (demo) 4:30
** Rotterdam, Ahoy, 10.03.1990*

EEC EMI, 560-20 3946 2

»Internal exile«

(UK release 09.09.1991)

7" 7" 7" 7" 7" 7" 7" 7" 7" 7" 7" 7" 7" 7" 7" 7"
Side 1) Internal exile (7" edit) 3:30
Side 2) Carnival man 6:20

UK Polydor, Fishy 1
EEC Polydor, 867 750 7
FRA Polydor, 867 750 7

12" 12" 12" 12" 12" 12" 12" 12" 12" 12" 12"
Side 1) Internal exile (album version) 4:36
Side 2) Internal exile (karaoke mix) 3:30
Carnival man 6:20

UK Polydor, FISHS 1 DJ
promo, no ps
UK Polydor, FISHS 1
numbered picture disc, insert
EEC Polydor, 867 751-1

CD CD CD CD CD CD CD CD CD CD CD CD
Internal exile (7" edit) 3:30
Internal exile (album version) 4:36
Carnival man 6:20
Internal exile (karaoke mix) 3:30

UK	Polydor, FISCD 1
EEC	Polydor, 867 887-2
digi pack	
EEC	Polydor, 867 751-2

LP LP LP LP LP LP LP LP LP LP LP LP LP LP

Side 1)	Shadowplay	6:23
	Credo	6:39
	Just good friends (close)	6:00
	Favourite stranger	5:58
Side 2)	Lucky	4:49
	Dear friend	4:08
	Tongues	6:22
	Internal exile	4:44

EEC	Polydor, 511 049-1
release 28.10.1991	
KOR	Polydor, 513 401-1/RG 3041
korean lyric sheet	

CD CD CD CD CD CD CD CD CD CD CD CD

Shadowplay	6:23
Credo	6:39
Just good friends (close)	6:00
Favourite stranger	5:58
Lucky	4:49
Dear friend	4:08
Tongues	6:22
Internal exile	4:44
Something in the air •	5:08

• Bonus track

EEC	Polydor, 511 049-1
release 28.10.1991	
CZ	Popron, 5051-2
RUS	CD Media Records, N 2139
JAP	Polydor, POCP 1162
promo	
JAP	Polydor, POCP 1162
USA	Polydor, 314513765-2
different cover	

••

Shadowplay	6:23
Credo	6:39
Just good friends (close)	6:00
Favourite stranger	5:58
Lucky	4:49
Dear friend	4:08
Tongues	6:22
Internal exile	4:44
Something in the air	5:08
Poet's moon •	4:26
Carnival man •	6:20

Remastered, • bonus tracks

EEC	Roadrunner, 8687-2
release 28.10.1998	

»Credo«

(UK release 02.12.1991)

7" 7" 7" 7" 7" 7" 7" 7" 7" 7" 7" 7" 7" 7" 7" 7"

Side 1)	Credo (7" edit)	4:06
Side 2)	Poet's moon	4:25

UK	Polydor, Fishy 2
EEC	Polydor, 865 118-7

••

Side 1)	Credo (album version)	6:42
Side 2)	Credo (7" edit)	4:06
	Tongues (demo)	

UK	Polydor, FISH X 2

12" 12" 12" 12" 12" 12" 12" 12" 12" 12" 12"

Side 1)	Credo (album version)	6:42
Side 2)	Credo (7" edit)	4:06
	Poet's moon	4:25

UK	Polydor, FISHS 2DJ
promo, no ps	
UK	Polydor, FISHS 2
large numbered box with poster	

CD CD CD CD CD CD CD CD CD CD CD CD

Side 1)	Credo (album version)	6:42
Side 2)	Credo (7" edit)	4:06
	Poet's moon	4:25

UK	Polydor, FISCD 2
numbered digi pack	
EEC	Polydor, 865 119-2
numbered digi pack	
USA	Polydor, CDP 728
promo	

»BBC Transcription«

(UK-only release 5/'92)

CD CD CD CD CD CD CD CD CD CD CD CD

Vigil	10:07
Credo	7:57
Tongues	7:03
Incubus	9:49
The company	4:16
Big wedge	6:49
Internal exile/	
Market square heroes	10:32
Heart of Lothian	4:01

Recorded live in Nottingham, Royal Court Theatre, 15.11.1991

UK	BBC, TCD 0291
radio show, less than 100 copies	

»Something in the air«

(UK release 22.06.1992)

7" 7" 7" 7" 7" 7" 7" 7" 7" 7" 7" 7" 7" 7" 7" 7"

Side 1) Something in the air (radio edit) 3:57
Side 2) Dear friend 4:23
Hamburg, 16.12.1991

UK Polydor, Fishy 3
EEC Polydor, 863 118-7

12" 12" 12" 12" 12" 12" 12" 12" 12" 12" 12"

Side 1) Something in the air (Teddy bear mix) 6:46
Side 2) Something in the air (album mix) 5:07
Dear friend 4:23
Hamburg, 16.12.1991

UK Polydor, FISHX X 3

CD CD CD CD CD CD CD CD CD CD CD CD

Something in the air (radio edit) 3:57
Something in the air (album mix) 5:07
Something in the air (Teddy bear mix) 6:46
Dear friend 4:23
Hamburg, 16.12.1991

UK Polydor, FISH P 3
white plastic long pack, poster
EEC Polydor, 863 119-2

••

Something in the air (album edit) 5:06
Something in the air (Christopher Robin mix) 4:59
Credo 7:22
Enschede, 19.12.1991
Shadowplay 6:45
Hamburg, 16.12.1991

UK Polydor, FISH L 3
black plastic long pack, backstage pass

»Never mind the bullocks«

(UK release 12.12.1992)

7" 7" 7" 7" 7" 7" 7" 7" 7" 7" 7" 7" 7" 7" 7" 7"

Side 1) Hold your head up (edited version) 3:24
Side 2) Question (edited version) 4:23

UK Polydor, Fishy 4
EEC Polydor, 863 938-7

CD CD CD CD CD CD CD CD CD CD CD CD

Hold your head up (edited version) 3:24
Question (album version) 6:38
Hold your head up (album version) 4:11
Five years (album version) 5:18

UK Polydor, FISCD 4
EEC Polydor, 422 863 939

»Songs from the mirror«

(UK release 20.01.1993)

LP LP LP LP LP LP LP LP LP LP LP LP LP LP

Side 1) Question 6:38
Boston tea party 4:35
Fearless 6:15
Apeman 5:54
Side 2) Hold your head up 3:43
Solo 4:09
I know what I like 4:17
Five years 5:19

UK Polydor, 517 499-1
with promo stickers on label and cover
UK Polydor, 517 499-1

CD CD CD CD CD CD CD CD CD CD CD CD

Question 6:38
Boston tea party 4:35
Fearless 6:15
Apeman 5:54
Hold your head up 3:43
Solo 4:09
I know what I like 4:17
Jeepster • 4:30
Five years 5:19

• Bonus track

UK Polydor, 7 314 517 499-2 6
promo print
UK Polydor, 7 314 517 499-2 6
EEC Polydor, INT 517 499 2

••

Question 6:38
Boston tea party 4:35
Fearless 6:15
Apeman 5:54
Hold your head up 3:43
Solo 4:09
Time and a word • 4:24
The seeker • 3:16
I know what I like 4:17
Five years 5:19

Remastered, • bonus tracks

EEC Roadrunner, 8682-2

»Five years«

(EEC promo release only 1993)

CD CD CD CD CD CD CD CD CD CD CD CD

	Five years (radio edit)	3:59

EEC Polydor, LC 0309
promo

»Toiling at the Reeperbahn«

(UK-only release 6/'93)

2CD 2CD 2CD 2CD 2CD 2CD 2CD 2CD 2CD

Disc 1)	Credo	7:29
	The voyeur (I like to watch)	4:39
	Punch and Judy	6:08
	Just good friends	6:32
	Pipeline	8:32
	Out of my life	4:25
	Incubus	9:58
	Raw meat	5:51
Disc 2)	Something in the air	6:51
	Lady Nina	6:50
	The company	5:46
	Lucky	5:38
	Big wedge	8:21
	Kayleigh	4:08
	Lavender	2:43
	Heart of Lothian	3:33
	Internal exile	13:33
	incl. Market square heroes	
	incl. Roadhouse blues	

Recorded live in Hamburg, Grosse Freiheit, 23.06.1992

UK Battleside Limited, FIS001

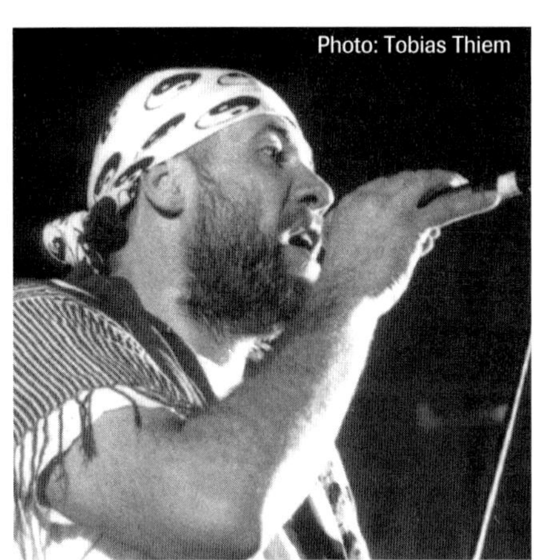
Photo: Tobias Thiem

»Pigpen's birthday«

(UK release 6/'93)

2CD 2CD 2CD 2CD 2CD 2CD 2CD 2CD 2CD

Disc 1)	The voyeur (I like to watch)	6:31
	Punch and Judy	5:17
	State of mind	6:17
	Family business	5:50
	Assassing	6:41
	The company	7:06
	Intro to Script for a jester's tear	5:34
	Script for a jester's tear	7:13
	A gentleman's excuse me	4:23
Disc 2)	Sugar mice	8:53
	Vigil in a wilderness of mirrors	9:43
	Kayleigh	4:04
	Lavender	2:22
	Heart of Lothian	4:58
	Cliche	7:20
	Big wedge	6:24
	Internal exile *	6:34

*Recorded live in London, Hammersmith Odeon, 02.04.1990, except * live in Edinburgh, Playhouse, 27.03.1990*

UK Battleside Limited, FIS002
UK Dick Bros Records, DDICK16
re-release 1996
EEC Roadrunner, RR 8684 2
release 28.10.1998, remastered
USA Griffin, GN 0831-2
USA Griffin, F 1103
250 copies in a walnut-wooden box
USA Renaissance Records, RMED 00159-2
release 24.09.1996

»Derek Dick and his amazing electric bear«

(UK release 6/'93)

2CD 2CD 2CD 2CD 2CD 2CD 2CD 2CD 2CD

Disc 1)	Vigil in a wilderness of mirrors	9:48
	Credo	7:58
	State of mind	6:57
	Tongues	8:02
	Family business	7:13
	Incubus	11:10
	Shadowplay	6:38
Disc 2)	Dear friend	7:02
	Lucky	5:22
	Big wedge	7:35
	Fugazi	8:49
	Heart of Lothian	5:36
	The company	5:20

	Forgotten sons	12:33
	Internal exile	10:17
	incl. Market square heroes	

Recorded live in Haddington, Corn Exchange, 03.11.1991 at the first convention of the Company Scotland

UK	Battleside Limited, FIS003
CAN	Griffin, GN 1031-2
USA	Griffin, GN 1031-2

»Uncle Fish and the crypt creepers«

(UK release 6/'93)

2CD 2CD 2CD 2CD 2CD 2CD 2CD 2CD 2CD

Disc 1)	Vigil in a wilderness of mirrors	9:26
	Credo	7:38
	Tongues	7:54
	Family business	6:53
	Incubus	11:21
	Shadowplay	9:17
	Dear friend	4:22
Disc 2)	The company	4:25
	Lucky	5:02
	Big wedge	6:45
	Windswept thumb/	5:07
	Heart of Lothian/Fugazi	11:49
	Internal exile	10:42
	incl. Market square heroes	
	Forgotten sons *	10:29

*Recorded live in Düsseldorf, Philipshalle, 07.12.1991, except * live in Paris, Olympia, 09.12.1991*

UK	Battleside Limited, FIS004
UK	Dick Bros Records, DDICK17CD
re-release 1996	
EEC	Roadrunner, RR 8685 2
release 28.10.1998, remastered	
USA	Griffin, GN 1032-2
USA	Renaissance Records, RMED00160-2
release 24.09.1996	

»For whom the bells toll«

(UK release 6/'93)

2CD 2CD 2CD 2CD 2CD 2CD 2CD 2CD 2CD

Disc 1)	Vigil in a wilderness of mirrors	9:08
	Credo	8:14
	Tongues	7:31
	Family business	6:16
	Incubus	15:03
	The company	9:19
	Shadowplay	6:50
Disc 2)	Shadowplay	12:44
	Dear friend	9:58
	Lucky	6:01
	Big wedge	6:32
	Heart of Lothian	5:25
	Forgotten sons	9:47
	Internal exile *	11:42
	incl. Market square heroes	

*Recorded live in Edinburgh, Playhouse, 31.12.1991, except * live in Paris, Olympia, 09.12.1991*

UK	Battleside Limited, FIS005
USA	Griffin, GN 0832-2
USA	Griffin, F1102
250 copies in a walnut-wooden box	

»Sushi«

(UK release 15.03.1994)

2CD 2CD 2CD 2CD 2CD 2CD 2CD 2CD 2CD

Disc 1)	Fearless	6:49
	Big wedge	5:33
	Boston tea party	4:14
	Credo	7:29
	Family business	5:43
	View from a hill	3:01
	He knows you know	2:43
	She chameleon	3:59
	Kayleigh	4:12
	White russian	9:19
	The company	7:10
Disc 2)	Just good friends	8:11
	Jeepster	3:54
	Hold your head up	3:08
	Lucky	5:04
	Internal exile	7:33
	Cliche	7:04
	The last straw	7:39
	Poets moon	4:13
	5 years	7:58

Recorded live in Utrecht, Vredenburg, 18.03.1993

UK	Dick Bros Records, DDICK2CD
EEC	Dick Bros Records, DDICK2CD
with promo print	
EEC	Dick Bros Records, DDICK2CD
EEC	Roadrunner, RR 8680 2
remastered, release 28.10.1998	
EEC	IRS Intercord, 991.051
JAP	Pony Canyon, PCCY-01117
USA	Renaissance Records, RMED00135-2
release 24.09.1996	

»Lady let it lie«

(UK release 05.04.1994)

12" 12" 12" 12" 12" 12" 12" 12" 12" 12" 12"

Side 1) Lady let it lie (album version) 6:53
Out of my life (Suits '94 session) 3:45
Side 2) Black canal 8:26

UK Dick Bros Records, DDICK003PIC
picture disc

CD CD CD CD CD CD CD CD CD CD CD CD

Lady let it lie (album version) 6:53
Out of my life (Suits '94 session) 3:45
Black canal 8:26
Lady let it lie 3:47
Rheinberg, 30.10.1993

UK Dick Bros Records, DDICK3CD1
digi pack
EEC Dick Bros Records, DDICK3CD1
digi pack

••

Lady let it lie (album version) 6:53
Emperor's song * 6:17
Just good friends 6:20
Utrecht, 18.03.1993
Out of my life * 3:47

** Rheinberg, 30.10.1993*

UK Dick Bros Records, DDICK3CD2
EEC Dick Bros Records, DDICK3CD2

»Suits«

(UK release 16.05.1994)

2LP 2LP 2LP 2LP 2LP 2LP 2LP 2LP 2LP 2LP

Side 1) Mr. 1470 6:05
Lady let it lie 6:53
Emperor's song 6:18
Side 2) Fortunes of war 7:51
Somebody special 5:22
No dummy 6:16
Side 3) Pipeline 6:43
Black canal • 8:27
Out of my life • 8:42
Side 4) Jumpsuit city 6:49
Bandwagon 5:07
Raw meat 7:20

• Bonus tracks

UK Dick Bros Records, DDICK4LP

LP LP LP LP LP LP LP LP LP LP LP LP LP LP

Side 1) Mr. 1470 6:05
Lady let it lie (single edit) 4:08
Emperor's song 6:18
Fortunes of war 7:51
Side 2) Somebody special 5:22
No dummy 6:16
Jumpsuit city 6:49
Raw meat (edit) 6:31

UK Dick Bros Records, DDICK4PIC
picture disc

CD CD CD CD CD CD CD CD CD CD CD CD

Mr. 1470 6:05
Lady let it lie 6:53
Emperor's song 6:18
Fortunes of war 7:51
Somebody special 5:22
No dummy 6:16
Pipeline 6:43
Jumpsuit city 6:49
Bandwagon 5:07
Raw meat 7:20

UK Dick Bros Records, DDICK4CD
first release with photobook
UK Dick Bros Records, DDICK4CD
EEC Dick Bros Records, DDICK4CD
JAP Pony Canyon, PCCY-01117
USA Renaissance Records, RMED00134
release 17.09.1996

••

Mr. 1470 6:05
Lady let it lie 6:53
Emperor's song 6:18
Fortunes of war 7:51
Somebody special 5:22
No dummy 6:16
Pipeline 6:43
Black canal • 8:27
Out of my life • 8:42
Jumpsuit city 6:49
Bandwagon 5:07
Raw meat 7:20

Remastered, • bonus tracks

EEC Roadrunner, RR 8686 2
release 28.10.1998

»Acoustic session«

(UK release 1994)

CD CD CD CD CD CD CD CD CD CD CD CD

Lucky 4:27
Internal exile 4:33
Kayleigh 4:16
Fortunes of war 6:11

Dear friend 3:46
Sugar mice 5:47
Somebody special 4:53
Jumpsuit city 4:48
Lady let it lie 5:24

A Dick Bros Records, DDICK6CDFAN
fan club-only release
A Dick Bros Records, DDICK6CDPROMO
with promo print
A Dick Bros Records, DDICK6CD
POL Metal Mind Records, PROGCD 0019
re-release
USA Renaissance Records, RMED00136
release 17.09.1996

»Fortunes of war«

(UK release 19.09.1994)

CD CD CD CD CD CD CD CD CD CD CD CD

Fortunes of war (radio edit) 3:35
Fortunes of war (single edit) 5:05
Fortunes of war 6:29
London, Mean Fiddler, 29.06.1994

UK Dick Bros Records, DDICK8CDPROMO
promo-CD, digi pack

Fortunes of war (single edit) 5:05
Somebody special 4:46
Norwich, Waterfront, 21.06.1994
State of mind 7:15
London, Mean Fiddler, 29.06.1994
Lucky 6:08
Newport, TJ's, 27.06.1994

EEC Dick Bros Records, DDICK8CD1
digi pack with space for four CDs

Fortunes of war * 6:29
Warm wet circles 6:04
Newport, TJ's, 27.06.1994
Jumpsuit city * 5:48
The company * 4:12
** Recorded live in London, Mean Fiddler, 29.06.1994*

EEC Dick Bros Records, DDICK8CD2
clear plastic sleeve with sticker

Fortunes of war (acoustic) 6:08
(session June '94)
Kayleigh * 4:29
Internal exile * 4:48
Just good friends (acoustic) 6:10
(session July '94)
** Recorded live in London, Mean Fiddler, 29.06.1994*

EEC Dick Bros Records, DDICK8CD3
clear plastic sleeve with sticker

Fortunes of war (acoustic) 6:25
(session July '94)
Sugar mice * 6:58
Dear friend * 4:02
Lady let it lie (acoustic) 5:54
(session July '94)
** Recorded live in London, Mean Fiddler, 29.06.1994*

EEC Dick Bros Records, DDICK8CD4
clear plastic sleeve with sticker

»Emperor's song«

(UK release 1994)

CD CD CD CD CD CD CD CD CD CD CD CD

Emperor's song (album version) 6:19
Fortunes of war (album version) 7:51

EEC Dick Bros Records, DDICK9CDPROMO
promo

»Yin«

(UK release 04.09.1995)

CD CD CD CD CD CD CD CD CD CD CD CD

Incommunicado ('95 re-recording) 5:08
Family business (original
album version) 5:14
Just good friends ('95 re-recording
with Sam Brown) 5:46
Pipeline (original album version) 6:55
Institution waltz ('95 recording) 4:03
Tongues (original album version) 6:17
Time and a word (original
album version) 4:22
The company (original
album version) 4:05
Incubus ('95 re-recording) 9:40
Solo (original album version) 4:10
Favourite stranger ('95 re-recording) 6:03
Boston tea party ('95 re-recording
with Alex Harvey) 4:58
Raw meat (original album version) 6:52

UK Dick Bros Records, DDICK11CDPRO
promo
UK Dick Bros Records, DDICK11CD
EEC IRS, 991.056
USA Renaissance Records, RMED00127
release 10.09.1996
RSA Dick Bros Records, DDICK11CD

»Yang«

(UK release 04.09.1995)

CD CD CD CD CD CD CD CD CD CD CD CD

Lucky ('95 re-recording)	4:55
Big wedge ('95 remix)	5:49
Lady let it lie ('95 remix)	6:56
Lavender ('95 re-recording)	4:59
Credo ('95 re-recording)	6:46
A gentleman's excuse me (original album version)	4:16
Kayleigh ('95 re-recording)	4:10
State of mind ('95 re-recording)	6:50
Somebody special ('95 re-recording)	4:23
Sugar mice ('95 re-recording)	6:19
Punch and Judy ('95 re-recording)	3:28
Fortunes of war (original albumversion)	8:08
Internal exile ('89 recording from the »Vigil...« sessions)	4:48

UK promo	Dick Bros Records, DDICK12CDPROMO
UK	Dick Bros Records, DDICK12CD
EEC	IRS, 991.055
JAP promo	Pony Canyon, PCCY 00775
JAP	Pony Canyon, PCCY 00775
RSA	Dick Bros Records, DDICK12CD
USA release 10.09.1996	Renaissance Records, RMED00128

»Yin and Yang« (fan club-only box)

CD CD CD CD CD CD CD CD CD CD CD CD

There was a limited edition box sold via "The Company Scotland" mailorder-only. This box contained a booklet with lyrics and comments by Fish about the songs of »Yin« and »Yang«. Also free with the box was the "Funny Farm Interviews" promo CD (DDICK 15CD PROMO). Inside the box was space left for the official CD issues »Yin« and »Yang«, because these CD's were not included.

»Yin and Yang« (Radio Edits)

(UK-only release 1995)

CD CD CD CD CD CD CD CD CD CD CD CD

Spoken introduction by Fish	2:10
Kayleigh	4:11
Spoken introduction by Fish	1:08
Lucky	3:30
Spoken introduction by Fish	1:11
Boston tea party	3:56
Spoken introduction by Fish	0:58
Lavender	4:17
Spoken introduction by Fish	0:45
Somebody special	3:59
Spoken introduction by Fish	1:16
Just good friends	4:11
Spoken introduction by Fish	1:08
Lady let it lie	4:06
Spoken introduction by Fish	0:57
Punch and Judy	3:29

UK promo	Dick Bros Records, DDICK13CDPROMO
UK	Dick Bros Records, DDICK13CDFAN

»Just good friends«

(UK release 14.09.1995)

CD CD CD CD CD CD CD CD CD CD CD CD

Just good friends (single edit)	3:58
Somebody special (radio edit)	3:59
State of mind (»Yang« version)	6:50

UK	Dick Bros Records, DDICK14CD1
EEC	Dick Bros Records, 5 020667214542
EEC	IRS, 977.045

Just good friends (»Yin« version)	5:46
Roadhouse blues Grenoble, Le Summum, 09.06.1995	7:14
Raw meat Lyon, Le Transbordeur, 10.06.1995	9:29

UK	Dick Bros Records, DDICK14CD2
EEC	Dick Bros Records, 5 020667201492

»The Funny Farm Interviews«

(UK-only release 9/'95)

CD CD CD CD CD CD CD CD CD CD CD CD

The concept behind Yin and Yang	2:52
The artwork, the symbols, the cover design...	2:30
Institution waltz, the early years, joining Marillion...	7:03
Signing to EMI, early influences, stage and costumes..	6:15
Derek to Fish, the nickname...	2:05
The selection of the tracks for Yin and Yang	3:40
The special guests, working with	

	other musicians...	6:30
	Personal experiences, the lyrics...	8:10
	Leaving Marillion 1988, the split...	5:54
	The litigations, Internal exile, Suits...	8:03
	Misplaced childhood, Berlin 1985...	7:22
	Re-recordings	1:30
	Progressive rock 1984, Incubus...	3:11
	Returning to Scotland 1988, the politics...	4:44
	The breaks, Lucky...	1:31
	The career curve, Songs from the mirror...	5:47
	Dick Bros Record Company, the label...	2:41

UK Dick Bros Records, DDICK15CDPROMO
cardboard sleeve

»Fish head curry«

(UK-only release 7/'96)

2CD 2CD 2CD 2CD 2CD 2CD 2CD 2CD 2CD

Disc 1)	Black canal	6:46
	Jumpsuit city	6:42
	Big wedge	4:36
	Emperor's song	5:47
	Intro: See Rome and die	2:07
	Lady let it lie	6:07
	Intro: The observer	3:56
	Vigil in the wilderness of mirrors	9:32
	Shadowplay (medley)	4:09
	Fugazi	3:20
	Slainte mhath	5:50
	Credo	7:17
Disc 2)	Intro: Where's the wine from	2:23
	Kayleigh	4:30
	Pipeline	7:32
	Incommunicado	4:18
	Internal exile	5:32
	Lucky	16:45
	Lavender	6:45

Recorded live in Luzern/Switzerland, 12.11.1995

UK Dick Bros Records, DDICK18CD
5,000 numbered copies
UK Dick Bros Records, DDICK18CD
promo with number 000

»Krakow«

(UK release 8/'96)

2CD 2CD 2CD 2CD 2CD 2CD 2CD 2CD 2CD

Disc 1)	Black canal	7:04
	Jumpsuit city	4:59
	Big wedge	6:07
	Emperor's song	7:06
	Lady let it lie	6:18
	Vigil in a wilderness of mirrors	9:10
	Shadowplay (medley)	4:03
	Fugazi	3:21
	Slainte mhath	4:54
Disc 2)	Credo	10:23
	Kayleigh	4:43
	Pipeline	7:17
	Incommunicado	4:24
	Internal exile	5:29
	Lucky	15:48
	Lavender	7:00
	Boston tea party	5:49

Recorded live in Krakow/ Poland, 11.10.1995

UK Dick Bros Records, DDICK19CD
EEC Roadrunner, RR 8681 2
release 28.10.1998, remastered
USA Renaissance Records, REMD00166-2
release 10.09.1996

••

Big wedge (fade in)	1:24
Big wedge	4:44
Emperor's song	6:18
Lady let it lie (intro chat)	0:47
Lady let it lie	6:20
Credo (fade in)	0:16
Credo	9:00
Kayleigh (intro chat)	0:56
Kayleigh	4:38
Applause (fade out)	0:17
Lucky	15:35
Lavender (applause fade out)	0:11
Lavender	7:03

Recorded live in Krakow/ Poland, 11.10.1995

UK Dick Bros Records, DDICK20CDPROMO
promo

»Brother 52«

(UK release 28.04.1997)

12" 12" 12" 12" 12" 12" 12" 12" 12" 12" 12"

Side 1)	Brother 52 (stateline mix)	8:45
	Brother 52 (album version)	6:03
Side 2)	Brother 52 (dub mix)	7:05
	Brother 52 (stateline single edit)	3:40
	Brother 52 (single edit)	3:55

UK Dick Bros Records, DDICK24PIC
release 28.04.1997, picture disc

••

Side 1)	Brother 52 (stateline mix)	8:45
Side 2)	Brother 52 (dub mix)	7:05

UK Dick Bros Records, DDICK24P
white label promo

CD CD CD CD CD CD CD CD CD CD CD CD

Brother 52 (single edit)	3:55
Brother 52 (stateline single edit)	3:40
Do not walk outside this area	6:29
Brother 52 (album version)	6:03

UK Dick Bros Records, DDICK24CD1
white cover

••

Brother 52 (single edit)	3:55
Brother 52 (stateline mix)	8:45
Brother 52 (dub mix)	7:05

UK Dick Bros Records, DDICK24CD2
black cover

••

Brother 52 (single edit)	3:55

USA Viceroy/Lightyear, PRCD 3037
promo

»Sunsets on empire«

(UK release 19.05.1997)

CD CD CD CD CD CD CD CD CD CD CD CD

The perception of Johnny Punter	8:37
Goldfish and clowns	6:36
Change of heart	3:41
What colour is god?	5:50
Tara	5:12
Jungle ride	7:34
Worm in a bottle	6:24
Brother 52	6:03
Sunsets on empire	6:54
Say it with flowers	4:15

UK Dick Bros Records, DDICK25CDPROMO
promo
UK Dick Bros Records, DDICK25CD
EEC Dick Bros Records, 4844602
EEC Roadrunner, RR 8679 2
release 28.10.1998, remastered

••

The perception of Johnny Punter	8:37
Goldfish and clowns	6:36
Change of heart	3:41
What colour is god?	5:50
Tara	5:12
Jungle ride	7:34
Worm in a bottle	6:24
Brother 52	6:03
Sunsets on empire	6:54
Say it with flowers	4:15
Do not walk outside this area •	6:29

• Bonus track

JAP Pony Canyon, PCCY-01110
release 18.04.1997, remastered

••

The perception of Johnny Punter	8:37
Goldfish and clowns	6:36
Change of heart	3:41
What colour is god?	5:50
Tara	5:12
Jungle ride	7:34
Worm in a bottle	6:24
Brother 52	6:03
Sunsets on empire	6:54
Say it with flowers	4:15
Brother 52 (CD-ROM video clip) •	

• Bonus track

USA Vinceroy/Lightyear, 54197-2
release 05.06.1997, enhanced CD

CD CD CD CD CD CD CD CD CD CD CD CD

Brother 52 (single edit)	3:58
Change of heart (album version)	3:44
What colour is god? (edit)	4:08
Tara (edit)	4:04
Goldfish and clowns (radio edit)	4:13

UK Dick Bros Records, DDICK24CDPROMO
promo

2CD 2CD 2CD 2CD 2CD 2CD 2CD 2CD 2CD

Disc 1)	The perception of Johnny Punter	8:37
	Goldfish and clowns	6:36
	Change of heart	3:41
	What colour is god?	5:50
	Tara	5:12
	Jungle ride	7:34
	Worm in a bottle	6:24
	Brother 52	6:03
	Sunsets on empire	6:54
	Say it with flowers	4:15
Disc 2)	The themes behind Sunsets on empire, Yin and Yang tour…	2:45
	The concept running and comparison with Marillion…	0:50
	The album title, inspiration, artwork…	3:29
	Bosnia, Forgotten sons, war…	3:55
	Writing the album, band problems…	2:52

Musical styles, the fan base...	2:31
The recording progress and instruments...	2:52
The perception of Johnny Punter, influences...	2:04
Goldfish and clowns, images and marital problems...	1:58
Change of heart, relationships...	1:55
Classic pop songs, Kayleigh, Scottish world cup dreams...	1:25
What colour is god?, Tara, Malcolm X...	4:11
Tara, Soweto, Brasil, growing up in the sunsets...	2:38
Jungle ride, beat poetry, the watering hole...	2:41
Worm in a bottle, the sad man's Happy Birthday song...	1:27
Brother 52, grooves and loops...	2:12
Brother 52, the first live tattoo in a video...	3:36
Sunsets on empire, night of the big awakening...	1:20
Say it with flowers, sick lullabies, problems during mixing...	2:07

UK Dick Bros Records, DDICK26CD
digi pack, 15,000 copies
EEC Dick Bros Records, 4844632
digi pack, 15,000 copies

»Change of heart«

(UK-only release 11.08.1997)

CD CD CD CD CD CD CD CD CD CD CD CD

Change of heart (album version)	3:40
Goldfish and clowns (radio edit)	4:11
The perception of Johnny Punter (US radio edit)	8:37

UK Dick Bros Records, DDICK27CDPROMO
release 28.07.1997, promo
UK Dick Bros Records, DDICK27CD

»Fortunes of war«

(UK release 5/'98)

CD CD CD CD CD CD CD CD CD CD CD CD

Somebody special *	4:46
State of mind	7:15
Fortunes of war	6:29
Warm wet circles **	6:04
Jumpsuit city	5:48
The company	4:12
Kayleigh	4:29
Internal exile	4:48
Just good friends °	6:10
Sugar mice	6:58
Dear friend	4:02
Lady let it lie °	5:54
Lucky **	6:08

*Recorded live in London, Mean Fiddler, 29.06.1994, except * live in Norwich, Waterfront, 21.06.1994, ** live in Newport, TJ's, 27.06.1994, ° acoustic session July '94*

UK Dick Bros Records, DDICK30CD
EEC Roadrunner, RR 8689 2

»Tales from the big bus«

(UK release 7/'98)

2CD 2CD 2CD 2CD 2CD 2CD 2CD 2CD 2CD

Disc 1)	The perception of Johnny Punter	11:41
	What colour is god?	7:21
	Family business	6:24
	Mr. 1470	5:32
	Conversation	4:25
	Jungle ride	8:15
	Medley incl. Assassing, Credo, Tongues, Fugazi, White feather	20:25
Disc 2)	Conversation	6:25
	Cliche	8:35
	Brother 52	6:08
	Lucky	20:14
	Internal exile/The company	8:48

Recorded live in Cologne, Rhein-Rock-Hallen, 19.11.1997

UK Dick Bros Records, DDICK29CD
EEC Roadrunner, RR 8688 2
release 28.10.1998

»Kettle of Fish«

(EEC-only release 28.10.1998)

CD CD CD CD CD CD CD CD CD CD CD CD

Big wedge (original '90 version)	5:19
Just good friends ('95 »Yin« version)	5:48
Brother 52 (original '97 version)	6:06
Chasing Miss Pretty (unreleased song)	4:53
Credo (original '91 version)	6:41
A gentleman's excuse me (original '90 version)	4:20
Goldfish and clowns (original '97 version)	6:38

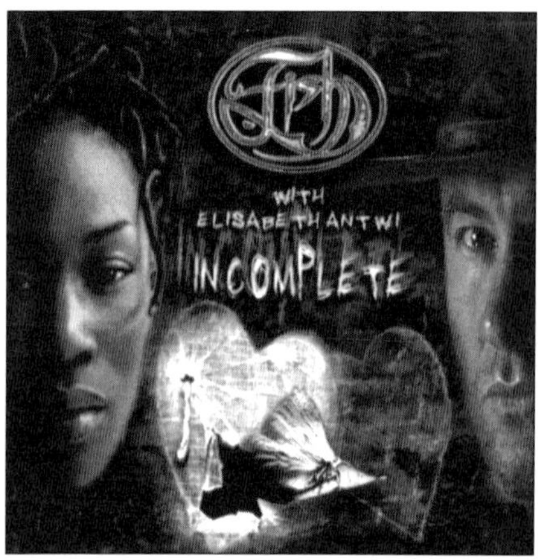

EEC cover »Incomplete« CD

	Lady let it lie ('94 single edit)	4:12
	Lucky ('95 »Yang« version)	4:58
	State of mind (original '90 version)	4:45
	Mr. Buttons (unreleased song)	4:36
	Fortunes of war (original '94 version)	7:54
	Internal exile (original '91 version)	4:41
Bonus CD-ROM •		
	This CD-ROM contains 3 video clips and back catalogue informations	

EEC — Roadrunner, RR 8678-8
first 30,000 copies + bonus CD •
EEC — Roadrunner, RRPROMO 365
promo in cardboard sleeve

»Incomplete«

(EEC-only release 22.03.1999)

CD CD CD CD CD CD CD CD CD CD CD CD

Incomplete (album version)	3:44
Wake up call (acoustic version)	3:20
Incomplete (demo version)	3:40

EEC — Roadrunner, RR2185-3
EEC — Roadrunner
CD-R, company sleeve

»Haddington convention 1998«

(UK-only release 29.03.1999)

2CD 2CD 2CD 2CD 2CD 2CD 2CD 2CD 2CD

Disc 1)	Lucky	5:43
	Mr. 1470	6:52
	Family business	6:10
	Hotel hobbies/Warm wet circles/ That time of the night	14:09
	What colour is god?	7:16
	Brother 52	6:03
	Assassing	2:27
	Credo	3:39
	Tongues	7:02
Disc 2)	Cliche	9:45
	The perception of Johnny Punter	10:22
	Kayleigh	5:51
	Lavender	6:35
	Heart of Lothian	4:16
	GI's a bun	3:45
	Worm in a bottle	10:49

Recorded live in Haddington, Corn Exchange, 30.05.1998 at "The Company Scotland" fan convention

UK — no label, D3789/D3790
2,000 copies, all signed, fan club-only

»Raingods with Zippos«

(UK release 19.04.1999)

CD CD CD CD CD CD CD CD CD CD CD CD

Tumbledown	5:52
Mission statement	4:00
Incomplete	3:44
Titled cross	4:19
Faith healer	5:01
Rites of passage	7:42
Plague of ghosts	
- Old haunts	3:13
- Digging deep	6:49
- Chocolate frogs	4:04
- Waving at stars	3:12
- Raingods dancing	4:16
- The wake up call-Make it happen	3:32

UK — Roadrunner, 386
promo in paper sleeve
UK — Roadrunner 8677-2
EEC — Roadrunner, 498 611 2
JAP — Pony Canyon, PCCY-01389
OBI, japanese lyrics, promo print around the hole of the CD
JAP — Pony Canyon, PCCY-01389
OBI, japanese lyrics

»The complete BBC sessions«

(EEC release 11.06.1999)

2CD 2CD 2CD 2CD 2CD 2CD 2CD 2CD 2CD

Disc 1)	Faithhealer	6:30

	The voyeur (I like to watch)	5:33
	Punch and Judy	5:52
	The company	4:16
	Script for a jester's tear	9:49
	Family business	6:18
	Warm wet circles	4:18
	Slainte mhath	7:03
	Vigil in a wilderness of mirrors	9:05
	Big wedge	5:55
	Fugazi	8:42
Disc 2)	Kayleigh	4:35
	Lavender	2:30
	Heart of Lothian	3:39
	Vigil in a wilderness of mirrors *	9:41
	Credo *	7:31
	Tongues *	7:09
	Incubus *	9:23
	The company *	4:02
	Big wedge *	6:29
	Internal exile *	4:34
	Market square heroes *	5:24
	Heart of Lothian *	4:57

*Recorded live in London, Town and Country Club 11.11.1989, except * recorded live in Nottingham, Royal Concert Hall, 15.11.1991*

EEC Blueprint/BBC, BP 297 CD
JAP Voiceprint, VPJ 109-110

»Issue 30«

(UK-only release 5/'00)

CD CD CD CD CD CD CD CD CD CD CD CD

Medley	10:41
- Emperor's song	
- Credo	
- What colour is god?	
- Mr. 1470	
Plague of ghosts	28:27
Medley	9:09
- Cliche	
- Perception of Johnny Punter	
Incomplete	4:40
Sunsets on empire	9:37
The company	5:39

Recorded live in Haddington, Corn Exchange, 29.08.1999 at the second night of "The Company Scotland" fan convention

UK Chocolate Frog Records, CFVP 007 CD
mailorder for "The Company"-members

»Candlelight in fog«

(UK-only release 7/'00)

2CD 2CD 2CD 2CD 2CD 2CD 2CD 2CD 2CD

Disc 1)	Faith healer	6:19
	Lucky	5:21
	Intro: American football and Jason's story	3:40
	Just good friends	6:29
	Intro: Happy birthday and Doc's memorial	4:23
	Brother 52	6:18
	Intro: Air conditioning and the fog	4:18
	Hotel hobbies	4:37
	Warm wet circles	6:20
	That time of the night	4:48
	Tumbledown	6:15
	Intro: Gas cooker rap	7:23
Disc 2)	Plague of ghosts	35:36
	- Old haunts	
	- Digging deep	
	- Chocolate frogs	
	- Waving at stars	
	- Raingods dancing	
	- The wake up call - Make it happen	
	Cliche	6:39
	The perception of Johnny Punter	3:40
	Intro: The company address	6:42
	The company	5:39
	Hotel hobbies *	4:37
	Warm wet circles *	4:19
	That time of the night *	6:17

*Recorded live in Philadelphia, Theater of Living Arts, 16.01.2000, except * live in New York City, Irving Plaza, 17.01.2000*

UK Chocolate Frog Records
mailorder-only, 3,000 copies, no number

»Acoustic sessions«

(UK-only release 06.11.2000)

2CD 2CD 2CD 2CD 2CD 2CD 2CD 2CD 2CD

Disc 1)	Lucky	4:27
	Internal exile	4:33
	Kayleigh	4:16
	Fortunes of war	6:11
	Dear friend	3:46
	Sugar mice	5:47
	Somebody special	4:53
	Jumpsuit city	4:48
	Lady let it lie	5:24
Disc 2)	Somebody special	
	Jumpsuit city	

Lady let it lie
Out of my life
State of mind
Kayleigh
Solo
The company
Lavender

UK Voiceprint/Chocolate Frog Records, CFVP006CD
Disc 1 is a remastered version of the »Acoustic session« CD (DDICK 6), disc 2 is the »Krakow« video acoustic set

»Fellini days – Radio edits«

(UK-only release 11.04.2001)

CD CD CD CD CD CD CD CD CD CD CD CD

So Fellini (radio edit)	4:13
Tiki 4 (radio edit)	4:27
Our smile (radio edit)	4:15
Tiki 4 (album version)	7:32
Our smile (album version)	5:25
What are Fellini Days? (Interview)	4:21
Writing & recording the album (Interview)	3:30
So Fellini intro (Interview)	2:20
Tiki 4 (Interview)	2:56
Our smile (Interview)	1:26
The tour (Interview)	3:23
The band (Interview)	2:14
The website/Internet (Interview)	3:08
Future plans/Acting (Interview)	2:17
Album release schedule (Interview)	2:14

UK Chocolate Frog Records
promo

»Fellini days«

(UK-only release 02.05.2001)

CD CD CD CD CD CD CD CD CD CD CD CD

3D	9:11
So Fellini	4:06
Tiki 4	7:32
Our smile	5:25
Long cold day	5:33
Dancing in the fog	5:30
Obligatory ballad	5:15
The Pilgrim's address	7:18
Clock moves sideways	7:17

UK Chocolate Frog Records, CFVP007CD

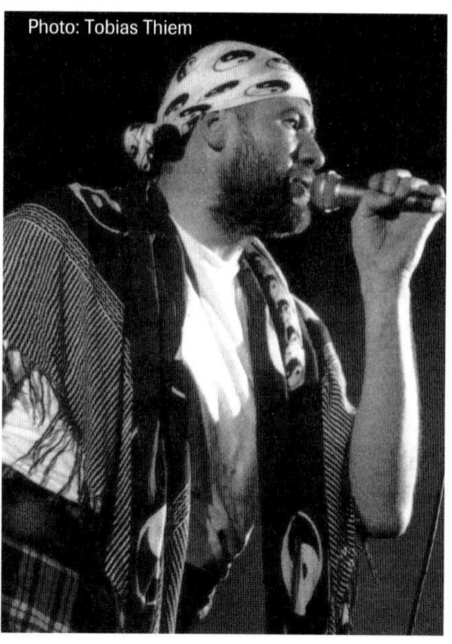
Photo: Tobias Thiem

»Sashimi«

(UK-only release 03.05.2001)

2CD 2CD 2CD 2CD 2CD 2CD 2CD 2CD 2CD

Disc 1)	Faithhealer	5:09
	Lucky	6:04
	Just good friends	6:18
	Brother 52	6:32
	Goldfish and clowns	8:13
	Hotel hobbies	4:22
	Warm wet circles	4:19
	That time of the night	6:18
	Tumbledown	5:49
	Intro: Riff Raff – the wine waiter	1:37
Disc 2)	Plague of ghosts	28:42
	i) Old haunts	
	ii) Digging deep	
	iii) Chocolate frogs	
	iv) Waving at stars	
	v) Raingods dancing	
	vi) Wake-up call (Make it happen)	
	Cliche	7:04
	The perception of Johnny Punter	3:21
	Sunsets on empire	10:11
	The company	5:35

Recorded live in Poznan, Zamek Centre of Culture, 03.10.1999

UK Chocolate Frog Records, CFVP008CD
mailorder-only

Projects with Fish

Various Artists - Soundtrack from the film »Quicksilver«

(UK release 1986)

LP LP LP LP LP LP LP LP LP LP LP LP LP LP

Side 1) ROGER DALTREY - Quicksilver lightning 4:45
FIONA - Casual thing 3:42
PETER FRAMPTON - Nothing at all 4:10
Fish + TONY BANKS - Short cut to somewhere * 3:35
J.PARR + M.MARTIN - Lovesong (Quicksilver) 4:04
Side 2) R.PARKER JR. + H.TERRY - One sunny day 4:04
LARRY J. MCNALLY - The motown song 3:50
Suite streets from Quicksilver 2:39
TONY BANKS - Quicksilver suite I. 6:31
TONY BANKS - Quicksilver suite II. 2:44

** Fish on vocals*

UK Atlantic
ARG Atlantic, 80003
JAP
USA Atlantic, 81631-1-E

CD CD CD CD CD CD CD CD CD CD CD CD

ROGER DALTREY - Quicksilver lightning 4:45
FIONA - Casual thing 3:42
PETER FRAMPTON - Nothing at all 4:10
Fish + TONY BANKS - Short cut to somewhere * 3:35
J.PARR + M.MARTIN - Lovesong (Quicksilver) 4:04
R.PARKER JR. + H.TERRY - One sunny day 4:04
LARRY J. MCNALLY - The motown song 3:50
Suite streets from Quicksilver 2:39
TONY BANKS - Quicksilver suite I. 6:31
TONY BANKS - Quicksilver suite II. 2:44

** Fish on vocals*

USA Atlantic, 81631-2

TONY BANKS

»Soundtracks«

(UK release 6/'86)

LP LP LP LP LP LP LP LP LP LP LP LP LP LP

Side 1) Short cut to somewhere * 3:35
Smilin' Jack Casey 3:12
Rebirth 2:56
Gypsy 3:36
Final chase 2:44
You call this victory 5:12
Side 2) Lion of symmetry 7:18
Redwing 5:34
Lorca 3:47
Kid and detective Droid 2:07
Lift off 3:04
Death of Abby 1:38

** Fish on vocals*

UK Charisma, CAS 1173
EEC Charisma/Virgin, 207 761-620

CD CD CD CD CD CD CD CD CD CD CD CD

Short cut to somewhere * 3:35
Smilin' Jack Casey 3:12
Rebirth 2:56
Gypsy 3:36
Final chase 2:44
You call this victory 5:12
Lion of symmetry 7:18
Redwing 5:34
Lorca 3:47
Kid and detective Droid 2:07
Lift off 3:04
Death of Abby 1:38

** Fish on vocals*

UK Charisma, CASCD 1173

Fish + TONY BANKS

»Shortcut to somewhere«

(UK release 13.10.1986)

7" 7" 7" 7" 7" 7" 7" 7" 7" 7" 7" 7" 7" 7" 7" 7"

Side 1) Short cut to somewhere * 3:38
Side 2) Smilin' Jack Casey 3:13

** Fish on vocals*

UK Charisma, CB 426

Side 1) Short cut to somewhere * 3:38
Side 2) - not playable -

** Fish on vocals*

UK Charisma/Townhouse, CB 426
one-sided white label test pressing, 19.09.1986

Side 1) Short cut to somewhere * 3:38
Side 2) Short cut to somewhere * 3:38

** Fish on vocals*

USA Atlantic, 7-89339
promo, no ps, 1986

12" 12" 12" 12" 12" 12" 12" 12" 12" 12" 12"

Side 1) Short cut to somewhere * 3:38
Side 2) Smilin' Jack Casey 3:13
K 2 3:56
** Fish on vocals*

UK Charisma, CB 426-12
promo
UK Charisma, CB 426-12

The Anti-Heroin Project

»Live-in world«

(UK release 10/'86)

7" 7" 7" 7" 7" 7" 7" 7" 7" 7" 7" 7" 7" 7" 7" 7"
Side 1) Live-in world 4:07
(additional vocals by Fish)
Side 2) Something better 4:12

UK EMI, AHP 1
EEC EMI, 1A 006-20 1525 7
EEC EMI, 1C 006-20 1525 7

12" 12" 12" 12" 12" 12" 12" 12" 12" 12" 12"
Side 1) Live-in world 4:07
(additional vocals by Fish)
On the street
Side 2) Something better 4:12
You know it makes sense

UK EMI, 12 AHP 1
EEC EMI, 1A K060-201524 6
EEC EMI, 1C K060-201524 6

»It's a Live-in world«

(UK release 11/'86)

2LP 2LP 2LP 2LP 2LP 2LP 2LP 2LP 2LP 2LP
Side 1) Lizzy Welch and the Anti-Smack Band – Smack 3:37
Sarah Miles – Cold turkey 1:29
Chris Sutton – Hot line 3:36
Elvis Costello – The end of the rainbow 3:15
The Anti-Heroin Project – Live-in world (additional vocals by Fish) 4:12
Bonnie Tyler – It's not easy 4:11
Jonno & Dennis – Don't use drugs 3:12
The Icicle Works/Pete Wylie – The needle and the damage done 2:33
Side 2) Charley Foskett – Freak street 1:26
Charley Foskett – Scagg
Hayley Mills/Dave Evans – Suspended pool 5:33
P.Wilson/K.Wilde/D.Pandy/ B.Whitlock – Something better 4:15
Ringo Starr – You know it makes sense 2:00
Precious Wilson – Waiting in the dark 4:00
Dave Stewart/Barbara Gaskin – The world spins so slow 4:44
Holly Johnson – Slay the dragon 3:22
Side 3) Paul McCartney – Simple as that 4:15
John Cleese/Bill Oddie/Ringo Starr – Naughty atom bomb 3:00
Chris Rea – Candles 4:40
Boon (Level 42) – Head full of shadows 3:54
Eurythmics – Aqua 4:36
Saxon – We came here to rock 4:20
New Model Army – Heroin 4:14
Side 4) Howard Jones – Little bit of snow 4:25
Feargal Sharkey – Never never (live) 3:36
Bananarama – Hooked on love 3:48
Dire Straits – The man's too strong 4:26
Wham – Blue (armed with love) (live in China) 3:53
Bucks Fizz – Magical 4:30
John Parr – She's gonna love ya to death 3:43

UK EMI, AHP LP 1
foc
EEC EMI, 240669-3
label yellow, foc

Artists By Nature

»Spirit of the forest«

(UK release 1989)

7" 7" 7" 7" 7" 7" 7" 7" 7" 7" 7" 7" 7" 7" 7" 7"
Track 1: "Spirit of the forest" 4:53
(additional vocals by Fish)

UK Virgin, VS 1191

12" 12" 12" 12" 12" 12" 12" 12" 12" 12" 12"
Track 1: "Spirit of the forest" 4:53
(additional vocals by Fish)

USA Virgin, 09655-1

Rock against Repatriation

»Sailing«

(UK release 16.02.1990)

7" 7" 7" 7" 7" 7" 7" 7" 7" 7" 7" 7" 7" 7" 7" 7"

Side 1) Sailing (vocal) 4:12
(additional vocals by Fish)
Side 2) Sailing (instrumental) 4:14

UK I.R.S., EIRS 139
USA I.R.S., IRS 40

Side 1) Sailing (vocal) 4:12
(additional vocals by Fish)
Side 2) – not playable –

UK Audio 1, 01-734 9901
one sided acetate

CD CD CD CD CD CD CD CD CD CD CD CD

Sailing (vocal) 4:12
(additional vocals by Fish)
Sailing (instrumental) 4:14

UK I.R.S., EIRSCD 139
USA I.R.S., IRSCD 40
3" CD

Various Artists »El Dorado – Saving the tropical forest charity album of the WWF-Project«

(EEC-only release 1990)

LP LP LP LP LP LP LP LP LP LP LP LP LP LP

Side 2, track 2 "Spirit of the forest" (5:18)
(additional vocals by Fish)

EEC CBS, 466324 1
postcard, booklet

The Scottish World Cup Squad and Friends

»Say it with pride«

(UK-only release 6/'90)

7" 7" 7" 7" 7" 7" 7" 7" 7" 7" 7" 7" 7" 7" 7" 7"

Side 1) Say it with pride 3:27
(additional vocals by Fish)
Side 2) Rise up 3:30

UK RCA, PB 43791

10" 10" 10" 10" 10" 10" 10" 10" 10" 10" 10"

Side 1) Say it with pride 3:32
(additional vocals by Fish)
Side 2) – not playable –

UK Copymasters, PB 43791
one-sided metal acetate

12" 12" 12" 12" 12" 12" 12" 12" 12" 12" 12"

Side 1) Say it with pride 3:27
(additional vocals by Fish)
Side 2) Rise up 3:30
Say it with pride (tartan version)
(additional vocals by Fish)

UK RCA, PB 43792

Tony Banks

»Still«

(UK release 31.05.1991)

LP LP LP LP LP LP LP LP LP LP LP LP LP LP

Side 1) Red day on blue street 5:48
Angel face * 5:16
The gift 3:49
Still it takes me by surprise 6:25
Hero for an hour 4:52
Side 2) I wanna change the score 4:27
Water out of wine 4:37
Another murder of a day * 9:02
Back to back 4:30
The final curtain 5:07

** Fish on vocals*

UK Virgin, V 2658
EEC Virgin, 211 638

CD CD CD CD CD CD CD CD CD CD CD CD

Red day on blue street 5:48
Angel face * 5:16
The gift 3:49
Still it takes me by surprise 6:25
Hero for an hour 4:52
I wanna change the score 4:27
Water out of wine 4:37
Another murder of a day * 9:02
Back to back 4:30
The final curtain 5:07

** Fish on vocals*

UK Virgin, CDV 2658
EEC Virgin, 261 638
JAP Virgin, VJCP-28041
promo
JAP Virgin, VJCP-28041

»Angel face«

(USA-only release 18.07.1990)

CD CD CD CD CD CD CD CD CD CD CD CD

	Angel face (radio version) *	4:38
	Angel face (album version) *	5:16

* *Fish on vocals*

USA — Giant Records, CDPRO-5308
promo-only

Jeff Wayne

»Musical version of Spartacus«

(EEC-only release 9/'92)

2CD 2CD 2CD 2CD 2CD 2CD 2CD 2CD 2CD

Disc 1)	Destiny	5:26
	Animal and man I.	7:26
	Animal and man II.	8:27
	For all time	7:21
	Whispers	6:20
	(spoken words by Fish)	
	The eagle & the hawk	15:28
Disc 2)	Going home	7:59
	The parting of the ways *	7:09
	We carry on	8:23
	Trust me	7:22
	Two souls with a single dream	8:14
	The last battle	8:46
	The appian way	9:44
	Epilogue I.	1:04
	Epilogue II.	1:51

* *Fish on vocals*

EEC — Columbia, 472 030-2

The Rainforest Project

»Earthrise«

(EEC-only release 10/'92)

LP LP LP LP LP LP LP LP LP LP LP LP LP LP

Track 15: "Spirit of the forest" 4:53
(additional vocals by Fish)

EEC — Polydor, 515 561-1

CD CD CD CD CD CD CD CD CD CD CD CD

Track 15: "Spirit of the forest" 4:53
(additional vocals by Fish)

EEC — Polydor, 515 561-2

Sciennes Primary Children

»Better world«

(UK-only release summer 1993)

CD CD CD CD CD CD CD CD CD CD CD CD

Better world *	3:59
Better world (instrumental)	4:12

* *Fish on vocals*

UK — Bruces Records, VOSTOK CD 3

The Funny Farm Project

»Outpatients '93«

(UK release 11/'93)

CD CD CD CD CD CD CD CD CD CD CD CD

Fish and Steve Howe – Time and a word	4:25
Dream Disciples – Mark 13	4:32
One Eternal – One love	4:02
Joyriders – Don't ask me	5:19
Fish – The seeker	3:17
Guaranteed Pure – Swing your bag	3:09
Avalon – Travellers tales	5:35
Fish – Out of my life (acoustic)	3:47
Joyriders – Best friend	5:24
Dream Disciples – Dream is dead	4:00

UK — Fishy Records, FishyCD 1
first edition of 7,000 copies, released November 93, 1,000 numbered and signed with golden "Company Scotland" print; 1,000 numbered including 200 signed with golden "Company Holland" print; 500 numbered including 200 signed with golden "Company Germany" print; 4,500 regular copies, not numbered or signed, without print
A — Fishy Records, FishyCD 1
UK — Dick Bros, DDick 1 CD
re-release
USA — Renaissance Records, RMED 00158
re-release 17.09.1996

Gomorrah

»Reflections of inanimate matter«

(UK release autumn 1994)

CD CD CD CD CD CD CD CD CD CD CD CD

Human trophies 6:43
(Fish speaks a few lines in that song)

UK Megapulse Records, MEGAP CD 1
EEC Black Market productions, BMCD 67

Scotia Nostra

»Scotland by our side«

(UK-only release 01.06.1998)

CD CD CD CD CD CD CD CD CD CD CD CD

Scotland by our side 4:19
Lucky (re-recorded version 1995) * 4:54
** Fish on vocals*

UK SNCD 001

Various Artists »Scottish world cup anthems«

(UK-only release 6/'98)

CD CD CD CD CD CD CD CD CD CD CD CD

Track 12: "Say it with pride"
(World Cup Squad 1992) 3:27
(additional vocals by Fish)

UK Cherry Red Records, CD GAFFER 26

Various Artists »The tartan army«

(UK-only release 6/'98)

CD CD CD CD CD CD CD CD CD CD CD CD

Track 9: "Say it with pride"
(World Cup Squad 1992) 3:27
(additional vocals by Fish)

UK TVD Entertainment, TV CD 2

Ayreon

»Into the electric castle«

(EEC release 05.09.1998)

2CD 2CD 2CD 2CD 2CD 2CD 2CD 2CD 2CD

Disc 1) Welcome to a new dimension 3:05
Isis and Osiris * 11:11
Amazing flight 10:15
Time beyond time 6:05
The decision tree (We're alive) * 6:24
Tunnel of light * 4:05
Across the rainbow bridge 6:20
Disc 2) The garden of emotions 6:40
Valley of the queens 2:25
The castle hall 5:49
Tower of hope 4:54
Cosmic fusion 7:27
The mirror maze 6:34
** Fish on vocals*

EEC Transmission Records, TM 14
JAP VICP 60478/9
OBI, promo, japanese lyrics
JAP VICP 60478/9
OBI, japanese lyrics

T 42 & Friends

»This big wonderful night«

(LUX-only release 16.12.2000)

CD CD CD CD CD CD CD CD CD CD CD CD

Hello, hello, hello, goodbye & Here we are again/The further we stretch
Alex
Oranges
Saxon street
Call you tomorrow
Marie-Anne
The company (with Fish and Marcus Kuffer from No Name on vocals)
Broomielaw *
Friends in low places
Great song of indifference
Roadhouse blues (with Fish, Ezio and Booga on vocals)
Stay with me (with Fish, Tara, Ezio and Booga on vocals)

*Recorded live in Dudelange (Luxembourg), Fete de la Musique, 17.06.2000, * Fish on vocals*

LUX T42, CD-08
private release

Discography of other Marillion Members

Steve Hogarth Steve Hogarth Steve Hogarth

Born 14.05.1956 in Kendal/England.

His first band in 1976 was The last Call. He did his first recording with Harlow in 1978. Steve joined the Europeans in spring 1981. They worked with John Otway in 1982, he also was a founding member of How we Live in 1986.

Being a session musician between 1983 and 1987, he played with The The , Julian Cope, Do-Re-Mi, Annabel Lamb, Blue Yonder, Toni Childs and Sharon O'Neill.

Steve Hogarth joined Marillion officially on the 02.02.1989.

Under the name of H he did some solo work in 1997 followed by guest appearances with John Wesley, Chucho Merchan and Ange in 1998.

Steve wurde am 14.05.1956 in Kendal/England geboren.

Seine erste Band, The last Call, hatte er im Jahre 1976, seine erste Plattenaufnahme folgte 1978 mit Harlow. Im Frühling 1981 wurde Steve Mitglied der Europeans. Die Band arbeitete 1982 u.a. mit John Otway zusammen. Außerdem war er Gründungsmitglied von How we Live 1986.

Als Session-Musiker arbeitete Steve zwischen 1983 und 1987 mit The The , Julian Cope, Do-Re-Mi, Annabel Lamb, Blue Yonder, Toni Childs und Sharon O'Neill zusammen.

Steve Hogarth wurde offizieller Sänger bei Marillion am 02.02.1989.

Unter dem Namen H machte er 1997 eine Solo-CD und sang 1998 als Gast bei John Wesley, Chucho Merchan und Ange.

Steve as a Band Member

Harlow

»Harry de Mazzio«

(UK-only release 8/'78-9/'78)

7" 7" 7" 7" 7" 7" 7" 7" 7" 7" 7" 7" 7" 7" 7"

Side 1) Harry de Mazzio 2:38
Side 2) Nothing to you 2:10

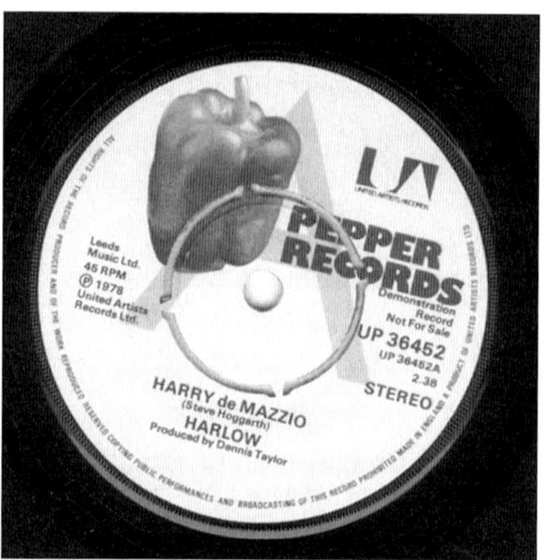

UK label »Harry de Mazzio« promo 7"

UK Pepper, UP 36452
demo sample, no ps, Steve's name is spelled "Hoggarth" on the label

John Otway

»All balls and no Willy«

(UK-only release 1982)

LP LP LP LP LP LP LP LP LP LP LP LP LP LP

Side 1) In dreams
Too much air, not enough oxygen
Telex
Montreal
Baby, it's the real thing
Turn off your dream (don't watch the nightmare)
Side 2) Mass communication
House is burning
Halloween
Nothing's gone (except no. 1)
Middle of winter (original version)

UK Empire Records, HAMLP 1

CD CD CD CD CD CD CD CD CD CD CD CD

In dreams
Too much air, not enough oxygen
Telex
Montreal
Baby, it's the real thing
Turn off your dream (don't watch the nightmare)
Mass communication

House is burning
Halloween
Nothing's gone (except no. 1)
Middle of winter (original version)

Some bonus tracks included, without the EUROPEANS

UK The music cooperation, TMC 9605
re-release 1996

»In dreams«

(UK-only release 1982)

7" 7" 7" 7" 7" 7" 7" 7" 7" 7" 7" 7" 7" 7" 7" 7"

Side 1) In dreams 2:44
Side 2) You ain't seen nothing yet

UK Empire Records, HAM 3

»Mass communication«

(UK-only release 1983)

7" 7" 7" 7" 7" 7" 7" 7" 7" 7" 7" 7" 7" 7" 7" 7"

Side 1) Mass communication 3:24
Side 2) Baby it's the real thing 3:20

UK Empire Records, HAM 6

EUROPEANS

»The animal song«

(UK release 9/'82)

7" 7" 7" 7" 7" 7" 7" 7" 7" 7" 7" 7" 7" 7" 7" 7"

Side 1) The animal song 3:28
Side 2) Someone's changing 3:42

UK A+M, AMS 8245
A-label promo, company sleeve
UK A+M, AMS 8245
EEC A+M, AMS 9239
ESP A+M, AMS 9239
one-sided promo with ps

12" 12" 12" 12" 12" 12" 12" 12" 12" 12" 12"

Side 1) The animal song
(Cross country version) 7:00
Side 2) The animal song 3:49
Someone's changing 3:42

UK A+M, AMSX 8245
EEC A+M, AMS 12.9239
ESP A+M, AMS 12.9239
"super single"

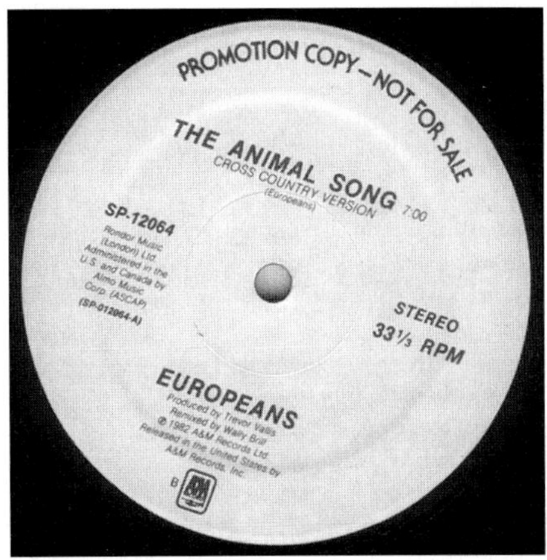

US label »The animal song« promo 12"

USA A+M, SP-12064
white label promo, no ps

»A.E.I.O.U.«

(UK release 7/'83)

7" 7" 7" 7" 7" 7" 7" 7" 7" 7" 7" 7" 7" 7" 7" 7"

Side 1) A.E.I.O.U. 3:40
Side 2) Voice on the telephone 3:36

UK A+M, AM 113
promo
UK A+M, AM 113
ESP A+M, AMS 9708
different backcover (with lyrics), golden promo stamp on cover
ESP A+M, AMS 9708
different backcover (with lyrics)

12" 12" 12" 12" 12" 12" 12" 12" 12" 12" 12"

Side 1) A.E.I.O.U. (alphabet soup) 6:09
Side 2) Voice on the telephone 3:36
A.E.I.O.U. (album version) 3:40

UK A+M, AMX 113
ESP A+M, AMS 12.9708
"super single"

»Recognition«

(UK release 8/'83)

7" 7" 7" 7" 7" 7" 7" 7" 7" 7" 7" 7" 7" 7" 7" 7"

Side 1) Recognition 3:25
Side 2) New industry 3:06

UK A+M, AM 138
A-label promo with ps
UK, A+M, AM 138
EEC A+M, AMS 9714
different cover

12" 12" 12" 12" 12" 12" 12" 12" 12" 12" 12"

Side 1) Recognition (New York Dance Mix) 5:20
Side 2) Recognition (English Dance Mix) 7:08

UK A+M, AMX 138

••

Side 1) Recognition 3:25
Side 2) The animal song 3:49
A.E.I.O.U. 3:40

EEC A+M, AMS 12.9714
different cover

••

Side 1) Recognition (English Mix) 7:08
Side 2) Recognition (American Mix) 5:20

USA A+M, SP-17248
white label promo, no ps

Mini-LP Mini-LP Mini-LP Mini-LP Mini-LP

Side 1) A.E.I.O.U. 4:00
Recognition 4:15
Innocence 3:56
Side 2) Spirit of youth 3:35
American people 3:35
Kingdom come * 6:10

* *Lead vocals by Steve Hogarth*

USA A+M, SP-12502
golden promo stamp on cover
USA A+M, SP-12502
release 10/'83

»Vocabulary«

(UK release 10/'83)

LP LP LP LP LP LP LP LP LP LP LP LP LP LP

Side 1) The animal song 3:50
A.E.I.O.U. 4:00
Voice on the telephone 3:43
American people 3:10
Falling 5:20
Side 2) Recognition 3:35
Innocence 4:00
Spirit of youth 3:34
Modern homes 3:21
Kingdom come * 6:00

* *Lead vocals by Steve Hogarth*

UK A+M, AMLX 68558
lyric sheet
EEC A+M, AMLX 68558
lyric sheet
NZ A+M, L 38148

»American people«

(UK-only release 11/'83)

7" 7" 7" 7" 7" 7" 7" 7" 7" 7" 7" 7" 7" 7" 7" 7"

Side 1) American people 3:10
Side 2) Going to work (long version) 6:08

UK A+M, AM 158
A-label promo with ps
UK A+M, AM 158

12" 12" 12" 12" 12" 12" 12" 12" 12" 12" 12"

Side 1) American people 3:10
Going to work (long version) 6:08
Side 2) Someone's changing 3:42
New industry 3:06

UK A+M, AMX 158

»Europeans Live«

(UK release 24.01.1984)

LP LP LP LP LP LP LP LP LP LP LP LP LP LP

Side 1) Typical 3:16
American people 3:23
Joining dots * 4:22
Innocence 3:28
Spirit of youth 5:38
Going to work * 5:02
Side 2) A.E.I.O.U. 5:00
The animal song 5:30
Tunnel vision * 5:20
Falling 7:00

*Recorded live in London, 15./16.12.1983, * lead vocals by Steve Hogarth*

UK A+M, SCOT 1
white label test pressing, no ps
UK A+M, SCOT 1
golden promo stamp on cover, pink writing on spine
UK A+M, SCOT 1
red writing on spine
UK A+M, SCOT 1
white writing on spine
ESP A+M, AMNP 193

»Animal song«

(ESP-only release 1984)

7" 7" 7" 7" 7" 7" 7" 7" 7" 7" 7" 7" 7" 7" 7" 7"

Side 1)	Animal song	5:30
Side 2)	American people	3:23

Recorded live in London, 15./16.12.1983

ESP — A+M
promo, no number

»Typical «

(UK-only release 2/'84)

7" 7" 7" 7" 7" 7" 7" 7" 7" 7" 7" 7" 7" 7" 7" 7"

Side 1)	Typical	3:16
Side 2)	Falling	7:00

UK — A+M, AM 184
A-label promo with ps
UK — A+M, AM 184

»Listen«

(UK-only release 1984)

7" 7" 7" 7" 7" 7" 7" 7" 7" 7" 7" 7" 7" 7" 7" 7"

Side 1)	Listen *	3:50
Side 2)	Climb the wall	3:45

** Lead vocals by Steve Hogarth*

UK — A+M, AM 201
A-label promo with ps
UK — A+M, AM 201

12" 12" 12" 12" 12" 12" 12" 12" 12" 12" 12"

Side 1)	Listen *	3:56
Side 2)	Climb the wall (extended version)	6:06

** Lead vocals by Steve Hogarth*

UK — A+M, AMX 201
clear vinyl

»Recurring dreams«

(UK release 30.10.1984)

LP LP LP LP LP LP LP LP LP LP LP LP LP LP

Side 1)	1001 arguments	4:15
	Home town	5:23
	Burning inside you *	4:43
	You don't want me (in your life) *	5 : 1
Side 2)	Writing for survival *	4:58
	Love has let me down	4:14
	Don't give your heart to anybody *	5:57
	Acid rain *	6:24

** Lead vocals by Steve Hogarth*

UK — A+M, AMA 5034
white label test pressing, no ps
UK — A+M, AMA 5034
EEC — A+M, AMA 5034
EEC — A+M, AMA 5034
with promo sticker

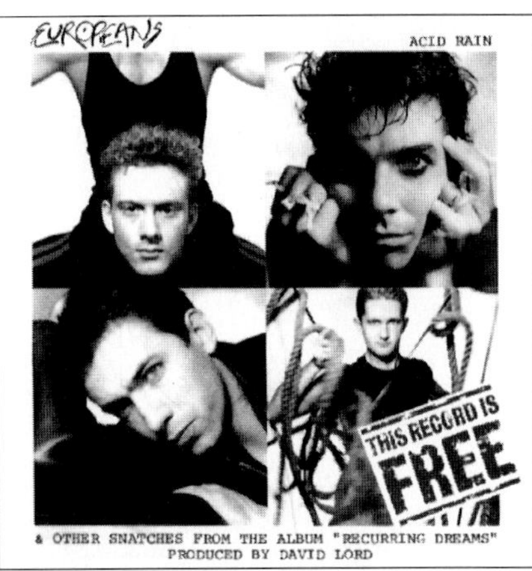

UK cover »Acid rain« promo 7"

»Acid rain«

(UK promo release only 1984)

7" 7" 7" 7" 7" 7" 7" 7" 7" 7" 7" 7" 7" 7" 7" 7"

Side 1)	Acid rain	6:24
Side 2)	Edits from: 1001 arguments/ Burning inside you/Home town	3:29

UK — A+M, FREE 1
promo with ps

»You don't want me (in your life)«

(EEC promo release only19.11.1984)

12" 12" 12" 12" 12" 12" 12" 12" 12" 12" 12"

Side 1)	You don't want me (in your life) (remixed)	6:19
Side 2)	Burning inside you	4:44

EEC — A+M, SAMP 86
promo

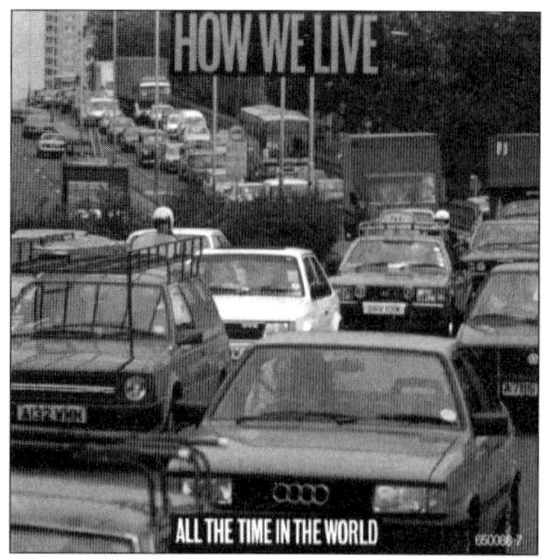

UK cover »All the time in the world« 7" version 1

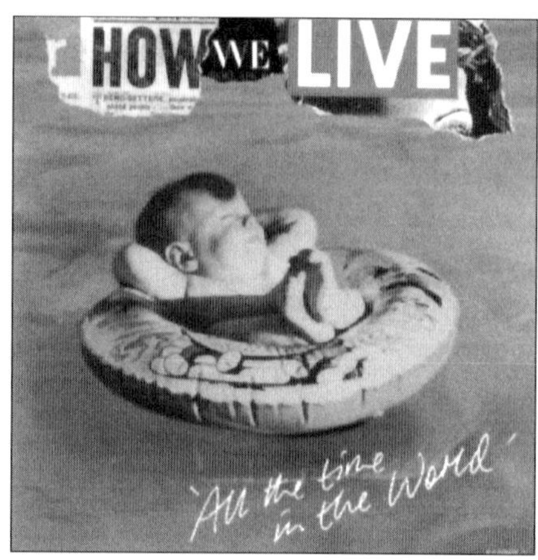

UK cover »All the time in the world« 7" version 2

HOW WE LIVE

»Working town«

(UK-only release 07.07.1986)

7" 7" 7" 7" 7" 7" 7" 7" 7" 7" 7" 7" 7" 7" 7" 7"

Side 1)	Working town	3:43
Side 2)	India	5:03

UK — Portrait, A 7290

12" 12" 12" 12" 12" 12" 12" 12" 12" 12" 12"

Side 1)	Working town	3:43
Side 2)	India	5:03

UK — Portrait, TA 7290

»All the time in the world«

(UK release 1986)

7" 7" 7" 7" 7" 7" 7" 7" 7" 7" 7" 7" 7" 7" 7" 7"

Side 1)	All the time in the world	3:51
Side 2)	Lost at sea	4:22

UK — Portrait, 650088-7
first release with "traffic" sleeve

••

Side 1)	All the time in the world	3:51
Side 2)	Lost at sea	4:22

+ Free promo tape (Portrait XPC 650088)

	Interview with Phil Ward-Large	6:38
	Working town	3:43
	Interview with Phil Ward-Large	4:28

UK — Portrait, 650088-7
re-release with blue "baby" sleeve + free tape

12" 12" 12" 12" 12" 12" 12" 12" 12" 12" 12"

Side 1)	All the time in the world (12" mix)	6:11
Side 2)	All the time in the world (7" version)	3:51
	Lost at sea	4:22

UK — Portrait, 650088-6
first release with "highway view from inside a car" sleeve
UK — Portrait, 650088-6
re-release with red "baby" sleeve April 1987
EEC — Portrait, PRT 650088-6
release 1987 with "highway view from inside a car"-sleeve

»Dry land«

(UK release 1/'87)

LP LP LP LP LP LP LP LP LP LP LP LP LP LP

Side 1)	Working girl	3:57
	All the time in the world	4:46
	Dry land	4:34
	Games in Germany	4:30
	India	5:03
Side 2)	The rainbow room	5:12
	Lost at sea	4:22
	In the city	5:32
	Working town	3:43
	A beat in the heart	4:27

UK — Portrait, PRT 450618
white label test pressing

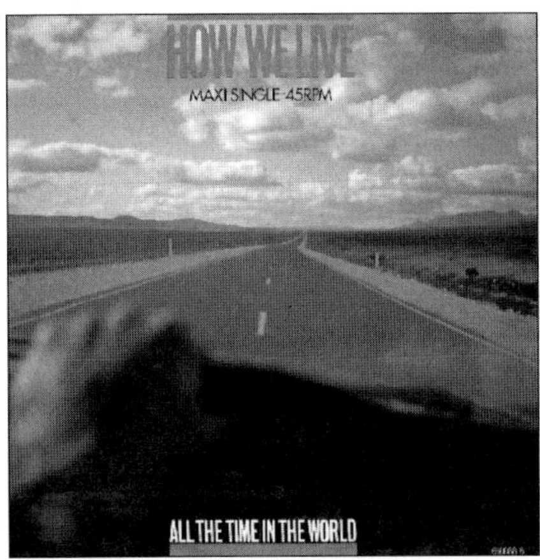

UK cover »All the time in the world« 12"

UK — Portrait, PRT 450618 1
ois, with golden promo stamp on cover
UK — Portrait, PRT 450618 1
ois
NL — Portrait, PRT 450618 1
ois

CD CD CD CD CD CD CD CD CD CD CD CD

Working girl	3:57
All the time in the world	4:46
Dry land	4:34
Games in Germany	4:30
India	5:03
The rainbow room	5:12
Lost at sea	4:22
In the city	5:32
Working town	3:43
A beat in the heart	4:27
You don't need anyone	4:45
Simon's car	4:46

UK — Portrait, PRT 450618 2
UK — Racket Records, RACKET 13
re-release 08.08.2000

»Games in Germany«

(UK-only release 1987)

7" 7" 7" 7" 7" 7" 7" 7" 7" 7" 7" 7" 7" 7" 7" 7"

Side 1) Games in Germany — 4:30
Side 2) Lost at sea — 4:22

UK — Portrait, PRT 650956 7

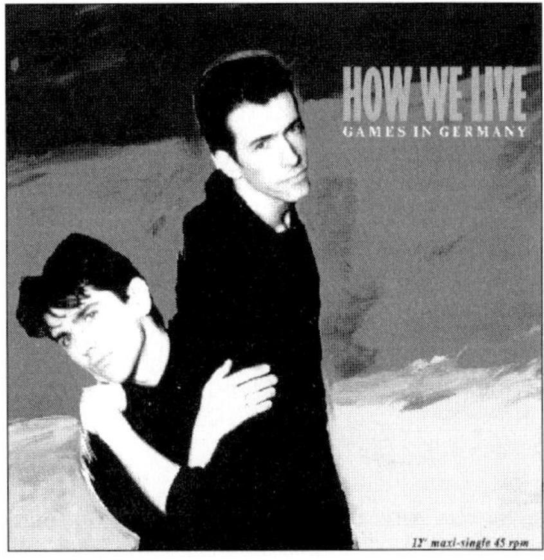

UK cover »Games in Germany« 12"

12" 12" 12" 12" 12" 12" 12" 12" 12" 12" 12"

Side 1) Games in Germany — 4:30
Side 2) Lost at sea — 4:22
India — 5:03

UK — Portrait, PRT 650956 6

»Working girl«

(UK-only release 7/'87)

7" 7" 7" 7" 7" 7" 7" 7" 7" 7" 7" 7" 7" 7" 7" 7"

Side 1) Working girl — 4:10
Side 2) In the city — 5:32

UK — Portrait, HWL 1

12" 12" 12" 12" 12" 12" 12" 12" 12" 12" 12"

Side 1) Working girl — 4:10
Side 2) In the city — 5:32
English summer — 3:26

UK — Portrait, HWLT 1

H

»Ice cream genius«

(UK release 05.11.1996)

CD CD CD CD CD CD CD CD CD CD CD CD

The evening shadows	4:27
Really like	5:19

You dinosaur thing	4:59
The deep water	7:59
Cage	7:02
Until you fall	3:55
Better dreams	7:20
Nothing to declare	6:32
The last thing *	8:15

UK Castle/Chop em out
golden CD-R, company sleeve
UK Castle, wen pr 016
promo CD with info sheet
UK Castle, wen cd 016
release 17.02.1997
USA Resurgence, RES 134 CD
re-release with different cover 25.08.1998 and bonus track *

You dinosaur thing	5:03
Cage	7:04
Nothing to declare	6:33

UK Castle, wen p 1017
promo in foc

»You dinosaur thing«

(UK-only release 03.03.1997)

CD CD CD CD CD CD CD CD CD CD CD CD

You dinosaur thing	4:16
The deep water	8:02
The last thing	8:13

UK Castle, wenx 1021

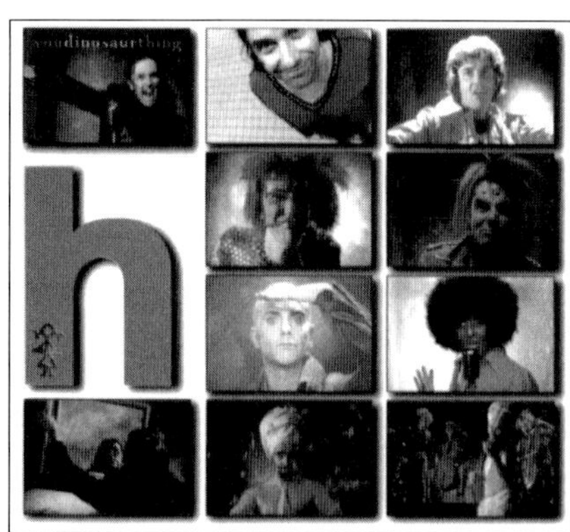

UK cover »You dinosaur thing« CD

Steve as Guest

Ange

»Grands Crus - live«

(FRA-only release 1998)

CD CD CD CD CD CD CD CD CD CD CD CD

Track 9: "Cantique (Hymne a la vie)" 4:37
(vocals by Steve Hogarth in french)

FRA PDM 04

Annabel Lamb

»Once bitten«

(EEC-only release 1983)

LP LP LP LP LP LP LP LP LP LP LP LP LP LP

Side 1)	Riders on the storm	6:00
	Once bitten	3:17
	Take me in your arms	3:27
	Heartland	3:22
	Backwards through the looking glass	3:28
Side 2)	Dividing the spoils of love (Steve plays piano)	5:12
	Hold fast (Colin Woore on guitar)	3:46
	Snake Pliskin	2:22
	Missing	4:14
	No cure	4:50

EEC A+M, AMLH 64969
EEC A+M, AMLH 68555

Blue Yonder

»Blue Yonder«

(UK release 1987)

LP LP LP LP LP LP LP LP LP LP LP LP LP LP

Side 1)	Windsong	4:11
	House of love	4:59
	When grace is falling	4:39
	In the rain	3:36
	Still I love	5:07
Side 2)	The long haul *	4:49
	Something for the pain	5:09
	Indigo	5:38
Secret miracle *		4:47

** Steve Hogarth on backing vocals*

UK	Atlantic, 781 686-1
EEC	Atlantic, 781 686-1
USA	Atlantic, 81 686-1
ois	

Chucho Merchan

»Ocean songs«

(UK-only release autumn 1998)

CD CD CD CD CD CD CD CD CD CD CD CD

Ocean blue *	5:38
Save the oceans for life on earth *	5:29
People uniting	5:02
Solito	5:15
Precious water	5:05
O'sea	3:37
Recycle	4:07
Out in the country (all vocals by Steve Hogarth)	6:07
It's a jungle out there	4:12
Mar Azul	5:38

** Additional lead vocals by Steve Hogarth*

UK, United Nations Enviroment Programme, OSCD 01

Do-Re-Mi

»Man overboard«

(GER-only release 1985)

7" 7" 7" 7" 7" 7" 7" 7" 7" 7" 7" 7" 7" 7" 7"

Side 1)	Man overboard	3:42
Side 2)	Fishtank	2:51

GER	Virgin, 107 609-100

12" 12" 12" 12" 12" 12" 12" 12" 12" 12" 12"

Side 1)	Man overboard	3:42
	Idiot grin	3:17
Side 2)	Warnings moving clockwise	3:53
	Fishtank	2:51

GER	Virgin, 602 006-213

»Domestic harmony«

(UK release 4/'85)

LP LP LP LP LP LP LP LP LP LP LP LP LP LP

Side 1)	The theme from Jungle Jim	3:49
	After the volcano	3:18
	Idiot grin	2:26
	Cuttlefish beach	4:21
	Black crocodiles	3:13
Side 2)	Man overboard	4:11
	Big accident	3:20
	Racing to zero	4:26
	New taboos	3:04
	1000 mouths	4:01

UK	Virgin, V 2367
EEC	Virgin, 207 357-620
ois	

CD CD CD CD CD CD CD CD CD CD CD CD

The theme from Jungle Jim	3:49
After the volcano	3:18
Idiot grin (12" version)	5:21
Cuttlefish beach	4:21
Warnings moving clockwise	3:47
Man overboard	4:11
Big accident	3:20
Racing to zero	4:26
New taboos	3:04
1000 mouths	4:01
Black crocodiles	3:13
No fury	2:59
Shake this place	3:17
Man overboard (12" version)	5:47
Burning the blues	1:50

UK	Virgin, CDV 2367
EEC	Virgin, 610 662-225
AUS	Virgin, 432 070-2

John Wesley

»The emperor falls«

(UK-only release 11/'98)

CD CD CD CD CD CD CD CD CD CD CD CD

Out of your league	4:30
Come and gone	4:25
An ordinary man *	6:04
Days that won't let go	4:13
There I go	4:58
One step behind	3:38
Last man by your side	4:46
Gift of a woman	2:46
The emperor falls	8:05
Someone for a day	2:50
Are you alive?	3:40
The desperation angel	4:20
So bad *	2:09
A time to dance	4:56

** Backing vocals by Steve Hogarth*

UK	Dream Catcher, CRIDE 7

Julian Cope

»St. Julian«

(UK release 1987)

LP LP LP LP LP LP LP LP LP LP LP LP LP LP

Side 1)	Trampolene	3:35
	Shot down	3:59
	Eves' volcano (covered in sin)	4:16
	Spacehopper	3:20
	Planet ride	5:42
Side 2)	World shut your mouth	3:33
	St. Julian	3:06
	Pulsar	2:46
	Screaming secrets	3:27
	A crack in the clouds	7:59

UK — Island, ILPS 9861
EEC — Island, 208 215-8
ois
USA — Island, 422842686 1

CD CD CD CD CD CD CD CD CD CD CD CD

Trampolene	3:35
Shot down	3:59
Eves' volcano (covered in sin)	4:16
Spacehopper	3:20
Planet ride	5:42
World shut your mouth	3:33
St. Julian	3:06
Pulsar	2:46
Screaming secrets	3:27
A crack in the clouds	7:59

UK — Island, CID 9861
UK — Island, IMCD 137
re-release 1991
EEC — Island, 258 215
USA — Island, 422842686 2

»Eve's volcano (covered in sin)«

(UK release 1987)

12" 12" 12" 12" 12" 12" 12" 12" 12" 12" 12"

Side 1)	Eves' volcano (covered in sin)	3:50
	Almost beautiful child (I & II)	5:23
Side 2)	Pulsar NX *	2:54
	Shot down *	3:51

** Live London, Westminster Central Hall 01/1987*

GER — Island, 609 003

CD CD CD CD CD CD CD CD CD CD CD CD

Eves' volcano (covered in sin)	3:50
Almost beautiful child (I & II)	5:23
Pulsar NX *	2:54
Shot down *	3:51
Spacehopper – annexe	4:54

** Live London, Westminster Central Hall 01/1987*

UK — Island, CID 318
fold-out cardboard sleeve

Sharon O'Neill

»Danced in the fire«

(EEC-only release 1987)

LP LP LP LP LP LP LP LP LP LP LP LP LP LP

Side 1)	Physical favours	4:35
	We're only human	3:28
	Trojan horse *	4:26
	Far away *	4:26
	Take me to Paris *	4:01
Side 2)	Danced in the fire	4:01
	Shock to the heart	3:45
	Thirst for love	3:50
	Under suspicion	4:39
	In control	3:26

** Backing vocals by Steve Hogarth*

EEC — Polydor, 833 577-1
ois

CD CD CD CD CD CD CD CD CD CD CD CD

Physical favours	4:35
We're only human	3:28
Trojan horse *	4:26
Far away *	4:26
Take me to Paris *	4:01
Danced in the fire	4:01
Shock to the heart	3:45
Thirst for love	3:50
Under suspicion	4:39
In control	3:26
Silk or stone	

** Backing vocals by Steve Hogarth*

EEC — Polydor, 833 577-2

The The

»Heartland«

(UK-only release 8/'86)

7" 7" 7" 7" 7" 7" 7" 7" 7" 7" 7" 7" 7" 7" 7" 7"

Side 1) Heartland (Steve Hogarth on piano)
Side 2) Born in the new USA

UK Epic/CBS, TRUTH 2

12" 12" 12" 12" 12" 12" 12" 12" 12" 12" 12"

Side 1) Heartland (Steve Hogarth on piano)
Side 2) Flesh and bones
Born in the new USA

UK Some Bizarre, EPCA 12.6983

»Infected«

(UK release 9/'86)

LP LP LP LP LP LP LP LP LP LP LP LP LP LP

Side 1)	Infected	4:49
	Out of the blue (into the fire)	5:10
	Heartland	5:01
	(Steve Hogarth on piano)	
	Angels of deception	4:37
Side 2)	Sweet bird of truth	5:22
	Slow train to dawn	4:14
	Twilight of a champion	4:22
	The mercy beat	7:22

UK Epic, EPC 26770
ois
EEC Epic, EPC 26770
ois
USA Epic, BFE 40471
release 1/'87

CD CD CD CD CD CD CD CD CD CD CD CD

Infected	4:49
Out of the blue (into the fire)	5:10
Heartland	5:01
(Steve Hogarth on piano)	
Angels of deception	4:37
Sweet bird of truth	5:22
Slow train to dawn	4:14
Twilight of a champion	4:22
The mercy beat	7:22
Infected (12" version)	6:12
Sweet bird of truth (12" version)	7:37
Slow train to dawn (12" version)	6:35

EEC Epic, CDCBS 26770
USA Epic, EK 40471
release 1/'87
USA CBS, 49813 (CD)

Toni Childs

»Union«

(UK release 1988)

LP LP LP LP LP LP LP LP LP LP LP LP LP LP

Side 1)	Don't walk away	3:58
	Walk and talk like angels	5:46
	Stop your fussin'	4:40
	Dreamer	5:01
	Let the rain come down	4:47
Side 2)	Zimbabwe	6:17
	Hush	4:04
	Tin drum	5:40
	Where's the ocean	4:41

UK A+M, AMA 5175
EEC A+M, 395 175-1
ois

CD CD CD CD CD CD CD CD CD CD CD CD

Don't walk away	3:58
Walk and talk like angels	5:46
Stop your fussin'	4:40
Dreamer	5:01
Let the rain come down	4:47
Zimbabwae	6:17
Hush	4:04
Tin drum	5:40
Where's the ocean	4:41

UK A+M, CD 5175/DX 3002
UK A+M, 395 175-2
re-release 1995
EEC A+M, 395 175-2
USA A+M, 750215175 2

»Stop your fussin'«

(GER-only release 1988)

7" 7" 7" 7" 7" 7" 7" 7" 7" 7" 7" 7" 7" 7" 7" 7"

Side 1)	Stop your fussin' (edit)	4:05
Side 2)	Where's the ocean	4:41

GER A+M, 390 313-7

12" 12" 12" 12" 12" 12" 12" 12" 12" 12" 12"

Side 1)	Stop your fussin' (edit)	4:05
Side 2)	Where's the ocean	4:41
	Walk and talk like angels	5:46

GER A+M, 390 313-1

»Don't walk away«

(GER-only release 1988)

12" 12" 12" 12" 12" 12" 12" 12" 12" 12" 12"

Side 1)	Don't walk away (extended)	7:30
Side 2)	Don't walk away (7" edit)	3:56
	Don't walk away (LP version)	3:58

GER A+M, 390 351-1

ROCK AGAINST REPATRIATION

»Sailing«

(UK release 16.02.1990)

7" 7" 7" 7" 7" 7" 7" 7" 7" 7" 7" 7" 7" 7" 7" 7"

Side 1)	Sailing (vocal)	4:12
	(additional vocals by Fish)	
Side 2)	Sailing (instrumental)	4:14

UK I.R.S., EIRS 139
USA I.R.S., IRS 40

••

Side 1)	Sailing (vocal)	4:12
	(additional vocals by Fish)	
Side 2)	– not playable –	

UK Audio 1, 01-734 9901
one sided acetate

CD CD CD CD CD CD CD CD CD CD CD CD

Sailing (vocal)	4:12
(additional vocals by Fish)	
Sailing (instrumental)	4:14

UK I.R.S., EIRSCD 139
USA I.R.S., IRSCD 40
3" CD

Mark Kelly Mark Kelly Mark Kelly Mark Kelly

Born as Mark Colbert Kelly 09.04.1961 in Dublin/Ireland.

His first band was CHEMICAL ALICE in 1980. They made a 4-track E.P. in 1981.

Mark joined MARILLION in November 1981. He did the producer job for JOHN WESLEY (first CD in 1994) and JUMP (1995) and appears as a guest on their CD's.

Geboren als Mark Colbert Kelly am 09.04.1961 in Dublin/Irland war CHEMICAL ALICE im Jahre 1980 seine erste Band.

Mark stieg im November 1981 bei MARILLION ein. Er war Produzent für JOHN WESLEY (erste CD 1994) und für JUMP (1995) und spielte auch auf deren CDs mit.

Mark as a Band Member

CHEMICAL ALICE

»Curiouser and curiouser«

(UK-only release 8/'81)

12" 12" 12" 12" 12" 12" 12" 12" 12" 12" 12"

Side 1)	Goodnight vienna	3:44
	The judge	6:36
Side 2)	Henry the king	5:43
	Lands of home	3:51

UK ACIDIC Records (GNOME 1)
1,000 copies, self-financed

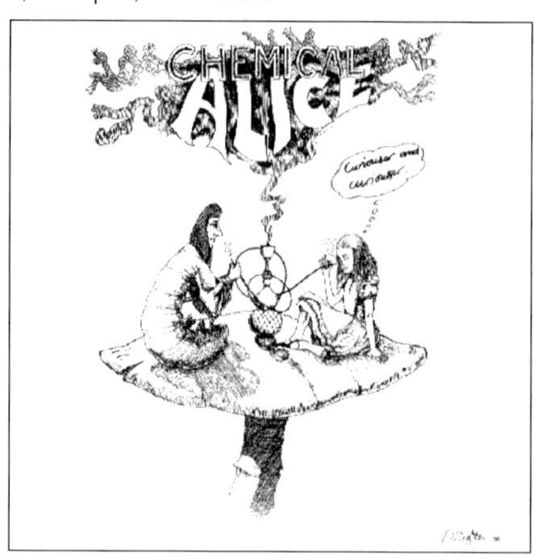

UK cover »Curiouser and curiouser« 12" E.P.

Mark as Guest

John Wesley

»Under the red and white sky«

(UK release 1994)

CD CD CD CD CD CD CD CD CD CD CD CD

Into the night	4:46
None so beautiful	4:26
Thirteen days	4:50
Waiting for the sun	5:01
She said no	3:41
The last light	4:48
To reach out	5:27
Rome is burning	3:04
Our hero	4:39
What you really want	4:11
Cuttin' the tree	4:09
Silver	3:42

UK Racket Records, RACKET 4
release of 10,000 copies
UK Racket Records, RACKET 4
re-release 1998
USA CBS

»The last light«

(FRA-only release 1994)

CD CD CD CD CD CD CD CD CD CD CD CD

The last light	4:54
Gold mine	4:08

FRA CNR 300 426

»John Wesley«

(FRA promo release only 1994)

CD CD CD CD CD CD CD CD CD CD CD CD

Domino	3:12
So bad	2:09
I know, I know	3:36

FRA CNR 300 727
free promo with a magazine

»The closing of the pale blue eyes«

(UK release 1995)

CD CD CD CD CD CD CD CD CD CD CD CD

Right here inside me	3:57
To share a dream	1:35
Alone together	2:46
In Ohio	2:33
Say goodbye to the pale blue eyes	3:09
A long way down	3:50
Death of a friend	2:27
Right here beside me	2:41

FRA CNR 30 0004-2
USA BVB
re-release 1998, ltd. ed.

»Waiting for the sun to shine in Paris«

(USA-only release 09.10.1998)

CD-R CD-R CD-R CD-RCD-R CD-R CD-R

Domino	3:54
Alone together	4:53
Goodbye to the pale blue eyes	3:38
Death of a friend	2:26
To reach out	4:54
Waiting for the sun	7:29
She said no	3:44
The last night	4:33
Into the night (first attempt)	2:35
Mark Kelly keyboard interlude	1:11
tuning up	0:49
Into the night	5:54
Thirteen days	4:02
Rome is burning	3:36
Cuttin' the tree	5:22
The hollow man	4:55
Warm wet circles	5:10
Sugar mice	4:54

Recorded live in Paris, Arapaho, 06.04.1995

USA WesFest productions, wesfest 1
ltd. ed. of 100 signed CD-R

»The emperor falls«

(UK-only release 11/'98)

CD CD CD CD CD CD CD CD CD CD CD CD

Out of your league	4:30
Come and gone	4:25
An ordinary man	6:04
Days that won't let go	4:13
There I go	4:58
One step behind	3:38
Last man by your side	4:46
Gift of a woman	2:46
The emperor falls	8:05

Someone for a day	2:50
Are you alive?	3:40
The desperation angel	4:20
So bad	2:09
A time to dance	4:56

UK — Dream Catcher, CRIDE 7

»Under the red and white sky/ The closing of the pale blue eyes«

(UK-only release 1999)

2CD 2CD 2CD 2CD 2CD 2CD 2CD 2CD 2CD

Disc 1) »Under the red and white sky«
Disc 2) »The closing of the pale blue eyes«

UK — Dream Catcher, CRIDE 14
re-release, remastered

JUMP

»The myth of independence«

(UK-only release 1995)

CD CD CD CD CD CD CD CD CD CD CD CD

Tower of babel	7:19
Princess of the people	5:11
On the wheel	3:55
Heaven and earth	3:40
Valediction (keyboards by Mark)	4:19
Runaway	1:57
Keep the blues	5:25
Blind birds	5:33
The shallow man	4:38
Drive time	4:02
On my side	6:47

UK — Cyclops CYCL 027

Ian Mosley Ian Mosley Ian Mosley Ian Moslay

Born 16.06.1953 in Paddington/England.

His first band was the jazz orchestra at school in 1966. He joined WALRUS in 1970 and for a (short) second period after the following jobs at the WEST END THEATRE ORCHESTRA and the musical »Hair« around '71.

Session works with different musicians over the years showed us a wandering Ian Mosley. He joined DARRYL WAY'S WOLF in early 1973 and playing with PETER GORDINO in 1975. After that period he joined the dutch band TRACE later this year and with LATIN EXPLOSION in the end of the year 1976.

Again he played with a few different musicians e.g. GREENSLADE, BIG BIG SUN and ADRIAN SNELL around 1977/1978. In 1978 he joined the GORDON GILTRAP BAND and began to work with STEVE HACKETT in 1981. One year later he appears with SALLY OLDFIELD (1982) and played with RENAISSANCE in 1983.

Ian Mosley joined MARILLION officially in January 1984.

He worked with PROPAGANDA in 1985. Guest appearance with JOHN WESLEY in 1994. He worked on an instrumental project called IRIS in 1995/1996.

In 2000 STEVE HACKETT released his 1986 album with Ian. A year later, Ian's solo-project with BEN CASTLE was released.

Geboren wurde Ian Mosley am 16.06.1953 in Paddington/England.

Seine erste Band war das Jazz Orchester in der Schule 1966. 1970 stieg er bei WALRUS ein. Bei dieser Band hängte er nach »Hair« noch einmal eine kurze Zeit an. Bei besagtem Musical spielte er 1971 genau wie mit dem WEST END THEATRE ORCHESTRA.

In den nächsten Jahren spielte er als Session-Schlagzeuger mit verschiedenen Musikern und zu Beginn des Jahres 1973 bei DARRYL WAY'S WOLF. 1975 folgte ein Engagement bei PETER GORDINO. Ian ging jedoch noch im gleichen Jahr zur holländischen Band TRACE und wurde Ende des Jahres 1976 bei LATIN EXPLOSION als Schlagzeuger gesichtet. Die Unstetigkeit hielt auch in den beiden kommenden Jahren an, er spielte u.a. bei GREENSLADE, BIG BIG SUN und ADRIAN SNELL. Im Jahre 1978 stieg er bei der GORDON GILTRAP BAND ein. Mit STEVE HACKETT begann Ian 1981 zu arbeiten und spielte auch mit SALLY OLDFIELD (1982) worauf noch ein Platz bei RENAISSANCE im Jahre 1983 folgte.

Ian Mosley wurde offizieller Schlagzeuger bei MARILLION im Januar 1984.

Nebenher arbeitete er (1985) mit PROPAGANDA. Er hatte auch einen Gastauftritt auf einer CD von JOHN WESLEY 1994 und war an einem Instrumental-Projekt namens IRIS zwischen 1995 und 1996 beteiligt.

Im Jahr 2000 veröffentlichte STEVE HACKETT sein Album von 1986 mit Ian und im darauffolgenden Jahr erschien Ian's Solo-Projekt mit BEN CASTLE.

Ian as a Band Member

DARRYL WAY'S WOLF

»Canis lupus«

(UK release 5/'73)

LP LP LP LP LP LP LP LP LP LP LP LP LP LP

Side 1) The void
Isolation waltz
Go down
Side 2) Wolf
Cadenza
Chanson sans paroles
Mc Donald's lament

UK — Deram, SDL 14
foc
JAP — London, LAX 1036

CD CD CD CD CD CD CD CD CD CD CD CD

The void
Isolation waltz
Go down
Wolf
Cadenza
Chanson sans paroles
Mc Donald's lament

JAP — Deram, P 25 L-25057
re-release 1989

»Saturation point«

(UK release 10/'73)

LP LP LP LP LP LP LP LP LP LP LP LP LP LP

Side 1) Ache
Two sisters
Slow rag
Market ouverture
Side 2) Game of X
Saturation point
Toy symphony

UK — Deram, SML 1104
foc
EEC — Deram, SHSP 1104
JAP — London, LAX 1037

»5 in the morning«

(GER-only release 1973)

7" 7" 7" 7" 7" 7" 7" 7" 7" 7" 7" 7" 7" 7" 7" 7"

Side 1) 5 in the morning
Side 2) Bunch of 5's

GER — Deram, DM 395

»Wolf«

(UK-only release 1973)

7" 7" 7" 7" 7" 7" 7" 7" 7" 7" 7" 7" 7" 7" 7" 7"

Side 1) Wolf
Side 2) Spring fever

UK — Deram, DM 378

»Two sisters«

(EEC-only release 1974)

7" 7" 7" 7" 7" 7" 7" 7" 7" 7" 7" 7" 7" 7" 7" 7"

Side 1) Two sisters
Side 2) Go down

EEC — Nova, DL 26002
promo

»Night music«

(UK release 6/'74)

LP LP LP LP LP LP LP LP LP LP LP LP LP LP

Side 1) The envoy
Black september
Flat 2-55
Anteros
Side 2) We're watching you
Steal the world
Comrade of the nine

UK — Deram, SML 1116
EEC — Nova, 6.22079
re-release 1976
JAP — London, LAX 1116

»Darryl Way's Wolf«
(USA-only release 1974)

LP LP LP LP LP LP LP LP LP LP LP LP LP LP

Side 1) The ache
Two sisters
Saturation point
Cadenza
Side 2) Go down
Toy symphony
Mc Donald's lament

USA London, PS 644

»BBC Transcription Disc«
(UK-only release 1974)

LP LP LP LP LP LP LP LP LP LP LP LP LP LP

Side 1) Wolf
Mc Donald's lament
Side 2) Isolation waltz
The ache
Recorded live in London, Paris Theatre, 1974

UK BBC

»One and Two«
(UK release 1975)

2LP 2LP 2LP 2LP 2LP 2LP 2LP 2LP 2LP 2LP

LP 1) »Canis lupus«
LP 2) »Saturation point«

UK London, 23 113
EEC Nova, 8005/1-2
EEC Nova, 6.281131/2
foc

»Isolation«
(JAP-only release 1997)

CD CD CD CD CD CD CD CD CD CD CD CD

Wolf *
Mc Donald's lament *
Isolation waltz *
The ache *
5 in the morning **
A bunch of fives **
** Recorded live in London, Paris Theatre, 1974, ** taken from the »5 in the morning« 7"*

JAP Highland, H 2041 W 1

»Anthology«
(UK-only release 1976)

LP LP LP LP LP LP LP LP LP LP LP LP LP LP

UK King, J 1008
compilation

»Concerto for electric violin«
(UK release 1978)

LP LP LP LP LP LP LP LP LP LP LP LP LP LP

Side 1) 1st movement: Allegro moderato 9:26
2nd movement: Slow 10:44
Side 2) 3rd movement: Scherzo 3:46
4th movement: Finale (Gigue) 11:32
(Ian Mosley on drums/percussion)

UK Island, ILPS 9550
EEC Island, 200 521

TRACE

»Birds«
(UK release 10/'75)

LP LP LP LP LP LP LP LP LP LP LP LP LP LP

Side 1) King bird 4:08
First avenue 0:31
Sculptor bird 1:29
Second avenue 0:15
Preacher bird 2:10
Third avenue 0:27
Birdcorps 0:52
Firecorps 0:43
Birdcorps 0:12
Mail bird 0:29
Fourth avenue 1:54
Soul bird 1:41
Mail bird 1:24
Sculptor bird 1:29
Second avenue 0:15
Preacher bird 2:16
Last avenue 0:12
King bird 1:20
Reflection 1:09
Side 2) Bourree 2:26
Snuff 2:24
In a mist 1:12
Opus 1065 7:44
Penny 2:42
Trixie-Dixie 0:22

UK Vertigo, 6413 080
EEC Vertigo, 6413 080
EEC Vertigo, 6012 704
re-release
EEC Vertigo, 7111 187
re-release
EEC Philips, 6413080
USA Sire, SASD 7514

CD CD CD CD CD CD CD CD CD CD CD CD

King bird	4:08
First avenue	0:31
Sculptor bird	1:29
Second avenue	0:15
Preacher bird	2:10
Third avenue	0:27
Birdcorps	0:52
Firecorps	0:43
Birdcorps	0:12
Mail bird	0:29
Fourth avenue	1:54
Soul bird	1:41
Mail bird	1:24
Sculptor bird	1:29
Second avenue	0:15
Preacher bird	2:16
Last avenue	0:12
King bird	1:20
Reflection	1:09
Bourree	2:26
Snuff	2:24
In a mist	1:12
Opus 1065	7:44
Penny	2:42
Trixie-Dixie	0:22
Birds (short edit)	3:39
Tabu (second version)	4:14

FRA Musea, FBGB 4176.AR
re-release 4/'96

Gordon Giltrap Band

»The peacock party«

(UK release 1979)

LP LP LP LP LP LP LP LP LP LP LP LP LP LP

Side 1)	Headwind – the eagle	3:00
	Magpie rag	2:37
	Hocus pocus	2:20
	Turkey trot – a country bluff	2:44
	Tailor bird	2:30
	Black rose – the raven	4:15
Side 2)	Birds of a feather	3:37
	Jester's rig	2:36
	Gypsy lane	2:56
	Party piece	2:41
	Chanticleer	3:29
	Dodo's dream	4:12

UK PVK, GIL 1
UK Prestige Records limited, PRST 507
EEC Electric Intercord, 161543
re-release 1982

CD CD CD CD CD CD CD CD CD CD CD CD

Headwind – the eagle	3:00
Magpie rag	2:37
Hocus pocus	2:20
Turkey trot – a country bluff	2:44
Tailor bird	2:30
Black rose – the raven	4:15
Birds of a feather	3:37
Jester's rig	2:36
Gypsy lane	2:56
Party piece	2:41
Chanticleer	3:29
Dodo's dream	4:12

UK Prestige Records limited, CDPT 507

»Magpie rag«

(UK-only release 03.03.1979)

7" 7" 7" 7" 7" 7" 7" 7" 7" 7" 7" 7" 7" 7" 7" 7"

Side 1) Magpie rag 2:37
Side 2) Gypsy lane

UK PVK, PV 101

»Fear of the dark«

(UK-only release 1979)

12" 12" 12" 12" 12" 12" 12" 12" 12" 12" 12"

Side 1) Fear of the dark
Side 2) Catwalk blues
Inner dream

UK Electric Records, LWOP 29
ltd. ed. 12" picture of 15,000 copies, no ps

»Jerusalem«

(UK-only release 1979)

7" 7" 7" 7" 7" 7" 7" 7" 7" 7" 7" 7" 7" 7" 7" 7"

Side 1) Jerusalem
Side 2) Party piece

UK Electric Records, WOT42

»Theme from the Waltons«

(UK-only release 1980)

7" 7" 7" 7" 7" 7" 7" 7" 7" 7" 7" 7" 7" 7" 7" 7"
Side 1) Theme from The Waltons
Side 2) Birds of a Feather

UK Cube Records, BUG 89

»Heartsong«

(UK-only release 1980)

7" 7" 7" 7" 7" 7" 7" 7" 7" 7" 7" 7" 7" 7" 7" 7"
Side 1) Heartsong
Side 2) The Deserter

UK Cube Records, BUG 95

»Hocus Pocus«

(UK-only release 1981)

7" 7" 7" 7" 7" 7" 7" 7" 7" 7" 7" 7" 7" 7" 7" 7"
Side 1) Hocus Pocus
Side 2) Dodo's dream

UK PVK, PV111

»Gordon Giltrap live«

(UK-only release 1981)

LP LP LP LP LP LP LP LP LP LP LP LP LP LP
Side 1) Awakening
Robes and crowns
Quest
The deserter
Fast approaching
Catwalk blues
Roots 1 & 2
Side 2) Nightrider
Inner dream
Fear of the dark
Visitation
Heartsong
Lucifer's cage
Recorded live 09.03.1979

UK Cube/Electric, ICS 1001

»Live at the BBC«

(UK-only release 198?)

CD CD CD CD CD CD CD CD CD CD CD CD
Track 11: "Fear of the dark" (live 06.03.1979)
(featuring Ian Mosley on drums)

UK Windsong, WHISC 009

Steve Hackett

»Cell 151«

(UK release 1983)

7" 7" 7" 7" 7" 7" 7" 7" 7" 7" 7" 7" 7" 7" 7" 7"
Side 1) Cell 151 3:17
Side 2) Time lapse at Milton Keynes 3:53

UK Charisma, CELL 1
NL Charisma, 811 341-7
Label says "Time lapse in Milton Keynes"

12" 12" 12" 12" 12" 12" 12" 12" 12" 12" 12"
Side 1) Cell 151 6:25
Side 2) Time lapse at Milton Keynes

UK Charisma, CELL 12

»Till we have faces«

(UK release 9/'84)

LP LP LP LP LP LP LP LP LP LP LP LP LP LP
Side 1) Duel (based on the Steven Spielberg film) 4:43
Mathilda Smith-Williams home for the aged 8:00
Let me count the ways 6:02
A doll that's made in Japan 3:55
Side 2) Myopia 2:54
What's my name 7:02
The Rio connection 3:16
Taking the easy way out 3:46
When you wish upon a star 0:50

UK Lamborghini, LMGLP 4000
UK Start, STL 1
re-release 1987
EEC Lamborghini/Teldec, 6.25987
USA Chrysalis, FV 41571

CD CD CD CD CD CD CD CD CD CD CD CD
Duel (based on the Steven Spielberg film) 4:43
Mathilda Smith-Williams home for the aged 8:00
Let me count the ways 6:02

A doll that's made in Japan	3:55
Myopia	2:54
What's my name	7:02
The Rio connection	3:16
Taking the easy way out	3:46
When you wish upon a star	0:50

UK — Lamborghini, LMGCD 4000
release September 1984
UK — Start, SCD 11
re-release 1987
EEC — SPV Records, SPV 89132
EEC — Castle Legends, CLC 5004
re-release 1990
EEC — Polygram, R 603423
EEC — Rigu, R 66782
FRA — Baillemont productions
re-release 1992
FRA — Musea, FGBG 4421.AR
JAP — Mercury Music, PHCR 4302
JAP — Lamborghini, CDLMG 4000
re-release 1985
USA — Herald/Caroline, HRL 10

Duel (based on the Steven Spielberg film)	4:43
Mathilda Smith-Williams home for the aged	8:00
Let me count the ways	6:02
A doll that's made in Japan	3:55
Myopia	2:54
What's my name	7:02
The Rio connection	3:16
Taking the easy way out	3:46
The gulf •	6:33
Stadiums of the damned •	4:37
When you wish upon a star	0:50

• Bonus tracks

UK — Kudos Permanent, PERMLCD 19
re-release May 1994
UK — Camino Records, CAMCD 9
re-release 1997

»A doll that's made in Japan«

(UK release 1984)

7" 7" 7" 7" 7" 7" 7" 7" 7" 7" 7" 7" 7" 7" 7" 7"

Side 1)	A doll that's made in Japan	4:00
Side 2)	A doll that's made in Japan (instrumental)	2:10

UK — Lamborghini, LMG 16
GER — Lamborghini, 6.14205
promo info on back cover
GER — Lamborghini, 6.14205
NL — Lamborghini, 145.121

12" 12" 12" 12" 12" 12" 12" 12" 12" 12" 12"

Side 1)	A doll that's made in Japan	5:55
Side 2)	Just the bones	6:58

UK — Lamborghini, 12 LMG 16

»Time lapse live-compilation«

(UK release 1994)

CD CD CD CD CD CD CD CD CD CD CD CD

Camino royale	8:41
Please don't touch	4:36
Everyday	7:02
In that quiet earth	3:50
Depth charge	3:19
Jacuzzi *	4:28
The steps *	5:56
Ace of wands *	7:34
Hope I don't wake *	4:13
The red flower of Ta Chai blooms everywhere *	2:42
Tigermouth *	3:23
A tower struck down	2:57
Special mornings	5:18
Clocks – the angel of mons	4:55

** With Ian Mosley; recorded live in New York, Savoy, 11/'81*

UK — Kudos Permanent, PERMLCD 22
UK — Camino Records, CAMCD 11
EEC — SPV Records, SPV 89162
EEC — Polydor, R 52508
EEC — Rigu, R 611 764
FRA — Baillemont Productions
JAP — Mercury Music, PHCR 4305
USA — Blue Plate, CAROL 1839-2
release 1992
USA — Caroline, 1839
release 1992

»Highly strung«

(UK release 3/'83)

LP LP LP LP LP LP LP LP LP LP LP LP LP LP

Side 1)	Camino royale	5:25
	Cell 151	3:30
	Always somewhere else	3:50
	Walking through walls	3:45
Side 2)	Give it away	4:05

	Weightless	3:30
	Group therapy	5:45
	India rubber man	2:50
	Hackett to pieces	2:35

UK — Charisma, HACK 1
UK — Charisma/Virgin, CHC 40
re-release late 1983
EEC — Charisma/Phonogram, 811 209-1
ois
JAP — Charisma, 25 S-161
USA — Epic, 38515
USA — Charisma, BFE-38515
different track order

CD CD CD CD CD CD CD CD CD CD CD CD

	Camino royale	5:25
	Cell 151	6:25
	Always somewhere else	3:50
	Walking through walls	3:45
	Give it away	4:05
	Weightless	3:30
	Group therapy	5:45
	India rubber man	2:50
	Hackett to pieces	2:35

UK — Charisma, HACKCD 1
re-release 1989
EEC — Virgin, VIRG 7872442
EEC — Virgin, R 64866
JAP — Virgin, VJCP 23035
USA — Blue Plate, CAROL 1860-2
re-release 1991
? — Plan 9-1860

»Feedback '86«

(UK release 09.10.2000)

CD CD CD CD CD CD CD CD CD CD CD CD

Cassandra (Ian Mosley on drums)
Prizefighters
Slot machine
Stadiums of the damned
Don't fall
Oh how I love you
Notre Dame des fleurs
The gulf

20 MP3s as bonus on enhanced section

UK — Camino, CAMCD 21
enhanced CD
EEC — SPV, 3192851
enhanced CD, with extra paper-cover

Sally Oldfield

»In concert«

(EEC-only release 1982)

LP LP LP LP LP LP LP LP LP LP LP LP LP LP

Side 1)	Weaver	3:38
	Nenya	3:38
	Morning of my life	5:31
	You set my gypsy blood free	3:41
	River of my childhood	3:57
Side 2)	Woman of the night	5:29
	Song of the healer	3:53
	Mirrors	3:18
	Mandala	4:40
	The sun in my eyes	3:57

EEC — Bronze/Ariola, 204 782-320

CD CD CD CD CD CD CD CD CD CD CD CD

	Weaver	3:38
	Nenya	3:38
	Morning of my life	5:31
	You set my gypsy blood free	3:41
	River of my childhood	3:57
	Woman of the night	5:29
	Song of the healer	3:53
	Mirrors	3:18
	Mandala	4:40
	The sun in my eyes	3:57

EEC — Bronze/Ariola, 610 165-22
release 1984

Renaissance

»Time line«

(UK release 1983)

LP LP LP LP LP LP LP LP LP LP LP LP LP LP

Side 1)	Flight	4:09
	Missing persons	3:36
	Chagrin Boulevard	4:23
	Richard IX.	3:40
	The entertainer	4:45
Side 2)	Electric avenue	4:57
	Majik	3:10
	Distant horizons	3:58
	Orient express	3:55
	Autotech	5:21

UK — IRS, SP 70 033
EEC — Illegal, ILP 25532
EEC — IRS/CBS, ILP 25 532
USA — IRS, IRS 70 033

CD CD CD CD CD CD CD CD CD CD CD CD

	Flight	4:09
	Missing persons	3:36
	Chagrin Boulevard	4:23
	Richard IX.	3:40
	The entertainer	4:45
	Electric avenue	4:57
	Majik	3:10
	Distant horizons	3:58
	Orient express	3:55
	Autotech	5:21

UK HTD, HTDCD 42
EEC Edel/Repertoire, 0004655 REP
release 1997

»Da capo«

(UK-only release 1995)

2CD 2CD 2CD 2CD 2CD 2CD 2CD 2CD 2CD

Disc 1)	Kings and queens	10:58
	Island	5:59
	Love goes on	2:48
	Love is all	3:39
	Prologue	5:36
	Bound for infinity	4:22
	Carpet on the sun	3:33
	Ashes are burning	11:21
	Black flame	6:27
	Running hard	9:34
	Mother Russia	9:21
	Africa	4:43
Disc 2)	Trip to the fair	11:54
	Ocean gypsy	7:07
	The young prince and princess as told	2:33
	Midas man	5:45
	Captive heart	4:16
	Northern lights	4:07
	Song for all seasons	10:56
	Forever changing	4:48
	Flood at Lyons	4:55
	Bonjour swansong	3:39
	Ukraine ways	6:28
	The entertainer (Ian Mosley on drums)	4:45
	Writers wronged	3:59

UK Repertoire, RR 4511
Compilation

Ian as Guest

John Wesley

»Under the red and white sky«

(UK release 1994)

CD CD CD CD CD CD CD CD CD CD CD CD

Into the night	4:46
None so beautiful *	4:26
Thirteen days *	4:50
Waiting for the sun	5:01
She said no	3:41
The last light	4:48
To reach out	5:27
Rome is burning	3:04
Our hero	4:39
What you really want	4:11
Cuttin' the tree	4:09
Silver	3:42

** Ian Mosley on drums*

UK Racket Records, RACKET 4
release of 10,000 copies
UK Racket Records, RACKET 4
re-release from 1998
USA CBS

»Under the red and white sky/ The closing of the pale blue eyes«

(UK-only release 1999)

2CD 2CD 2CD 2CD 2CD 2CD 2CD 2CD 2CD

Disc 1) »Under the red and white sky«
Disc 2) »The closing of the pale blue eyes«

UK Dream Catcher, CRIDE 14
re-release, remastered

Rock against Repatriation

»Sailing«

(UK release 16.02.1990)

7" 7" 7" 7" 7" 7" 7" 7" 7" 7" 7" 7" 7" 7" 7" 7"

Side 1)	Sailing (vocal) (additional vocals by Fish)	4:12
Side 2)	Sailing (instrumental)	4:14

UK I.R.S., EIRS 139
USA I.R.S., IRS 40

Side 1) Sailing (vocal) 4:12
(additional vocals by Fish)
Side 2) – not playable –

UK Audio 1, 01-734 9901
one sided acetate

CD CD CD CD CD CD CD CD CD CD CD CD

Sailing (vocal) 4:12
(additional vocals by Fish)
Sailing (instrumental) 4:14

UK I.R.S., EIRSCD 139
USA I.R.S., IRSCD 40
3" CD

Iris

»Crossing the desert«

(UK-only release 22.04.1996)

CD CD CD CD CD CD CD CD CD CD CD CD

Indian dream	7:48
Train de vie	4:29
Memory of eagle	8:53
Tap on top	4:35
War	8:16
Obsession	2:26
Crossing the desert	10:03
Ocean song	3:36

UK IRIS CD 1 (SPV 085-28232)

Propaganda

»A secret wish«

(UK release 9/'85)

LP LP LP LP LP LP LP LP LP LP LP LP LP LP

Side 1) Dream within a dream 8:04
(Ian Mosley on drums)
The murder of love 5:13
Jewel 3:10
Duel 4:47
Side 2) P-machinery 3:49
Sorry for laughing 3:27
Dr. Mabuse (first life) 5:03
The chase 4:05
The last word 3:01

UK Island/ZTT, ZTTIQ 3
EEC Island/ZTT, 207.027
POR Island/ZTT, 10.207027.46
USA Island, 90288

CD CD CD CD CD CD CD CD CD CD CD CD

Dream within a dream (Ian Mosley on drums)	8:04
The murder of love	5:13
Jewel	6:22
Duel	4:47
Frozen faces•	4:22
P-machinery	3:49
Sorry for laughing	3:27
Dr. Mabuse (first life)	5:03
The chase	4:05
The last word	3:01

• *Bonus track*

EEC Warner/ZTT, 4509-94749-2
EEC Island/ZTT/Ariola, 610540
release 1986
USA Island, CID 90288-2
release 1986

Ian Mosley & Ben Castle

»Postmankind«

(UK-only release 4/'01)

CD CD CD CD CD CD CD CD CD CD CD CD

Someday in may	7:39
Glass eye	4:16
The continuing adventures of Colonel Svene	6:08
The flying scroll	6:06
Any time	4:25
Why me?	5:45
Postmankind	4:52
The viewpoint	7:36

UK Racket Records, RACKET 16
mailorder-only

Steve Rothery Steve Rothery Steve Rothery

Steve Rothery was born on 25.11.1959 in Brampton/England.

His first band was DARK HORSE after finishing school (1976/'77?). He also recorded a demo tape with Edwin Hart, the singer of that band. Other bands Steve played with were PEGASUS and PURPLE HAZE.

Joined SILMARILLION in July 1979 with Doug Irvine and Mick Pointer, later they changed the name into MARILLION.

At the end of the '80ies, he also began to work outside of MARILLION, starting with an album production for JADIS in 1989 and a guest appearance with ARRAKEEN in 1990. With the band ENCHANT he combined both, album production and guest appearance in 1993.

Several guest appearances followed: JOHN WESLEY in 1994 and 1998, ARENA in 1995 and 1997 and MR. SO AND SO in 1998.

He also worked on a solo project called THE WISHING TREE in 1996 and worked with Ian Mosley on his solo-project together with Ben Castle.

Steve Rothery wurde am 25.11.1959 in Brampton/England geboren.

Seine erste Band war DARK HORSE nachdem Steve die Schule beendet hatte (1976/'77). Er nahm später auch ein Demo-Tape mit dem Sänger dieser Band, Edwin Hart, auf. Andere Bands in denen Steve spielte waren PEGASUS und PURPLE HAZE.

Er stieß im Juli 1979 zu SILMARILLION mit Doug Irvine and Mick Pointer, später nannten sie sich im MARILLION um.

Nach fast einer Dekade ging er erstmals "fremd" und produzierte für JADIS 1989 ein Album. 1990 folgte ein Gastauftritt auf einer CD mit ARRAKEEN. Bei ENCHANT verband er dann beides 1993.

Es folgten noch diverse Gastauftritte: JOHN WESLEY 1994 und 1998, ARENA 1995 und 1997 sowie MR. SO AND SO 1998.

1996 wurde es "Zeit" für ein Solo Projekt: THE WISHING TREE. Außerdem wurde er von Ian Mosley für dessen Soloprojekt zusammen mit Ben Castle eingespannt.

Steve as Guest

JADIS

»Jadis«

(UK-only release 12/'89)

LP LP LP LP LP LP LP LP LP LP LP LP LP

Side 1)	This changing face *	4:09
	Follow me to Salzburg *	4:23
	Scratching the surface *	3:15
	Taking your time *	4:39
Side 2)	G 13 **	5:48
	Out of reach **	4:04
	Don't keep me waiting **	3:17
	In the dark **	4:00

** New recording April 1989, ** old demo 12/'86 - 9/'87*

UK — Backbeat Records, 004/12

ARRAKEEN

»Patchwork«

(FRA-only release 1990)

CD CD CD CD CD CD CD CD CD CD CD CD

Le monde du quoi	5:35
Differences	11:25
L'entaluve	4:30
Folle Marie (live in Paris, 1990)	9:15
(including guitar solo by Steve Rothery)	

FRA — 2C production, 218753

ENCHANT

»A blueprint of the world«

(release 1993)

CD CD CD CD CD CD CD CD CD CD CD CD

The thirst	6:15
(produced by Steve Rothery, and e-bow)	
Catharsis *	5:53
Oasis	8:12
Acquaintance *	6:31
Mae dae	3:24
At death's door	7:17
East of Eden *	5:49
Nighttime sky *	8:57
(guitar solo by Steve Rothery)	

Enchanted 7:17
Open eyes •
** Produced by Steve Rothery*

EEC Dream circle Records, DCD 9310
JAP
re-release with bonus track •
USA IRS, IRS CD 987.709
USA
re-release 1995 with bonus track •

John Wesley

»Under the red and white sky«

(UK release 1994)

CD CD CD CD CD CD CD CD CD CD CD CD

Into the night	4:46
None so beautiful	4:26
Thirteen days	4:50
(guitar solo by Steve Rothery)	
Waiting for the sun	5:01
She said no	3:41
The last light	4:48
To reach out	5:27
Rome is burning	3:04
Our hero	4:39
What you really want	4:11
Cuttin' the tree	4:09
Silver	3:42

UK Racket Records, RACKET 4
release of 10,000 copies
UK Racket Records, RACKET 4
re-release from 1998
USA CBS

»The emperor falls«

(UK-only release 11/'98)

CD CD CD CD CD CD CD CD CD CD CD CD

Out of your league	4:30
Come and gone	4:25
An ordinary man	6:04
Days that won't let go	4:13
There I go	4:58
One step behind	3:38
Last man by your side	4:46
Gift of a woman	2:46
(guitar outro solo by Steve Rothery)	
The emperor falls	8:05
Someone for a day	2:50
Are you alive?	3:40
The desperation angel	4:20
So bad	2:09
A time to dance	4:56

UK Dream Catcher, CRIDE 7

»Under the red and white sky/ The closing of the pale blue eyes«

(UK-only release 1999)

2CD 2CD 2CD 2CD 2CD 2CD 2CD 2CD 2CD

Disc 1) »Under the red and white sky«
Disc 2) »The closing of the pale blue eyes«

UK Dream Catcher, CRIDE 14
re-release, remastered

Rock against Repatriation

»Sailing«

(UK release 16.02.1990)

7" 7" 7" 7" 7" 7" 7" 7" 7" 7" 7" 7" 7" 7" 7" 7"

Side 1)	Sailing (vocal)	4:12
	(additional vocals by Fish)	
Side 2)	Sailing (instrumental)	4:14

UK I.R.S., EIRS 139
USA I.R.S., IRS 40

••

Side 1)	Sailing (vocal)	4:12
	(additional vocals by Fish)	
Side 2)	– not playable –	

UK Audio 1, 01-734 9901
one sided acetate

CD CD CD CD CD CD CD CD CD CD CD CD

Sailing (vocal)	4:12
(additional vocals by Fish)	
Sailing (instrumental)	4:14

UK I.R.S., EIRSCD 139
USA I.R.S., IRSCD 40
3 " CD

Arena

»Songs from the lions cage«

(UK release 1995)

CD CD CD CD CD CD CD CD CD CD CD CD

Out of the wilderness	8:02
Crying for help I	1:22
Valley of the kings	10:10
Crying for help II	2:08
Jericho	6:50
Crying for help III	4:24
Midas vision	4:36
Crying for help IV	5:05
(guitar solo by Steve Rothery)	
Solomon	14:37

UK Verglas music, VGCD 001
USA Griffin music, GCD-402-2

»The cry«

(UK release 1997)

CD CD CD CD CD CD CD CD CDCD CD CD CD

Theme	0:55
The cry	3:10
The offering	2:33
Problem line	4:02
Isolation	1:59
Fallen idols	4:12
Guidance	5:09
Only child	5:03
(guitar solo by Steve Rothery)	
Stolen promise	2:58
The healer	5:44

UK Verglas music, VGCD 005
EEC SPV, 076-28302 C.D.

The wishing Tree

»Carnival of souls«

(UK-only release 9/'96)

CD CD CD CD CD CD CD CD CD CD CD CD

Evergreen	5:52
Starfish	3:09
Nightwater	4:23
Hall of memories	4:11
Midnight show	6:02
Night of the hunter	3:58
Fire-bright	3:06
Thunder in Tinseltown	4:34
Empire of lies	5:33
The dance	2:58
Hall of memories (live video) •	
Starfish (live video) •	
Man the hunter (demo) •	
She moves through the fair (demo) •	

Steve Rothery guitars and keyboards, Pete Trewavas bass

UK Dorian Music, DM WT 001
promo CD, no ps
UK Dorian Music, DM WT 001
UK Racket Records, RACKET 14
re-release 1/'01 with enhanced bonus tracks •

Mr. So and So

»The overlap«

(UK-only release 27.07.1998)

CD CD CD CD CD CD CD CD CD CD CD CD

Metaphor	6:11
Spacewalk	7:34
("atmospheres" by Steve Rothery)	
Drowners	6:13
Isn't it amazing	4:12
Salamander	8:26
Subtifuge	5:50
Coup de grace	6:33
("providing solo" by Steve Rothery)	
The overlap	8:12

UK Dorian Music, DM SS 001 CD

Ian Mosley & Ben Castle

»Postmankind«

(UK-only release 4/'01)

CD CD CD CD CD CD CD CD CD CD CD CD

Someday in may	7:39
Glass eye	4:16
The continuing adventures of	
Colonel Svene *	6:08
The flying scroll *	6:06
Any time	4:25
Why me?	5:45
Postmankind *	4:52
The viewpoint *	7:36

** Steve Rothery on guitar*

UK Racket Records, RACKET 16
mailorder-only

Pete Trewavas Pete Trewavas Pete Trewavas

Pete Trewavas was born in Middlesborough/ England, 15.01.1959.

His first school band was called MANANTUS (1972). There, he played together with Robin Boult. The next station was a band called ORTHI from Aylesbury (1975). They changed the line-up and the name of the band (into THE ROBINS) in 1978. Later on, they changed vocalist and name once more: this time into HEARTBEAT. That was in 1980. The band produced a 5-track demo-tape, but found no record label.

Later in 1980, Peter joined a band called TAMBERLANE. Eventually they first changed their name to THE CAMERAS and then to THE RED STARS. In January 1981, the band was called THE METROS.

His next venture in early 1982 was a band called EAST GOES WEST before he joined MARILLION in March 1982.

He worked on an instrumental project called IRIS in 1995/1996 and played bass with THE WISHING TREE in 1996, also in a project called TRANSATLANTIC in 2000 and he worked with Ian Mosley on his solo-project together with Ben Castle.

Geboren wurde Pete Trewavas am 15.01.1959 in Middlesborough/England.

Seine erste Band war zu Schulzeiten MANANTUS zusammen mit Robin Boult.

Danach spielte er in einer Band aus Aylesbury namens ORTHI. Diese Band wechselte einige Mitglieder aus und nannte sich 1978 in THE ROBINS um. 1980 wurde der Sänger und mit ihm gleich wieder der Name gewechselt, und zwar in HEARTBEAT. Die Band stellte ein Demo mit 5 Stücken fertig, fand aber keine Plattenfirma.

Später im Laufe des Jahres 1980 wechselte Pete zu TAMBERLANE, die ebenfalls ihren Namen mehrfach änderten, erst in THE CAMERAS und anschließend in THE RED STARS. Im Januar 1981 folgte ein erneuter Namenswechsel in THE METROS und damit gelang endlich die erste Plattenproduktion.

Zu Beginn des Jahres 1982 spielte Pete noch kurzzeitig in einer Band namens EAST GOES WEST bevor er im März 1982 bei MARILLION einstieg.

1995/1996 arbeitete er an einem Instrumentalprojekt namens IRIS mit und spielte Baß bei einem Projekt mit dem Namen THE WISHING TREE. Ebenfalls an “seinem” Instrument war er in den Jahren 2000/1 mit TRANSATLANTIC zu hören. Auch er wurde von Ian Mosley für sein Soloprojekt zusammen mit Ben Castle eingespannt.

Pete as a Band Member

THE METROS

»The first 33 1/3 E.P. – Driving us crazy«

(UK-only release summer 1981)

12" 12" 12" 12" 12" 12" 12" 12" 12" 12"

Side 1) I don't have your number
Platered in Paris
I saw her standing there
Side 2) Love me tomorrow
You think of her
Devil rock

UK
private pressing without pressing number, 2,000 copies

TRANSATLANTIC

»SMPTe«

(EEC release 27.03.2000)

CD CD CD CD CD CD CD CD CD CD CD CD

Track	Time
All of the above	30:59
We all need some light	5:45
Mystery train	6:52
My new world	16:16
In held (Twas) in I	17:21

EEC Inside Out/SPV, IOMCD 057
promo CD in cardboard sleeve
EEC Inside Out/SPV, SPV 085-31972
USA Radiant/Metal Blade
release 4/'00

2CD 2CD 2CD 2CD 2CD 2CD 2CD 2CD 2CD

Disc	Track	Time
Disc 1)	All of the above	30:59
	We all need some light	5:45
	Mystery train	6:52
	My new world	16:16
	In held (Twas) in I	17:21
Disc 2)	My new world (part 1) *	7:40
	My new world (part 2) *	8:39
	We all need some light (Alternative mix, Roine leadvoice)	5:38
	Honky tonk woman (Studio jam)	1:54
	Oh darlin' (Studio jam)	2:30
	My cruel world (Original demo)	10:43
	Interactive section incl. video	

** Alternative take, Neal lead, different lyrics, disc 2 enhanced bonus CD*

EEC Inside Out/SPV, SPV 087-31970
ltd. ed. 2CD-set in book-cover
EEC Inside Out/SPV
re-release of 2CD-set without book-cover

»Live in America«

(EEC-only release 12.03.2001)

2CD 2CD 2CD 2CD 2CD 2CD 2CD 2CD 2CD

Disc 1)	All of the above	30:47
	BEATLES medley: Mystery train/ Magical mystery tour/Strawberry fields forever	15:32
	We all need some light	6:51
Disc 2)	GENESIS medley: Watcher of the skies/Firth of fifth	10:47
	My new world	16:51
	Medley: There is more to this world (THE FLOWER KINGS)/Go the way you go (SPOCK'S BEARD)/The great escape (MARILLION) (with Pete on vocals)/ Finally free (DREAM THEATER)/She's so heavy (BEATLES)	19:10

Recorded live on the USA-tour june/july 2000

EEC Inside Out, SPV 089-41512
promo sticker on cover back
EEC Inside Out, SPV 089-41512

»Bridge across forever«

(EEC-only release 9/'01)

CD CD CD CD CD CD CD CD CD CD CD CD

Duel with the devil	26:34
i. Motherless children	
ii. Walk away	
iii. Silence of the night	
iv. You're not alone	
v. Almost home	
Suite Charlotte Pike	14:30
i. If she runs	
ii. Mr. Wonderful	
iii. Lost and found (part 1)	
iv. Temple of the gods	
v. Motherless children/If she runs (reprise)	
Bridge across forever	5:32
Stranger in your soul	26:06
i. Sleeping wide awake	
ii. Hanging in the balance	
iii. Lost and found (part 2)	
iv. Awakening the stranger	
v. Slide	
vi. Stranger in your soul	

EEC Inside Out/SPV
promo, cardboard sleeve
EEC Inside Out/SPV

2CD 2CD 2CD 2CD 2CD 2CD 2CD 2CD 2CD

Disc 1)	Duel with the devil	26:34
	i. Motherless children	
	ii. Walk away	
	iii. Silence of the night	
	iv. You're not alone	
	v. Almost home	
	Suite Charlotte Pike	14:30
	i. If she runs	
	ii. Mr. Wonderful	
	iii. Lost and found (part 1)	
	iv. Temple of the gods	
	v. Motherless children/If she runs (reprise)	
	Bridge across forever	5:32
	Stranger in your soul	26:06
	i. Sleeping wide awake	
	ii. Hanging in the balance	
	iii. Lost and found (part 2)	
	iv. Awakening the stranger	
	v. Slide	
	vi. Stranger in your soul	
Disc 2)	Shine on you crazy diamond	15:05
	Studio chat	4:51
	And I love her	7:56
	Smoke on the water	4:24
	Dance with the devil (demo)	9:07
	Roine's demo bits	9:00
	Interactive video section	

EEC Inside Out/SPV 088-41700 DCD
ltd. ed. in book-cover

Pete as Guest

IRIS

»Crossing the desert«

(UK-only release 22.04.1996)

CD CD CD CD CD CD CD CD CD CD CD CD

Indian dream	7:48
Train de vie	4:29
Memory of eagle	8:53
Tap on top	4:35
War	8:16
Obsession	2:26
Crossing the desert	10:03
Ocean song	3:36

UK SPV, IRIS CD 1 (SPV 085-28232)

The wishing Tree

»Carnival of souls«

(UK-only release 9/'96)

CD CD CD CD CD CD CD CD CD CD CD CD

Evergreen	5:52
Starfish	3:09
Nightwater	4:23
Hall of memories	4:11
Midnight show	6:02
Night of the hunter	3:58
Fire-bright	3:06
Thunder in Tinseltown	4:34
Empire of lies	5:33
The dance	2:58

Steve Rothery guitars and keyboards, Pete Trewavas bass

UK — Dorian Music, DM WT 001
promo CD, no ps
UK — Dorian Music, DM WT 001

••

Evergreen	5:52
Starfish	3:09
Nightwater	4:23
Hall of memories	4:11
Midnight show	6:02
Night of the hunter	3:58
Fire-bright	3:06
Thunder in Tinseltown	4:34
Empire of lies	5:33
The dance	2:58
Hall of memories (live video) •	
Starfish (live video) •	
Man the hunter (demo) •	
She moves through the fair (demo) •	

Steve Rothery guitars and keyboards, Pete Trewavas bass, • enhanced bonus tracks

UK — Racket Records, RACKET 14
re-release 1/'01

Rock Against Repatriation

»Sailing«

(UK release 16.02.1990)

7" 7" 7" 7" 7" 7" 7" 7" 7" 7" 7" 7" 7" 7" 7" 7"

Side 1) Sailing (vocal) 4:12
(additional vocals by Fish)
Side 2) Sailing (instrumental) 4:14

UK — I.R.S., EIRS 139
USA — I.R.S., IRS 40

••

Side 1) Sailing (vocal) 4:12
(additional vocals by Fish)
Side 2) – not playable –

UK — Audio 1, 01-734 9901
one sided acetate

CD CD CD CD CD CD CD CD CD CD CD CD

Sailing (vocal) 4:12
(additional vocals by Fish)
Sailing (instrumental) 4:14

UK — I.R.S., EIRSCD 139
USA — I.R.S., IRSCD 40
3" CD

Steve Hackett

»Feedback '86«

(UK release 09.10.2000)

CD CD CD CD CD CD CD CD CD CD CD CD

Cassandra
(Pete Trewavas on bass)
Prizefighters
Slot machine
Stadiums of the damned
Don't fall
Oh how I love you
Notre Dame des fleurs
The gulf

20 MP3s as bonus on enhanced section

UK — Camino, CAMCD 21
enhanced CD
EEC — SPV, 3192851
enhanced CD, with extra paper-cover

Ian Mosley & Ben Castle

»Postmankind«

(UK-only release 4/'01)

CD CD CD CD CD CD CD CD CD CD CD CD

Someday in may	7:39
Glass eye	4:16
The continuing adventures of Colonel Svene	6:08
The flying scroll	6:06
Any time	4:25
Why me?	5:45
Postmankind	4:52
The viewpoint	7:36

UK — Racket Records, RACKET 16
mailorder-only

Cover Versions, Cover Bands, Tributes

You will find any other item which is related to MARILLION in any way in this chapter (especially cover versions).

JESTER HOAX

»Cover dei Marillion«

(ITA-only release 12/'98)

CD-R CD-R CD-R CD-R CD-R CD-R CD-R

Cinderella search	5:06
Punch & Judy	3:06
He knows you know	4:53
Kayleigh	3:48

ITA
private pressing

MICHAEL HUNTER

»River«

(UK-only release 1994)

CD CD CD CD CD CD CD CD CD CD CD CD

Part I.	14:46
Part II.	3:07
Part III.	4:01
Part IV.	7:59
Part V.	1:04
Part VI.	1:33
Part VII.	9:57

This music was played at the "Brave"-tour before MARILLION entered the stage.

UK Racket Records, Racket 5

SEASONS END

»Demo«

(GER-only release spring 2000)

CD-R CD-R CD-R CD-R CD-R CD-R CD-R

Warm wet circles/That time of the night	10:26
Easter	5:54
The great escape/Falling from the moon	6:13

GER
private pressing

»Live«

(GER-only release 2001)

2CD-R 2CD-R 2CD-R 2CD-R 2CD-R 2CD-R

Disc 1) Splintering heart
Alone again in the lap of luxury
Sugar mice
Seasons end
Script for a jester's tear
The great escape
Bridge
Living with the big lie
Out of this world
Afraid of sunlight
Disc 2) Pseudo silk kimono
Kayleigh
Lavender
Lords of the backstage
Blind curve
Childhood's end?
Warm wet circles
White russian
This strange engine
Fugazi

Recorded live in Heidelberg, 11.08.2001

GER
private pressing

SPLINTERING HEART

»Demo«

(GER-only release spring 1997)

CD-R CD-R CD-R CD-R CD-R CD-R CD-R

Splintering heart
Kayleigh
Lavender
Bitter suite
iii) Blue angel
The space

GER
private pressing

Various Artists »Hope for the future« (A Marillion tribute album)
(USA-only release 1999)

CD CD CD CD CD CD CD CD CD CD CD CD

John Wesley - Fallin' from the moon	5:00
Timescape - The space	5:45
Braintree - Going under	4:48
And again - Out of this world	7:25
Evil Genius - Just for the record	3:00
Chicken Fried Funk - Cannibal surf babe	5:10
Scott Jones - Sugar mice	2:59
Accelerated Decreptitude - Afraid of sunlight/That time of the night	5:23
Twist Of F 8 - Tux on	8:08
Body - She chameleon	7:22
The Wish - The answering machine	2:46
Tracy la Barbera - Beautiful	5:34

USA Out of this world Records, Out 1
ltd. ed. of 1,000 copies, mailorder-only

Bliss

"Made again"
»Heavenly shades of night are falling« CD, 2000
USA Bliss Records, BlissCD1

Darius

"Kayleigh"
»Somewhere alive in the crowd« CD, 1999
GER Zizania Music Ltd. ZEG 0299
acoustic version

John Wesley

"King of sunset town"
»Wesfest '98 - Live in New York« CD-R, 1999
USA WesFest Productios, wesfest 1
ltd. ed.

"Easter"
»Wesfest '98 - Live in New York« CD-R, 1999
USA WesFest Productios, wesfest 1
ltd. ed.

"Sugar mice"
»Wesfest '98 - Live in New York« CD-R, 1999
USA WesFest Productios, wesfest 1
ltd. ed.

Lana Lane

"Seasons end"
»Queen of the ocean« CD, 1999
JAP Avalon, MICY-1100
»Ballad collection« 2CD, 2000
EEC Pseudonym Records, CDP-1078-DD
»Seasons end«, CD, 2000
EEC Pseudonym Records, CDEP-1083-DD
in "normal" version and a live version: Tokyo, 20.04.1999

Tone

"Kayleigh"
»Kayleigh«, CD
EEC EMI
never commercially available, but copies exist

Twist of F 8

"Heart of Lothian"
»Demo«, CD-R, 2000
USA
private pressing

Vanden Plas

"Theme from Pseudo silk kimono"
»Accult« CD, 1996
GER Dream Circle Records, DCD 9629

"Kayleigh"
»Accult« CD, 1996
GER Dream Circle Records, DCD 9629
acoustic version

Marillion/Related - Top 20 Collectibles

The prices in the list below are based on my own experiences (at record fairs and online auctions), with a little help from Marillion collectors and dealers worldwide.

Die Preise in der unten aufgeführten Liste ergeben eine Zusammenfassung aus meinen eigenen Erfahrungen (auf Platten Börsen und Internet Auktionen) sowie dem Wissen von vielen mir bekannten Marillion-Sammlern und Händlern weltweit.

01) **Garden party** 400,- Euro
(uncut shaped picture disc, 10+ copies)

02) **Clutching at...** 300,- Euro
(video-CD, test pressing with ps, 50+ copies)

03) **Warm wet circles** 200,- Euro
(12" metal acetate, tape-mix 37, 1 copy only)

04) **Kayleigh** 200,- Euro
(JAP-promo, 7",ps)

05) **The Metros** 150,- Euro
»The first 33 1/3 E.P.«
(12" E.P. with Pete Trewavas)

06) **Marillion Rochester** 130,- Euro
(2CD, tour fund, signed and numbered copies)

07) **The story so far** 120,- Euro
(CAN-only promo, LP, ps)

08) **Harlow**
»Harry de Mazzio« 100,- Euro
(7" demo with Steve Hogarth, no ps)

09) **How we live »Dry land«** 75,- Euro
(official CD with Steve Hogarth)

10) **»Fugazi«** 75,- Euro
(CZ-only LP, multicoloured vinyl, 30 copies

11) **»Real to reel«** 75,- Euro
(ESP-only 12" promo sampler)

12) **»Marillion acoustic«** 75,- Euro
(FRA-only promo)

13) **Chemical Alice** 75,- Euro
»Curiouser and curiouser«
(12" E.P. with Mark Kelly)

14) **»Marillion Rochester«** 75,- Euro
(2CD, tour fund, not signed)

15) **»Fugazi«** 70,- Euro
(GER test pressing, LP plays side A on both sides)

16) **»Script for a jester's tear«** 60,- Euro
(LP test pressing with fully signed sleeve, 200 copies)

17) **»Fugazi«** 60,- Euro
(LP test pressing with fully signed sleeve, 200 copies)

18) **»Market square heroes«** 60,- Euro
(12" picture disc, 3,000 copies)

19) **»Punch and Judy«** 60,- Euro
(JAP-promo, 7" with very different ps)

20) **»Lavender«** 60,- Euro
(CAN 7" with very different ps)

Important Label Discographies

Racket Records

RACKET 1 MARILLION »Live at the Borderline« (CD) 1993
RACKET 2 MARILLION »Live in Caracas« (CD) 1993
RACKET 3 MARILLION »Live in Glasgow« (CD) 1993
RACKET 4 JOHN WESLEY »Under the red and white sky« (CD) 1994
RACKET 5 MICHAEL HUNTER »River« (CD) 1994
RACKET 6 MARILLION »The making of Brave« (2CD) 1995
RACKET 7 MARILLION/THE POSITIVE LIGHT »Tales from the engine room« 1998
RACKET 8 MARILLION »Marillion Rochester« (2CD) 1998
RACKET 9 MARILLION »Piston broke« (2CD) 1998
WEBFREE 01 MARILLION »The web Christmas 1998« (CD) 1998
RACKET 10 MARILLION »Unplugged at the Walls« (2CD) 1999
RACKET 11 MARILLION »Zodiac« (CD) 1999
WEBFREE 2 MARILLION »marillion.christmas 1999« (CD) 1999
RACKET 12 MARILLION »marillion.co.uk« (CD) 2000
RACKET 13 HOW WE LIVE »Dry land« (re-issue CD with 2 bonus tracks) 2000
RACKET 91 N MARILLION »Shot in the dark« (NTSC-Video) 2000
RACKET 91 P MARILLION »Shot in the dark« (PAL-Video) 2000
RACKET 14 THE WISHING TREE »Carnival of souls« (re-issue CD with bonus) 2001
WEBFREE 03 MARILLION »Marillion Christmas 2000-A piss-up in a brewery« (CD) 2001
RACKET 15 MARILLION »Crash course – An introduction to Marillion« (CD) 2001
RACKET 16 IAN MOSLEY + BEN CASTLE »Postmankind« (CD) 2001
RACKET 17 MARILLION »Refracted – The making of "Afraid of sunlight"« (2CD) 2001
RACKET 18 MARILLION »Another DAT at the office – The making of "This strange engine"« (2CD) 2001

Dick Bros Record Company

DDICK 1 CD Various Artists »Outpatients '93« (CD re-issue) 1993
DDICK 2 CD FISH »Sushi« (2CD) 1994
DDICK 3 PIC FISH »Lady let it lie« (12" picture disc) 1994
DDICK 3 CD1 FISH »Lady let it lie« (digipack) 1994
DDICK 3 CD2 FISH »Lady let it lie« (jewel-case) 1994
DDICK 4 LP FISH »Suits« (2LP) 1994
DDICK 4 PIC FISH »Suits« (LP picture disc) 1994
DDICK 4 CD FISH »Suits« (CD) 1994
DDICK 4 MC FISH »Suits« (MC) 1994
DDICK 5 PROMO1 FISH »No dummy« (promo) 1994
DDICK 5 PROMO2 FISH »No dummy« (promo) 1994
DDICK 6 CD FAN FISH »Acoustic session« (fan club-CD) 1994
DDICK 6 CD PROMO FISH »Acoustic session« (promo) 1994
DDICK 6 CD FISH »Acoustic session« 1994
DDICK 7 CD PROMO DREAM DISCIPLES »In amber« (3 track promo) 1994
DDICK 7 CD DREAM DISCIPLES »In amber« 1994
DDICK 8 CD PROMO DREAM DISCIPLES »Fortunes of war« (promo) 1994
DDICK 8 CD 1 DREAM DISCIPLES »Fortunes of war« (CD 1) 1994
DDICK 8 CD 2 FISH »Fortunes of war« (CD 2) 1994
DDICK 8 CD 3 FISH »Fortunes of war« (CD 3) 1994
DDICK 8 CD 4 FISH »Fortunes of war« (CD 4) 1994
DDICK 9 CD PROMO FISH »Emperor's song« (promo) 1994
DDICK 10 CD DREAM DISCIPLES »In amber« (CD) 1994
DDICK 10 SIN DREAM DISCIPLES »In amber« (7" single) 1994
DDICK 11 CD PROMO FISH »Yin« (promo CD) 1995
DDICK 11 CD FISH »Yin« (CD) 1995
DDICK 11 MC FISH »Yin« (MC) 1995
DDICK 12 CD PROMO FISH »Yang« (promo) 1995
DDICK 12 CD FISH »Yang« (CD) 1995
DDICK 12 MC FISH »Yang« (MC) 1995
DDICK 13 CD PROMO FISH »Yin and Yang radio edits« (promo) 1995
DDICK 13 CD FAN FISH »Yin and Yang radio edits« (fan club-CD) 1995
DDICK 14 CD 1 FISH »Just good friends« (CD 1) 1995

DDICK 14 CD 2 FISH »Just good friends« (CD 2) 1995
DDICK 14 MC FISH »Just good friends« (MC) 1995
DDICK 15 CD PROMO FISH »The Funny Farm Interviews« (promo) 1995
DDICK 16 CD FISH »Pigpen's birthday« (2CD re-issue) 1996
DDICK 17 CD FISH »Uncle Fish and the crypt creepers« (2CD re-issue) 1996
DDICK 18 CD FISH »Fish head curry« (2CD) 1996
DDICK 19 CD FISH »Krakow« (2CD) 1996
DDICK 20 CD PROMO FISH »Krakow« radio promo (promo) 1996
DDICK 21 VID FISH »Krakow video« (electric set) 1996
DDICK 22 VID FISH »Krakow video« (acoustic set) 1996
DDICK 23 CD TAM WHITE »Mandacin« (CD) 1996
DDICK 24 P FISH »Brother 52« (12" promo) 1997
DDICK 24 PIC FISH »Brother 52« (12" picture disc) 1997
DDICK 24 CD 1 FISH »Brother 52« (CD 1) 1997
DDICK 24 CD 2 FISH »Brother 52« (CD 2) 1997
DDICK 24 CD PROMO FISH »Sunsets on empire« (promo sampler) 1997
DDICK 25 CD PROMO FISH »Sunsets on empire« (promo) 1997
DDICK 25 CD FISH »Sunsets on empire« (CD) 1997
DDICK 25 MC FISH »Sunsets on empire« (MC) 1997
DDICK 26 CD FISH »Sunsets on empire« (2CD, ltd. ed.) 1997
DDICK 27 CD PROMO FISH »Change of heart« (promo) 1997
DDICK 27 CD FISH »Change of heart« (CD) 1997
DDICK 28 CD FISH »Vigil in a wilderness of mirrors« (remastered CD) 1998
DDICK 29 CD FISH »Tales from the big bus« (2CD) 1998
DDICK 30 CD FISH »Fortunes of war« (CD) 1998

MARILLION Tour History

1978 - 1979

SILMARILLION and later MARILLION played some rehearsals and live gigs around this time.
But there are no further details known about dates or locations.

1980

01.03.1980 Berkhamsted, Civic Centre, England
3/'80 Hertford, Enid Studios, England (Demo recordings)

They played nearly 14 gigs between March 1980 and November 1980. The dates and locations are mostly unknown. But confirmed venues of some of these shows are The Metal Hospital in St.Albans, The Street Traders Fair in Watford and gigs in Luton and High Wycombe.

06.06.1980 Unknown Studio, England ("Demo summer")
11/'80 Bicester, Red Lion Pub, England
11/'80 Colsford, Farmyard Studios, England (last work with Doug Irvine)

1981

02.01.1981 Buckinghamshire, Leyland Farm Studios, England (Fish's audition)
14.03.1981 Bicester, Red Lion Pub, England (First gig with Fish and Diz Minnitt)
16.03.1981 Stoke, Mandeville Hospital, England
18.03.1981 Bletchley, White Heart, England
27.03.1981 High Wycombe, SU Bar, England
31.03.1981 Aylesbury, The Britannia, England
04.04.1981 Berkhamsted, Kings Arms Hall, England
16.04.1981 Amersham, Annie's Wine Bar, England
24.04.1981 Milton Keynes, Starting Gate, England
26.04.1981 Bicester, Red Lion Pub, England
30.04.1981 Hemel Hempstead, Dacorum College, England
01.05.1981 Berkhamsted, Kings Arms Hall, England
02.05.1981 St.Albans, Horn of Plenty, England
05.05.1981 Aylesbury, The Britannia, England
09.05.1981 Woolaston, Nags Head, England
10.05.1981 Maidenhead, The Bell, England
22.05.1981 Milton Keynes, Starting Gate, England

29.05.1981 Aylesbury, Friars Maxwell Hall, England
30.05.1981 Bicester, Red Lion Pub, England
03.06.1981 Aylesbury, The Britannia, England
06.06.1981 St.Albans, Horn of Plenty, England
07.06.1981 Maidenhead, The Bell, England
10.06.1981 Bletchley, White Heart, England
12.06.1981 Bedford, Horse and Groom, England
13.06.1981 Woolaston, Nags Head, England
14.06.1981 Reading, Target Club, England
23.06.1981 High Wycombe, Nags Head, England
25.06.1981 Luton, Technical College, England
26.06.1981 Milton Keynes, Starting Gate, England
27.06.1981 Southall, Hanborough Tavern, England
01.07.1981 Aylesbury, The Britannia, England
08.07.1981 Halton, Hospital, England
15.07.1981 Dunstable, Wheatsheaf, England
18.07.1981 Watlington, Roxon Studios, England (Demo recordings)
19.07.1981 Watlington, Roxon Studios, England (Demo recordings)
21.07.1981 Aylesbury, Walton Garden Party, England
28.07.1981 Aylesbury, The Britannia, England
29.07.1981 Aston Clinton, Street Party, England
01.08.1981 Aylesbury, Friars Maxwell Hall, England
21.08.1981 Bedford, Horse and Groom, England
26.08.1981 Bletchley, White Heart, England
28.08.1981 Bicester, Nowhere Club, England
04.09.1981 Milton Keynes, Starting Gate, England
09.09.1981 Aylesbury, The Britannia, England
14.09.1981 St.Albans, City Hall, England
17.09.1981 High Wycombe, College, England
25.09.1981 Stoke, Mandeville Hospital, England
26.09.1981 Reading, Target Club, England
08.10.1981 Oxford, Pennyfarthing, England
09.10.1981 Chadwell Heath, Electric Stadium, England
10.10.1981 Northhampton, Black Lion, England
12.10.1981 Luton, Mad Hatters, England
14.10.1981 Dunstable, Wheatsheaf, England
15.10.1981 Leamington Spa, Crown Hotel, England
19.10.1981 Chalfont St.Peter, Newland's Park College, England
20.10.1981 London, Marquee Club, England
22.10.1981 Chesham, Elgiva Hall, England
23.10.1981 Harrow, Northwich Park Hospital, England
24.10.1981 High Wycombe, Nags Head, England
26.10.1981 Oxford, Polytechnic, England
29.10.1981 Cambridge, Great Northern Club, England
30.10.1981 Bedford, Horse and Groom, England
31.10.1981 Aylesbury, Friars Maxwell Hall, England
01.11.1981 Gravesend, Red Lion, England
04.11.1981 Oxford, Scamps, England
05.11.1981 Milton Keynes, Compass Club, England
07.11.1981 Woolaston, Nags Head, England
11.11.1981 Chadwell Heath, Electric Stadium, England
12.11.1981 Clapham, 101 Club, England
13.11.1981 Milton Keynes, Starting Gate, England
20.11.1981 Chesham, Elgiva Hall, England
21.11.1981 Chesham, Elgiva Hall, England (last gig with Brian Jelliman on keyboards)
28.11.1981 Aston Clinton, Village Hall, England (played without keyboarder)
30.11.1981 Aston Clinton, Studio session, England (Demo recordings)
01.12.1981 Cambridge, Great Northern, England (first gig with Mark Kelly on keyboards)
02.12.1981 Chadwell Heath, Electric Stadium, England
03.12.1981 Dunstable, Wheatsheaf, England
15.12.1981 Dunstable, Wheatsheaf, England
16.12.1981 Chadwell Heath, Electric Stadium, England
24.12.1981 Milton Keynes, Starting Gate, England

1982

03.01.1982 London, Marquee Club, England
25.01.1982 London, Marquee Club, England
27.01.1982 Chadwell Heath, Electric Stadium, England
29.01.1982 London, BBC Studios, England (Friday Rock Show)
12.02.1982 Bangor, University, Wales
20.02.1982 Aylesbury, Friars Maxwell Hall, England
26.02.1982 Canterbury, College of Technology, England
27.02.1982 London, Starlight Rooms West Hampstead, England

01.03.1982 London, Dingwalls Club, England
06.03.1982 Bedford, College, England
07.03.1982 London, Marquee Club, England
09.03.1982 Chalfont St.Peter, Newland's Park College, England (last show with Diz Minnitt)
26.03.1982 Milton Keynes, Starting Gate, England (show without bass player)
02.04.1982 Coventry, General Wolfe Club, England (first gig with Pete Trewavas on bass)
08.04.1982 Scarborough, Taboo, England
11.04.1982 Bathgate, Cairn Park Hotel, Scotland
12.04.1982 Bannockburn, The Tandhu, Scotland
14.04.1982 Dunbar, Golden Stones Hotel, Scotland
15.04.1982 Edinburgh, Nite Club, Scotland
16.04.1982 Greenock, Victorian Carriage, Scotland
17.04.1982 Dunoon, Tor-Na-De Hotel, Scotland
18.04.1982 Balloch, Ben Lomand Hotel, Scotland
19.04.1982 Broxburn, Astor Hotel, Scotland
21.04.1982 Glasgow, The Dial Inn, Scotland (afternoon show)
21.04.1982 Glasgow, The Dial Inn, Scotland (evening show)
22.04.1982 Inverness, Ice Rink, Scotland
23.04.1982 Keith, Longmore Hall, Scotland
24.04.1982 Grangemouth, Hotel Intercontinental, Scotland
25.04.1982 Kelso, Cross Keys, Scotland
27.04.1982 Edinburgh, University, Scotland
29.04.1982 Galashields, University of Textiles, Scotland
30.04.1982 Alloa, Town Hall, Scotland
01.05.1982 Kirkcaldy, Kinghorn Cunzie Neuk, Scotland
02.05.1982 Glasgow, The Mayfair, Scotland
06.05.1982 Aberdeen, The Venue, Scotland
07.05.1982 Glenrothes, Rothes Arms, Scotland
08.05.1982 Penrith, Newtonrigg College, England
09.05.1982 Lancaster, University, England
10.05.1982 Stafford, Riverside Recreation Centre, England
11.05.1982 Colwyn Bay, Pier, Wales
12.05.1982 Bangor, University, Wales
14.05.1982 London, Starlight Rooms West Hampstead, England
19.05.1982 London, Marquee Club, England
21.05.1982 London, Marquee Club, England
25.05.1982 Derby, Tiffanies, England
29.05.1982 Cambridge, Sound Cellar, England
19.06.1982 Aylesbury, Friars Maxwell Hall, England
21.06.1982 London, Clarendon Hotel, England
01.07.1982 London, Marquee Club, England
02.07.1982 London, Marquee Club, England
09.07.1982 East Retford, The Porterhouse, England
12.07.1982 Manchester, The Gallery, England
14.07.1982 Coventry, General Wolfe Club, England
16.07.1982 Cambridge, Sound Cellar, England
17.07.1982 Bath, Moles Club, England
22.07.1982 London, Marquee Club, England
24.07.1982 Milton Keynes, Starting Gate, England
12.08.1982 London, Marquee Club, England
13.08.1982 London, Marquee Club, England
14.08.1982 Cambrigde, Rock Club, England
16.08.1982 Southend, 0-6 Club, England
17.08.1982 Gloucester, Leisure Centre, England
19.08.1982 Sheffield, Limit Club, England
20.08.1982 Middlesbrough, Cavern Club, England
26.08.1982 Liverpool, The Warehouse, England
28.08.1982 Wakefield, Theakstone's Music Festival, England (Open Air)
29.08.1982 Reading, Thamesside Arena, England (Reading Rock-Open Air)
06.09.1982 London, Fair Deal Studios, England (first EMI Demo recordings)
13.09.1982 Glasgow, The Mayfair, Scotland
25.09.1982 London, Marquee Club, England
26.10.1982 London, University, England
27.10.1982 London, Marquee Club, England
28.10.1982 London, Marquee Club, England
29.10.1982 Coventry, General Wolfe Club, England
30.10.1982 East Retford, The Porterhouse, England
01.11.1982 Grimsby, Community Centre, England
02.11.1982 Manchester, The Gallery, England
03.11.1982 Bangor, University, Wales
04.11.1982 Liverpool, The Warehouse, England
06.11.1982 Guildford, Civic Hall, England
08.11.1982 Glasgow, Night Moves, England
09.11.1982 Ayr, Pavillon, Scotland
10.11.1982 Keith, Longmore Hall, Scotland
11.11.1982 Inverness, Ice Rink, Scotland
12.11.1982 Edinburgh, Nite Club, Scotland
13.11.1982 Dundee, University, Scotland

14.11.1982 Redcar, Coatham Bowl, England
15.11.1982 Southend, 0-6 Club, England
16.11.1982 Swindon, Brunel Rooms, England
17.11.1982 Gloucester, Leisure Centre, England
18.11.1982 Norwich, Gala Ballroom, England
20.11.1982 Dunstable, Queensway Hall, England
21.11.1982 Witney Oxen, Palace Theatre, England
22.11.1982 Canterbury, University, England
23.11.1982 Bristol, The Granary, England
24.11.1982 Stoke, Wagon and Horses, England
25.11.1982 Sheffield, Limit Club, England
26.11.1982 London, The Venue, England
28.12.1982 London, Marquee Club, England
29.12.1982 London, Marquee Club, England
30.12.1982 London, Marquee Club, England

1983

21.01.1983 Manchester, TV Studios, England (Oxford Road Show)
25.02.1983 Swindon, Brunel Rooms, England
26.02.1983 Plymouth, Polytechnical College, England
09.03.1983 Chelsea, College, England
15.03.1983 Norwich, University of East Anglia, England
16.03.1983 Reading, Top Rank, England
17.03.1983 Guildford, Civic Hall, England
18.03.1983 Aylesbury, Friars, England
19.03.1983 Folkestone, Lees Cliffe Hall, England
20.03.1983 Portsmouth, Guildhall, England
22.03.1983 Cardiff, Top Rank, Wales
23.03.1983 Malvern, Winter Gardens, England
24.03.1983 Bradford, Caesar's, England
25.03.1983 Newcastle, Mayfair Ballroom, England
27.03.1983 Bornemouth, Winter Gardens, England
28.03.1983 Bristol, Colston Hall, England
29.03.1983 Hanley, Victoria Hall, England
30.03.1983 Nottingham, Rock City, England
31.03.1983 Birmingham, Odeon, England
01.04.1983 Ipswich, Gaumont, England
02.04.1983 St.Albans, City Hall, England
05.04.1983 Hull, City Hall, England
06.04.1983 Middlesbrough, Town Hall, England
07.04.1983 Edinburgh, The Playhouse Theatre, Scotland
08.04.1983 Glasgow, Pavillon, Scotland
09.04.1983 Dundee, Caird Hall, Scotland
11.04.1983 Aberdeen, Capitol Theatre, Scotland
12.04.1983 Lancaster, University, England
13.04.1983 Sheffield, City Hall, England
14.04.1983 Liverpool, Royal Court Theatre, England
15.04.1983 Manchester, Apollo Theatre, England
17.04.1983 London, Hammersmith Odeon, England
18.04.1983 London, Hammersmith Odeon, England (last gig with Mick Pointer on drums)
12.05.1983 London, Marquee Club, England (played as SKYLINE DRIFTERS, first gig with Andy Ward on drums)
20.05.1983 London, BBC Studios, England (Old Grey Whistle Test)
21.05.1983 Mannheim, Rhein-Neckar-Stadion, Germany (Open Air)
22.05.1983 Würzburg, Talavera Messegelände, Germany (Open Air)
16.06.1983 Gorseinon, Penyrheol Theatre, Wales (Open Air)
17.06.1983 Glastonbury, CND Festival, England (Open Air)
01.07.1983 Roskilde, Festival, Denmark (Open Air)
03.07.1983 Den Haag, Zuiderpark, Holland (Parkpop-Open Air)
14.07.1983 Youngstown OH, USA
15.07.1983 Akron OH, Agora Ballroom, USA
17.07.1983 Alpine Valley WI, East Troy Music Theater, USA
18.07.1983 Lowell (Grand Rapids) MI, Showboat, USA
19.07.1983 Cincinatti OH, Bogart's, USA
20.07.1983 Columbus OH, Harrington Center, USA
22.07.1983 Chicago IL, Park West, USA
23.07.1983 Detroit MI, Grand Circus Theatre, USA
26.07.1983 Buffalo NY, Skytops, USA
27.07.1983 Poughkeepsie NY, The Chance, USA
29.07.1983 Waterbury CT, Toad's Place, USA
30.07.1983 Syracuse NY, The Lost Horizon, USA
31.07.1983 Montreal (Quebec), The Spectrum, Canada
01.08.1983 Quebec City (Quebec), Bars Univers, Canada
03.08.1983 Toronto (Ontario), Concert Hall, Cananda
04.08.1983 Rochester NY, Red Creek, USA
05.08.1983 New Haven CT, Toad's Place, USA
06.08.1983 Providence RI, The Living Room, USA
08.08.1983 New York City NY, Pier 84, USA (last show with Andy Ward on drums)

25.08.1983 Liverpool, Royal Court Theatre, England (first show with John Martyr on drums)
27.08.1983 Reading, Thamesside Arena, England (Reading Rock-Open Air)
18.09.1983 New York City NY, Radio City Hall, USA (Support for RUSH)
19.09.1983 New York City NY, Radio City Hall, USA (Support for RUSH)
20.09.1983 New York City NY, Radio City Hall, USA (Support for RUSH)
21.09.1983 New York City NY, Radio City Hall, USA (Support for RUSH)
22.09.1983 New York City NY, Radio City Hall, USA (Support for RUSH, last show with John Martyr on drums)
01.10.1983 Baunatal, Rundsporthalle, Germany (only gig with Jonathan Mover on drums)
27.10.1983 Aberystwyth, College, Wales (first show with Ian Mosley on drums)
28.10.1983 Swansea, University, Wales
29.10.1983 Bath, University, England
30.10.1983 London, Marquee Club, England (played as LUFTHANSA AIR TERMINAL)
27.12.1983 Nottingham, Rock City, England
28.12.1983 London, Hammersmith Odeon, England
29.12.1983 Aylesbury, Friars, England
30.12.1983 Birmimgham, Odeon, England
31.12.1983 Edinburgh, Playhouse Theatre, Scotland

1984

08.02.1984 Chippenham, Gold Diggers Club, England
09.02.1984 Hanley, Victoria Hall, England
10.02.1984 Manchester, TV Studios, England (Oxford Road Show)
11.02.1984 Leeds, University, England
12.02.1984 Lancaster, University, England
13.02.1984 Liverpool, Royal Court Theatre, England
14.02.1984 Manchester, Apollo Theatre, England
17.02.1984 Glasgow, Apollo, Scotland
18.02.1984 Aberdeen, Capitol Theatre, Scotland
19.02.1984 Edinburgh, Playhouse Theatre, Scotland
20.02.1984 Newcastle, City Hall, England
22.02.1984 Norwich, St.Andrews Hall, England
23.02.1984 Oxford, Apollo, England
24.02.1984 Cardiff, St.David's Hall, Wales
26.02.1984 Plymouth, Skating Rink, England
27.02.1984 Exeter, University, England
28.02.1984 Bristol, Colston Hall, England
29.02.1984 Southampton, Gaumont, England
02.03.1984 Brighton, The Dome, England
03.03.1984 Birmingham, Odeon, England
05.03.1984 Leicester, De Montfort Hall, England
06.03.1984 Sheffield, City Hall, England
08.03.1984 Southend, Cliff's Pavillon, England
09.03.1984 London, Hammersmith Odeon, England
10.03.1984 London, Hammersmith Odeon, England
11.03.1984 London, Hammersmith Odeon, England
12.03.1984 Chippenham, Gold Diggers Club, England
07.04.1984 Bourges, Festival, France (Open Air)
01.05.1984 Great Yarmouth, 3 in 1 Club, England (unannounced secret gig)
04.05.1984 Copenhagen, The Saga, Denmark
06.05.1984 Hamburg, Musikhalle, Germany
07.05.1984 Offenbach, Stadthalle, Germany
08.05.1984 Cologne, Sartory Saal, Germany
09.05.1984 Munich, Alabama Halle, Germany
11.05.1984 Paris, Eldorado, France
11.06.1984 Geleen, Sportpark, Holland (Pink Pop Open Air)
16.06.1984 Quebec City (Quebec), La Salle Albert Rousseau, Canada
17.06.1984 Quebec City (Quebec), La Salle Albert Rousseau, Canada
19.06.1984 Montreal (Quebec), Le Spectrum, Canada
20.06.1984 Montreal (Quebec), Le Spectrum, Canada
22.06.1984 Syracuse NY, The Lost Horizon, USA
25.06.1984 New Haven CT, Toad's Place, USA
26.06.1984 New York City NY, The Ritz, USA
30.06.1984 Schüttorf, Vechtwiese, Germany (Open Air)
02.07.1984 Stuttgart-Sindelfingen, Stadthalle, Germany
03.07.1984 Mannheim, Rosengarten, Germany
05.07.1984 Berlin, Metropol, Germany
06.07.1984 Paderborn, Hermann-Löns-Stadion, Germany (Open Air)
07.07.1984 Giessen, VFB-Waldstadion, Germany (Open Air)
08.07.1984 St.Wendel, Bosenbach-Stadion, Germany (Open Air)
10.07.1984 Zürich, Volkshaus, Switzerland
14.07.1984 Saint Pabu-Finisters, 6e Elixier Festival, France
21.07.1984 Milton Keynes, Concert Bowl, England (Open Air)

27.08.1984 Wakefield, Norstell Priory, England (Open Air)
03.11.1984 Liverpool, Royal Court Theatre, England
05.11.1984 Poole, Arts Centre, England
06.11.1984 Gloucester, Leisure Centre, England
07.11.1984 Cardiff, University, Wales
08.11.1984 Hanley, Victoria Hall, England
10.11.1984 Guildford, Surrey University, England
11.11.1984 Paris, Casino de Paris, France
12.11.1984 Nantes, Parc Exposition, France
13.11.1984 Brest, Petite Salle de Penfeld, France
15.11.1984 Paris, Espace Ballard, France
16.11.1984 Strasbourg, Hall Tivoli, France
17.11.1984 Amsterdam, Paradiso, Holland
19.11.1984 Stockholm, Göta Lejon, Sweden
20.11.1984 Copenhagen, The Saga, Denmark
21.11.1984 Zürich-Kloten, Schlüfwegzentrum, Switzerland
22.11.1984 Utrecht, Muziekcentrum, Vredenburg, Holland
23.11.1984 Kerkrade, Rodahal, Holland
24.11.1984 Poperinge, Meacker Blyde, Belgium
25.11.1984 Schifflange, Polyalent, Luxembourg
27.11.1984 Clermont-Ferrand, Palais des Congres, France
28.11.1984 Lyon, Palais D' Hiver, France
29.11.1984 Geneva, Salle de Fetes de Thonex, Switzerland
01.12.1984 Nancy, Parc Exposition, France
03.12.1984 Augsburg, Kongresshalle, Germany
04.12.1984 Fürth, Stadthalle, Germany
05.12.1984 Saabrücken, Kongresshalle, Germany
06.12.1984 Mainz, Rheingoldhalle, Germany
08.12.1984 Kassel, Stadthalle, Germany
10.12.1984 Bonn-Bad Godesberg, Stadthalle, Germany
11.12.1984 Essen, Grugahalle, Germany
13.12.1984 London, Hammersmith Odeon, England
14.12.1984 London, Hammersmith Odeon, England
15.12.1984 London, Hammersmith Odeon, England
17.12.1984 Manchester, Apollo Theatre, England
18.12.1984 Nottingham, Theatre Royal, England
19.12.1984 Glasgow, Barrowland Ballroom, Scotland (afternoon show)
19.12.1984 Glasgow, Barrowland Ballroom, Scotland (evening show)
20.12.1984 Edinburgh, Playhouse Theatre, Scotland
21.12.1984 Birmingham, Odeon, England
22.12.1984 Aylesbury, Civic Centre, England

1985

25.05.1985 Adenau, Nürburgring, Germany (Rock am Ring-Open Air)
27.05.1985 St.Gallen, Festivalgelände, Switzerland (Open Air)
01.06.1985 Nürnberg, Messegelände, Germany (Open Air)
03.06.1985 Barcelona, Salon Sibelle, Spain
05.06.1985 Madrid, Sala Canciller, Spain
06.06.1985 Madrid, Sala Canciller, Spain
08.06.1985 Lisbon, Pavilhao Belenenses, Portugal
09.06.1985 Oporto, Pavilhao Infante Sagres, Portugal
11.06.1985 Toulouse, Palais des Sports, France
15.06.1985 Nice, Theatre de Verdure, France
17.06.1985 Milan, Rolling Stone, Italy
18.06.1985 Bologna, Arena Puccini, Italy
17.08.1985 Donnington, Castle Donnington, England (Monsters of Rock-Open Air)
04.09.1985 Dublin, SFX Centre, Ireland
05.09.1985 Dublin, SFX Centre, Ireland
06.09.1985 Belfast, Maysfield Leisure Centre, Northern Ireland
10.09.1985 London, Marquee Club, England ("The Web UK" Fan Club Gig)
29.09.1985 Leicester, De Montfort Hall, England
06.10.1985 Tel Aviv, Festival, Israel
09.10.1985 Oslo, Asker Hall, Norway
11.10.1985 Stockholm, Eriksdalhallen, Sweden
12.10.1985 Göteborg, Frolundaborg Isshall, Sweden
13.10.1985 Copenhagen, Falkoner Theatre, Denmark
15.10.1985 Utrecht, Muziekcentrum Vredenburg, Holland
16.10.1985 Utrecht, Muziekcentrum Vredenburg, Holland
19.10.1985 Lausanne, Hall 18 Beaulieu, Switzerland
20.10.1985 Winterthur, Eulach-Halle, Switzerland
22.10.1985 Rome, Teatro Tenda, Italy
23.10.1985 Scandicci, Palasport, Italy
24.10.1985 Milan, Teatro Tenda, Italy
26.10.1985 Clermont-Ferrand, Maison des Sportes, France
27.10.1985 Toulon, Gymnase du Port Marchand, France
29.10.1985 Lyon, Bourse du Travail, France
30.10.1985 Strasbourg, Hall Tivoli, France
31.10.1985 Nancy, Parc Exposition, France
01.11.1985 Brussels, Voorst Nationaal, Belgium
04.11.1985 Bonn, Biskuithalle, Germany

05.11.1985 Frankfurt, Eissporthalle, Germany
07.11.1985 Rouen, Exo 7, France
08.11.1985 Paris, Le Zenith, France
09.11.1985 Mulhouse, Parc Exposition, France
11.11.1985 Stuttgart, Hans-Martin-Schleyer-Halle, Germany
12.11.1985 Karlsruhe, Gartenhalle, Germany
13.11.1985 Ludwigshafen, Friedrich-Ebert-Halle, Germany
14.11.1985 Munich, Sedelmayer-Halle, Germany
16.11.1985 Düsseldorf, Philipshalle, Germany
17.11.1985 Hamburg, Audimax, Germany
18.11.1985 Berlin, Eissporthalle, Germany
19.11.1985 Bremen, Stadthalle II, Germany
21.11.1985 Osnabrück, Stadthalle, Germany
22.11.1985 Kassel, Stadthalle, Germany
23.11.1985 Hannover, Stadion-Sporthalle, Germany
25.11.1985 Aachen, Eurogress, Germany
26.11.1985 Völklingen, Sporthalle, Germany
27.11.1985 Mainz, Rheingold-Halle, Germany
28.11.1985 Fürth, Stadthalle, Germany
03.12.1985 Osaka, Kosei Nenkin Hall, Japan
04.12.1985 Nagoya, Unryo Hall, Japan
05.12.1985 Nagoya, Unryo Hall, Japan
06.12.1985 Tokyo, Nihon Seinen Kan, Japan
07.12.1985 Tokyo, Nihon Seinen Kan, Japan
10.12.1985 London, Marquee Club, England
13.12.1985 London, Brixton Academy Theatre, England
14.12.1985 St.Austell, Cornwall Coliseum, England
15.12.1985 Brighton, Conference Centre, England
17.12.1985 Glasgow, Scottish Exhibition Centre, Scotland
18.12.1985 Blackpool, The Opera House, England
19.12.1985 Birmingham, National Exhibition Centre, England
20.12.1985 Southampton, Gaumont, England

1986

08.01.1986 London, Hammersmith Odeon, England
09.01.1986 London, Hammersmith Odeon, England
10.01.1986 London, Hammersmith Odeon, England
12.01.1986 Cardiff, St.David's Hall, Wales
13.01.1986 Cardiff, St.David's Hall, Wales
14.01.1986 Nottingham, Royal Centre, England
16.01.1986 Manchester, Apollo Theatre, England
17.01.1986 Manchester, Apollo Theatre, England
18.01.1986 Warrington, The Spectrum, England
20.01.1986 Aberdeen, Capitol Theatre, Scotland
21.01.1986 Edinburgh, Playhouse Theatre, Scotland
22.01.1986 Newcastle, City Hall, England
24.01.1986 Bristol, Colston Hall, England
25.01.1986 Birmingham, Odeon, England
26.01.1986 Birmingham, Odeon, England
28.01.1986 Sheffield, City Hall, England
29.01.1986 Leicester, De Montfort Hall, England
31.01.1986 Norwich, University of Anglia, England
03.02.1986 London, Hammersmith Odeon, England
04.02.1986 London, Hammersmith Odeon, England
05.02.1986 London, Hammersmith Odeon, England
06.02.1986 London, Hammersmith Odeon, England (Double o Charity Benefit)
26.02.1986 Utica NY, Mowhawk Valley Community College, USA
27.02.1986 Buffalo NY, Memorial Auditorium, USA (Support for Rush)
28.02.1986 Waterloo (Ontario), Super Skate Seven, Canada
01.03.1986 Toronto (Ontario), Concert Hall, Canada
03.03.1986 Quebec City (Quebec), Le Colise, Canada (Support for Rush)
04.03.1986 Montreal (Quebec), The Forum, Canada (Support for Rush)
07.03.1986 Winnipeg (Manitoba), Le-Rendez-Vous, Canada
09.03.1986 Calgary (Alberta), Mc Ewen Hall Ballroom at University, Canada
10.03.1986 Vancouver (British Columbia), Commodore Ballroom, Canada
11.03.1986 Seattle WA, Parker's, USA
12.03.1986 Portland OR, USA
14.03.1986 San Francisco CA, The Old Filmore, USA
15.03.1986 Los Angeles CA, The Roxy, USA
16.03.1986 Los Angeles CA, The Roxy, USA
20.03.1986 Indianapolis IN, Market Square Arena, USA (Support for Rush)
21.03.1986 Chicago IL, Rosemont Horizon, USA (Support for Rush)
22.03.1986 Chicago IL, Rosemont Horizon, USA (Support for Rush)
24.03.1986 Milwaukee WI, Mecca Arena, USA (Support for Rush)
25.03.1986 St.Paul MN, Civic Center, USA (Support for Rush)
27.03.1986 Grand Rapids MI, Devos Hall, USA
28.03.1986 Detroit MI, Joe Louis Arena, USA (Support for Rush)
29.03.1986 Cincinatti OH, Riverfront Coliseum, USA (Support for Rush)

31.03.1986 East Rutherford NJ, Brendan Byrne Arena, USA (Support for RUSH)
01.04.1986 East Rutherford NJ, Brendan Byrne Arena, USA (Support for RUSH)
02.04.1986 Springfield MA, Civic Center, USA (Support for RUSH)
04.04.1986 New York City NY, The Ritz, USA
27.04.1986 San Diego CA, California Theater, USA
28.04.1986 Los Angeles CA, Beverly Theater, USA
29.04.1986 Los Angeles CA, Beverly Theater, USA
11.06.1986 Göteborg, Liseberg, Sweden
12.06.1986 Stockholm, Grönalund, Sweden
14.06.1986 Paris, Hippodrome de Vincennes, France
15.06.1986 Munich, Olympiastadion, Germany (Open Air)
17.06.1986 Vienna, Stadthalle, Austria
19.06.1986 Rotterdam, Ahoy, Holland
21.06.1986 Mannheim, Maimarktgelände, Germany (Open Air)
26.06.1986 Berlin, Waldbühne, Germany (Open Air)
28.06.1986 Milton Keynes, Concert Bowl, England (Open Air)
17.07.1986 Milan, Stadio San Siro, Italy (Open Air)
19.07.1986 Cologne, Müngersdorfer Stadion, Germany (Open Air)
27.07.1986 St.Helens, Soap-Aid-Festival, England (Open Air)
03.08.1986 London, Olympia Theatre, England (British Music Fair)
27.12.1986 Aylesbury, Civic Centre, England
28.12.1986 Aylesbury, Civic Centre, England
29.12.1986 Liverpool, Royal Court Theatre, England
30.12.1986 Liverpool, Royal Court Theatre, England
31.12.1986 Glasgow, Barrowland Ballroom, Scotland

1987

14.04.1987 London, Marquee Club, England ("Incommunicado" Video Shot)
14.05.1987 Milan, Ristorante La Fanfula, Italy ("Pizza gig" with Fish and Pete)
22.06.1987 Gdansk, Olivia Hall, Poland
23.06.1987 Gdansk, Olivia Hall, Poland
25.06.1987 Zabrze, Hala Widowiskowo Sportowa, Poland
26.06.1987 Zabrze, Hala Widowiskowo Sportowa, Poland
27.06.1987 Poznan, Arena Hall, Poland
28.06.1987 Poznan, Arena Hall, Poland
30.06.1987 Padova, Palasport, Italy
01.07.1987 Torino, Assedio Park, Italy (Open Air, Soundcheck only, gig cancelled)
03.07.1987 Rome, E.U.R., Italy
05.07.1987 Locarno, Piazza Grande, Switzerland (Open Air)
06.07.1987 Genoa, Parco dei Torchi Nervi, Italy (Open Air)
08.07.1987 Annecy, Hall Exposition, France
09.07.1987 Paris, Le Zenith, France
10.07.1987 Frauenfeld, Pferderennbahn, Switzerland (Out in the Green-Open Air)
11.07.1987 Leysin, Festival, Switzerland (Open Air)
14.07.1987 Antibes, La Pinede, France
15.07.1987 Marseilles, Theatre du Pharao, France
16.07.1987 Lyon, Theatre Antique de Fourviere, France
18.07.1987 St.Goarshausen, Loreley-Freilichtbühne, Germany (Open Air)
16.09.1987 San Juan Capistrano CA, The Coach House, USA
18.09.1987 Riverside CA, Deanza Theater, USA
19.09.1987 Los Angeles CA, Hollywood Palladium, USA
20.09.1987 San Francisco CA, Warfield Theater, USA
21.09.1987 San Jose CA, Cabaret, USA
23.09.1987 Boulder CO, Glenn Miller Ballroom at University, USA
25.09.1987 Milwaukee WI, Billy's Old Mill, USA
26.09.1987 Minneapolis MN, First Avenue, USA
27.09.1987 Grand Rapids MI, Devos Hall, USA
29.09.1987 Detroit MI, The Ritz, USA
30.09.1987 Cincinatti OH, Bogart's, USA
02.10.1987 Poughkeepsie NY, The Chance, USA
03.10.1987 New York City NY, The Ritz, USA
05.10.1987 Kingston RI, Edwards Auditorium at University of Rhode Island, USA
06.10.1987 Washington DC, The Bayou, USA
08.10.1987 Ottawa (Ontario), Colloseum, Canada
09.10.1987 Quebec City (Quebec), Le Colise, Canada
10.10.1987 Verdun (Quebec), Auditorium, Canada

11.10.1987 Boston MA, Paradise Theater, USA
12.10.1987 Albany NY, Palace Theater, USA
13.10.1987 Toronto (Ontario), Massey Hall, Canada
14.10.1987 Rochester NY, Renaissance Theater, USA
15.10.1987 Poughkeepsie NY, The Chance, USA
03.11.1987 London, Wembley Arena, England
04.11.1987 London, Wembley Arena, England
05.11.1987 London, Wembley Arena, England
07.11.1987 Brussels, Voorst Nationaal, Belgium
08.11.1987 Rotterdam, Ahoy, Holland
09.11.1987 Rotterdam, Ahoy, Holland
11.11.1987 Copenhagen, Valby Hall, Denmark
12.11.1987 Oslo, Skedsmo Hall, Norway
13.11.1987 Göteborg, Scandinavium, Sweden
14.11.1987 Stockholm, Isstadion, Sweden
16.11.1987 Hannover, Stadion-Sporthalle, Germany
17.11.1987 Stuttgart, Hans-Martin-Schleyer-Halle, Germany
19.11.1987 Cologne, Sporthalle, Germany
20.11.1987 Saarbrücken, Messehalle, Germany
21.11.1987 Offenburg, Ortenau-Halle, Germany
23.11.1987 Essen, Grugahalle, Germany
24.11.1987 Münster, Halle Münsterland I, Germany
25.11.1987 Berlin, Deutschlandhalle, Germany
26.11.1987 Bremen, Stadthalle I, Germany
28.11.1987 Hamburg, Alsterdorfer Sporthalle, Germany
30.11.1987 Munich, Olympiahalle, Germany
01.12.1987 Eppelheim, Rhein-Neckar-Halle, Germany
02.12.1987 Mulhouse, Palais des Sports, France
03.12.1987 Metz, Parc Exposition, France
05.12.1987 Frankfurt, Festhalle, Germany
06.12.1987 Strasbourg, Hall Tivoli, France
07.12.1987 Lyon, Palais des Sports, France
08.12.1987 Toulon, Espace des Lices, France
10.12.1987 Toulouse, Palais des Sports, France
11.12.1987 Pau, Parc Exposition, France
13.12.1987 Nantes, La Beaujoire, France
14.12.1987 Paris, Palais Omnisports Bercy, France
17.12.1987 Edinburgh, Playhouse Theatre, Scotland
18.12.1987 Edinburgh, Playhouse Theatre, Scotland
19.12.1987 Edinburgh, Playhouse Theatre, Scotland
21.12.1987 Birmingham, National Exhibition Centre, England
22.12.1987 Birmingham, National Exhibition Centre, England

1988

07.01.1988 Aberdeen, Capitol Theatre, Scotland
08.01.1988 Newcastle, City Hall, England
09.01.1988 Hanley, Victoria Hall, England
11.01.1988 Manchester, Apollo Theatre, England
15.01.1988 London, Hammersmith Odeon, England
16.01.1988 London, Hammersmith Odeon, England
17.01.1988 London, Hammersmith Odeon, England
18.01.1988 London, Hammersmith Odeon, England
22.01.1988 Zürich, Hallenstadion, Switzerland
23.01.1988 Lausanne, Hall 7 Salle de Fetes Beaulieu, Switzerland
25.01.1988 Torino, Palasport, Italy
26.01.1988 Milan, Palatrussardi, Italy
27.01.1988 Florence, Palasport, Italy
30.01.1988 Napoli, Teatro Tenda, Italy
01.02.1988 Rome, Teatro Olympico, Italy
02.02.1988 Modena, Palasport, Italy
12.02.1988 St.Austell, Cornwall Coliseum, England
14.02.1988 Nottingham, Theatre Royal, England
15.02.1988 Sheffield, City Hall, England
24.03.1988 Guernsey, Centre Beau Sejnor, England
26.03.1988 Jersey, Centre Fort Regent, England
29.03.1988 Petange, Centre Sportif, Luxembourg
04.04.1988 Bourges, Le Stadium, France
24.04.1988 London, Marquee Club, England
27.05.1988 Aylesbury, Wendover Wellhead Inn, England
18.06.1988 East-Berlin, Radrennbahn Weissensee, East-Germany (Open Air)
23.07.1988 St.Andrews, Craightown Country Park, Scotland (Fife Aid II-Open Air, last gig with Fish)
16.09.1988 Rotterdam, De Glazen Zaal, Holland (Ibanez Music Fair, Steve Rothery only)
12.11.1988 Utrecht, Tivoli, Holland ("Freaks" Fan Club Convention, Pete Trewavas on vocals)
10.12.1988 Liverpool, Royal Court Theatre, England ("The Web UK" Fan Club Convention, Dave Lloyd on vocals)

1989

08.06.1989 Stoke Row, The Crooked Billet, England (played as LOW FAT YOGHURTS, first gig with Steve Hogarth)

01.08.1989 London, Brixton Academy Theatre, England ("Hooks in you" Video Shoot)
08.09.1989 Rotterdam, De Glazen Zaal, Hollan (Music Harmony Show with Steve H. and Steve R.)
05.10.1989 Besancon, Palais des Sports, France
06.10.1989 Lyon, Le Transbordeur, France
07.10.1989 Vitrolles, Stadium de Vitrolles, France
09.10.1989 Milan, Rolling Stone, Italy
10.10.1989 Zofingen, Mehrzweckhalle, Germany
11.10.1989 Düsseldorf, Philipshalle, Germany
12.10.1989 Berlin, Metropol, Germany
13.10.1989 Munich, Circus Krone, Germany
15.10.1989 Brussels, Ancienne Belgique, Belgium
16.10.1989 Utrecht, Muziekcentrum Vredenburg, Holland
17.10.1989 Utrecht, Muziekcentrum Vredenburg, Holland
18.10.1989 Hamburg, Concert Centrum Hamburg I, Germany
20.10.1989 Copenhagen, The Saga, Denmark
22.10.1989 Petange, Centre Sportif, Luxembourg
23.10.1989 Offenbach, Stadthalle, Germany
24.10.1989 Geneva, Salle de Fetes de Thonex, Switzerland
25.10.1989 Paris, Le Zenith, France
07.11.1989 London, Astoria Theatre, England
14.11.1989 New York City NY, The Ritz, USA
21.11.1989 Los Angeles CA, The Roxy, USA
03.12.1989 Newcastle, City Hall, England
04.12.1989 Glasgow, Barrowland Ballroom, Scotland
06.12.1989 Bristol, Colston Hall, England
07.12.1989 Newport, Newport Centre, Wales
09.12.1989 Hanley, Victoria Hall, England
10.12.1989 Bradford, St.Georges Hall, England
11.12.1989 Sheffield, City Hall, England
13.12.1989 Liverpool, Royal Court Theatre, England
14.12.1989 Manchester, Apollo Theatre, England
15.12.1989 Wolverhampton, Civic Hall, England
17.12.1989 Aston Villa, Leisure Centre, England
18.12.1989 London, Hammersmith Odeon, England

1990

19.01.1990 Sao Paulo, Morumbi Stadion, Brazil (Open Air)
27.01.1990 Rio de Janeiro, Sambadromo, Brazil (Hollywood Rock-Open Air)
01.02.1990 Toronto (Ontario), Diamond Club, Canada
02.02.1990 Montreal (Quebec), Le Spectrum, Canada
03.02.1990 Montreal (Quebec), Le Spectrum, Canada
05.02.1990 Cambrigde (Ontario), The Highlands, Canada
06.02.1990 Ottawa (Ontario), Barrymore's, Canada
07.02.1990 Boston MA, Paradise Theater, USA
09.02.1990 Springfield MA, Paramount Theater, USA
10.02.1990 New York City NY, The Ritz, USA
11.02.1990 Rochester NY, Renaissance Theater, USA
12.02.1990 New Haven CT, Toad's Place, USA
14.02.1990 Philadelphia PA, Theater of Living Arts, USA
15.02.1990 Philadelphia PA, Theater of Living Arts, USA
16.02.1990 Baltimore MD, Hammerjacks, USA
17.02.1990 Charlotte NC, Club 4808, USA
18.02.1990 Atlanta GA, The Roxy, USA
20.02.1990 Cincinatti OH, Bogart's, USA
21.02.1990 Grand Rapids MI, Club Eastbrook, USA
22.02.1990 Roseville (Detroit) MI, The Ritz, USA
23.02.1990 Milwaukee WI, Riverside Theater, USA
24.02.1990 Chicago IL, Park West, USA
01.03.1990 San Diego CA, Bacchanal, USA
02.03.1990 Hollywood CA, The Palace, USA
03.03.1990 San Jose CA, Cabaret, USA
08.03.1990 Madrid, Jacara, Spain
09.03.1990 Barcelona, Zeleste, Spain
11.03.1990 Toulouse, Gymnase, France
12.03.1990 Talence, La Medoquine, France
13.03.1990 Angers, Parc Exposition, France
14.03.1990 Clermont-Ferrand, Palais des Congres, France
15.03.1990 Nice, Theatre de Verdure, France
17.03.1990 Rome, Teatro Tenda, Italy
18.03.1990 Reggio Emilia, Festa dell' Unita Primavera, Italy
19.03.1990 Torino, Teatro Colosseo, Italy
21.03.1990 Augsburg, Schwabenhalle, Germany
22.03.1990 Aalen, Greuthalle, Germany
23.03.1990 St.Wendel, Sporthalle, Germany
24.03.1990 Heilbronn, Harmonie, Germany
25.03.1990 Bonn, Biskuithalle, Germany
27.03.1990 Bremen, Stadthalle II, Germany
28.03.1990 Osnabrück, Stadthalle, Germany
29.03.1990 Ludwigshafen, Friedrich-Ebert-Halle, Germany
30.03.1990 Mulhouse, Le Phoenix, France
01.04.1990 Paris, Le Zenith, France

02.04.1990 Lille, Espace Foire, France
03.04.1990 Rotterdam, Ahoy, Holland
05.04.1990 Oslo, Rockefeller, Norway
06.04.1990 Stockholm, Konserthuset, Sweden
24.04.1990 Leicester, De Montfort Hall, England
05.06.1990 Syracuse NY, The Lost Horizon, USA
06.06.1990 Boston MA, Paradise Theater, USA
07.06.1990 Northampton MA, Pearl Street Club, USA
08.06.1990 Asbury Park NJ, The Stone Pony, USA
09.06.1990 Bayshore NY, Sundance, USA
10.06.1990 Norfolk VA, The Boathouse, USA
12.06.1990 Washington DC, The Bayou, USA
13.06.1990 Glendale (Philadelphia) PA, Pulsations, USA
14.06.1990 Latham (Albany) NY, Saratoga Winners, USA
15.06.1990 Poughkeepsie NY, The Chance, USA
16.06.1990 Rochester NY, Penny Arcade, USA
17.06.1990 Cheektowaga NY, Sindbad's, USA
19.06.1990 Toledo OH, Roxanne's, USA
20.06.1990 Columbus OH, Newport Music Hall, USA
21.06.1990 Lakewood OH, Phantasy Theater, USA
23.06.1990 Maple (Ontario), Kingswood Music Theater, Canada
24.06.1990 London (Ontario), Kiplings, Canada
25.06.1990 Kitchener (Ontario), Stages, Canada
27.06.1990 Ottawa (Ontario), Barrymore's, Canada
28.06.1990 Ottawa (Ontario), Barrymore's, Canada
29.06.1990 Montreal (Quebec), La Ronde, Canada
30.06.1990 Port (Quebec), L' Agora du Vieux, Canada
07.07.1990 Brest, Plouenan, France
09.07.1990 Hull, City Hall, England
11.07.1990 Birmingham, National Exhibition Centre, England
12.07.1990 London, Wembley Arena, England
22.09.1990 Utrecht, Tivoli, Holland ("Freaks" Fan Club Convention)
10.12.1990 Bath, Moles Club, England ("The Web UK" Fan Club Show, played as Low Fat Yoghurts)
11.12.1990 Bath, Moles Club, England ("The Web UK" Fan Club Show, played as Low Fat Yoghurts)
12.12.1990 Bath, Moles Club, England ("The Web UK" Fan Club Show, played as Low Fat Yoghurts)
18.12.1990 Nottingham, Rock City, England
19.12.1990 Bristol, Bierkeller, England
20.12.1990 Walsall, Junction 10, England
21.12.1990 Manchester, The International II, England
22.12.1990 London, Town and Country Club, England

1991

22.05.1991 London, Bordeline Club, England (Unplugged show without Ian Mosley)
01.06.1991 Cologne, Luxor, Germany ("The Release" Fan Club Unplugged show without Ian Mosley)
10.06.1991 Milan, My Club, Italy (Steve Hogarth and Mark Kelly with a local band)
10.07.1991 Coventry, Tic Toc Club, England
13.07.1991 Workington, Festival, England (Cumbria-Rock-Open Air)
19.07.1991 Sopot, Festival, Poland
24.07.1991 Cologne, Live Music Hall, Germany
17.09.1991 Liverpool, Royal Court Theatre, England
18.09.1991 Oxford, Apollo, England
19.09.1991 Cambridge, Corn Exchange, England
21.09.1991 Manchester, Apollo Theatre, England
22.09.1991 Edinburgh, Playhouse Theatre, Scotland
23.09.1991 Bradford, St.Georges Hall, England
25.09.1991 Nottingham, Royal Centre, England
26.09.1991 Cardiff, St.David's Hall, Wales
27.09.1991 Aston Villa, Leisure Centre, England
29.09.1991 London, Hammersmith Odeon, England
30.09.1991 London, Hammersmith Odeon, England
03.10.1991 Rotterdam, Ahoy, Holland
05.10.1991 Paris, Le Zenith, France
06.10.1991 Düsseldorf, Philipshalle, Germany
07.10.1991 Munich, Circus Krone, Germany
08.10.1991 Berlin, Tempodrom, Germany
10.10.1991 Hamburg, Concert Centrum Hamburg III, Germany
11.10.1991 Copenhagen, The Saga, Denmark
12.10.1991 Stockholm, Palladium, Sweden
14.10.1991 Ludwigsburg, Forum, Germany
15.10.1991 Offenbach, Stadthalle, Germany
16.10.1991 Winterthur, Eulach-Halle, Switzerland
18.10.1991 Milan, Teatro Orfeo, Italy
19.10.1991 Lausanne, Hall 18 Beaulieu, Switzerland
21.10.1991 Brussels, Ancienne Belgique, Belgium
02.11.1991 Lisbon, Pavillon Carlos Lopez, Portugal

03.11.1991 Oporto, Coliseum, Portugal
06.11.1991 Madrid, Sala Canciller, Spain
07.11.1991 Barcelona, Zelesete, Spain
08.11.1991 Nice, Theatre de Verdure, France
10.11.1991 Cascina (Pisa), Teatro Politeama, Italy
11.11.1991 Genoa, Teatro Genovese, Italy
12.11.1991 Rome, Palladium, Italy
14.11.1991 Dolo (Venice), Teatro Excelsior, Itlay
16.11.1991 Locarno, Palazzo Fevi, Switzerland
18.11.1991 Vienna, CA Zelt, Austria
05.12.1991 Utrecht, Muziekcentrum Vredenburg, Holland
06.12.1991 Utrecht, Muziekcentrum Vredenburg, Holland
08.12.1991 Dortmund, Westfalenhalle III, Germany
09.12.1991 Hannover, Capitol, Germany
11.12.1991 Augsburg, Schwabenhalle, Germany
12.12.1991 Bonn, Biskuithalle, Germany
13.12.1991 Mulhouse, Le Phoenix, France
15.12.1991 Bristol, Victoria Rooms, England
16.12.1991 Aylesbury, Civic Hall, England
17.12.1991 Glasgow, Barrowland Ballroom, Scotland
18.12.1991 Middlesborough, Town Hall, England
20.12.1991 London, Town and Country Club, England

1992

16.03.1992 Allentown PA, Zodiac, USA (Pete T. with Steve H. and Steve R. acoustic)
18.03.1992 Danbury CT, Tuxedo Junction, USA, (Pete T. with Steve H. and Steve R. acoustic)
19.03.1992 Burlington VT, K.D. Churchills's, USA (Pete T. with Steve H. and Steve R. acoustic)
23.03.1992 Ste Foy (Quebec), Salle Albert Rousseau, Canada
24.03.1992 Montreal (Quebec), La Brique, Canada
25.03.1992 Toronto (Ontario), The Phoenix, Canada
27.03.1992 Utica NY, Lily's, USA (Afternoon show with Pete T., Steve H. and Steve R. acoustic)
27.03.1992 Syracuse NY, The Lost Horizon, USA (Evening show, full gig)
28.03.1992 New York City NY, The Ritz, USA
29.03.1992 Washington DC, The Bayou, USA
30.03.1992 Philadelphia PA, Chesnut Cabaret, USA
01.04.1992 Columbus OH, Newport Music Hall, USA
02.04.1992 Cleveland OH, Empire Concert Club, USA
03.04.1992 Ferndale MI, Magic Bag, USA (Afternoon show without Ian, acoustic)
03.04.1992 Roseville (Ferdale) MI, The Ritz, USA (Evening show, full gig)
04.04.1992 Chicago IL, Park West, USA
05.04.1992 Grand Rapids MI, Vinyl Solution, USA (Pete T. with Steve H. and Steve R. acoustic)
06.04.1992 Grand Rapids MI, Club Eastbrook, USA
07.04.1992 Bloomington IN, Jake's, USA
08.04.1992 Cincinatti OH, Bogart's, USA
09.04.1992 St.Louis MO, Mississippi Nights, USA
11.04.1992 Boulder CO, Fox Theater, USA
14.04.1992 Los Angeles CA, Variety Arts Theater, USA
15.04.1992 San Jose CA, Cabaret, USA
16.04.1992 Sunnyvale CA, CD Warehouse, USA (Afternoon show, acoustic)
16.04.1992 San Francisco CA, Bimbo's 365 Club, USA (Evening show, full gig)
09.05.1992 London, Borderline Club, England ("The Web UK" Fan Club 10th anniversary show)
06.06.1992 Adenau, Nürburgring, Germany (Rock am Ring-Open Air)
03.07.1992 Midtfyns, Festival, Denmark (Open Air)
10.07.1992 Tallinn, Festival, Estonia (Rock Summer-Open Air)
18.07.1992 Mexico City, National Auditorium, Mexico
23.07.1992 Milan, Dorema Cafe, Italy (Steve H. and Steve R. acoustic, Fan Club only)
25.07.1992 Riga, Festival, Lativa (Open Air, Mark Sugden on drums for an ill Ian Mosley)
29.07.1992 Lisbon, Aqualua do Restelo, Portugal (Acoustic show without Ian Mosley)
21.08.1992 Leysin, Gampel Festival, Switzerland
02.09.1992 Cologne, E-Werk, Germany ("The Release" Fan Club show)
03.09.1992 Rotterdam, Ahoy, Holland
05.09.1992 London, Wembley Arena, England
26.09.1992 Buenos Aires, Obras Stadium, Argentinia
30.09.1992 Caracas, Poliedro Arena, Venezuela
01.10.1992 Caracas, Poliedro Arena, Venezuela
04.10.1992 Manaus, Brylho, Brazil
05.10.1992 Sao Paulo, Olympia Concert Hall, Brazil
06.10.1992 Sao Paulo, Olympia Concert Hall, Brazil
08.10.1992 Rio de Janeiro, Canecao, Brazil
11.10.1992 Boston MA, Paradise Theater, USA
12.10.1992 New Haven CT, Toad's Place, USA
14.10.1992 Toronto (Ontario), The Phoenix, Canada

15.10.1992 Montreal (Quebec), La Brique, Canada
16.10.1992 Quebec City (Quebec), Solide Rock, Canada
17.10.1992 Quebec City (Quebec), Solide Rock, Canada
20.10.1992 Allentown PA, Zodiac, USA
21.10.1992 Poughkeepsie NY, The Chance, USA
22.10.1992 Philadelphia PA, Chesnut Cabaret, USA
23.10.1992 Baltimore MD, Hammerjacks, USA

1993

19.06.1993 Utrecht, Tivoli, Holland ("The Web Holland" Fan Club Convention, Steve H. and Pete T. playing with dutch band SINISTER STREET)

1994

09.02.1994 Cologne, Altes Presswerk, Germany ("The Release" Fan Club show, "Brave" pre-release party)
10.02.1994 Milan, Village Rock Cafe, Italy (Italian Fan Club show)
20.02.1994 Liverpool, Royal Court Theatre, England
22.02.1994 Cardiff, St.David's Hall, Wales
23.02.1994 Norwich, University of East Anglia, England
24.02.1994 Leeds, Town and Country, England
26.02.1994 Glasgow, Barrowland Ballroom, Scotland
28.02.1994 Wolverhampton, Civic Hall, England
01.03.1994 Aylesbury, Civic Hall, England
02.03.1994 Cambridge, Corn Exchange, England
04.03.1994 London, Forum, England
05.03.1994 London, Forum, England
15.03.1994 Bremen, Aladin, Germany
16.03.1994 Berlin, Huxley's, Germany
17.03.1994 Bonn, Biskuithalle, Germany
19.03.1994 Hannover, Capitol, Germany
20.03.1994 Bielefeld, PC 69, Germany
22.03.1994 Hamburg, Docks, Germany
23.03.1994 Hamburg, Docks, Germany
24.03.1994 Groningen, Envenementenhal, Holland
26.03.1994 Geleen, Hanehof, Holland
28.03.1994 Amsterdam, Paradiso, Holland ("The Web Holland" Fan Club show)
29.03.1994 Amsterdam, Paradiso, Holland
31.03.1994 Utrecht, Muziekcentrum Vredenburg, Holland
05.04.1994 Neu-Isenburg, Hugenottenhalle, Germany
06.04.1994 Fürth, Stadthalle, Germany
07.04.1994 Ludwigsburg, Forum, Germany
08.04.1994 Waldkirch, Stadthalle, Germany
10.04.1994 Munich, Terminal I, Germany
11.04.1994 Linz, Posthof, Austria
12.04.1994 Vienna, CA Zelt, Austria
14.04.1994 Milan, City Square, Italy
15.04.1994 Genoa, Teatro Verdi, Italy
17.04.1994 Zürich, Kongress Spirrgarten, Switzerland
18.04.1994 Nice, Theatre de Verdure, France
20.04.1994 Geneva, Palladium, Switzerland
22.04.1994 Madrid, Sala Canciller II, Spain
23.04.1994 Lerida, Sala Xelsa, Spain
26.04.1994 Aucamville, Salle des Fetes, France
27.04.1994 Lyon, Le Transbordeur, France
28.04.1994 Paris, La Cigale, France
29.04.1994 Paris, La Cigale, France
30.04.1994 Paris, La Cigale, France
02.05.1994 Besancon, Le Montjoye, France
03.05.1994 Reims, Le Cirque, France
04.05.1994 Gent, Vooruit, Belgium
05.05.1994 Rastatt, Badener Halle, Germany
06.05.1994 Enschede, Muziekcentrum, Holland
08.05.1994 Guildford, Civic Hall, England
09.05.1994 Sheffield, City Hall, England
11.05.1994 Oxford, Apollo, England
12.05.1994 Manchester, Apollo Theatre, England
13.05.1994 Newcastle, City Hall, England
14.05.1994 Nottingham, Royal Concert Hall, England
16.05.1994 Bristol, Colston Hall, England
17.05.1994 Birmingham, Town Hall, England
18.05.1994 London, Hammersmith Odeon, England
21.05.1994 Helsinki, Tavastia, Finland
23.05.1994 Stockholm, Circus, Sweden
24.05.1994 Oslo, Sentrum, Norway
25.05.1994 Malmö, Kulturbolaget, Sweden
27.05.1994 Copenhagen, Pumpehusset, Denmark
28.05.1994 Copenhagen, Pumpehusset, Denmark
11.06.1994 Luzern, Eschenbach-Festival, Switzerland (Open Air)
12.06.1994 Cologne, Tanzbrunnen, Germany (Open Air)
14.06.1994 Poznan, Poznan Arena, Poland
15.06.1994 Warsaw, Congresshaus, Poland
18.06.1994 Weert, Bospop-Festival, Holland (Open Air)
13.07.1994 Osaka, W'ohol, Japan

15.07.1994 Kawasaki, Club Citta, Japan
16.07.1994 Kawasaki, Club Citta, Japan
06.08.1994 Chur, Festival, Switzerland (Open Air)
07.08.1994 Colmar, Festival, France (Open Air)
02.09.1994 Mexico City, National Auditorium, Mexico
03.09.1994 Mexico City, La Diabla, Mexico (unannounced special Club gig)

1995

31.01.1995 London, Ronnie Scott's, England (Steve H. and Steve R. perform with Dream Theater)
17.06.1995 Utrecht, Tivoli, Holland ("The Web Holland" Fan Club show, semi-acoustic)
18.06.1995 London, The Mean Fiddler, England ("The Web UK" Fan Club show, semi-acoustic)
23.06.1995 Arnhem, Luxor Theatre, Holland
02.08.1995 Washington DC, The Bayou, USA
03.08.1995 Philadelphia PA, Theater of Living Arts, USA
04.08.1995 Boston MA, The Paradise, USA
05.08.1995 Toronto (Ontario), RPM Warehouse, Canada
07.08.1995 New Haven CT, Toad's Place, USA
08.08.1995 New York City NY, Tramps, USA
09.08.1995 South Amboy NJ, Club Bene, USA
11.08.1995 Cleveland OH, The Odeon, USA
12.08.1995 Pittsburgh PA, Graffiti Showcase, USA (Afternoon show for "The Web USA" Fan Club)
12.08.1995 Pittburgh PA, Graffiti Showcase, USA (Evening show, full gig)
13.08.1995 Columbus OH, Newport Music Hall, USA
14.08.1995 Grand Rapids MI, Orbit Room, USA
15.08.1995 Chicago IL, Park West, USA
17.08.1995 Montreal (Quebec), Le Spectrum, Canada
18.08.1995 Ste-Foy (Quebec), Salle Albert Rousseau, Canada
19.08.1995 Poughkeepsie NY, The Chance, USA
15.09.1995 Oxford, Apollo, England
16.09.1995 London, Forum, England
17.09.1995 Cambridge, Corn Exchange, England
19.09.1995 Wolverhampton, Civic Hall, England
20.09.1995 Manchester, Apollo Theatre, England
21.09.1995 Leeds, Town and Country, England
23.09.1995 Glasgow, Barrowland Ballroom, Scotland
24.09.1995 Nottingham, Royal Concert Hall, England
25.09.1995 Cardiff, St.David's Hall, Wales
27.09.1995 London, Shepherd's Bush Empire, England
29.09.1995 Rotterdam, Ahoy, Holland
30.09.1995 Luxembourg, Dudelange Sports Hall, Luxembourg
01.10.1995 Hamburg, Grosse Freiheit, Germany
02.10.1995 Hamburg, Grosse Freiheit, Germany
04.10.1995 Paris, Le Zenith, France
05.10.1995 Saarbrücken, Kultur-Fabrik, Germany
06.10.1995 Bonn, Biskuithalle, Germany
07.10.1995 Hannover, Capitol, Germany
09.10.1995 Bielefeld, PC 69, Germany
10.10.1995 Neu-Isenburg, Hugenottenhalle, Germany
11.10.1995 Stuttgart-Filderstadt, Philharmonie, Germany

1996

21.04.1996 Hilversum, KRO-FM-Radio-Studio, Holland (Acoustic gig)
22.04.1996 Utrecht, Muziekcentrum Vredenburg, Holland
23.04.1996 Cologne, E-Werk, Germany
24.04.1996 Paris, La Cigale, France
28.04.1996 London, Forum, England

1997

30.04.1997 Glasgow, Glasgow Garage, Scotland
02.05.1997 Cambridge, Corn Exchange, England
03.05.1997 Cardiff, St.David's Hall, Wales
04.05.1997 Aylesbury, Civic Centre, England
06.05.1997 Wolverhampton, Civic Hall, England
07.05.1997 Norwich, University of East Anglia, England
08.05.1997 Leeds, Town and Country, England
09.05.1997 Nottingham, Royal Concert Hall, England
10.05.1997 Poole, Arts Centre, England
12.05.1997 London, Shepherd's Bush Empire, England
13.05.1997 London, Shepherd's Bush Empire, England
15.05.1997 Manchester, Apollo Theatre, England
16.05.1997 Redcar, Coatham Bowl, England
19.05.1997 Gent, Vooruit, Belgium
20.05.1997 Paris, Bataclan, France
23.05.1997 Geleen, Hanehof, Holland
24.05.1997 Utrecht, Muziekcentrum Vredenburg, Holland

25.05.1997 Den Haag, Congresgebouw, Holland
26.05.1997 Groningen, Oosterpoort, Holland
28.05.1997 Eindhoven, MC Frits Phillips, Holland
29.05.1997 Utrecht, Tivoli, Holland ("The Web Holland" Fan Club show)
30.05.1997 Esbjerg, Gl. Vardevej, Denmark (Esbjerg-Rock-Festival)
14.06.1997 Brasilia, Nilson Nelson Stadium, Brazil (Skol-Rock-Festival)
15.06.1997 Goiania, Jao Sportscenter, Brazil
20.06.1997 Sao Paulo, Olympia, Brazil
21.06.1997 Sao Paulo, Olympia, Brazil
22.06.1997 Buenos Aires, Hard Rock Cafe, Argentinia (Afternoon show, short gig)
22.06.1997 Buenos Aires, Opera Teatre, Argentinia (Evening show, full gig)
24.06.1997 Porto Alegre, Gigantinho, Brazil
25.06.1997 Santiago de Chile, Estadio Chile, Chile
27.06.1997 Campinas, Pedreira do Chapadao, Brazil (Skol-Rock-Festival)
28.06.1997 Rio de Janeiro, Metropolitan, Brazil
29.06.1997 Belo Horizonte, Serraria Souza Pinto, Brazil
05.07.1997 Madrid, Communidad de Madrid Stadium, Spain (Rock'in Madrid-Festival)
27.07.1997 Bellinzona, Festival, Switzerland (Kingdom-Open Air)
24.08.1997 San Juan Capistrano CA, Coach House, USA
25.08.1997 Los Angeles CA, House of Blues, USA
26.08.1997 San Francisco CA, The Fillmore, USA
30.08.1997 Pittsburgh PA, Graffiti Showcase, USA (Afternoon Fan Club session)
30.08.1997 Pittsburgh PA, Graffiti Showcase, USA (Evening show, full gig)
31.08.1997 Rochester NY, House of Guitars, USA (Afternoon electric set, without Steve R.)
31.08.1997 Rochester NY, The Spectrum, USA (Evening show, full gig)
01.09.1997 Poughkeepsie NY, The Chance, USA
04.09.1997 Toronto (Ontario), The Guverment, Canada
05.09.1997 Quebec City (Quebec), Salle Albert Rousseau, Canada
06.09.1997 Montreal (Quebec), The Spectrum, Canada
09.09.1997 New Haven CT, Toad's Place, USA
10.09.1997 Sommerville MA, Sommerviller Theater, USA
11.09.1997 New York City NY, Irving Plaza, USA
13.09.1997 South Amboy NJ, Club Bene, USA
15.09.1997 Alexandria VA, The Birchmere, USA
16.09.1997 Philadelphia PA, Theater of Living Arts, USA
18.09.1997 Cincinatti OH, Bogart's, USA
19.09.1997 Cleveland OH, The Odeon, USA
20.09.1997 Milwaukee WI, The Rave, USA
21.09.1997 Grand Rapids MI, Aris' Disc Shop, USA (Pete T. with Steve H. and Steve R. acoustic)
21.09.1997 Grand Rapids MI, Orbit Room, USA (Evening show, full gig)
23.09.1997 Chicago IL, Park West, USA
26.09.1997 Mexico City, Radio Activo, Mexico (Afternoon Surprise show with Pete T., Steve H. and Steve R. acoustic)
26.09.1997 Mexico City, Hard Rock Cafe, Mexico (Evening Surprise show, full band)
27.09.1997 Mexico City, National Auditorium, Mexico
04.10.1997 Munich, Colloseum, Germany
05.10.1997 Nürnberg, Forum, Germany
06.10.1997 Luxembourg, Atelier, Luxembourg
07.10.1997 Bonn, Biskuithalle, Germany
09.10.1997 Halle, Easy Schorre, Germany
10.10.1997 Berlin, Huxley's, Germany
12.10.1997 Bielefeld, PC 69, Germany
13.10.1997 Hamburg, Docks, Germany
14.10.1997 Hannover, Capitol, Germany
15.10.1997 Stuttgart, Longhorn, Germany
16.10.1997 Neu-Isenburg, Hugenottenhalle, Germany
19.10.1997 Aucamville, Salle Georges Brassens, France
20.10.1997 Nice, Theatre de Verdure, France
21.10.1997 Lyon, Le Transbordeur, France
22.10.1997 Reims, L'Usine, France
23.10.1997 Lille, Le Splendid Jenlain, France
25.10.1997 Strasbourg, La Laiterie, France
27.10.1997 Amsterdam, Paradiso, Holland ("The Web Holland" Fan Club show)

1998

10.01.1998 Barcelona, Ateneu Popular de Nou Barris, Spain (Fan Club acoustic gig with Pete T., Steve H. and Streve R.)
24.05.1998 Steeple Barton, Hopcroft Hotel, England (Short gig, wedding of engineer Stewart Every, without Pete T.)
25.06.1998 Oswestry, The Walls Restaurant, England (Intimate gig for a few fans from all over the world, acoustic)

26.06.1998 Oswestry, The Walls Restaurant, England (second night of the Intimate gig called "Candlelight Dinner Concert")
17.08.1998 Hilversum, Radio-Studio, Holland (Short acoustic show with Mark K., Steve H. and Steve R.)
29.08.1998 Oxford, Zodiac Club, England ("The Web UK" Fan Club Convention, full gig)
05.09.1998 Utrecht, Tivoli, Holland ("The Web Holland" Fan Club show)
12.09.1998 Cologne, Alter Wartesaal, Germany ("The Release" Fan Club show)
14.09.1998 London, Jazz Cafe, England (Album-release-party, with electric set)
19.09.1998 Göteborg, Pusterviksteatern, Sweden (Album-launch with electric set)
09.10.1998 Paris, Virgin Megastore, France (Album-launch with acoustic set by Pete T., Steve H. and Steve R.)
17.10.1998 Madrid, Sala Caracol, Spain (Album-launch with electric set)
30.10.1998 Reading, University, England
01.11.1998 Manchester, The Academy, England
02.11.1998 Manchester, Rock City, England
04.11.1998 Wolverhampton, Civic Hall, England
05.11.1998 Aylesbury, Civic Centre, England
06.11.1998 London, Forum, England
08.11.1998 Munich, Babylon, Germany
09.11.1998 Dieberg, Ludwigshalle, Germany
10.11.1998 Bielefeld, PC 69, Germany
12.11.1998 Hamburg, Docks, Germany
13.11.1998 Hannover, Capitol, Germany
14.11.1998 Cologne, E-Werk, Germany
16.11.1998 Rotterdam, Ahoy, Holland
18.11.1998 Paris, L'Elysee Montmartre, France
14.12.1998 Aylesbury, Grapes Pub, England ("The Web UK" meets Steve H. for singing to X-mas karaoke-CD)

1999

09.04.1999 Essex, The Maypole, England (Steve R. surprises Fish at his acoustic gig, they perform "Sugar mice")
29.05.1999 Bernex, Feast of Hope-Festival, Switzerland (Fish as a guest with Steve H. on stage during "Hope for the future", later they perform "Lavender" together)
24.07.1999 Oxford, The Zodiac, England ("The Web UK" Fan Club Convention, full electric set)
25.07.1999 Oxford, The Zodiac, England (second night of "The Web UK" Fan Club Convention, full electric set)
26.07.1999 Oxford, The Zodiac, England (Club gig, open to the public)
27.07.1999 Oxford, The Zodiac, England (second night, Club gig, open to the public)
06.10.1999 Paris, MCM Cafe, France (Live show for French TV)
16.11.1999 Dudley, JB's, England
17.11.1999 Nottingham, Rock City, England
18.11.1999 Manchester, The Academy, England
20.11.1999 London, Shepard's Bush Empire, England
22.11.1999 Groningen, Oosterpoort, Holland
23.11.1999 Tilburg, 013, Holland
24.11.1999 Enschede, Music Centre, Holland
25.11.1999 Amsterdam, Paradiso, Holland
27.11.1999 Hamburg, Saturn-Music-Store, Germany (afternoon 3 song acoustic gig)
27.11.1999 Hamburg, Docks, Germany (evening show)
28.11.1999 Berlin, Columbia Halle, Germany
29.11.1999 Cologne, E-Werk, Germany
30.11.1999 Stuttgart, Longhorn, Germany
02.12.1999 Dresden, Schlachthof, Germany
03.12.1999 Hannover, Capitol, Germany
04.12.1999 Mannheim, Capitol, Germany
05.12.1999 Aachen, Cafe Roncalli, Germany (intimate semi-acoustic "Christmas goose"-gig, incl. dinner for "The Web"-members)

2000

27.05.2000 Geneva, Stade du Bout-du-Monde, Switzerland "Feast of Hope-Festival" (H Band)
18.06.2000 Bethlehem PA, Zoellner Arts Center, USA "NEARfest" (Transatlantic)
20.06.2000 Cambridge MA, The Middle East, USA (Transatlantic)
21.06.2000 Philadelphia PA, Theater of Living Arts, USA (Transatlantic)
22.06.2000 New Haven CT, Toad's Place, USA (Transatlantic)
23.06.2000 New York City NY, Wetlands, USA (Transatlantic)
24.06.2000 Washington DC, 9:30 Club, USA (Transatlantic)
08.08.2000 London, Dingwalls, England "An evening of Genius" (H Band with new line-up)

09.08.2000 London, Dingwalls, England "An evening of Genius" (H Band with new line-up + special guest Colin Woore = How we live reunion)
01.09.2000 Los Angeles CA, La Mirada Civic Theater for the Performing Arts, USA "Progfest 2000" (Transatlantic)
31.10.2000 Utrecht, Tivoli, Holland (H Band with Pete Trewavas)
16.11.2000 Burton-upon-Trent, The Bass Museum, England (acoustic set)
17.11.2000 Burton-upon-Trent, The Bass Museum, England (acoustic set)
20.11.2000 Dublin, The HQ, Ireland
24.11.2000 Mailand, Binario Zero, Italy
28.11.2000 Oslo, Rockefeller, Norway
01.12.2000 Leeds, The Cockpit, England
02.12.2000 London, La Scala, England
04.12.2000 Paris, Cafe de la Danse, France
07.12.2000 Cologne, Rhein Rock Hallen, Germany
09.12.2000 Rotterdam, Nighttown, Holland
10.12.2000 Rotterdam, Nighttown, Holland
12.12.2000 Barcelona, Bikini, Spain

2001

20.01.2001 Anaheim CA, NAMM Show, USA (Transatlantic)
12.02.2001 London, Royal Albert Hall, England (Jordan Formula 1 Team-party, All-Star-Band with Pete Trewavas, Ian Mosley and Steve Rothery)
13.02.2001 Bath, The Venue, England
15.02.2001 Durham, The Ballroom, England
16.02.2001 Leeds, The Cockpit, England
18.02.2001 Sheffield, The Fusion, England
19.02.2001 Liverpool, Stanley Theatre, England
20.02.2001 Nottingham, Glow Bar, England
22.02.2001 Cambridge, The Boat Race, England
23.02.2001 Oxford, Zodiac, England
25.02.2001 Swansea, Divas, Wales
28.02.2001 London, Dingwalls, England
16.03.2001 Oswestry, The Walls Restaurant, England ("Stranger by the Minute"-gig with Steve Hogarth, Steve Rothery and Pete Trewavas)
04.05.2001 Codevilla, Thunder Road, Italy
05.05.2001 Lucca, Circuito, Italy (gig was cancelled)
15.05.2001 Dublin, Vicar Street, Ireland
18.05.2001 Hemel Hempstead, Dacorum Pavilion, England
19.05.2001 Manchester, Academy, England
20.05.2001 Wolverhampton, Civic Centre, England
22.05.2001 London, Forum, England
23.05.2001 Paris, Virgin Megastore, France (short acoustic gig with Steve Rothery, Steve Hogarth and Pete Trewavas)
23.05.2001 Paris, Bataclan, France (500. gig of Steve Hogarth with Marillion)
24.05.2001 Cologne, E-Werk, Germany
26.05.2001 Amsterdam, Heineken Hal, Holland
28.05.2001 Lille, Le Splendid, France
29.05.2001 Strasbourg, La Laiterie, France
31.05.2001 Lyon, Le Transbordeur, France
02.06.2001 Tolouse, Le Bikini, France
04.06.2001 Barcelona, Sala Bikini, Spain
05.06.2001 Barcelona, Sala Bikini, Spain
06.06.2001 Madrid, Sala Arena, Spain
22.06.2001 Bex, Grandes Iles d'Amont Rock Festival (Open Air), Switzerland
23.06.2001 Wohlen Aargau, Sound Arena Rock Festival (Open Air), Switzerland
07.07.2001 Bellinzona, Rock Circus, Switzerland (Open Air)
08.08.2001 London, Dingwalls, England (H-Band, the 2nd annual "Evenings of Genius"-Spirit Evening)
09.08.2001 London, Dingwalls, England (H-Band, the 2nd annual "Evenings of Genius"-Spirit Evening)
10.08.2001 Bonn-Beuel, Brückenforum, Germany (H-Band, German Fan Convention "A box of surprises", encores with Ian Mosley + Pete Trewavas)
15.09.2001 Lucca, Palazzo Ducale, Italy
17.09.2001 Lisbon, Paradise Garage, Portugal
18.09.2001 Porto, Estado Novo, Portugal
22.09.2001 San Miguel (Azores), Ponta Delgada, Portugal
04.10.2001 Rome, Alpheus Club, Italy
05.10.2001 Forti, Naima Club, Italy
06.10.2001 Pontoglio (BS), Palabosco, Italy
09.10.2001 Leeds, Metropolitan University, England
10.10.2001 London, Astoria, England
12.10.2001 Paris, Elysee Montmartre, France
13.10.2001 Tilburg, 013, Holland
14.10.2001 Groningen, Oosterpoort, Holland
15.10.2001 Utrecht, Muziekcentrum Vredenburg, Holland
17.10.2001 Hamburg, Grosse Freiheit, Germany
18.10.2001 Düsseldorf, Tor 3, Germany
19.10.2001 Bielefeld, PC 69, Germany

21.10.2001 Mannheim, Capitol, Germany
22.10.2001 Stuttgart, Longhorn, Germany
23.10.2001 Berlin, ColumbiaFritz, Germany
25.10.2001 Krakow, Kinoteatr UPC Zwiazkowiec, Poland
26.10.2001 Bydgoszcz, Astoria Sport Hall, Poland
10.11.2001 London, Astoria, England (TRANSATLANTIC)
11.11.2001 Paris, Elysee Montmartre, France (TRANSATLANTIC)
12.11.2001 Tilburg, 013, Holland (TRANSATLANTIC)
13.11.2001 Cologne, Live Music Hall, Germany (TRANSATLANTIC)
15.11.2001 Brussels, Ancienne Belgique, Belgium (TRANSATLANTIC)
16.11.2001 Hamburg, Grosse Freiheit, Germany (TRANSATLANTIC)
17.11.2001 Berlin, Music Hall, Germany (TRANSATLANTIC)
18.11.2001 Karlsruhe, Festhalle Durlach, Germany (TRANSATLANTIC)
19.11.2001 Munich, Elserhalle, Germany (TRANSATLANTIC)
20.11.2001 Milan, Palavobis, Italy (TRANSATLANTIC)

FISH Tour History

1989

21.03.1989 Lockerbie, Rex Cinema, Scotland
30.09.1989 Utrecht, Tivoli, Holland ("Freaks" Fan Club Convention)
11.10.1989 Haddington, Corn Exchange, Scotland
12.10.1989 Haddington, Corn Exchange, Scotland
13.10.1989 North-Berwick, Beach Pavillon, Scotland
15.10.1989 Dingwall, Legends, Scotland
16.10.1989 Elgin, Town Hall, Scotland
17.10.1989 Ullapool, Village Hall, Scotland
19.10.1989 Stornoway (Isle of Lewis), Seaforth Hotel, Scotland
20.10.1989 Portree (Isle of Skye), Gathering Hall, Scotland
21.10.1989 Aviemore, Crofter's Pub, Scotland (Jam-session because of cancelled gig in the Osprey-Suite)
23.10.1989 Edinburgh, Queens Hall, Scotland
24.10.1989 Stirling, Albert Hall, Scotland
25.10.1989 Ayr, Pavillon, Scotland
26.10.1989 Leeds, University, England
28.10.1989 Blackburn, St.Georges Hall, England
29.10.1989 Manchester, The Ritz, England
30.10.1989 Glasgow, Barrowlands, Scotland
31.10.1989 Newcastle, City Hall, England
02.11.1989 Wolverhampton, Civic Hall, England
03.11.1989 Cambridge, Corn Exchange, England
04.11.1989 Sheffield, University Octagon, England
05.11.1989 Liverpool, Royal Court Theatre, England
07.11.1989 Portsmouth, Guildhall, England
08.11.1989 Guildford, Civic Hall, England
09.11.1989 Newport, Gwent Centre, Wales
11.11.1989 London, Town and Country Club, England
12.11.1989 London, Town and Country Club, England
14.12.1989 Glasgow, College of Art, Scotland ("Cash for Kids"-Acoustic gig with Fish, Robin Boult, Frank Usher and Mickey Simmonds)

1990

28.02.1990 Liverpool, Royal Court Theatre, England
01.03.1990 Newcastle, Polytechnic, England
02.03.1990 Norwich, University of East Anglia, England
05.03.1990 Milan, Rolling Stone, Italy
06.03.1990 Zürich, Volkshaus, Switzerland
09.03.1990 Düsseldorf, Philipshalle, Germany
10.03.1990 Rotterdam, Ahoy, Holland
11.03.1990 Brussels, Ancienne Belgique, Belgium
12.03.1990 Paris, Olympia, France
14.03.1990 Offenbach, Stadthalle, Germany
15.03.1990 Pentange, Centre Sportif, Luxembourg
16.03.1990 Münster, Halle Münsterland, Germany
18.03.1990 Oslo, Rockefeller, Norway
19.03.1990 Copenhagen, The Saga, Denmark
20.03.1990 Hamburg, Concert Centrum Hamburg III, Germany
22.03.1990 Berlin, Neue Welt, Germany
24.03.1990 Kassel, Stadthalle, Germany
26.03.1990 Birmingham, Aston Villa Leisure Centre, England

27.03.1990 Edinburgh, Playhouse Theatre, Scotland
28.03.1990 Manchester, Apollo, England
29.03.1990 Cardiff, St.David's Hall, Wales
31.03.1990 Nottingham, Royal Court Hall, England
01.04.1990 London, Hammersmith Odeon, England
02.04.1990 London, Hammersmith Odeon, England
07.04.1990 Edinburgh, Buster Brown's, Scotland
13.05.1990 Dunfermline, East End Park, Scotland (Fish with Frank Usher and NAZARETH, Charity-Open Air)
24.05.1990 Coventry, Tic Toc Club, England
26.05.1990 Konstanz, Bodenseestadion, Germany (Open Air)
02.06.1990 Salzgitter, Insel, Germany (Open Air)
03.06.1990 St.Wendel, Bosenbachstadion, Germany (Open Air)
04.06.1990 Cologne, Luxor, Germany (Intimate Club gig)
05.06.1990 Hamburg, Logo, Germany (Intimate Club gig)
08.06.1990 Jübeck, Festival, Germany (Open Air)
09.06.1990 Gelsenkirchen, Parkstadion, Germany (Open Air)
10.06.1990 Mulhouse, Le Phoenix, France
11.06.1990 Lyon, Le Transbordeur, France
13.06.1990 Utrecht, Muziekcentrum Vredenburg, Holland
14.06.1990 Utrecht, Muziekcentrum Vredenburg, Holland ("Freaks" Fan Club members only)
17.06.1990 Berlin, Radrennbahn Weissensee, Germany (Open Air)
18.06.1990 Genoa, Parco di Nervi, Italy (Open Air)
20.06.1990 Turin, Arena Metropolis, Italy
21.06.1990 Modena, Festa del 'Unita, Italy
22.06.1990 Rome, Teatro Tenda, Italy
24.06.1990 Nice, Theatre Deveroure, France
25.06.1990 Marseilles, Theatre du Moulin, France
26.06.1990 Barcelona, Zeleste, Spain
28.06.1990 Oporto, Portugal
29.06.1990 Lisbon, Portugal
02.07.1990 Poole, Arts Centre, England
03.07.1990 St.Austell, Cornwall Coliseum,England
04.07.1990 Aylesbury, Civic Centre, England
07.07.1990 Leysin, Festival, Switzerland
09.07.1990 London, Royal Albert Hall, England

1991

25.05.1991 Siegburg, Schulzentrum Neuenhof, Germany ("The Company Germany" Fan Club Convention, Fish without his own band, but with SINISTER STREET)
26.10.1991 Utrecht, Tivoli, Holland ("Freaks" Fan Club Convention)
30.10.1991 Dalkeith, St.David's School, Scotland (Charity-gig)
01.11.1991 Elgin, Town Hall, Scotland
02.11.1991 Aviemore, Speyside Theatre, Scotland
03.11.1991 Haddington, Corn Exchange, Scotland ("The Company Scotland" Fan Club Convention)
07.11.1991 Dundee, Caird Hall, Scotland
08.11.1991 Belfast, Mandela Hall, Northern Ireland
09.11.1991 Haddington, Corn Exchange, Scotland
14.11.1991 Wolverhampton, Civic Centre, England
15.11.1991 Nottingham, Royal Centre, England
16.11.1991 Liverpool, Royal Court Theatre, England
18.11.1991 Bristol, Colston Hall, England
20.11.1991 Cambridge, Corn Exchange, England
22.11.1991 London, Hammersmith Odeon, England
23.11.1991 London, Hammersmith Odeon, England
26.11.1991 Offenbach, Stadthalle, Germany
01.12.1991 St.Wendel, Sporthalle, Germany
02.12.1991 Munich, Theaterfabrik, Germany
03.12.1991 Milan, Teatre Orfeo, Italy
05.12.1991 Zürich, Volkshaus, Switzerland
06.12.1991 Neutachel, New York Club, Switzerland
07.12.1991 Düsseldorf, Philipshalle, Germany
09.12.1991 Paris, Olympia, France
10.12.1991 Ludwigsburg, Bürgersaalforum am Schlosspark, Germany
11.12.1991 Berlin, Metropol, Germany
13.12.1991 Copenhagen, Pumpehuset, Denmark
14.12.1991 Stockholm, Palladium, Sweden
16.12.1991 Hamburg, Concert Centrum Hamburg III, Germany
17.12.1991 Utrecht, Vredenburg, Holland
18.12.1991 Geleen, Hanehof, Holland
20.12.1991 Enschede, Muziekcentrum, Holland
21.12.1991 Brussels, Ancienne Belgique, Belgium
22.12.1991 Birmingham, Aston Villa Leisure Centre, England

23.12.1991 Manchester, Apollo Theatre, England
27.12.1991 Glasgow, Barrowland Ballroom, Scotland
28.12.1991 Dundee, Caird Hall, Scotland
30.12.1991 Aberdeen, Capitol, Scotland
31.12.1991 Edinburgh, Playhouse Theatre, Scotland

1992

02.01.1992 Utrecht, Tivoli, Holland
03.01.1992 Utrecht, Tivoli, Holland
04.01.1992 Utrecht, Tivoli, Holland
05.01.1992 Utrecht, Tivoli, Holland
11.01.1992 London, Tuffnell Park Dome, England
18.03.1992 Dalkeith, Miners Social Club, Scotland
20.03.1992 London, Hammersmith Odeon, England (Andy Field-Tribute)
03.04.1992 London, Hammersmith Odeon, England
17.04.1992 Dingwall, Legends, Scotland
18.04.1992 Aberdeen, Pelican, Scotland
24.04.1992 Dundee, Fat Sam's, Scotland
25.04.1992 Carlisle, Front Page, England
26.04.1992 Newcastle, Riverside, England
30.04.1992 Glasgow, King Tuts, Scotland
01.05.1992 Glasgow, King Tuts, Scotland
02.05.1992 Edinburgh, Preservation Hall, Scotland
03.05.1992 Edinburgh, Preservation Hall, Scotland
06.05.1992 Dalkeith, Miners Social Club, Scotland
08.05.1992 Melrose, Corn Exchange, Scotland
09.05.1992 Hamilton, Town Hall, Scotland
14.05.1992 Dumfries, Loreburn Hall, Scotland
15.05.1992 Inverness, Hayloft, Scotland
16.05.1992 Loch Gelly, Town Hall, Scotland
22.05.1992 Ayr, The Powerhouse, Scotland
23.05.1992 Edinburgh, University, Scotland
24.05.1992 Berwick Upon Tweed, The Maltings, Scotland
26.05.1992 Liverpool, Krazy House, England
27.05.1992 Norwich, Oval Rock House, England
31.05.1992 Bathgate, Rock City, England
06.06.1992 Arhus, Festival, Denmark (Open Air)
07.06.1992 Arhus, Festival, Denmark (Open Air)
20.06.1992 Weert, De Lichtenberg, Holland (Bospop-Festival)
21.06.1992 Weert, De Lichtenberg, Holland (Bospop-Festival)
23.06.1992 Hamburg, Grosse Freiheit, Germany
24.06.1992 Cologne, Tanzbrunnen, Germany (Open Air)
26.06.1992 Neu-Ulm, Gorki Park, Germany (Open Air)
27.06.1992 St.Gallen, Festival, Switzerland (Open Air)
29.06.1992 Sheffield, City Hall, England
03.07.1992 Dumfries, Loreburn Hall, Scotland
05.07.1992 Hawick, Teviotdale Leisure Centre, Scotland
17.07.1992 Aberdeen, Pelican, Scotland
18.07.1992 Aberdeen, Pelican, Scotland
19.07.1992 Tairlair, Mac Duff Music Festival, Scotland (Open Air)
06.08.1992 Glasgow, The Cathouse, Scotland
07.08.1992 Glasgow, The Cathouse, Scotland
08.08.1992 Carlisle, Front Page, England
14.08.1992 Edinburgh, Preservation Hall, Scotland
15.08.1992 Edinburgh, Preservation Hall, Scotland
23.08.1992 Haddington, Corn Exchange, Scotland ("The Company Scotland" Fan Club Convention)
27.11.1992 Glasgow, Rocking House, Scotland (Fish with "The Party Boys")
05.12.1992 Glasgow, Rocking House, Scotland (Fish with "The Party Boys")
14.12.1992 Glasgow, College of Arts, Scotland (Charity gig)
17.12.1992 Edinburgh, Musicbox, Scotland (Fish with "The Party Boys")
23.12.1992 Dunfermline, Scotland (Fish with "The Party Boys")

1993

25.01.1993 Glasgow, Arches, Scotland (FISH with "The Party Boys")
15.02.1993 Elgin, Bishop Mills Hotel, Scotland
16.02.1993 Dingwall, Tulloch Castle, Scotland
17.02.1993 Livingston, Forum, Scotland
18.02.1993 Livingston, Forum, Scotland
19.02.1993 Loch Gelly, Town Hall, Scotland
21.02.1993 Manchester, Academy, England
22.02.1993 London, Town and Country Club, England
23.02.1993 London, Town and Country Club, England
25.02.1993 Bristol, Colston Hall, England
26.02.1993 Cambridge, Corn Exchange, England
27.02.1993 Leeds, Town and Country Club, England

01.03.1993	Offenbach, Stadthalle, Germany
02.03.1993	Lichtenfels, Stadthalle, Germany
04.03.1993	Hannover, Music Hall, Germany
05.03.1993	Berlin, Neue Welt, Germany
07.03.1993	Oslo, Sentrum Kino, Norway
08.03.1993	Stockholm, Melody, Sweden
10.03.1993	Hamburg, Music Hall, Germany
11.03.1993	Düsseldorf, Philipshalle, Germany
12.03.1993	Völklingen, Sporthalle, Germany
13.03.1993	Mulhouse, Le Phoenix, France
15.03.1993	Paris, Le Zenith, France
16.03.1993	Gent, Voorhuit, Belgium
17.03.1993	Utrecht, Muziekcentrum Vredenburg, Holland
18.03.1993	Utrecht, Muziekcentrum Vredenburg, Holland
20.03.1993	Munich, Terminal I, Germany
22.03.1993	Bern, National Theater, Switzerland
23.03.1993	Zürich, Volkshaus, Switzerland
24.03.1993	Milan, City Square, Italy
25.03.1993	Rome, Palladium, Itlay
27.03.1993	Linz, Posthof, Austria
28.03.1993	Vienna, Bank Austria Zelt, Austria
30.03.1993	Mannheim, Rosengarten, Germany
31.03.1993	Ludwigsburg, Forum, Germany
01.04.1993	Erlangen, Stadthalle, Germany
02.04.1993	Osnabrück, Stadthalle, Germany
04.04.1993	Nottingham, Rock City, England
05.04.1993	Birmingham, Town Hall, England
07.04.1993	Glasgow, Barrowlands, Scotland
08.04.1993	Aberdeen, Music Hall, Scotland
10.04.1993	Caister, Neptunes's Palace, England
05.06.1993	Uden, Festival, Holland
19.06.1993	Frankfurt, Musik Arena, Germany
27.06.1993	Den Haag, Festival, Holland (Parkpop-Open Air)
18.07.1993	Macduff, Tarlair-Music Festival, Scotland
21.08.1993	Kortenaken, Boerenrock-Festival, Belgium
01.10.1993	Edinburgh, Music Box, Scotland
03.10.1993	Edinburgh, Music Box, Scotland
04.10.1993	Motherwell, Civic Centre, Scotland
05.10.1993	Sheffield, Lead Mill, England
07.10.1993	Warrington, Parr Hall, England
08.10.1993	Aylesbury, Civic Centre, England
10.10.1993	Brentwood, Leisure Centre, England
11.10.1993	Croydon, Fairfield Hall, England
12.10.1993	Southampton, Mayflower, England
13.10.1993	Hastings, White Rock Theatre, England
15.10.1993	Wolverhampton, Wulfrun Hall, England
16.10.1993	Norwich, Oval, England
17.10.1993	Barnsley, Civic Theatre, England
19.10.1993	Lincoln, Ritz Theatre, England
20.10.1993	Ipswich, Corn Exchange, England
21.10.1993	Halifax, Victoria Hall, England
23.10.1993	London, Borderline Club, England
24.10.1993	Bristol, Bierkeller, England
25.10.1993	Southampton, Mayflower, England
26.10.1993	Wolverhampton, Civic Hall, England
27.10.1993	Oberhausen, Music Circus Ruhr, Germany
28.10.1993	Bremen, Aladin, Germany
30.10.1993	Rheinberg, Stadthaus, Germany ("The Company Germany" Fan Club Convention)
01.11.1993	Tilburg, Noorderligt, Holland
02.11.1993	Rotterdam, Nightown, Holland
03.11.1993	Amsterdam, Melkweg, Holland
05.11.1993	Enschede, The Twente, Holland
06.11.1993	Utrecht, Tivoli, Holland ("The Company Holland" Fan Club Convention)
07.11.1993	Utrecht, Tivoli, Holland
08.11.1993	Leeuwarden, Salenschaaf, Holland

1994

05.04.1994	Glasgow, HMV, Scotland
05.04.1994	East Kilbride, HMV, Scotland
06.04.1994	Newcastle, HMV, England
06.04.1994	Middlesborough, HMV, England
07.04.1994	Manchester, HMV, England
07.04.1994	Liverpool, HMV, England
08.04.1994	Birmingham, HMV, England
08.04.1994	Northampton, HMV, England
11.04.1994	Cardiff, HMV, Wales
11.04.1994	Bristol, HMV, England
12.04.1994	Swindon, HMV, England
12.04.1994	Reading, HMV, England
13.04.1994	Aylesbury, HMV, England
14.04.1994	London, HMV (Oxford Street), England
13.05.1994	Banff, Uncle Sam's, Scotland
24.05.1994	Cumbernauld, Sax Club
25.05.1994	Newcastle, Riverside, England
28.05.1994	Haddington, Corn Exchange, Scotland
04.06.1994	Eschwege, Open Flair-Festival, Germany (Open Air)
10.06.1994	Paris, Euro Disney, France
16.06.1994	Glasgow, The Garage, Scotland
17.06.1994	Liverpool, Lomax, England

18.06.1994 Worcester, Nortwick, England
20.06.1994 Leeds, Irish Centre, England
21.06.1994 Norwich, Waterfront, England
22.06.1994 Northampton, Roadmenders, England
23.06.1994 Manchester, Middlehall University, England
25.06.1994 Bonn, Rheinkultur-Festival, Germany
27.06.1994 Newport, TJ's, Wales
28.06.1994 Wolverhampton, Wulfrun Hall, England
29.06.1994 London, Mean Fiddler, England
06.08.1994 Estavayer-le-Lac, Festival, Switzerland
26.08.1994 Edinburgh, Waverley Centre, Scotland
27.08.1994 Kilmarnock, Grand Hall, Scotland
01.09.1994 Groningen, Oosterpoort, Holland
02.09.1994 Huijbergen, Feesttent, Holland
03.09.1994 Oslo, Sentrum, Norway
13.09.1994 Leeuwarden, Saalenschaaf, Holland
14.09.1994 Utrecht, Tivoli, Holland
15.09.1994 Rotterdam, Nightown, Holland
17.09.1994 Enschede, De Twente, Holland
18.09.1994 Geleen, Hanehof, Holland
19.09.1994 Amsterdam, Paradiso, Holland
22.09.1994 Hamburg, Docks, Germany
23.09.1994 Osnabrück, Halle Gartlage, Germany
24.09.1994 Berlin, Neue Welt, Germany
26.09.1994 Hannover, Music Hall, Germany
27.09.1994 Bonn, Biskuithalle, Germany
28.09.1994 Ludwigsburg, Forum, Germany
29.09.1994 Neu-Isenburg, Hugenottenhalle, Germany
01.10.1994 Mannheim, Capitol, Germany
02.10.1994 Ulm, Arts and Craft, Germany
03.10.1994 Nürnberg, Resi, Germany
05.10.1994 Munich, Terminal I, Germany
06.10.1994 Betzdorf, Stadthalle, Gernmany
08.10.1994 Zabrze, DMIT, Poland
09.10.1994 Warsaw, Stoldola Club, Poland
10.10.1994 Ostrava, Sportovni Hall Tatran, Czech Republik
03.12.1994 Sinzig, Brauhaus Helenensaal, Germany
04.12.1994 Heidelberg, Billy Blues, Germany
06.12.1994 Haltern, Old Daddy Club, Germany
07.12.1994 Essen, Schloß Borbeck, Germany
08.12.1994 Utrecht, Muziekcentrum Vredenburg, Holland
09.12.1994 Duisburg, Gertrud-Bäumler-Schule, Germany ("The Company Germany" Fan Club Convention)
12.12.1994 Florence, The flog, Italy
13.12.1994 Rome, Palladium, Italy
14.12.1994 Milan, Factory, Italy
16.12.1994 Zürich, Electric Ballroom, Switzerland
18.12.1994 Ris Orangis, Le Plan, France
19.12.1994 Paris, Hot Brass, France
20.12.1994 Opwijk, Nijdrop, Belgium
22.12.1994 Manchester, Boardwalk, England
27.12.1994 Liverpool, Lomax, England
28.12.1994 London, Mean Fiddler, England
29.12.1994 Falkirk, Martell Nightclub, Scotland
30.12.1994 Glasgow, The Garage, Scotland

1995

07.05.1995 Edinburgh, Usher Hall, Scotland
14.05.1995 Oslo, Sentrum Kino, Norway
19.05.1995 Sparks Nightclub, Singapore
22.05.1995 Hong Kong City, Hard Rock Cafe, Hong Kong
27.05.1995 Gasperich, Croix de Gasperich, Luxembourg (Carity-Festival)
30.05.1995 Istanbul, Acikhava Tiyatrosu, Turkey (Harbiye-Open Air)
06.06.1995 Reims, Le Cirque, France
07.06.1995 Rouen, Rock and Roll Circus, France
09.06.1995 Grenoble, Le Summum, France
10.06.1995 Lyon, Le Transbordeur, France
12.06.1995 Strasbourg, Ancienne Laiterie, France
14.06.1995 Caen, Salle Georges Brassens, France
15.06.1995 Bordeaux, La Chat Blue, France
16.06.1995 Montpellier, Victoire, France
17.06.1995 Toulouse, Le Bikini, France
18.06.1995 Zürich, Rock gegen Hass-Festival, Switzerland (Open Air)
19.06.1995 Marseille, Espace Julien, France
11.08.1995 Nottingham, Wollarton Park, England
02.09.1995 Edinburgh, Princess Street Gardens, Scotland (Open Air)
07.09.1995 Liverpool, Royal Court Theatre, England
08.09.1995 Wolverhampton, Wulfrun Hall, England
09.09.1995 London, Willesdon Empire, England
12.09.1995 Vosselaar, Biepop, Belgium
14.09.1995 Groningen, Oosterpoort, Holland
15.09.1995 Esbjerg, Tobaksfabrikken, Denmark
16.09.1995 Copenhagen, Alexandra Rockteater, Denmark
18.09.1995 Malmö, KB, Sweden

19.09.1995 Odense, Rytemeposten, Denmark
21.09.1995 Oslo, Rockefeller, Norway
22.09.1995 Bergen, Maxime Club, Norway
25.09.1995 Göteborg, FM Stadion, Sweden
26.09.1995 Stockholm, Stadion, Sweden
28.09.1995 Helsinki, Tavastia Club, Finland
30.09.1995 Tallinn, Club Pirat, Estonia
01.10.1995 Tartu, University Sport Hall, Estonia
04.10.1995 Warsaw, Stoldola Club, Poland
06.10.1995 Poznan, Hall Arena, Poland
07.10.1995 Katowice, Dom Muzyka i Tanca, Poland
08.10.1995 Bresslau, Hall WWF, Poland
10.10.1995 Ostrava, Sportovni Hall Tatran, Czech Republik
11.10.1995 Krakow, Hall of TV, Poland
12.10.1995 Prague, KD Eden, Czech Republik
14.10.1995 Krakow, Bucklein Theatre, Poland
16.10.1995 Vienna, Metropol, Austria
18.10.1995 Babenhausen, Stadthalle, Germany
19.10.1995 Gelsenkirchen, Forum im Zelt, Germany
20.10.1995 Bremerhaven, Stadthalle, Germany
22.10.1995 Stuttgart, Longhorn, Germany
23.10.1995 Halle, Easy Schorre, Germany
25.10.1995 Munich, Charterhalle, Germany
26.10.1995 Mannheim, Alte Feuerwache, Germany
27.10.1995 Nürnberg, Löwensaal, Germany
29.10.1995 Bielefeld, PC 69, Germany
30.10.1995 Hamburg, Grosse Freiheit, Germany
31.10.1995 Cloppenburg, Stadthalle, Germany
02.11.1995 Hannover, Capitol, Germany
03.11.1995 Kiel, Pumpe, Germany
05.11.1995 Cologne, Theater am Rudolfplatz, Germany
06.11.1995 Berlin, Metropol, Germany
07.11.1995 Bresslau, Hall WWF, Poland
10.11.1995 Zürich, Electric Ballroom, Switzerland
11.11.1995 Milan, Factory, Italy
12.11.1995 Luzern, Schüür Club, Switzerland
14.11.1995 Rubigen, Hunziken Mühle, Switzerland
15.11.1995 Nancy, Terminal Export, France
16.11.1995 Dijon, L'anser, France
17.11.1995 Bettenburg, Centre Sportif, Luxembourg
19.11.1995 Lüttich (Liege), La Chapelle, Belgium
20.11.1995 Paris, New Morning, France
05.12.1995 Falkirk, Martell Club, Scotland
06.12.1995 Glenrothes, Rothes Hall, Scotland
07.12.1995 Aberdeen, Lemon Tree, Scotland
08.12.1995 Dingwall, The Club, Scotland
10.12.1995 Glasgow, The Garage, Scotland
11.12.1995 Newcastle, Riverside, England
12.12.1995 Cambridge, The Junction, England
13.12.1995 London, Clapham Grand, England
15.12.1995 Belfast, The Empire, Northern Ireland
16.12.1995 Dublin, Olympia, Ireland

1996

20.04.1996 Santiago de Chile, Santa Rosa, Chile
21.04.1996 Santiago de Chile, Santa Rosa, Chile
23.04.1996 Buenos Aires, Broadway Theatre, Argentinia
24.04.1996 Buenos Aires, Broadway Theatre, Argentinia
26.04.1996 Curitiba, Aeroanta, Brazil
28.04.1996 Rio de Janeiro, Brazil
29.04.1996 Sao Paulo, Palace, Brazil
30.04.1996 Sao Paulo, Palace, Brazil
09.05.1996 Dubai (with SAS-Charity-Band)
10.05.1996 Dubai (with SAS-Charity-Band)
16.05.1996 Glasgow, Renfrew, Scotland
18.05.1996 Varsselder, Huntenpop, Holland
22.05.1996 Tomislavgrad, Bosnia
23.05.1996 Gornji Vakuf, Bosnia
24.05.1996 Sarajevo, Bosnia
25.05.1996 Sarajevo, Bosnia
26.05.1996 Vitez, Bosnia
27.05.1996 Sipovo, Bosnia
29.05.1996 Kupres, Bosnia
30.05.1996 Mrkonjicgrad, Richard III. Hotel, Bosnia
31.05.1996 Banja Luka, Bosnia
01.06.1996 Sanski Most, Bosnia
02.06.1996 Split, Croatia
06.06.1996 Ulm, (with SAS-Charity-Band)
08.06.1996 Rotterdam, Holland
03.08.1996 Lokeren, Festival, Belgium
10.08.1996 Skanderborg, Festival, Denmark
18.08.1996 Dortmund, Friedensplatz, Germany (Rock for Bosnia-Open Air)
25.08.1996 Haddington, Corn Exchange, Scotland ("The Company Scotland" Fan Club Convention)

1997

30.01.1997 Kilburn, National Ballroom, Scotland (with SAS-Charity-Band)
11.04.1997 Bern, Switzerland (with SAS-Charity-Band)

16.05.1997 London, Natural History Museum, England (with SAS-CHARITY-BAND)
17.05.1997 Tartu, Arena, Estonia (with SAS-CHARITY-BAND)
24.05.1997 Haddington, Railway Tavern, Scotland
26.05.1997 Aberdeen, Lemon Tree, Scotland
27.05.1997 Edinburgh, The Venue, Scotland
28.05.1997 Glasgow, The Garage, Scotland
30.05.1997 Dublin, Olympia, Ireland
31.05.1997 Belfast, The Empire, Northern Ireland
01.06.1997 Sheffield, Lead Mill, England
03.06.1997 Newcastle, Riverside, England
04.06.1997 Manchester, Hope and Grape, England
05.06.1997 Liverpool, L 2, England
06.06.1997 Blackwood, Miners Club, Wales
08.06.1997 Wolverhampton, Wulfrun Hall, England
09.06.1997 Portsmouth, Wedgewood Rooms, England
10.06.1997 Cambridge, The Junction, England
12.06.1997 London, Shepherd Bush Empire, England
14.06.1997 Dudelange, Festival, Luxembourg
15.06.1997 Eindhoven, Holland ("The Company Holland" Fan Club Convention)
16.06.1997 Paris, Divan du Monde, France
18.06.1997 Istanbul, Acikhava Tiyatrosu, Turkey (Open Air)
19.06.1997 Ankara, Turkey
21.06.1997 Weert, Bospop-Festival, Holland
22.06.1997 Biebop, Festival, Belgium
23.06.1997 Reading, Alley Cat, England
24.06.1997 Bristol, Fleece and Firkin, England
28.06.1997 Berlin, Haus des Rundfunks, Germany
10.07.1997 Rome, Cus Roma, Italy
11.07.1997 Rimini, Velvet, Italy
12.07.1997 Vigevano, Castello, Italy
18.07.1997 Pittsburgh PA, Graffitti Showcase, USA
19.07.1997 Philadelphia PA, Theater of Living Arts, USA
20.07.1997 Washington DC, The Bayou, USA
22.07.1997 New York City NY, Tramps, USA
23.07.1997 Morgan NJ, Club Bene, USA
24.07.1997 Danbury CN, Tuxedo Junction, USA
25.07.1997 Poughkeepsie NY, The Chance, USA
27.07.1997 Providence RI, Strand Theatre, USA
28.07.1997 Boston MA, Paradise Rock Club, USA
30.07.1997 Toronto (Ontario), The Guverment, Canada
31.07.1997 Quebec City (Quebec), Bar Spectacle d' Auteuil, Canada
01.08.1997 Hull (Quebec), Parc des Fees, Canada (Rock for new frontiers-Festival)
03.08.1997 Montreal (Quebec), Le Spectrum, Canada
04.08.1997 Quebec City (Quebec), Bar Spectacle d' Auteuil, Canada
05.08.1997 Sherbrooke (Quebec), Cafe du Palais, Canada
07.08.1997 Buffalo NY, The Tralf, USA
08.08.1997 Pontiac MI, 7th House, USA
10.08.1997 Cleveland OH, The Odeon, USA
11.08.1997 Grand Rapids MI, The Intersection, USA
12.08.1997 Columbus OH, Ludlow's, USA
14.08.1997 Milwaukee WI, Shank Hall, USA
15.08.1997 Chicago IL, Park West, USA
18.08.1997 Denver CO, Bluebird Theater, USA
21.08.1997 Vancouver (British Columbia), Starfish Room, Canada
22.08.1997 Seattle WA, The Fenix, USA
24.08.1997 San Francisco CA, Slim's, USA
25.08.1997 Fremont CA, Club Kaos, USA
27.08.1997 West Hollywood CA, Roxy Theater, USA
31.08.1997 Malta
05.09.1997 Bolton, Albert Hall, England
06.09.1997 Nottingham, The Rig, England
07.09.1997 Cheltenham, Town Hall, England
09.09.1997 Burnley, Mechanics, England
11.09.1997 Bradford, Rios, England
12.09.1997 Norwich, Oval Rockhouse, England
14.09.1997 Utrecht, Tivoli, Holland
15.09.1997 Groningen, Oosterpoort, Holland
16.09.1997 Tilburg, The Noorderligt, Holland
18.09.1997 Sittard, Schouwburg, Holland
19.09.1997 Amsterdam, Paradiso, Holland
20.09.1997 Rotterdam, Nightown, Holland
22.09.1997 Arhus, Huset, Denmark
23.09.1997 Copenhagen, Pumpehuset, Denmark
24.09.1997 Odense, Rytmeposten, Denmark
26.09.1997 Malmö, KB, Sweden
27.09.1997 Stockholm, Studion, Sweden
29.09.1997 Oslo, Rockefeller, Norway
01.10.1997 Helsinki, Tavastia, Finland
02.10.1997 Tallinn, Club Dekoltee, Estonia
04.10.1997 Tartu, Estonia
05.10.1997 Olstyn, Club Komin, Poland
06.10.1997 Lublin, Sport Hall, Poland
07.10.1997 Warsaw, Proxima, Poland
08.10.1997 Rzesgow, Academy, Poland

10.10.1997 Przemysl, TV Studio, Poland
11.10.1997 Zabrze, DMIT, Poland
12.10.1997 Wroclaw, WHH Hall, Poland
14.10.1997 Bydgoszcz, Filharmonia, Poland
16.10.1997 Szczecin, WDK Trans, Poland
18.10.1997 Poznan, Eskulap, Poland
19.10.1997 Krakow, Studio Leg, Poland
25.10.1997 Bern, Rubigen, Switzerland
26.10.1997 Zürich, Spirrgarten, Switzerland
28.10.1997 Alstatten, La Cucaracha, Switzerland
29.10.1997 Olten, Terminus, Switzerland
30.10.1997 Treviso, Sonny Boy, Italy
31.10.1997 Rome, Frontiera, Italy
02.11.1997 Milan, Magazzini Generali, Italy
03.11.1997 Neu Ulm, Arts and Crafts, Germany
05.11.1997 Regensburg, QU, Germany
06.11.1997 Mannheim, Alte Feuerwache, Germany
07.11.1997 Karlsruhe, Tollhaus, Germany
09.11.1997 Stuttgart, Longhorn, Germany
10.11.1997 Oberhausen, Musik Circus Ruhr, Germany
11.11.1997 Hamburg, Docks, Germany
13.11.1997 Potsdam, Lindenpark, Germany
14.11.1997 Hannover, Capitol, Germany
15.11.1997 Kiel, Traumfabrik, Germany
17.11.1997 Halle, Easy Schorre, Germany
18.11.1997 Braunschweig, FBZ, Germany
19.11.1997 Uebach-Palenberg, Rockfabrik, Germany
20.11.1997 Cologne, Rhein Rock Hallen, Germany
22.11.1997 Lille, Le Splendid, France
23.11.1997 Ris Orangis, Le Plan, France
25.11.1997 Toulouse, Le Yellow, France
26.11.1997 Marseille, Espace Julien, France
29.11.1997 Barcelona, Zeleste I, Spain
01.12.1997 Grenoble, L' Entrepot, France
02.12.1997 Lyon, Le Pez Ner, France
08.12.1997 Dudley, JB's, England
09.12.1997 Guildford, Civic Hall, England
10.12.1997 Buckley, Tivoli, Wales
13.12.1997 Devon, Ashburton Lanterns, England
14.12.1997 Salisbury, Arts Centre at City Hall, England
15.12.1997 London, Mean Fiddler, England
17.12.1997 Cumbernauld, Allender Hall, Scotland
18.12.1997 Edinburgh, Liquid Room, Scotland
20.12.1997 Öhringen, Kultura, Germany (Christmas-Rock-Nacht 1997,with SAS-Charity Band)

1998

22.02.1998 Alton, Lord Mayor Trelour College, England (with SAS-Charity Band)
02.05.1998 Norwich, Oval Rockhouse, England
23.05.1998 Schorndorf, Manufaktur Hammerschlag, Germany (Gitarrenfest, with SAS-Charity Band)
30.05.1998 Haddington, Corn Exchange, Scotland ("The Company Scotland" Fan Club Convention)
07.06.1998 London, Battersea Park, England (with SAS-Charity Band)
28.08.1998 Trier, Wiltingen, Germany
29.08.1998 Duisburg, Glück-Auf-Halle, Germany ("The Company Germany" Fan Club Convention)
19.09.1998 Rabat, Ta' Qali National Park Greek Theatre, Malta
11.12.1998 Chiddingfold (Surrey), Chiddingfold Club, England (with SAS-Charity Band)
12.12.1998 Chiddingfold (Surrey), Chiddingfold Club, England (with SAS-Charity Band)

1999

09.04.1999 Chigwell Row (Essex), The Maypole, England
10.04.1999 Utrecht, Oude Pothuis, Holland
11.04.1999 Hertogenbosch, Poitin Irish Pub, Holland
13.04.1999 Amsterdam, Paradiso, Holland
14.04.1999 Amsterdam, Fame, Holland (In-Store Acoustic gig)
15.04.1999 Paris, Virgin Megastore, France (In-Store Acoustic gig)
16.04.1999 Lyon, FNAC Bellecour, France (In-Store Acoustic gig)
17.04.1999 Marseille, Virgin Megastore, France (In-Store Acoustic gig)
18.04.1999 Karlsruhe, Treacy's Irish Pub, Germany
19.04.1999 Mannheim, Prinz, Germany (In-Store Acoustic gig)
20.04.1999 Cologne, Saturn, Germany (18:00, In-Store Acoustic gig)
20.04.1999 Cologne, Flanagan's Irish Pub, Germany (22:30)
21.04.1999 Berlin, Kulturkaufhaus Dussmann, Germany (In-Store Acoustic gig)
22.04.1999 London, HMV Oxford Street, England (In-Store Acoustic gig)
23.04.1999 Edinburgh, HMV Princess Street, Scotland (In-Store Acoustic gig)

29.05.1999 Geneva, Feast of Hope Festival, Switzerland (see also MARILLION tour dates)
30.05.1999 Bern, Mühle Hunziken, Switzerland
31.05.1999 Winterthur, Albani, Switzerland
28.08.1999 Haddington, St.Mary's Church, Scotland (Acoustic Fan Club Gig)
29.08.1999 Haddington, Corn Exchange, Scotland (The Company Scotland convention)
11.09.1999 Groningen, Oosterpoort, Holland
12.09.1999 Utrecht, Muziekcentrum Vredenburg, Holland
13.09.1999 Tilburg, 013, Holland
14.09.1999 Amsterdam, Paradiso, Holland
16.09.1999 Aarhus, Train, Denmark
18.09.1999 Malmö, KB, Sweden
19.09.1999 Oslo, Rockefellers, Norway
20.09.1999 Stockholm, Klubben Fryshuset, Sweden
21.09.1999 Gothenberg, Tredgarden, Sweden
23.09.1999 Copenhagen, Pumphuset, Sweden
24.09.1999 Bremen, Tivoli, Germany
25.09.1999 Hamburg, Grosse Freiheit, Germany
27.09.1999 Leipzig, Der Anker, Germany
28.09.1999 Prague, Rock Cafe, Czech Republik
30.09.1999 Basel, Sommer-Casino, Switzerland
01.10.1999 Yverdon-les-Bains, Amalgame, Switzerland
03.10.1999 Poznan, Centrum Kultury Zamek, Poland
04.10.1999 Berlin, Columbia-Fritz, Germany
05.10.1999 Offenbach, Capitol, Germany
06.10.1999 Stuttgart, Longhorn, Germany
09.10.1999 Rotterdam, Nightown, Holland
10.10.1999 Cologne, Live Music Hall, Germany
12.10.1999 Bern, Bierhubelei, Switzerland
13.10.1999 Vienna, Planet Music, Austria
15.10.1999 Milan, Binario Zero, Italy
17.10.1999 Luzern, Schuur, Switzerland
18.10.1999 Winterthur, Salzhaus, Switzerland
26.10.1999 Lille, Le Splendid, France
27.10.1999 Paris, MCM TV Cafe, France
28.10.1999 Ris Orangis, Le Plan, France
29.10.1999 Luxembourg, Den Atelier, Luxembourg
30.10.1999 Brussels, Ancienne Belgique, Belgium
01.11.1999 Wolverhampton, Wulfrun Hall, England
02.11.1999 London, The Mean Fiddler, England

2000

08.01.2000 Tampa FL, Hattricks, USA (with JOHN WESLEY BAND)
13.01.2000 Atlanta GA, Variety Playhouse, USA
15.01.2000 Washington DC, 9:30 Club, USA
16.01.2000 Philadelphia PA, Theater of Living Arts, USA
17.01.2000 New York City NY, Irving Plaza, USA
19.01.2000 St.Petersburg FL, State Theater, USA
19.02.2000 London, Shepard's Bush Empire, UK (with SAS-CHARITY BAND)
27.05.2000 Geneva, Feast of Hope Festival, Switzerland
16.06.2000 Nidrum, The Twilight Cafe, Belgium (with T 42)
17.06.2000 Dudelange, Townhall Square, Luxembourg (with T 42)
07.07.2000 Banja Luka, Bosnia
08.07.2000 Banja Luka, Bosnia
09.07.2000 Mrjonic Grad, Bosnia
10.07.2000 Sipovo, Bosnia
11.07.2000 Sarajevo, Bosnia
13.07.2000 Split, Croatia
22.07.2000 Paradise Bay, Malta (with SAS-CHARITY BAND)
15.09.2000 San Diego, Microsoft, USA (private gig with SAS-CHARITY BAND)
17.09.2000 Los Angeles, Troubadour, USA (with SAS-CHARITY BAND)
29.10.2000 London, Charlie Browns Wood Green, England (Southern Fan Club Convention)
30.10.2000 London, Charlie Browns Wood Green, England
30.11.2000 Prishtina, Yugoslavia
01.12.2000 Prishtina, Yugoslavia
02.12.2000 Prishtina, Yugoslavia
03.12.2000 Prishtina, Yugoslavia
06.12.2000 Southampton, The Brook, England (with SAS-CHARITY BAND)
07.12.2000 Southampton, The Brook, England (with SAS-CHARITY BAND)
08.12.2000 Surrey, Chiddingfold, England (with SAS-CHARITY BAND)
09.12.2000 Surrey, Chiddingfold, England (with SAS-CHARITY BAND)
10.12.2000 London, Shepard's Bush Empire, England (with SAS-CHARITY BAND)
11.12.2000 Cambridge, Corn Exchange, England (with SAS-CHARITY BAND)
12.12.2000 Liverpool, Royal Court Theatre, England (with SAS-CHARITY BAND)
13.12.2000 York, Barbican, England (with SAS-CHARITY BAND)

14.12.2000 Edinburgh, Usher Hall, Scotland (with SAS-CHARITY BAND)
15.12.2000 Manchester, Apollo, England (with SAS-CHARITY BAND)
18.12.2000 Northern Ireland
19.12.2000 Northern Ireland
20.12.2000 Northern Ireland
21.12.2000 Northern Ireland

2001

27.01.2001 Leeuwarden, Schaaf, Holland
28.01.2001 Utrecht, Tivoli, Holland (The Company Holland Fan convention)
02.02.2001 Oberhausen, Schilda Halle, Germany
03.02.2001 Oberhausen, Schilda Halle, Germany (5th The Company Germany Fan convention)
29.04.2001 Dalkeith, "Number 10" Masonic Lodge, Scotland (Warm-up show)
03.05.2001 Glasgow, Garage, Scotland
04.05.2001 Wolverhampton, Wulfrun Hall, England
06.05.2001 Cambridge, t.b.a.
07.05.2001 Luxembourg, Den Atelier, Luxembourg
09.05.2001 Tilburg, 013, Holland
10.05.2001 Rotterdam, Nighttown, Holland
11.05.2001 Amsterdam, Paradiso, Holland
13.05.2001 Groningen, Oosterport, Holland
15.05.2001 Odense, Rytemposten, Denmark
16.05.2001 Copenhagen, Pumpehuset, Denmark
17.05.2001 Stockholm, Klubben, Sweden
18.05.2001 Oslo, Rockefeller, Norway
20.05.2001 Hamburg, Schlachthof, Germany
21.05.2001 Aschaffenburg, Colos Saal, Germany
22.05.2001 Cologne, Live Music Hall, Germany
24.05.2001 Karlsruhe, Tollhaus, Germany
25.05.2001 Kreuztal, Otto-Flick-Halle, Germany
26.05.2001 Geneva, Feast of Hope-Festival, Switzerland
28.05.2001 Krakow, Kino Teatr, Poland
29.05.2001 Lodz, Klub Faraon, Poland
31.05.2001 Poznan, CK Zamek, Poland
02.06.2001 Herisau, Casino, Switzerland
03.06.2001 Ris Orangis, Le Plan, France
05.06.2001 Verviers, Spirit of 66, Belgium
06.06.2001 London, Mean Fiddler, England
07.06.2001 Liverpool, Stanley Theatre at University, England
09.06.2001 Edinburgh, Liquid Rooms, Scotland
13.06.2001 Southampton, The Brook, England (with SAS-CHARITY BAND)
14.06.2001 Southampton, The Brook, England (with SAS-CHARITY BAND)
15.06.2001 Aarhus, Train, Denmark (with SAS-CHARITY BAND)
16.06.2001 Esbjerg, Tobakken, Denmark (with SAS-CHARITY BAND)
22.06.2001 Wiel-Bielstein, Open Air, Germany (with SAS-CHARITY BAND)
29.07.2001 Nidrom, Roots Rock Festival, Belgium (with SAS-CHARITY BAND)
11.08.2001 Hants, Gosport Festival, England (with SAS-CHARITY BAND)
26.08.2001 Haddington, St.Mary's Church, Scotland (The Company Scotland convention)
26.08.2001 Haddington, Corn Exchange, Scotland (The Company Scotland convention)
01.09.2001 Chemnitz, Germany (with SAS-CHARITY BAND)
30.09.2001 Mexico City, Metropolitan Theatre, Mexico
01.10.2001 Mexico City, Metropolitan Theatre, Mexico
03.10.2001 San Jose, Teatro Melico Salazar, Coata Rica
05.10.2001 Caracas, Centro Sambil, Venezuela
06.10.2001 Caracas, Centro Sambil, Venezuela
10.10.2001 Sao Paulo, Direct TV Hall, Brazil
11.10.2001 Rio, Canecao, Brazil
13.10.2001 Curitiba, **T.B.C.**, Brazil
15.10.2001 Porto Alegre, Teatro Do Fiergas, Brazil
17.10.2001 La Plata, Teatro Coliseo Podesta, Argentinia
18.10.2001 Rosario, Teatro Astengo, Argentinia
19.10.2001 San Isidro, Teatro Don Bosco, Argentinia
20.10.2001 Buenos Aires, Teatro Coliseo, Argentinia
22.10.2001 Mendoza, Teatro Gran Rex, Argentinia
23.10.2001 Santiago, Teatro Providencia Santa Rosa De Las Condes, Chile
06.11.2001 London, Mean Fiddler, England
07.11.2001 Utrecht, Tivoli, Holland
10.11.2001 Aarhus, Vox Hall, Denmark
11.11.2001 Malmö, KB Halle, Sweden
12.11.2001 Copenhagen, Lille Vega, Denmark
14.11.2001 Kiel, Traumfabrik, Germany
15.11.2001 Bochum, Zeche, Germany
16.11.2001 Osnabrück, Hyde Park, Germany
18.11.2001 Berlin, ColumbiaFritz, Germany

20.11.2001	Poznan, ** T.B.C.**, Poland	28.11.2001	**T.B.C.** France
22.11.2001	Vienna, ** T.B.C.**, Austria	29.11.2001	**T.B.C.** France
23.11.2001	Aarburg, Moonwalker, Switzerland	15.12.2001	Chiddingfold, England (with SAS-Charity Band)
24.11.2001	Geneva, Undertown, Switzerland	16.12.2001	Chiddingfold, England (with SAS-Charity Band)
25.11.2001	Rubigen, Meuele Hunziken, Switzerland		
27.11.2001	Nürnberg, Hirsch, Germany		

Marillion Records Page

FISH Records — Page

Records with MARILLION Relationship — Page

Compilations — Page

Miscellaneous **Page**

MARILLION Songs
(Studio Versions only) Page

FISH Songs
(Studio Versions only) Page